THE LOEB CLASSICAL LIBRARY

FOUNDED BY JAMES LOEB, LL.D.

EDITED BY

G. P. GOOLD, PH.D.

FORMER EDITORS

† T. E. PAGE, C.H., LITT.D.   † E. CAPPS, PH.D., LL.D.

† W. H. D. ROUSE, LITT.D.   † L. A. POST, L.H.D.

E. H. WARMINGTON, M.A., F.R.HIST.SOC.

QUINTILIAN

IV

THE INSTITUTIO ORATORIA OF
QUINTILIAN

WITH AN ENGLISH TRANSLATION BY
H. E. BUTLER, M.A.,
PROFESSOR OF LATIN IN LONDON UNIVERSITY

IN FOUR VOLUMES
IV

CAMBRIDGE, MASSACHUSETTS
HARVARD UNIVERSITY PRESS
LONDON
WILLIAM HEINEMANN LTD
MCMLXXIX

American ISBN 0–674–99141–9
British ISBN 0 434 99127 9

First printed 1922
Reprinted 1936, 1953, 1958, 1961, 1968, 1979

Printed in Great Britain by
Fletcher & Son Ltd, Norwich

TABLE OF CONTENTS

SIGLA

A = Codex Ambrosianus, 11th century.

B = Agreement of Codices Bernensis, Bambergensis and Nostradamensis, 10th century.

G = Codex Bambergensis in those passages where gaps have been supplied by a later 11th-century hand.

BIBLIOGRAPHICAL NOTE (1979)

Critical edition:

Michael Winterbottom (*OCT*), 2 vols, Oxford 1970

Commentaries:

Book X, W. Peterson, Oxford 1891
Book XII, R. G. Austin (very full; excellent bibliography), Oxford 1954²

Studies:

Jean Cousin, *Études sur Quintilien*, Paris 1936
G. M. A. Grube, *The Greek and Roman Critics*, London 1965
George Kennedy, *Quintilian*, New York 1969
Michael Winterbottom, *Problems in Quintilian* (BICS Suppl. 25), London 1970

Lexicon:

E. Bonnell (vol. 6 of Spalding's edition), Leipzig 1834 (repr. 1963)

Survey:

Jean Cousin, 'Quintilien 1935–1959,' *Lustrum* 7 (1963) 289–331

QUINTILIAN

BOOK X

M. FABII QUINTILIANI
INSTITUTIONIS ORATORIAE

LIBER X

I. Sed haec eloquendi praecepta, sicut cogitationi
sunt necessaria, ita non satis ad vim dicendi valent,
nisi illis firma quaedam facilitas, quae apud Graecos
ἕξις nominatur, accesserit: ad quam scribendo plus
an legendo an dicendo conferatur, solere quaeri scio.
Quod esset diligentius nobis examinandum, si quali-
2 bet earum rerum possemus una esse contenti. Verum
ita sunt inter se conexa et indiscreta omnia ut, si
quid ex his defuerit, frustra sit in ceteris laboratum.
Nam neque solida atque robusta fuerit unquam
eloquentia nisi multo stilo vires acceperit, et citra
lectionis exemplum labor ille carens rectore fluitabit; et qui[1] sciet quae quoque sint modo dicenda,
nisi tamen in procinctu paratamque ad omnes
casus habuerit eloquentiam, velut clausis thesauris
3 incubabit.   Non autem ut quidquid praecipue neces-

---

[1] fluitabit et qui, *Halm*: fluvit autem qui, *G.*

THE INSTITUTIO ORATORIA
OF QUINTILIAN

BOOK X

I. But these rules of style, while part of the student's theoretical knowledge, are not in themselves sufficient to give him oratorical power. In addition he will require that assured facility which the Greeks call ἕξις. I know that many have raised the question as to whether this is best acquired by writing, reading or speaking, and it would indeed be a question calling for serious consideration, if we could rest content with any one of the three. But 2 they are so intimately and inseparably connected, that if one of them be neglected, we shall but waste the labour which we have devoted to the others. For eloquence will never attain to its full development or robust health, unless it acquires strength by frequent practice in writing, while such practice without the models supplied by reading will be like a ship drifting aimlessly without a steersman. Again, he who knows what he ought to say and how he should say it, will be like a miser brooding over his hoarded treasure, unless he has the weapons of his eloquence ready for battle and prepared to deal with every emergency. But the degree in 3

sarium est, sic ad efficiendum oratorem maximi
protinus erit momenti. Nam certe, cum sit in
eloquendo positum oratoris officium, dicere ante
omnia est, atque hinc initium eius artis fuisse manifestum est; proximam deinde imitationem, novissi-
4 mam scribendi quoque diligentiam. Sed ut perveniri
ad summa nisi ex principiis non potest, ita procedente iam opere etiam[1] minima incipiunt esse
quae prima sunt. Verum nos non, quomodo insti-
tuendus orator, hoc loco dicimus; nam id quidem
aut satis aut certe uti potuimus dictum est; sed
athleta, qui omnes iam perdidicerit a praeceptore
numeros, quo genere exercitationis ad certamina
praeparandus sit. Igitur eum, qui res invenire et
disponere sciet, verba quoque et eligendi et collocandi
rationem perceperit, instruamus, qua ratione quod
didicerit[2] facere quam optime, quam facillime possit.

5   Num ergo dubium est, quin ei velut opes sint
quaedam parandae, quibus uti, ubicunque desidera-
tum erit, possit? Eae constant copia rerum ac
6 verborum. Sed res propriae sunt cuiusque causae
aut paucis communes, verba in universas paranda;
quae si in rebus singulis essent singula, minorem

---

    [1] etiam, *Osann*: iam, *MSS*
    [2] qua ratione, *ed. Col.* 1527: qua   oratione, *MSS.*
didicerit, *Zumpt*: dicere, *G.*

which a thing is essential does not necessarily make it of immediate and supreme importance for the formation of the ideal orator. For obviously the power of speech is the first essential, since therein lies the primary task of the orator, and it is obvious that it was with this that the art of oratory began, and that the power of imitation comes next, and third and last diligent practice in writing. But as 4 perfection cannot be attained without starting at the very beginning, the points which come first in time will, as our training proceeds, become of quite trivial importance. Now we have reached a stage in our enquiry where we are no longer considering the preliminary training of our orator; for I think the instructions already given should suffice for that; they are in any case as good as I could make them. Our present task is to consider how our athlete who has learnt all the technique of his art from his trainer, is to be prepared by actual practice for the contests in which he will have to engage. Consequently, we must assume that our student has learned how to conceive and dispose his subject matter and understands how to choose and arrange his words, and must proceed to instruct him how to make the best and readiest use of the knowledge which he has acquired.

There can then be no doubt that he must accumu- 5 late a certain store of resources, to be employed whenever they may be required. The resources of which I speak consist in a copious supply of words and matter. But while the matter is necessarily 6 either peculiar to the individual case, or at best common to only a few, words must be acquired to suit all and every case. Now, if there were special

curam postularent, nam cuncta sese cum ipsis protinus rebus offerrent. Sed cum sint aliis alia aut magis propria aut magis ornata aut plus efficientia aut melius sonantia, debent esse non solum nota omnia sed in promptu atque, ut ita dicam, in conspectu, ut, cum se iudicio dicentis ostenderint, facilis
7 ex his optimorum sit electio. Et quae idem significarent solitos scio ediscere, quo facilius et occurreret unum ex pluribus et, cum essent usi aliquo, si breve intra spatium rursus desideraretur, effugiendae repetitionis gratia sumerent aliud quod idem intelligi posset. Quod cum est puerile et cuiusdam infelicis operae tum etiam utile parum; turbam tantum modo [1] congregat, ex qua sine discrimine occupet proximum quodque.
8 Nobis autem copia cum iudicio paranda est vim orandi non circulatoriam volubilitatem spectantibus. Id autem consequemur optima legendo atque audiendo; non enim solum nomina ipsa rerum cognoscemus hac cura, sed quod quoque loco sit
9 aptissimum. Omnibus enim fere verbis [2] praeter pauca, quae sunt parum verecunda, in oratione locus est. Nam scriptores quidem iamborum veterisque comoediae etiam in illis saepe laudantur, sed nobis

---

[1] turbam tantum modo, *Halm*: turbamtum modo, *G*: turbam enim tantum, *vulgo*.
[2] fere verbis, *cod Harl.* 4995 : ferebis vel, *G*.

---

[1] See §§ 59 and 96.

words adapted to each individual thing, they would require less care, since they would automatically be suggested by the matter in hand. But since some words are more literal, more ornate, more significant or euphonious than others, our orator must not merely be acquainted with all of them, but must have them at his fingers' ends and before his very eyes, so that when they present themselves for his critical selection, he will find it easy to make the appropriate choice. I know that some speakers 7 make a practice of learning lists of synonyms by heart, in order that one word out of the several available may at once present itself to them, and that if, after using one word, they find that it is wanted again after a brief interval, they may be able to select another word with the same meaning and so avoid the necessity of repetition. But this practice is childish and involves thankless labour, while it is really of very little use, as it merely results in the assembly of a disorderly crowd of words, for the speaker to snatch the first that comes to hand.

On the contrary, discrimination is necessary in 8 the acquisition of our stock of words; for we are aiming at true oratory, not at the fluency of a cheapjack. And we shall attain our aim by reading and listening to the best writers and orators, since we shall thus learn not merely the words by which things are to be called, but when each particular word is most appropriate. For there is a place in 9 oratory for almost every word, with the exception only of a very few, which are not sufficiently seemly. Such words are indeed often praised when they occur in writers of iambics [1] or of the old comedy,

nostrum opus intueri sat est. Omnia verba, exceptis de quibus dixi, sunt alicubi optima; nam et humilibus interim et vulgaribus est opus, et quae nitidiore in parte videntur sordida, ubi res poscit,
10 proprie dicuntur. Haec ut sciamus atque eorum non significationem modo sed formas etiam mensurasque norimus, ut, ubicunque erunt posita, conveniant, nisi multa lectione atque auditione assequi nullo modo possumus, cum omnem sermonem auribus primum accipiamus. Propter quod infantes a mutis nutricibus iussu regum in solitudine educati, etiamsi
11 verba quaedam emisisse traduntur, tamen loquendi facultate caruerunt. Sunt autem alia huius naturae, ut idem pluribus vocibus declarent, ita ut nihil significationis, quo potius utaris, intersit, ut *ensis* et *gladius;* alia vero,[1] etiamsi propria rerum aliquarum sint nomina, τροπικῶς quasi tamen[2] ad eundem
12 intellectum feruntur, ut *ferrum* et *mucro.* Nam per abusionem *sicarios* etiam omnes vocamus, qui caedem telo quocunque commiserint. Alia circuitu verborum plurium ostendimus, quale est *Et pressi copia lactis.*

---

[1] alia vero, *Frotscher*: aliave, *G.*
[2] quasi tamen, *edd.*: quare tam, *G*: quare tamen, *later MSS.*

---

[1] See Herodot. ii. 2. The children were alleged to have cried "bekos," Phrygian for bread.
[2] or *catachresis.* See VIII. ii. 5 and vi. 34.
[3] *Ecl.* i. 81.

but we need do no more than consider our own
special task. All words, with these exceptions,
may be admirably employed in some place or
other. For sometimes we shall even require low
and common words, while those which would
seem coarse if introduced in the more elegant
portions of our speech may, under certain circumstances, be appropriate enough. Now to acquire a 10
knowledge of these words and to be acquainted not
merely with their meaning, but with their forms and
rhythmical values, so that they may seem appropriate
wherever employed, we shall need to read and listen
diligently, since all language is received first through
the ear. It was owing to this fact that the children
who, by order of a king, were brought up by a dumb
nurse in a desert place, although they are said to
have uttered certain words, lacked the power of
speech.[1] There are, however, some words of such 11
a nature that they express the same sense by
different sounds, so that it makes no difference to
the meaning which we use, as, for instance, *gladius*
and *ensis*, which may be used indifferently when we
have to speak of a sword. Others, again, although
properly applied to specific objects, are used by
means of a *trope* to express the same sense, as, for
example, *ferrum* (steel) and *mucro* (point), which are
both used in the sense of sword. Thus, by the 12
figure known as *abuse*,[2] we call all those who commit
a murder with any weapon whatsoever *sicarii* (poni-
arders). In other cases we express our meaning
periphrastically, as, for instance, when Virgil [3]
describes cheese as

" Abundance of pressed milk."

Plurima vero mutatione figuramus: Scio *Non ignoro*
et *Non me fugit* et *Non me praeterit* et *Quis nescit?*
13 et *Nemini dubium est.* Sed etiam ex proximo mutuari
libet. Nam et *intelligo* et *sentio* et *video* saepe idem
valent quod *scio.* Quorum nobis ubertatem ac divitias
dabit lectio, ut non solum quomodo occurrent sed
14 etiam quomodo oportet utamur. Non semper enim
haec inter se idem faciunt; nec sicut de intellectu
animi recte dixerim *video* ita de visu oculorum *in-*
telligo, nec ut *mucro* gladium sic mucronem *gladius*
15 ostendit. Sed ut copia verborum sic paratur, ita
non verborum tantum gratia legendum vel audiendum
est. Nam omnium, quaecunque docemus, hoc[1] sunt
exempla potentiora etiam ipsis quae traduntur artibus, cum eo qui discit perductus est, ut intelligere
ea sine demonstrante et sequi iam suis viribus possit,
quia, quae doctor praecepit, orator ostendit.
16   Alia vero audientes, alia legentes magis adiuvant.
Excitat qui dicit spiritu ipso, nec imagine et ambitu

---

[1] hoc, *Regius*: haec, *MSS.*

---

[1] See I. viii. 16; IX. i. 11.

On the other hand, in a number of instances we employ *figures*[1] and substitute one expression for another. Instead of "I know," we say "I am not ignorant," or "the fact does not escape me," or "I have not forgotten," or "who does not know?" or "it can be doubted by none." But we may also 13 borrow from a word of cognate meaning. For "I understand," or "I feel" or "I see" are often equivalent to "I know." Reading will provide us with a rich store of expressions such as these, and will enable us not merely to use them when they occur to us, but also in the appropriate manner. For they are not always interchangeable: for 14 example, though I may be perfectly correct in saying, "I see" for "I understand," it does not follow that I can say "I understand" for "my eyes have seen," and though *mucro* may be employed to describe a sword, a sword does not necessarily mean the same as *mucro* (point). But, although a store 15 of words may be acquired by these means, we must not read or listen to orators merely for the sake of acquiring words. For in everything which we teach examples are more effective even than the rules which are taught in the schools, so long as the student has reached a stage when he can appreciate such examples without the assistance of a teacher, and can rely on his own powers to imitate them. And the reason is this, that the professor of rhetoric lays down rules, while the orator gives a practical demonstration.

But the advantages conferred by reading and 16 listening are not identical. The speaker stimulates us by the animation of his delivery, and kindles the imagination, not by presenting us with an elaborate

rerum sed rebus incendit. Vivunt omnia enim et
moventur, excipimusque nova illa velut nascentia
cum favore ac sollicitudine. Nec fortuna modo
iudicii sed etiam ipsorum qui orant periculo adficimur.
17 Praeter haec vox, actio decora, accommodata,[1] ut
quisque locus postulabit, pronuntiandi vel potentissima in dicendo ratio et, ut semel dicam, pariter
omnia docent. In lectione certius iudicium, quod
audienti frequenter aut suus cuique favor aut ille
18 laudantium clamor extorquet. Pudet enim dissentire,
et velut tacita quadam verecundia inhibemur plus
nobis credere, cum interim et vitiosa pluribus placent,
et a conrogatis laudantur etiam quae non placent.
19 Sed e contrario quoque accidit, ut optime dictis
gratiam prava iudicia non referant. Lectio libera est
nec actionis impetu transcurrit; sed repetere saepius
licet, sive dubites sive memoriae penitus adfigere
velis. Repetamus autem et retractemus,[2] et ut cibos
mansos ac prope liquefactos demittimus, quo facilius
digerantur, ita lectio non cruda, sed multa iteratione[3]
mollita et velut confecta, memoriae imitationique
tradatur.

[1] accommodata ut, *ed. Col.* 1527: commoda aut, *G*:
commodata ut, *Halm.*
[2] retractemus, *Spalding*: tractemus, *G.*
[3] iteratione, *some late MSS.*: altercatione, *G and others.*

picture, but by bringing us into actual touch with the things themselves. Then all is life and movement, and we receive the new-born offspring of his imagination with enthusiastic approval. We are moved not merely by the actual issue of the trial, but by all that the orator himself has at stake. More- 17 over his voice, the grace of his gestures, the adaptation of his delivery (which is of supreme importance in oratory), and, in a word, all his excellences in combination, have their educative effect. In reading, on the other hand, the critical faculty is a surer guide, inasmuch as the listener's judgment is often swept away by his preference for a particular speaker, or by the applause of an enthusiastic audience. For 18 we are ashamed to disagree with them, and an unconscious modesty prevents us from ranking our own opinion above theirs, though all the time the taste of the majority is vicious, and the *claque* may praise even what does not really deserve approval. On the other hand, it will sometimes also happen 19 that an audience whose taste is bad will fail to award the praise which is due to the most admirable utterances. Reading, however, is free, and does not hurry past us with the speed of oral delivery; we can re-read a passage again and again if we are in doubt about it or wish to fix it in the memory. We must return to what we have read and reconsider it with care, while, just as we do not swallow our food till we have chewed it and reduced it almost to a state of liquefaction to assist the process of digestion, so what we read must not be committed to the memory for subsequent imitation while it is still in a crude state, but must be softened and, if I may use the phrase, reduced to a pulp by frequent re-perusal.

20   Ac diu non nisi optimus quisque et qui credentem
sibi minime fallat legendus est, sed diligenter ac
paene ad scribendi sollicitudinem; nec per partes
modo scrutanda omnia, sed perlectus liber utique
ex integro resumendus, praecipueque oratio, cuius
virtutes frequenter ex industria quoque occultantur.

21 Saepe enim praeparat, dissimulat, insidiatur orator,
eaque in prima parte actionis dicit, quae sunt in summa
profutura.   Itaque suo loco minus placent, adhuc
nobis quare dicta sint ignorantibus, ideoque erunt

22 cognitis omnibus repetenda.   Illud vero utilissimum
nosse eas causas, quarum orationes in manus sump-
serimus et, quotiens continget, utrinque habitas
legere actiones: ut Demosthenis atque Aeschinis
inter se contrarias, et Servii Sulpicii atque Messalae,
quorum alter pro Aufidia, contra dixit alter, et
Pollionis et Cassii reo Asprenate aliasque plurimas.

23 Quinetiam si minus pares videbuntur aliquae, tamen
ad cognoscendam litium quaestionem recte requiren-
tur, ut contra Ciceronis orationes Tuberonis in
Ligarium et Hortensii pro Verre.   Quinetiam,
easdem causas ut quisque egerit utile[1] erit scire.

---

[1] utile, *edd. Ald. and Col.*: utrisque, *G and most MSS.*

---

[1] See iv. ii. 106 and vi. i. 20.
[2] See § 113.   [3] See § 116.
[4] C. Nonius Asprenas, a friend of Augustus, accused by
Cassius and defended by Pollio on a charge of poisoning.

For a long time also we should read none save the 20
best authors and such as are least likely to betray our
trust in them, while our reading must be almost as
thorough as if we were actually transcribing what we
read. Nor must we study it merely in parts, but
must read through the whole work from cover to
cover and then read it afresh, a precept which applies
more especially to speeches, whose merits are often
deliberately disguised. For the orator frequently 21
prepares his audience for what is to come, dissembles
and sets a trap for them and makes remarks at the
opening of his speech which will not have their full
force till the conclusion. Consequently what he
says will often seem comparatively ineffective where
it actually occurs, since we do not realise his motive
and it will be necessary to re-read the speech after
we have acquainted ourselves with all that it contains. Above all, it is most desirable that we should 22
familiarise ourselves with the facts of the case with
which the speech deals, and it will be well also,
wherever possible, to read the speeches delivered on
both sides, such as those of Aeschines and Demosthenes in the case of Ctesiphon, of Servius Sulpicius
and Messala for and against Aufidia,[1] of Pollio [2] and
Cassius [3] in the case of Asprenas,[4] and many others.
And even if such speeches seem unequal in point of 23
merit, we shall still do well to study them carefully
with a view to understanding the problems raised by
the cases with which they deal: for example, we
should compare the speeches delivered by Tubero
against Ligarius and by Hortensius in defence of
Verres with those of Cicero for the opposite side,
while it will also be useful to know how different
orators pleaded the same case. For example,

Nam de domo Ciceronis dixit Calidius, et pro Milone
orationem Brutus exercitationis gratia scripsit, etiamsi
egisse eum Cornelius Celsus falso existimat; et
Pollio et Messala defenderunt eosdem, et nobis
pueris insignes pro Voluseno Catulo Domitii Afri,
Crispi Passieni, Decimi Laelii orationes ferebantur.

24 Neque id statim legenti persuasum sit omnia
quae optimi auctores dixerint utique esse perfecta.
Nam et labuntur aliquando et oneri cedunt et indulgent ingeniorum suorum voluptati, nec semper
intendunt animum; nonnunquam fatigantur, cum
Ciceroni dormitare interim Demosthenes, Horatio
25 vero etiam Homerus ipse videatur. Summi enim
sunt, homines tamen, acciditque his qui, quidquid
apud illos repererunt, dicendi legem putant, ut
deteriora imitentur, (id enim est facilius) ac se
abunde similes putent, si vitia magnorum consequan-
26 tur. Modesto tamen et circumspecto iudicio de
tantis viris pronuntiandum est, ne, quod plerisque
accidit, damnent quae non intelligunt. Ac si necesse
est in alteram errare partem : omnia eorum legenti-
bus placere quam multa displicere maluerim.

27 Plurimum dicit oratori conferre Theophrastus
lectionem poetarum, multique eius iudicium sequuntur; neque immerito. Namque ab his in rebus

---

[1] Probably before some other tribunal. Cicero's *de Domo
Sua* was delivered before the *pontifices*.

[2] *cp.* III. vi. 93. Cornelius Celsus was an encyclopaedic
writer of the early empire, whose treatise on medicine has
survived.

[3] Liburnia. See IX. ii. 34.   [4] See § 118.

[5] Stepfather of Nero. See VI. i. 50.

[6] Probably the Laelius Balbus of Tac. *Ann.* VI. 47, 48.

[7] In a lost letter : *cp.* Plut. *Cic.* 24.   [8] *A. P.* 359.

[9] In one of his lost rhetorical treatises.

Calidius[1] spoke on the subject of Cicero's house,
Brutus wrote a declamation in defence of Milo, which
Cornelius Celsus wrongly believes to have been
actually delivered in court,[2] and Pollio and Messalla
defended the same clients,[3] while in my boyhood
remarkable speeches delivered by Domitius Afer,[4]
Crispus Passienus[5] and Decimus Laelius[6] in defence of Volusenus were in circulation.

The reader must not, however, jump to the conclu- 24
sion that all that was uttered by the best authors is
necessarily perfect. At times they lapse and stagger
beneath the weight of their task, indulge their bent
or relax their efforts. Sometimes, again, they give
the impression of weariness: for example, Cicero[7]
thinks that Demosthenes sometimes nods, and Horace[8]
says the same of Homer himself. For despite their 25
greatness they are still but mortal men, and it will
sometimes happen that their reader assumes that
anything which he finds in them may be taken as a
canon of style, with the result that he imitates their
defects (and it is always easier to do this than to
imitate their excellences) and thinks himself a
perfect replica if he succeeds in copying the
blemishes of great men. But modesty and circum- 26
spection are required in pronouncing judgment on
such great men, since there is always the risk of
falling into the common fault of condemning what
one does not understand. And, if it is necessary to
err on one side or the other, I should prefer that
the reader should approve of everything than that
he should disapprove of much.

Theophrastus[9] says that the reading of poets is 27
of great service to the orator, and has rightly been
followed in this view by many. For the poets will

spiritus et in verbis sublimitas et in adfectibus
motus omnis et in personis decor petitur, praecipueque velut attrita cotidiano actu forensi ingenia
optime rerum talium blanditia reparantur.   Ideoque
28 in hac lectione Cicero requiescendum putat.   Meminerimus tamen, non per omnia poetas esse oratori
sequendos nec libertate verborum nec licentia
figurarum ; genus ostentationi comparatum et praeter
id, quod solam petit voluptatem eamque etiam
fingendo non falsa modo sed etiam quaedam in-
29 credibilia sectatur, patrocinio quoque aliquo iuvari,
quod alligata ad certam pedum necessitatem non
semper uti propriis possit, sed depulsa recta via
necessario ad eloquendi quaedam deverticula con-
fugiat, nec mutare quaedam modo verba, sed ex-
tendere, corripere, convertere, dividere cogatur ;
nos vero armatos stare in acie et summis de rebus
30 decernere et ad victoriam niti.   Neque ergo arma
squalere situ ac rubigine velim, sed fulgorem inesse
qui terreat, qualis est ferri, quo mens simul visusque
praestringitur, non qualis auri argentique, imbellis
et potius habenti periculosus.
31   Historia quoque alere oratorem quodam uberi [1]
iucundoque suco potest ; verum et ipsa sic est

---

[1] uberi, *Spalding* : moveri, *G.*

[1] *Pro Arch.* 12.

give us inspiration as regards the matter, sublimity of language, the power to excite every kind of emotion, and the appropriate treatment of character, while minds that have become jaded owing to the daily wear and tear of the courts will find refreshment in such agreeable study. Consequently Cicero [1] recommends the relaxation provided by the reading of poetry. We should, however, remember that the 28 orator must not follow the poets in everything, more especially in their freedom of language and their license in the use of figures. Poetry has been compared to the oratory of display, and further, aims solely at giving pleasure, which it seeks to secure by inventing what is not merely untrue, but sometimes even incredible. Further, we must bear in mind 29 that it can be defended on the ground that it is tied by certain metrical necessities and consequently cannot always use straightforward and literal language, but is driven from the direct road to take refuge in certain by-ways of expression; and compelled not merely to change certain words, but to lengthen, contract, transpose or divide them, whereas the orator stands armed in the forefront of the battle, fights for a high stake and devotes all his effort to winning the victory. And yet I would not have his 30 weapons defaced by mould and rust, but would have them shine with a splendour that shall strike terror to the heart of the foe, like the flashing steel that dazzles heart and eye at once, not like the gleam of gold or silver, which has no warlike efficacy and is even a positive peril to its wearer.

History, also, may provide the orator with a nutri- 31 ment which we may compare to some rich and pleasant juice. But when we read it, we must

legenda, ut sciamus, plerasque eius virtutes oratori
esse vitandas. Est enim proxima poetis et quodammodo carmen solutum, et scribitur ad narrandum
non ad probandum, totumque opus non ad actum rei
pugnamque praesentem, sed ad memoriam posteritatis et ingenii famam componitur ; ideoque et verbis
remotioribus et liberioribus figuris narrandi taedium
32 evitat. Itaque, ut dixi, neque illa Sallustiana brevitas,
qua nihil apud aures vacuas atque eruditas potest
esse perfectius, apud occupatum variis cogitationibus
iudicem et saepius ineruditum captanda nobis est ;
neque illa Livii lactea ubertas satis docebit eum, qui
33 non speciem expositionis, sed fidem quaerit. Adde
quod [1] M. Tullius ne Thucydidem quidem aut
Xenophontem utiles oratori putat, quanquam illum
bellicum canere, huius ore *Musas esse locutas* existimet.
Licet tamen nobis in digressionibus uti vel historico
nonnunquam nitore, dum in his, de quibus erit
quaestio, meminerimus, non athletarum toris, sed
militum lacertis opus [2] esse ; nec versicolorem illam,
qua Demetrius Phalereus dicebatur uti, vestem bene
34 ad forensem pulverem facere. Est et alius ex

---

[1] adde quod, *Regius* : audeo quia, *G.*
[2] opus, *added by ed. Col.* 1527.

---

[1] IV. ii. 45.   [2] *Or.* 30 *sq.*
         [3] *cp.* § 80.

remember that many of the excellences of the historian require to be shunned by the orator. For history has a certain affinity to poetry and may be regarded as a kind of prose poem, while it is written for the purpose of narrative, not of proof, and designed from beginning to end not for immediate effect or the instant necessities of forensic strife, but to record events for the benefit of posterity and to win glory for its author. Consequently, to avoid monotony of narrative, it employs unusual words and indulges in a freer use of figures. Therefore, as I have already 32 said,[1] the famous brevity of Sallust, than which nothing can be more pleasing to the leisured ear of the scholar, is a style to be avoided by the orator in view of the fact that his words are addressed to a judge who has his mind occupied by a number of thoughts and is also frequently uneducated, while, on the other hand, the milky fullness of Livy is hardly of a kind to instruct a listener who looks not for beauty of exposition, but for truth and credibility. We must also remember that Cicero[2] thinks that not 33 even Thucydides or Xenophon will be of much service to an orator, although he regards the style of the former as a veritable call to arms and considers that the latter was the mouthpiece of the Muses. It is, however, occasionally permissible to borrow the graces of history to embellish our digressions, provided always that we remember that in those portions of our speech which deal with the actual question at issue we require not the swelling thews of the athlete, but the wiry sinews of the soldier, and that the cloak of many colours which Demetrius of Phalerum[3] was said to wear is but little suited to the dust and heat of the forum. There is, it is true, 34

historiis usus et is quidem maximus, sed non ad praesentem pertinens locum, ex cognitione rerum exemplorumque, quibus inprimis instructus esse debet orator, ne omnia testimonia exspectet a litigatore, sed pleraque ex vetustate diligenter sibi cognita sumat, hoc potentiora, quod ea sola criminibus odii et gratiae vacant.

35 A philosophorum vero lectione ut essent multa nobis petenda, vitio factum est oratorum, qui quidem illis optima sui operis parte cesserunt. Nam et de iustis, honestis, utilibus, iisque quae sint istis contraria, et de rebus divinis maxime dicunt et argumentantur acriter Stoici,[1] et altercationibus atque interrogationibus oratorem futurum optime Socratici 36 praeparant. Sed his quoque adhibendum est simile iudicium, ut etiam cum in rebus versemur iisdem, non tamen eandem esse condicionem sciamus litium ac disputationum, fori et auditorii, praeceptorum et periculorum.

37 Credo exacturos plerosque, cum tantum esse utilitatis in legendo iudicemus, ut id quoque adiungamus operi, qui sint legendi,[2] quae in auctore

---

[1] Stoici *added by Meister.*
[2] legendi *inserted by ed. Col.* 1527.

---

[1] *cp.* I *Pref.* 11.

another advantage which we may derive from the historians, which, however, despite its great importance, has no bearing on our present topic; I refer to the advantage derived from the knowledge of historical facts and precedents, with which it is most desirable that our orator should be acquainted; for such knowledge will save him from having to acquire all his evidence from his client and will enable him to draw much that is germane to his case from the careful study of antiquity. And such arguments will be all the more effective, since they alone will be above suspicion of prejudice or partiality.

The fact that there is so much for which we must 35 have recourse to the study of the philosophers is the fault of orators who have abandoned[1] to them the fullest portion of their own task. The Stoics more especially discourse and argue with great keenness on what is just, honourable, expedient and the reverse, as well as on the problems of theology, while the Socratics give the future orator a first-rate preparation for forensic debates and the examination of witnesses. But we must use the 36 same critical caution in studying the philosophers that we require in reading history or poetry; that is to say, we must bear in mind that, even when we are dealing with the same subjects, there is a wide difference between forensic disputes and philosophical discussions, between the law-courts and the lecture-room, between the precepts of theory and the perils of the bar.

Most of my readers will, I think, demand that, 37 since I attach so much importance to reading, I should include in this work some instructions as to what authors should be read and what their special

quoque praecipua virtus. Sed persequi singulos
38 infiniti fuerit operis. Quippe cum in Bruto M.
Tullius tot milibus versuum de Romanis tantum
oratoribus loquatur et tamen de omnibus aetatis suae,
quibuscum vivebat, exceptis Caesare atque Marcello,
silentium egerit, quis erit modus, si et illos et qui
39 postea fuerunt et Graecos omnes?[1] Fuit igitur
brevitas illa tutissima, quae est apud Livium in
epistola ad filium scripta, legendos Demosthenem
atque Ciceronem, tum ita, ut quisque esset De-
40 mostheni et Ciceroni simillimus. Non est tamen
dissimulanda nostri quoque iudicii summa. Paucos
enim vel potius vix ullum ex his qui vetustatem
pertulerunt existimo posse reperiri, quin iudicium
adhibentibus adlaturus sit utilitatis aliquid, cum se
Cicero ab illis quoque vetustissimis auctoribus, ingeniosis quidem, sed arte carentibus, plurimum
41 fateatur adiutum. Nec multo aliud de novis sentio.
Quotus enim quisque inveniri tam demens potest,
qui ne minima quidem alicuius certe fiducia partis
memoriam posteritatis speraverit? Qui si quis est,
intra primos statim versus deprehendetur et citius
nos dimittet, quam ut eius nobis magno temporis
42 detrimento constet experimentum. Sed non quidquid ad aliquam partem scientiae pertinet, protinus
ad phrasin, de qua loquimur, accommodatum.

Verum antequam de singulis, pauca in universum

---

[1] Graecos *is followed in the MSS.* by et philosophos, *which
is expurged by Schmidt.*

excellences may be. To do this in detail would be an endless task. Remember that Cicero in his 38 *Brutus*, after writing pages and pages on the subject of Roman orators alone, says nothing of his own contemporaries with the exception of Caesar and Marcellus. What limit, then, would there be to my labours if I were to attempt to deal with them and with their successors and all the orators of Greece as well? No, it was a safer course that Livy adopted 39 in his letter to his son, where he writes that he should read Cicero and Demosthenes and then such orators as most resembled them. Still, I must not conceal 40 my own personal convictions on this subject. I believe that there are few, indeed scarcely a single one of those authors who have stood the test of time who will not be of some use or other to judicious students, since even Cicero himself admits that he owes a great debt even to the earliest writers, who for all their talent were totally devoid of art. And my opinion about 41 the moderns is much the same. For how few of them are so utterly crazy as not to have the least shadow of hope that some portion or other of their work may have claims upon the memory of posterity? If there is such an one, he will be detected before we have perused many lines of his writings, and we shall escape from him before the experiment of reading him has cost us any serious loss of time. On the 42 other hand, not everything that has some bearing on some department of knowledge will necessarily be of service for the formation of style, with which we are for the moment concerned.

Before, however, I begin to speak of individual authors, I must make a few general remarks about the variety of judgments which have been passed

43 de varietate opinionum dicenda sunt. Nam quidam
solos veteres legendos putant neque in ullis aliis
esse naturalem eloquentiam et robur viris dignum
arbitrantur; alios recens haec lascivia deliciaeque et
omnia ad voluptatem multitudinis imperitae com-
44 posita delectant. Ipsorum etiam qui rectum dicendi
genus sequi volunt, alii pressa demum et tenuia et
quae minimum ab usu cotidiano recedant, sana et
vere Attica putant; quosdam elatior ingenii vis
et magis concitata et plena spiritus capit; sunt
etiam lenis et nitidi et compositi generis non pauci
amatores. De qua differentia disseram diligentius,
cum de genere dicendi quaerendum erit. Interim
summatim, quid et[1] a qua lectione petere possint,
qui confirmare facultatem dicendi volent, attingam.
Paucos enim qui[2] sunt eminentissimi excerpere in
5 animo est. Facile est autem studiosis, qui sint his
simillimi, iudicare; ne quisquam queratur omissos
forte quos ipse valde probet. Fateor enim plures[3]
legendos esse quam qui a me nominabuntur. Sed
nunc genera ipsa lectionum, quae praecipue convenire intendentibus ut oratores fiant, existimem,
persequar.

46 Igitur, ut Aratus *ab Iove incipiendum* putat, ita nos

---

[1] summatim quid et a qua, *vulgo* : sumat et a qua, *G* (quia
et a qua 2*nd hand*).
[2] qui *added by ed. Col.* 1527.
[3] plures, *vulgo* : plurimis, *G*.

---

[1] XII. **x.** 63 *sqq.*

upon them. For there are some who think that only 43
the ancients should be read and hold that they are
the sole possessors of natural eloquence and manly
vigour; while others revel in the voluptuous and
affected style of to-day, in which everything is designed to charm the ears of the uneducated majority.
And even if we turn to those who desire to follow 44
the correct methods of style, we shall find that some
think that the only healthy and genuinely Attic style
is to be found in language which is restrained and
simple and as little removed as possible from the
speech of every day, while others are attracted by a
style which is more elevated and full of energy and
animation. There are, too, not a few who are devoted to a gentle, elegant and harmonious style. Of
these different ideals I shall speak in greater detail,
when I come to discuss the question of the particular
styles best suited to oratory.[1] For the moment I
shall restrict myself to touching briefly on what the
student who desires to consolidate his powers of
speaking should seek in his reading and to what kind
of reading he should devote his attention. My design is merely to select a few of the most eminent
authors for consideration. It will be easy for the 45
student to decide for himself what authors most
nearly resemble these: consequently, no one will
have any right to complain if I pass over some of his
favourites. For I will readily admit that there are
more authors worth reading than those whom I propose to mention. But I will now proceed to deal
with the various classes of reading which I consider
most suitable for those who are ambitious of becoming
orators.

I shall, I think, be right in following the principle 46

rıte coepturi ab Homero videmur. Hic enim, quemadmodum ex Oceano dicit ipse omnium [1] amnium
fontiumque cursus initium capere, omnibus eloquentiae partibus exemplum et ortum dedit. Hunc nemo
in magnis rebus sublimitate, in parvis proprietate
superaverit. Idem laetus ac pressus, iucundus et
gravis, tum copia tum brevitate mirabilis, nec poetica
47 modo sed oratoria virtute eminentissimus. Nam ut
de laudibus, exhortationibus, consolationibus taceam,
nonne vel nonus liber, quo missa ad Achillem legatio
continetur, vel in primo inter duces illa contentio vel
dictae in secundo sententiae omnes litium ac consili-
48 orum explicant artes? Adfectus quidem vel illos
mites vel hos concitatos, nemo erit tam indoctus, qui
non in sua potestate hunc auctorem habuisse fateatur.
Age vero, non utriusque operis sui ingressu in paucissimis versibus legem prooemiorum non dico servavit
sed constituit? Nam benevolum auditorem invocatione
dearum, quas praesidere vatibus creditum est, et
intentum proposita rerum magnitudine et docilem
49 summa celeriter comprehensa facit. Narrare vero
quis brevius quam qui mortem nuntiat Patrocli, quis
significantius potest quam qui Curetum Aetolorumque
proelium exponit? Iam similitudines, amplificationes,

---

[1] omnium *added by Osann.*

---

[1] Arat. *Phaen.* 1.   [2] *Il.* xxi. 196.
[3] Antilochus, *Il.* xviii. 18.   [4] Phoenix, *Il.* ix. 529.

laid down by Aratus [1] in the line, "With Jove let us begin," and in beginning with Homer. He is like his own conception of Ocean,[2] which he describes as the source of every stream and river; for he has given us a model and an inspiration for every department of eloquence. It will be generally admitted that no one has ever surpassed him in the sublimity with which he invests great themes or the propriety with which he handles small. He is at once luxuriant and concise, sprightly and serious, remarkable at once for his fullness and his brevity, and supreme not merely for poetic, but for oratorical power as well. For, to say nothing of his eloquence, 47 which he shows in praise, exhortation and consolation, do not the ninth book containing the embassy to Achilles, the first describing the quarrel between the chiefs, or the speeches delivered by the counsellors in the second, display all the rules of art to be followed in forensic or deliberative oratory? As regards the emotions, there can be no one so ill- 48 educated as to deny that the poet was the master of all, tender and vehement alike. Again, in the few lines with which he introduces both of his epics, has he not, I will not say observed, but actually established the law which should govern the composition of the exordium? For, by his invocation of the goddesses believed to preside over poetry he wins the goodwill of his audience, by his statement of the greatness of his themes he excites their attention and renders them receptive by the briefness of his summary. Who can narrate more briefly than the hero [3] who 49 brings the news of Patroclus' death, or more vividly than he [4] who describes the battle between the Curetes and the Aetolians? Then consider his

exempla, digressus, signa rerum et argumenta ceteraque genera [1] probandi ac refutandi sunt ita multa, ut etiam qui de artibus scripserunt plurimi harum rerum
50 testimonium ab hoc poeta petant.   Nam epilogus quidem quis unquam poterit illis Priami rogantis Achillem precibus aequari?   Quid? in verbis, sententiis, figuris, dispositione totius operis nonne humani ingenii modum excedit? ut magni sit virtutes eius non aemulatione, quod fieri non potest, sed
51 intellectu sequi.   Verum hic omnes sine dubio et in omni genere eloquentiae procul a se reliquit, epicos tamen praecipue, videlicet quia clarissima [2] in materia
52 simili comparatio est.   Raro assurgit Hesiodus, magnaque pars eius in nominibus est occupata; tamen utiles circa praecepta sententiae levitasque verborum et compositionis probabilis, daturque ei
53 palma in illo medio genere dicendi.   Contra in Antimacho vis et gravitas et minime vulgare eloquendi genus habet laudem.   Sed quamvis ei secundas fere grammaticorum consensus deferat, et adfectibus et iucunditate et dispositione et omnino arte deficitur, ut plane manifesto appareat, quanto
54 sit aliud proximum esse aliud secundum. [3] Panyasin

---

[1] genera, *Caesar* : quae, *G.*
[2] clarissima, *most MSS. :* durissima, *G.*
[3] secundum, *various late MSS. omitted by G.*

---

[1] *Il.* xxiv. 486 *sqq.*   [2] Especially the *Theogony.*
[3] Antimachus of Colophon (*flor. circ.* 405 B.C.), author of a Thebaid.
[4] Uncle of Herodotus, author of a Heracleia.

similes, his amplifications, his illustrations, digressions, indications of fact, inferences, and all the other methods of proof and refutation which he employs. They are so numerous that the majority of writers on the principles of rhetoric have gone to his works for examples of all these things. And as for perorations, what can ever be equal to the prayers which Priam addresses to Achilles [1] when he comes to beg for the body of his son? Again, does he not transcend the limits of human genius in his choice of words, his reflexions, figures, and the arrangement of his whole work, with the result that it requires a powerful mind, I will not say to imitate, for that is impossible, but even to appreciate his excellences? But he has in truth outdistanced all that have come after him in every department of eloquence, above all, he has outstripped all other writers of epic, the contrast in their case being especially striking owing to the similarity of the material with which they deal. Hesiod rarely rises to any height, while a great part of his works is filled almost entirely with names [2]: none the less, his maxims of moral wisdom provide a useful model, the smooth flow of his words and structure merit our approval, and he is assigned the first place among writers of the intermediate style. On the other hand, Antimachus[3] deserves praise for the vigour, dignity and elevation of his language. But although practically all teachers of literature rank him second among epic poets, he is deficient in emotional power, charm, and arrangement of matter, and totally devoid of real art. No better example can be found to show what a vast difference there is to being near another writer and being second to him. Panyasis[4] is

ex utroque mixtum putant in eloquendo neutrius-
que aequare virtutes, alterum tamen ab eo materia
alterum disponendi ratione superari. Apollonius in
ordinem a grammaticis datum non venit, quia
Aristarchus atque Aristophanes, poetarum iudices,
neminem sui temporis in numerum redegerunt; non
tamen contemnendum reddidit opus aequali quadam
55 mediocritate. Arati materia motu caret, ut in qua
nulla varietas, nullus adfectus, nulla persona, nulla
cuiusquam sit oratio; sufficit tamen operi, cui se
parem credidit. Admirabilis in suo genere Theocritus, sed musa illa rustica et pastoralis non forum
56 modo, verum ipsam etiam urbem reformidat. Audire
videor undique congerentes nomina plurimorum
poetarum. Quid? Herculis acta non bene Pisandros?
Nicandrum frustra secuti Macer atque Vergilius?
Quid? Euphorionem transibimus? quem nisi pro-
basset Vergilius, idem nunquam certe *conditorum*
Chalcidico versu carminum fecisset in Bucolicis mentionem. Quid? Horatius frustra Tyrtaeum Homero
57 subiungit? Nec sane quisquam est tam procul a
cognitione eorum remotus, ut non indicem certe ex

---

[1] Apollonius of Rhodes, author of the Argonautica. The
list to which reference is made consisted of the four poets
just mentioned, with the addition of Pisandros, for whom
see § 56.

[2] Aristophanes of Byzantium.

[3] A Rhodian poet of the seventh century B.C.

[4] Nicander of Colophon (second century B.C.), author of
didactic poems, Theriaca and Alexipharmaca and Metamorphoses (ἑτεροιούμενα). Virgil imitated him in the *Georgics*,
Aemilius Macer, the friend of Ovid, in his *Theriaca*.

[5] Euphorion of Chalcis (220 B.C.) wrote elaborate short
epics. See *Ecl.* x. 50. The words are, however, put into
the mouth of Gallus with reference to his own imitations of
Euphorion.

regarded as combining the qualities of the last two
poets, being their inferior in point of style, but
surpassing Hesiod in the choice of his subject and
Antimachus in its arrangement. Apollonius [1] is not
admitted to the lists drawn up by the professors
of literature, because the critics, Aristarchus and
Aristophanes,[2] included no contemporary poets.
None the less, his work is by no means to be
despised, being distinguished by the consistency
with which he maintains his level as a repre-
sentative of the intermediate type. The subject 55
chosen by Aratus is lifeless and monotonous, afford-
ing no scope for pathos, description of character,
or eloquent speeches. However, he is adequate for
the task to which he felt himself equal. Theocritus
is admirable in his own way, but the rustic and
pastoral muse shrinks not merely from the forum,
but from town-life of every kind. I think I hear 56
my readers on all sides suggesting the names of
hosts of other poets. What? Did not Pisandros [3]
tell the story of Hercules in admirable style?
Were there not good reasons for Virgil and Macer
taking Nicander [4] as a model? Are we to ignore
Euphorion? [5] Unless Virgil had admired him, he
would never have mentioned

“ verses written in Chalcidic strain ”

in the *Eclogues*. Again, had Horace no justification
for coupling the name of Tyrtaeus [6] with that of
Homer? To which I reply, that there is no one so 57
ignorant of poetic literature that he could not, if he
chose, copy a catalogue of such poets from some

[6] See Hor. *A. P.* 401. Tyrtaeus, writer of war songs
(seventh century B.C.).

33

bibliotheca sumptum transferre in libros suos possit.
Nec ignoro igitur quos transeo nec utique damno, ut
58 qui dixerim esse in omnibus utilitatis aliquid. Sed
ad illos iam perfectis constitutisque viribus reverte-
mur; quod in cenis grandibus saepe facimus ut, cum
optimis satiati sumus, varietas tamen nobis ex vilio-
ribus grata sit.   Tunc et elegiam vacabit in manus
sumere, cuius princeps habetur Callimachus, secundas
59 confessione plurimorum Philetas occupavit.   Sed
dum adsequamur[1] illam firmam, ut dixi, facilitatem,
optimis adsuescendum est et multa magis quam multorum lectione formanda mens et ducendus color.
Itaque ex tribus receptis Aristarchi iudicio scriptoribus iamborum ad ἕξιν maxime pertinebit unus Archi-
60 lochus.   Summa in hoc vis elocutionis, cum validae
tum breves vibrantesque sententiae, plurimum sanguinis atque nervorum, adeo ut videatur quibusdam,
quod quoquam minor est, materiae esse non ingenii
61 vitium.   Novem vero Lyricorum longe Pindarus
princeps spiritus magnificentia, sententiis, figuris,
beatissima rerum verborumque copia et velut quodam
eloquentiae flumine; propter quae Horatius eum

---

[1] adsequamur, *Halm* : adsequimur, *G and most MSS.* :
adsequatur, *a few late MSS.*

---

[1] § 45.   [2] Philetas of Cos (290 B.C.).   [3] x. i. 1.
[4] *i.e.* invective. The other two writers are Simonides of
Amorgos and Hipponax of Ephesus. Archilochus (*fl.*
686 B.C.).
[5] The five not mentioned here are Alcman, Sappho, Ibycus,
Anacreon and Bacchylides.   [6] *Od.* IV. ii. 1.

library for insertion in his own treatises. I can
therefore assure my readers that I am well aware
of the existence of the poets whom I pass over in
silence, and am far from condemning them, since I
have already said that some profit may be derived
from every author.[1] But we must wait till our 58
powers have been developed and established to the
full before we turn to these poets, just as at banquets
we take our fill of the best fare and then turn
to other food which, in spite of its comparative
inferiority, is still attractive owing to its variety.
Not until our taste is formed shall we have leisure
to study the elegiac poets as well. Of these, Callimachus is regarded as the best, the second place
being, according to the verdict of most critics,
occupied by Philetas.[2] But until we have acquired 59
that assured facility of which I spoke,[3] we must
familiarise ourselves with the best writers only and
must form our minds and develop an appropriate tone
by reading that is deep rather than wide. Consequently, of the three writers of iambics [4] approved by
the judgment of Aristarchus, Archilochus will be far
the most useful for the formation of the facility in
question. For he has a most forcible style, is full of 60
vigorous, terse and pungent reflexions, and over-
flowing with life and energy: indeed, some critics
think that it is due solely to the nature of his
subjects, and not to his genius, that any poets are to
be ranked above him. Of the nine lyric poets [5] 61
Pindar is by far the greatest, in virtue of his inspired
magnificence, the beauty of his thoughts and figures,
the rich exuberance of his language and matter,
and his rolling flood of eloquence, characteristics
which, as Horace [6] rightly held, make him in-

62 merito credidit nemini imitabilem.   Stesichorus quam
sit ingenio validus, materiae quoque ostendunt,
maxima bella et clarissimos canentem duces et epici
carminis onera lyra sustinentem.   Reddit enim
personis in agendo simul loquendoque debitam
dignitatem, ac si tenuisset modum, videtur aemulari
proximus Homerum potuisse; sed redundat atque
effunditur, quod ut est reprehendendum, ita copiae

63 vitium est.   Alcaeus in parte operis *aureo plectro*
merito donatur, qua tyrannos insectatus multum
etiam moribus confert in eloquendo quoque brevis
et magnificus et dicendi vi[1] plerumque oratori similis;
sed et lusit[2] et in amores descendit, maioribus tamen

64 aptior.   Simonides, tenuis alioqui, sermone proprio
et iucunditate quadam commendari potest; praecipua
tamen eius in commovenda miseratione virtus, ut
quidam in hac eum parte omnibus eius operis
auctoribus praeferant.

65   Antiqua comoedia cum sinceram illam sermonis
Attici gratiam prope sola retinet, tum facundissimae
libertatis est et in[3] insectandis vitiis praecipua, plurimum tamen virium etiam in ceteris partibus habet.
Nam et grandis et elegans et venusta, et nescio an
ulla, post Homerum tamen, quem ut Achillem

---

[1] dicendi vi, *Halm* : dicendi et, *G.*
[2] sed et lusit, *several late MSS.* : et eius sit, *G.*
[3] est et in, *G. A. B. Wolff* : etsi est, *MSS.*

---

[1] Stesichorus of Himera in Sicily (*flor. circ.* 600 B.C.),
wrote in lyric verse on many legends, more especially on
themes connected with the Trojan war.
[2] Hor. *Od.* II. xiii. 26.   Alcaeus of Mitylene (*circa* 600
B.C.).
[3] Simonides of Ceos, 556–468 B.C., famous for all forms of
lyric poetry, especially funeral odes.

imitable. The greatness of the genius of Stesichorus [1] 62
is shown by his choice of subject: for he sings of the
greatest wars and the most glorious of chieftains,
and the music of his lyre is equal to the weighty
themes of epic poetry. For both in speech and
action he invests his characters with the dignity
which is their due, and if he had only been capable
of exercising a little more restraint, he might,
perhaps, have proved a serious rival to Homer.
But he is redundant and diffuse, a fault which,
while deserving of censure, is nevertheless a defect
springing from the very fullness of his genius.
Alcaeus has deserved the compliment of being said 63
to make music with *quill of gold* [2] in that portion
of his works in which he attacks the tyrants of his
day and shows himself a real moral force. He is,
moreover, terse and magnificent in style, while the
vigour of his diction resembles that of oratory. But
he also wrote poetry of a more sportive nature and
stooped to erotic poetry, despite his aptitude for
loftier themes. Simonides [3] wrote in a simple style, 64
but may be recommended for the propriety and
charm of his language. His chief merit, however,
lies in his power to excite pity, so much so, in fact,
that some rank him in this respect above all writers
of this class of poetry.

The old comedy is almost the only form of poetry 65
which preserves intact the true grace of Attic
diction, while it is characterised by the most eloquent freedom of speech, and shows especial power
in the denunciation of vice; but it reveals great
force in other departments as well. For its style
is at once lofty, elegant and graceful, and if we
except Homer, who, like Achilles among warriors,

semper excipi par est, aut similior sit oratoribus
66 aut ad oratores faciendos aptior. Plures eius
auctores; Aristophanes tamen et Eupolis Crati-
nusque praecipui. Tragoedias primus in lucem
Aeschylus protulit, sublimis et gravis et grandiloquus
saepe usque ad vitium, sed rudis in plerisque et
incompositus; propter quod correctas eius fabulas in
certamen deferre posterioribus poetis Athenienses
67 permiserunt, suntque eo modo multi coronati. Sed
longe clarius illustraverunt hoc opus Sophocles atque
Euripides, quorum in dispari dicendi via uter sit
poeta melior, inter plurimos quaeritur; idque ego
sane, quoniam ad praesentem materiam nihil pertinet,
iniudicatum relinquo. Illud quidem nemo non fateatur necesse est, iis qui se ad agendum comparant
68 utiliorem longe fore Euripiden. Namque is et
sermone (quod ipsum reprehendunt, quibus gravitas
et cothurnus et sonus Sophocli videtur esse subli-
mior) magis accedit oratorio generi et sententiis
densus et in iis quae a sapientibus tradita sunt
paene ipsis par, et dicendo ac respondendo cuilibet
eorum qui fuerunt in foro diserti comparandus; in
adfectibus vero cum omnibus mirus tum in iis qui
69 miseratione constant facile praecipuus. Hunc [1] admiratus maxime est, ut saepe testatur, et secutus, quanquam in opere diverso, Menander, qui vel unus, meo

---

[1] hunc, *several late MSS.* : et, *G.*

---

[1] Contemporaries: Cratinus (519–422), Aristophanes (448–
380), Eupolis (446–410).

is beyond all comparison, I am not sure that there is any style which bears a closer resemblance to oratory or is better adapted for forming the orator. There are a number of writers of the old comedy, 66 but the best are Aristophanes, Eupolis and Cratinus.[1] Aeschylus was the first to bring tragedy into prominence: he is lofty, dignified, grandiloquent often to a fault, but frequently uncouth and inharmonious. Consequently, the Athenians allowed later poets to revise his tragedies and to produce them in the dramatic contests, and many succeeded in winning the prize by such means. Sophocles 67 and Euripides, however, brought tragedy to far greater perfection: they differ in style, but it is much disputed as to which should be awarded the supremacy, a question which, as it has no bearing on my present theme, I shall make no attempt to decide. But this much is certain and incontrovertible, that Euripides will be found of far greater service to those who are training themselves for pleading in court. For his language, although actually censured 68 by those who regard the dignity, the stately stride and sonorous utterance of Sophocles as being more sublime, has a closer affinity to that of oratory, while he is full of striking reflexions, in which, indeed, in their special sphere, he rivals the philosophers themselves, and for defence and attack may be compared with any orator that has won renown in the courts. Finally, although admirable in every kind of emotional appeal, he is easily supreme in the power to excite pity. Menander, as he often testifies in his works, had 69 a profound admiration for Euripides, and imitated him, although in a different type of work. Now,

quidem iudicio, diligenter lectus ad cuncta, quae
praecipimus, effingenda sufficiat; ita omnem vitae
imaginem expressit, tanta in eo inveniendi copia et
eloquendi facultas, ita est omnibus rebus, personis,
70 adfectibus accommodatus. Nec nihil profecto vide-
runt, qui orationes, quae Charisii nomini addicuntur,[1]
a Menandro scriptas putant. Sed mihi longe magis
orator probari in opere suo videtur, nisi forte aut illa[2]
iudicia, quae Epitrepontes, Epicleros, Locroe habent,
aut meditationes in Psophodee, Nomothete, Hypo-
bolimaeo non omnibus oratoriis numeris sunt abso-
71 lutae. Ego tamen plus adhuc quiddam collaturum
eum declamatoribus puto, quoniam his necesse est
secundum condicionem controversiarum plures subire
personas, patrum, filiorum, militum, rusticorum,
divitum, pauperum, irascentium, deprecantium, mi-
tium, asperorum. In quibus omnibus mire custoditur
72 ab hoc poeta decor. Atque ille quidem omnibus
eiusdem operis auctoribus abstulit nomen et fulgore
quodam suae claritatis tenebras obduxit. Tamen
habent alii quoque Comici, si cum venia leguntur,
quaedam quae possis decerpere; et praecipue Phile-

---

[1] Charisii nomini addicuntur, a, *Frotscher*: charis in
homine adductura, *G.*: Charisii nomine eduntur, *vulgo.*
[2] *after* illa *G and a number of later MSS. read* mala,
*which is, however, omitted in a few MSS. and is expunged by
Andresen.*

---

[1] A contemporary of Demosthenes; his speeches have not
survived, but were considered to resemble those of Lysias.
[2] The greater portion of the Epitrepontes has been re-
covered from a papyrus. The other plays are lost. The
names may be translated: "The Arbitrators," "The Heiress,"
"The Locri," "The Timid Man," "The Lawgiver," "The
Changeling."

the careful study of Menander alone would, in my
opinion, be sufficient to develop all those qualities
with the production of which my present work
is concerned; so perfect is his representation of
actual life, so rich is his power of invention and
his gift of style, so perfectly does he adapt himself
to every kind of circumstance, character and emotion. Indeed, those critics are no fools who think 70
the speeches attributed to Charisius [1] were in reality
written by Menander. But I consider that he shows
his power as an orator far more clearly in his
comedies; since assuredly we can find no more
perfect models of every oratorical quality than the
judicial pleadings of his Epitrepontes,[2] Epicleros
and Locri, or the declamatory speeches in the Pso-
phodes, Nomothetes, and Hypobolimaeus. Still, for 71
my own part, I think that he will be found even more
useful by declaimers, in view of the fact that they
have, according to the nature of the various contro-
versial themes, to undertake a number of different
rôles and to impersonate fathers, sons, soldiers,
peasants, rich men and poor, the angry man and
the suppliant, the gentle and the harsh. And all
these characters are treated by this poet with
consummate appropriateness. Indeed, such is his 72
supremacy that he has scarce left a name to other
writers of the new comedy, and has cast them into
darkness by the splendour of his own renown.
Still, you will find something of value in the other
comic poets as well, if you read them in not too
critical a spirit; above all, profit may be derived
from the study of Philemon,[3] who, although it was

[3] Philemon of Soli (360–262); Menander of Athens (342–
290).

mon, qui ut prave sui temporis iudiciis Menandro
saepe praelatus est, ita consensu tamen omnium
meruit credi secundus.

73 Historiam multi scripsere praeclare, sed nemo
dubitat longe duos ceteris praeferendos, quorum
diversa virtus laudem paene est parem consecuta.
Densus et brevis et semper instans sibi Thucydides,
dulcis et candidus et fusus Herodotus ; ille concitatis
hic remissis adfectibus melior, ille contionibus hic
74 sermonibus, ille vi hic voluptate. Theopompus his
proximus ut in historia praedictis minor, ita oratori
magis similis, ut qui, antequam est ad hoc opus
sollicitatus, diu fuerit orator. Philistus quoque me-
retur, qui turbae quamvis bonorum post eos auctorum
eximatur, imitator Thucydidis et ut multo infirmior
ita aliquatenus lucidior. Ephorus, ut Isocrati visum,
75 calcaribus eget. Clitarchi probatur ingenium, fides
infamatur. Longo post intervallo temporis natus
Timagenes vel hoc est ipso probabilis, quod inter-
missam historias scribendi industriam nova laude
reparavit. Xenophon non excidit mihi, sed inter
philosophos reddendus est.

---

[1] Theopompus of Chios, born about 378 B.C., wrote a
history of Greece (*Hellenica*) from close of Peloponnesian war
to 394 B.C., and a history of Greece in relation to Philip of
Macedon (*Philippica*). His master, Isocrates, urged him to
write history.

[2] Philistus of Syracuse, born about 430 B.C., wrote a
history of Sicily.

[3] Ephorus of Cumae, *flor. circ.* 340 B.C., wrote a universal
history. He was a pupil of Isocrates. *Cp.* II. viii. 11.

a depraved taste which caused his contemporaries often to prefer him to Menander, has none the less deserved the second place which posterity has been unanimous in awarding him.

If we turn to history, we shall find a number of 73 distinguished writers; but there are two who must undoubtedly be set far above all their rivals: their excellences are different in kind, but have won almost equal praise. Thucydides is compact in texture, terse and ever eager to press forward: Herodotus is pleasant, lucid and diffuse: the former excels in vigour, speeches and the expression of the stronger passions; the latter in charm, conversations and the delineation of the gentler emotions. Theo- 74 pompus [1] comes next, and though as a historian he is inferior to the authors just mentioned, his style has a greater resemblance to oratory, which is not surprising, as he was an orator before he was urged to turn to history. Philistus [2] also deserves special distinction among the crowd of later historians, good though they may have been: he was an imitator of Thucydides, and though far his inferior, was some- what more lucid. Ephorus,[3] according to Isocrates, needed the spur. Clitarchus [4] has won approval by 75 his talent, but his accuracy has been impugned. Timagenes [5] was born long after these authors, but deserves our praise for the very fact that he revived the credit of history, the writing of which had fallen into neglect. I have not forgotten Xenophon, but he will find his place among the philosophers.

[4] Clitarchus of Megara wrote a history of Persia and of Alexander, whose contemporary he was.

[5] Timagenes, a Syrian of the Augustan age, wrote a history of Alexander and his successors.

76   Sequitur oratorum ingens manus, ut cum decem simul Athenis aetas una tulerit. Quorum longe princeps Demosthenes ac paene lex orandi fuit; tanta vis in eo, tam densa omnia, ita quibusdam nervis intenta sunt, tam nihil otiosum, is dicendi modus, ut nec quod desit in eo nec quod redundet

77 invenias.   Plenior Aeschines et magis fusus et grandiori similis, quo minus strictus est; carnis tamen plus habet, minus lacertorum.   Dulcis in primis et acutus Hyperides, sed minoribus causis, ut non dixerim

78 utilior, magis par.   His aetate Lysias maior, subtilis atque elegans et quo nihil, si oratori satis est docere, quaeras perfectius.   Nihil enim est inane, nihil arcessitum; puro tamen fonti quam magno flumini propior.

79 Isocrates in diverso genere dicendi nitidus et comptus et palaestrae quam pugnae magis accommodatus omnes dicendi veneres sectatus est, nec immerito; auditoriis enim se, non iudiciis compararat; in inventione facilis, honesti studiosus, in compositione

80 adeo diligens, ut cura eius reprehendatur.   Neque ego in his, de quibus sum locutus, has solas virtutes, sed has praecipuas puto, nec ceteros parum fuisse

---

[1] Antiphon, Andocides, Lysias (flor. 403–380), Isocrates (435-338), Isaeus, Demosthenes, Aeschines, Lycurgus, Hyperides and Dinarchus.

There follows a vast army of orators, Athens alone 76
having produced ten remarkable orators [1] in the
same generation. Of these Demosthenes is far the
greatest : indeed he came to be regarded almost as
the sole pattern of oratory. Such is the force and
compactness of his language, so muscular his style,
so free from tameness and so self-controlled, that
you will find nothing in him that is either too much
or too little. The style of Aeschines is fuller and 77
more diffuse, while his lack of restraint gives an
appearance of grandeur. But he has more flesh and
less muscle. Hyperides has extraordinary charm and
point, but is better qualified, not to say more useful,
for cases of minor importance. Lysias belongs to an 78
earlier generation than those whom I have just
mentioned. He has subtlety and elegance and, if
the orator's sole duty were merely to instruct, it
would be impossible to conceive greater perfection.
For there is nothing irrelevant or far-fetched in his
speeches. None the less I would compare him to a
clear spring rather than to a mighty river. Isocrates 79
was an exponent of a different style of oratory : he is
neat and polished and better suited to the fencing-
school than to the battlefield. He elaborated all the
graces of style, nor was he without justification. For
he had trained himself for the lecture-room and not
the law-courts. He is ready in invention, his moral
ideals are high and the care which he bestows upon
his rhythm is such as to be a positive fault. I do 80
not regard these as the sole merits of the orators of
whom I have spoken, but have selected what seemed
to me their chief excellences, while those whom I
have passed over in silence were far from being
indifferent. In fact, I will readily admit that the

magnos. Quin etiam Phalerea illum Demetrium,
quanquam is primus inclinasse eloquentiam dicitur,
multum ingenii habuisse et facundiae fateor, vel ob
hoc memoria dignum, quod ultimus est fere ex
Atticis, qui dici possit orator; quem tamen in illo
medio genere dicendi praefert omnibus Cicero.

81 Philosophorum, ex quibus plurimum se traxisse eloquentiae M. Tullius confitetur, quis dubitet Platonem
esse praecipuum sive acumine disserendi sive eloquendi facultate divina quadam et Homerica? Multum enim supra prosam orationem et quam pedestrem
Graeci vocant surgit, ut mihi non hominis ingenio
sed quodam Delphici videatur oraculo dei instinctus.[1]

82 Quid ego commemorem Xenophontis illam iucunditatem inadfectatam, sed quam nulla consequi adfec-
tatio possit? ut ipsae sermonem finxisse Gratiae
videantur et, quod de Pericle veteris comoediae
testimonium est, in hunc transferri iustissime possit,
in labris eius sedisse quandam persuadendi deam.

83 Quid reliquorum Socraticorum elegantiam? Quid
Aristotelem? quem dubito scientia rerum an scriptorum copia an eloquendi [2] suavitate an inventionum
acumine an varietate operum clariorem putem. Nam

---

[1] quodam Delphici . . . dei instinctus, *Frotscher* : quaedam
Delphico . . . de instrictus, *G* : quodam Delphico . . . instinctus, *vulgo*.

[2] eloquendi, *cod. Harl.* 4950, *cod. Dorv.* : eloquendi usus,
G and nearly all MSS. : eloquendi vi ac, *Geel*.

---

[1] Governed Athens as Cassander's vicegerent 317–307 :
then fled to Egypt, where he died in 283.
[2] *de Or.* ii. 95. *Orat.* 92. The "intermediate" style is
that which lies between the "grand" and the "plain"
styles.
[3] Eupolis, πειθώ τις ἐπεκάθιζεν ἐπὶ τοῖς χείλεσιν.

famous Demetrius of Phalerum,[1] who is said to
have been the first to set oratory on the down-
ward path, was a man of great talent and eloquence
and deserves to be remembered, if only for the
fact that he is almost the last of the Attic
school who can be called an orator : indeed Cicero [2]
prefers him to all other orators of the intermediate
school.

Proceeding to the philosophers, from whom Cicero 81
acknowledges that he derived such a large portion
of his eloquence, we shall all admit that Plato is
supreme whether in acuteness ot perception or in
virtue of his divine gift of style, which is worthy of
Homer. For he soars high above the levels of
ordinary prose or, as the Greeks call it, pedestrian
language, and seems to me to be inspired not by
mere human genius, but, as it were, by the oracles
of the god of Delphi. Why should I speak of the 82
unaffected charm of Xenophon, so far beyond the
power of affectation to attain? The Graces themselves seem to have moulded his style, and we may
with the utmost justice say of him, what the writer
of the old comedy [3] said of Pericles, that the goddess
of persuasion sat enthroned upon his lips. Why 83
should I dwell on the elegance of the rest of the
Socratics ? or on Aristotle,[4] with regard to whom I
hesitate whether to praise him more for his knowledge, for the multitude of his writings, the sweetness of his style, the penetration revealed by his
discoveries or the variety of the tasks which he

[4] "Sweet" is the last epithet to be applied to the
surviving works of Aristotle. But Dionysius of Halicarnassus
and Cicero praise him no less warmly, referring, no doubt,
to works that are lost.

in Theophrasto tam est loquendi nitor ille divinus,
84 ut ex eo nomen quoque traxisse dicatur. Minus
indulsere eloquentiae Stoici veteres; sed cum honesta
suaserunt tum in colligendo probandoque quae insti-
tuerant plurimum valuerunt, rebus tamen acuti magis
quam, id quod sane non adfectaverunt, oratione
magnifici.

85 Idem nobis per Romanos quoque auctores ordo
ducendus est. Itaque ut apud illos Homerus sic
apud nos Vergilius auspicatissimum dederit exordium,
omnium eius generis poetarum Graecorum nostro-
86 rumque haud dubie proximus. Utar enim verbis
iisdem, quae ex Afro Domitio iuvenis excepi; qui
mihi interroganti, quem Homero crederet maxime
accedere, *Secundus,* inquit, *est Vergilius, propior tamen
primo quam tertio.* Et hercule ut [1] illi naturae caelesti
atque immortali cesserimus, ita curae et diligentiae
vel ideo in hoc plus est, quod ei fuit magis laborandum, et quantum eminentibus vincimur, fortasse
87 aequalitate pensamus. Ceteri omnes longe sequ-
entur. Nam Macer et Lucretius legendi quidem,
sed non ut phrasin, id est, corpus eloquentiae faciant,
elegantes in sua quisque materia sed alter humilis,
alter difficilis. Atacinus Varro in iis, per quae nomen
est adsecutus, interpres operis alieni, non spernendus

---

[1] ut, *several late MSS.* : cum, *G and majority of MSS.*

---

[1] Theophrastus, Aristotle's successor as head of his school
(322–287). Diogenes Laertius (v. 38) says that his real name
was Tyrtamus, but that Aristotle called him Theophrastus
because of the "divine qualities of his style" (φράσις).

[2] Varro of Atax in Gaul (82–37 B.C.) was specially famous
for his translation of the *Argonautica* of Apollonius Rhodius.
He also wrote didactic poetry and historical epic.

essayed? In Theophrastus[1] we find such a superhuman brilliance of style that his name is said to be
derived therefrom. The ancient Stoics indulged 84
their eloquence comparatively little. Still, they
pleaded the cause of virtue, and the rules which
they laid down for argument and proof have been of
the utmost value. But they showed themselves
shrewd thinkers rather than striking orators, which
indeed they never aimed at being.

I now come to Roman authors, and shall follow 85
the same order in dealing with them. As among
Greek authors Homer provided us with the most
auspicious opening, so will Virgil among our own.
For of all epic poets, Greek or Roman, he, without
doubt, most nearly approaches to Homer. I will 86
repeat the words which I heard Domitius Afer use
in my young days. I asked what poet in his opinion
came nearest to Homer, and he replied, "Virgil
comes second, but is nearer first than third." And
in truth, although we must needs bow before the
immortal and superhuman genius of Homer, there
is greater diligence and exactness in the work
of Virgil just because his task was harder. And
perhaps the superior uniformity of the Roman's excellence balances Homer's pre-eminence in his out-
standing passages. All our other poets follow a long 87
way in the rear. Macer and Lucretius are, it is true,
worth reading, but not for the purpose of forming
style, that is to say, the body of eloquence: both
deal elegantly with their themes, but the former is
tame and the latter difficult. The poems by which
Varro of Atax[2] gained his reputation were translations, but he is by no means to be despised, although
his diction is not sufficiently rich to be of much

quidem,verum ad augendam facultatem dicendi parum
88 locuples.   Ennium sicut sacros vetustate lucos ador-
emus, in quibus grandia et antiqua robora iam non
tantam habent speciem quantam religionem.   Pro-
piores alii atque ad hoc, de quo loquimur, magis
utiles.   Lascivus quidem in herois quoque Ovidius
et nimium amator ingenii sui, laudandus tamen in
89 partibus.   Cornelius autem Severus, etiam si sit [1]
versificator quam poeta melior, si tamen, ut est
dictum, ad exemplar primi libri bellum Siculum
perscripsisset, vindicaret sibi iure secundum locum.
Serranum [2] consummari mors immatura non passa
est ; puerilia tamen eius opera et maximam indolem
ostendunt et admirabilem praecipue in aetate illa
90 recti generis voluntatem.   Multum in Valerio Flacco
nuper amisimus.   Vehemens et poeticum ingenium
Saleii Bassi fuit, nec ipsum senectute maturuit.
Rabirius ac Pedo non indigni cognitione, si vacet.
Lucanus ardens et concitatus et sententiis clarissimus
et, ut dicam quod sentio, magis oratoribus quam poetis
91 imitandus.   Hos nominavimus, quia Germanicum

---

[1] si sit, *Spalding* : *MSS. vary between* si, sit *and* sic.
[3] Serranum, *Lange* : ferrenum, *G.*

---

[1] Friend and contemporary of Ovid.   A considerable fragment is preserved by Sen. *Suas.* vi. 26.   The Sicilian War
was the war with Sextus Pompeius (38–36) and perhaps
formed a portion of a larger work on the Civil War.   The
surviving fragment deals with the death of Cicero.   The
primus liber may therefore perhaps be the first book of this
larger work.
[2] Nothing is known of this poet except the name.
[3] Nothing is known of this poet save that he is highly
praised by Tacitus in his *Dialogues*, and was patronised by
Vespasian.   The unfinished Argonautica of Valerius Flaccus
survives.

service in developing the resources of eloquence. Ennius deserves our reverence, but only as those 88 groves whose age has made them sacred, but whose huge and ancient trunks inspire us with religious awe rather than with admiration for their beauty. There are other poets who are nearer in point of time and more useful for our present purpose. Ovid has a lack of seriousness even when he writes epic and is unduly enamoured of his own gifts, but portions of his work merit our praise. On the other 89 hand, although Cornelius Severus [1] is a better versifier than poet, yet if, as has been said, he had written his poem on the Sicilian war in the same style throughout as his first book, he would have had a just claim to the second place. A premature death prevented the powers of Serranus [2] from ripening to perfection, but his youthful works reveal the highest talent and a devotion to the true ideal of poetry, which is remarkable in one so young. We have suffered serious loss 90 in the recent death of Valerius Flaccus. Saleius Bassus [3] showed an ardent and genuinely poetic genius, but, like that of Serranus, it was not mellowed by years. Rabirius [4] and Pedo [5] deserve to be studied by those who have the time. Lucan is fiery and passionate and remarkable for the grandeur of his general reflexions, but, to be frank, I consider that he is more suitable for imitation by the orator than by the poet. I have restricted my 91 list of poets to these names, because Germanicus

---

[4] A contemporary of Ovid, believed to be the author of a fragment on the battle of Actium, found at Herculaneum.

[5] C. Albinovanus Pedo wrote a poem on the voyage of Germanicus to the north of Germany. A fragment is preserved by Sen. *Suas.* i. 14.

Augûstum ab institutis studiis deflexit cura terrarum,
parumque dis visum est esse eum maximum poetarum. Quid tamen his ipsis eius operibus, in quae
donato imperio iuvenis secesserat, sublimius, doctius,
omnibus denique numeris praestantius? Quis enim
caneret bella melius, quam qui sic gerit? Quem
praesidentes studiis deae propius audirent? Cui
magis suas artes aperiret familiare numen Minerva?
92 Dicent haec plenius futura saecula, nunc enim
ceterarum fulgore virtutum laus ista praestringitur.
Nos tamen sacra litterarum colentes feres, Caesar, si
non tacitum hoc praeterimus et Vergiliano certe
versu testamur,

> *Inter victrices hederam tibi serpere laurus.*

93   Elegia quoque Graecos provocamus, cuius mihi
tersus atque elegans maxime videtur auctor Tibullus.
Sunt qui Propertium malint. Ovidius utroque lasci-
vior, sicut durior Gallus. Satira quidem tota nostra
est, in qua primus insignem laudem adeptus Lucilius
quosdam ita deditos sibi adhuc habet amatores, ut
eum non eiusdem modo operis auctoribus, sed
94 omnibus poetis praeferre non dubitent. Ego quantum ab illis tantum ab Horatio dissentio, qui Luci-

---

[1] Domitian.
[2] He claimed to be the son of Minerva. It is doubtful if
he ever wrote any poetry. Cp. Tac. *Hist.* iv. 86, Suet. *Dom.*
2 and 20.   [3] *Ecl.* viii. 13.
[4] Cornelius Gallus, the friend of Virgil, and the first distinguished writer of elegy at Rome.   [5] *Sat.* I. iv. 11.

Augustus [1] has been distracted from the study of
poetry on which he had embarked by his care for
the governance of the world, and the gods have
thought it scarce worthy of his powers that he
should be the greatest of poets. But what can be
more sublime, more learned, more perfect in every
detail than those works to which he devoted himself
in the seclusion to which he retired after conferring
the supreme power upon his father and his brother?
Who could sing of war better than he who wages it
with such skill? To whom would the goddesses
that preside over literature sooner lend an ear? To
whom would Minerva, his familiar deity, [2] more
readily reveal her secrets? Future ages shall tell of 92
these things more fully; to-day his glory as a poet
is dimmed by the splendour of his other virtues.
But you will forgive us, Caesar, who worship at the
shrine of literature, if we refuse to pass by your
achievements in silence and insist on testifying at
least that, as Virgil sings,

> "The ivy creeps amid your victor bays." [3]

We also challenge the supremacy of the Greeks in 93
elegy. Of our elegiac poets Tibullus seems to me
to be the most terse and elegant. There are, however, some who prefer Propertius. Ovid is more
sportive than either, while Gallus [4] is more severe.
Satire, on the other hand, is all our own. The first
of our poets to win renown in this connexion was
Lucilius, some of whose devotees are so enthusiastic
that they do not hesitate to prefer him not merely
to all other satirists, but even to all other poets.
I disagree with them as much as I do with Horace, [5] 94
who holds that Lucilius' verse has a "muddy flow,

53

lium fluere lutulentum et esse aliquid, quod tollere
possis, putat. Nam eruditio in eo mira et libertas
atque inde acerbitas et abunde salis. Multum
est tersior ac purus magis Horatius et, nisi labor
eius amore, praecipuus. Multum et verae gloriae
quamvis uno libro Persius meruit. Sunt clari
95 hodieque et qui olim nominabuntur. Alterum illud
etiam prius satirae genus, sed non sola carminum
varietate mixtum condidit Terentius Varro, vir Romanorum eruditissimus. Plurimos hic libros et doctis-
simos composuit, peritissimus linguae Latinae et
omnis antiquitatis et rerum Graecarum nostrarum-
que, plus tamen scientiae collaturus quam eloquen-
96 tiae. Iambus non sane a Romanis celebratus est ut
proprium opus, sed aliis[1] quibusdam interpositus;
cuius acerbitas in Catullo, Bibaculo, Horatio, quanquam illi epodos interveniat, reperietur. At Lyricorum idem Horatius fere solus legi dignus. Nam
et insurgit aliquando et plenus est iucunditatis
et gratiae et varius figuris et verbis felicissime
audax. Si quem adiicere velis, is erit Caesius

[1] sed aliis, *inserted by Christ.*

---

[1] His Menippean Satires, of which only fragments survive.
Although ostensibly an imitation of the work of the Greek
Menippus of Gadara, they can still be said to belong to the
older type of satire, the "medley" or "hotch-potch."

[2] The meaning is not clear. The words may mean (i) that
these writers did not confine themselves to the *iambus*, or
(ii) that the *iambus* alternates with other metres, cp. *epodos*
below.

[3] M. Furius Bibaculus, contemporary of Catullus, and
writer of similar invective against the Caesareans.

[4] *i. e.* the short iambic line interposed between the tri-
meters.

and that there is always something in him that might well be dispensed with." For his learning is as remarkable as his freedom of speech, and it is this latter quality that gives so sharp an edge and such abundance of wit to his satire. Horace is far terser and purer in style, and must be awarded the first place, unless my judgment is led astray by my affection for his work. Persius also, although he wrote but one book, has acquired a high and well-deserved reputation, while there are other distinguished satirists still living whose praises will be sung by posterity. There is, however, another 95 and even older type of satire which derives its variety not merely from verse, but from an admixture of prose as well. Such were the satires composed by Terentius Varro,[1] the most learned of all Romans. He composed a vast number of erudite works, and possessed an extraordinary knowledge of the Latin language, of all antiquity and of the history of Greece and Rome. But he is an author likely to contribute more to the knowledge of the student than to his eloquence. The 96 iambic has not been popular with Roman poets as a separate form of composition, but is found mixed up with other forms of verse.[2] It may be found in all its bitterness in Catullus, Bibaculus[3] and Horace, although in the last-named the iambic is interrupted by the epode.[4] Of our lyric writers Horace is almost the sole poet worth reading: for he rises at times to a lofty grandeur and is full of sprightliness and charm, while there is great variety in his figures, and his boldness in the choice of words is only equalled by his felicity. If any other lyric poet is to be mentioned, it will be Caesius Bassus, who has but

Bassus, quem nuper vidimus; sed eum longe prae-
cedunt ingenia viventium.

97   Tragoediae scriptores veterum Accius atque Pacuvius clarissimi[1] gravitate sententiarum, verborum
pondere, auctoritate personarum.   Ceterum nitor et
summa in excolendis operibus manus magis videri
potest temporibus quam ipsis defuisse.   Virium tamen
Accio plus tribuitur; Pacuvium videri doctiorem qui
98 esse docti adfectant volunt.   Iam Varii Thyestes
cuilibet Graecarum comparari potest.   Ovidii Medea
videtur mihi ostendere, quantam ille vir praestare
potuerit, si ingenio suo imperare quam indulgere
maluisset.   Eorum quos viderim longe princeps Pomponius Secundus, quem senes quidem parum tragicum
putabant, eruditione ac nitore praestare confite-
99 bantur.   In comoedia maxime claudicamus.   Licet
Varro Musas, Aelii Stilonis sententia, Plautino dicat
sermone locuturas fuisse, si Latine loqui vellent,
licet Caecilium veteres laudibus ferant, licet Terentii
scripta ad Scipionem Africanum referantur (quae
tamen sunt in hoc genere elegantissima et plus adhuc
habitura gratiae si intra versus trimetros stetissent),
100 vix levem consequimur umbram, adeo ut mihi sermo
ipse Romanus non recipere videatur illam solis con-
cessam Atticis venerem, cum eam ne Graeci quidem

    [1] clarissimi, *several late MSS.* : gravissima, G : gravissimus,
other late MSS. : grandissimus, *cod. Monac.* : grandissimi,
Halm.

---

    [1] Accius (170–90), Pacuvius (220–132).
    [2] L. Varius Rufus, friend of Virgil and Horace, editor of
the *Aeneid ;* wrote epic and a single tragedy.
    [3] Pomponius Secundus, died 60 A.D. ; wrote a tragedy
entitled *Aeneas.*
    [4] The first Roman philologist (144–70 B.C.).

lately passed from us. But he is far surpassed in talent by poets still living.

Among writers of tragedy Accius and Pacuvius[1] 97
are most remarkable for the force of their general reflexions, the weight of their words and the dignity of their characters. But they lack polish, and failed to put the finishing touches on their works, although the fault was perhaps rather that of the times in which they lived than of themselves. Accius is generally regarded as the most vigorous, while those who lay claim to learning regard Pacuvius as the more learned of the two. The Thyestes of Varius[2] 98
is a match for any Greek tragedy, and the Medea of Ovid shows, in my opinion, to what heights that poet might have risen if he had been ready to curb his talents instead of indulging them. Of the tragic writers whom I myself have seen, Pomponius Secundus[3] is by far the best : his older critics thought him insufficiently tragic, but admitted his eminence as far as learning and polish were concerned. Comedy 99
is our weakest point. Although Varro quotes Aelius Stilo[4] as saying that if the Muses wished to speak Latin, they would use the language of Plautus, although the ancients extol Caecilius,[5] and although Scipio Africanus is credited with the works of Terence (which are the most elegant of their kind, and would be still more graceful if the poet had confined himself to the iambic trimeter), we still 100
scarcely succeed in reproducing even a faint shadow of the charm of Greek comedy. Indeed, it seems to me as though the language of Rome were incapable of reproducing that graceful wit which was

[5] Caecilius (219-166), Terence (194-159), Afranius (flor. circ. 150). Only fragments of Caecilius and Afranius remain.

in alio genere linguae suae[1] obtinuerint. Togatis
excellit Afranius ; utinam non inquinasset argumenta
puerorum foedis amoribus mores suos fassus.

101   At non historia cesserit Graecis, nec opponere
Thucydidi Sallustium verear, neque indignetur sibi
Herodotus aequari T. Livium, cum in narrando
mirae iucunditatis clarissimique candoris, tum in
contionibus supra quam enarrari potest eloquentem ;
ita quae dicuntur omnia cum rebus tum personis
accommodata sunt ; adfectus quidem, praecipueque
eos qui sunt dulciores, ut parcissime dicam, nemo
102 historicorum commendavit magis.   Ideoque im-
mortalem illam Sallustii velocitatem diversis virtutibus consecutus est.   Nam mihi egregie dixisse
videtur Servilius Nonianus, pares eos magis quam
similes ; qui et ipse a nobis auditus est, clarus vi[2]
ingenii et sententiis creber, sed minus pressus quam
103 historiae auctoritas postulat.   Quam paulum aetate
praecedens eum Bassus Aufidius egregie, utique in
libris belli Germanici, praestitit genere ipso, probabilis in omnibus, sed in quibusdam suis ipse viribus
104 minor.   Superest adhuc et exornat aetatis nostrae
gloriam vir saeculorum memoria dignus, qui olim
nominabitur, nunc intelligitur.   Habet amatores nec

---

[1] suae, *Köhler* : quae, *G*.

[2] clarus vi, *Kiderlin* : clarius, *G* : clari vir, *vulgo*.

---

[1] Caecilius (219–166), Terence (194–159), Afranius (flor.
circ. 150) Only fragments of Caecilius and Afranius survive.

[2] Friend of Persius, and famous as orator, reciter and
historian ; died 60 A.D.

[3] He wrote a history of the empire down to the death of
Claudius.   The work on the German war was probably a
separate work.

[4] Probably Fabius Rusticus. Tacitus would have been too
young at this time to be mentioned in such terms.

granted to Athens alone, and was beyond the reach of other Greek dialects to achieve. Afranius [1] excels in the purely Roman comedy, but it is to be regretted that he revealed his own character by defiling his plots with the introduction of indecent paederastic intrigues.

In history, however, we hold our own with the 101 Greeks. I should not hesitate to match Sallust against Thucydides, nor would Herodotus resent Titus Livius being placed on the same level as himself. For the latter has a wonderful charm and transparency in narrative, while his speeches are eloquent beyond description; so admirably adapted is all that is said both to the circumstances and the speaker; and as regards the emotions, especially the more pleasing of them, I may sum him up by saying that no historian has ever depicted them to greater perfection. Thus it is that, although by 102 different means, he has acquired no less fame than has been awarded to the immortal rapidity of Sallust. For I strongly approve of the saying of Servilius Nonianus,[2] that these historians were equal rather than alike. Servilius, whom I myself have heard, is himself remarkable for the force of his intellect, and is full of general reflexions, but he is less restrained than the dignity of history demands. But 103 that dignity is admirably maintained, thanks to his style, by Aufidius Bassus,[3] a slightly earlier writer, especially in his work on the German war: he is always praiseworthy, though at times he fails to do his powers full justice. But there still survives to 104 add lustre to this glorious age a man [4] worthy to be remembered through all time: he is appreciated to-day, but after generations shall declare his name

immerito Cremuti[1] libertas, quanquam circumcisis quae dixisse ei nocuerat. Sed elatum abunde spiritum et audaces sententias deprehendas etiam in his quae manent. Sunt et alii scriptores boni, sed nos genera degustamus, non bibliothecas excutimus.

105 Oratores vero vel praecipue Latinam eloquentiam parem facere Graecae possint. Nam Ciceronem cuicunque eorum fortiter opposuerim. Nec ignoro quantam mihi concitem pugnam, cum praesertim non sit id propositi, ut eum Demostheni comparem hoc tempore; neque enim attinet, cum Demosthenem in primis legendum vel ediscendum potius

106 putem. Quorum ego virtutes plerasque arbitror similes, consilium, ordinem, dividendi,[2] praeparandi, probandi rationem, omnia denique quae sunt inventionis. In eloquendo est aliqua diversitas; densior ille hic copiosior, ille concludit adstrictius hic latius, pugnat ille acumine semper hic frequenter et pondere, illi nihil detrahi potest huic nihil adiici,

107 curae plus in illo in hoc naturae. Salibus certe et commiseratione, qui duo plurimum in adfectibus

---

[1] immerito Cremuti, *Nipperdey*: immerito rem * * * uti, *G*: *later MSS. vary between* immerito remitti *and* imitatores uti.

[2] dividendi, *Aldine ed.*: videndi, *G and nearly all MSS.*

---

[1] Cremutius Cordus wrote a history of the Civil wars and reign of Augustus. He was accused for his praise of Brutus and Cassius, and committed suicide in A.D. 25. It was he who called Cassius "the last of all the Romans."

[2] See XII. i. 14 *sqq.*, also XII. x. 12 *sqq.*

aloud. The bold utterances of Cremutius[1] also have their admirers, and deserve their fame, though the passages which brought him to his ruin have been expurgated; still that which is left reveals a rich store of lofty animation and fearless reflexions upon life. There are other good writers as well, but I am merely selecting from the different departments of literature, not reviewing complete libraries.

But it is our orators, above all, who enable us to 105 match our Roman eloquence against that of Greece. For I would set Cicero against any one of their orators without fear of refutation. I know well enough what a storm I shall raise by this assertion, more especially since I do not propose for the moment[2] to compare him with Demosthenes; for there would be no point in such a comparison, as I consider that Demosthenes should be the object of special study, and not merely studied, but even committed to memory. I regard the excellences of these 106 two orators as being for the most part similar, that is to say, their judgment, their gift of arrangement, their methods of division, preparation and proof, as well as everything concerned with invention. In their actual style there is some difference. Demosthenes is more concentrated, Cicero more diffuse; Demosthenes makes his periods shorter than Cicero, and his weapon is the rapier, whereas Cicero's periods are longer, and at times he employs the bludgeon as well: nothing can be taken from the former, nor added to the latter; the Greek reveals a more studied, the Roman a more natural art. As regards 107 wit and the power of exciting pity, the two most powerful instruments where the feelings are concerned, we have the advantage. Again, it is possible

valent, vincimus. Et fortasse epilogos illi mos civitatis
abstulerit; sed et nobis illa, quae Attici mirantur,
diversa Latini sermonis ratio minus permiserit.   In
epistolis quidem, quanquam sunt utriusque, dialo-
108 gisve, quibus nihil ille, nulla contentio est.   Ceden-
dum vero in hoc, quod et prior fuit et ex magna
parte Ciceronem, quantus est, fecit.   Nam mihi
videtur M. Tullius, cum se totum ad imitationem
Graecorum contulisset, effinxisse vim Demosthenis,
109 copiam Platonis, iucunditatem Isocratis.   Nec vero
quod in quoque optimum fuit, studio consecutus est
tantum; sed plurimas vel potius omnes ex se ipso
virtutes extulit immortalis ingenii beatissima ubertas.
Non enim pluvias, ut ait Pindarus, aquas colligit,
sed vivo gurgite exundat, dono quodam providentiae
genitus, in quo totas vires suas eloquentia experi-
110 retur.   Nam quis docere diligentius, movere vehe-
mentius potest?   Cui tanta unquam iucunditas
adfuit? ut ipsa illa quae extorquet impetrare eum
credas, et cum transversum vi sua iudicem ferat
111 tamen ille non rapi videatur, sed sequi.   Iam in

---

[1] *cp.* II. xvi. 4; VI. i 7. Quintilian refers to an alleged
law at Athens forbidding appeals to the emotion.
[2] The quotation is not found in Pindar's extant works.

that Demosthenes was deprived by national custom[1]
of the opportunity of producing powerful perorations, but against this may be set the fact that the
different character of the Latin language debars us
from the attainment of those qualities which are
so much admired by the adherents of the Attic
school. As regards their letters, which have in
both cases survived, and dialogues, which Demosthenes never attempted, there can be no comparison
between the two. But, on the other hand, there is 108
one point in which the Greek has the undoubted
superiority : he comes first in point of time, and it
was largely due to him that Cicero was able to attain
greatness. For it seems to me that Cicero, who
devoted himself heart and soul to the imitation of
the Greeks, succeeded in reproducing the force of
Demosthenes, the copious flow of Plato, and the
charm of Isocrates. But he did something more 109
than reproduce the best elements in each of these
authors by dint of careful study ; it was to himself
that he owed most of, or rather all his excellences,
which spring from the extraordinary fertility of his
immortal genius. For he does not, as Pindar[2] says,
" collect the rain from heaven, but wells forth with
living water," since Providence at his birth conferred
this special privilege upon him, that eloquence should
make trial of all her powers in him. For who can 110
instruct with greater thoroughness, or more deeply
stir the emotions ? Who has ever possessed such a
gift of charm ? He seems to obtain as a boon what
in reality he extorts by force, and when he wrests
the judge from the path of his own judgment, the
latter seems not to be swept away, but merely to
follow. Further, there is such weight in all that he 111

omnibus quae dicit tanta auctoritas inest, ut dissentire pudeat, nec advocati studium sed testis aut
iudicis adferat fidem, cum interim haec omnia, quae
vix singula quisquam intentissima cura consequi
posset, fluunt illaborata, et illa, qua nihil pulchrius
auditum est, oratio prae se fert tamen felicissimam
112 facilitatem.   Quare non immerito ab hominibus[1]
aetatis suae regnare in iudiciis dictus est, apud
posteros vero id consecutus, ut Cicero iam non
hominis nomen, sed eloquentiae habeatur.   Hunc
igitur spectemus, hoc propositum nobis sit exemplum, ille se profecisse sciat, cui Cicero valde
113 placebit.   Multa in Asinio Pollione invento, summa
diligentia, adeo ut quibusdam etiam nimia videatur,
et consilii et animi satis ; a nitore et iucunditate
Ciceronis ita longe abest, ut videri possit saeculo
prior.   At Messala nitidus et candidus et quadam
modo praeferens in dicendo nobilitatem suam, viri-
114 bus minor.   C. vero Caesar si foro tantum vacasset,
non alius ex nostris contra Ciceronem nominaretur.
Tanta in eo vis est, id acumen, ea concitatio, ut
illum eodem animo dixisse, quo bellavit, appareat ;
exornat tamen haec omnia mira sermonis, cuius

---

[1] ab hominibus, *Halm* : ab omnibus, *B* : hominibus, *a few
late MSS.*

---

[1] Asinius Pollio (75 B.C.–A.D. 4), the friend of Virgil,
distinguished as poet, historian and orator.
[2] M. Valerius Corvinus (64 B.C.–A.D. 8), the friend of
Tibullus and distinguished as an orator.

says that his audience feel ashamed to disagree with him, and the zeal of the advocate is so transfigured that it has the effect of the sworn evidence of a witness, or the verdict of a judge. And at the same time all these excellences, of which scarce one could be attained by the ordinary man even by the most concentrated effort, flow from him with every appearance of spontaneity, and his style, although no fairer has ever fallen on the ears of men, none the less displays the utmost felicity and ease. It was not, 112 therefore, without good reason that his own contemporaries spoke of his "sovereignty" at the bar, and that for posterity the name of Cicero has come to be regarded not as the name of a man, but as the name of eloquence itself. Let us, therefore, fix our eyes on him, take him as our pattern, and let the student realise that he has made real progress if he is a passionate admirer of Cicero. Asinius Pollio[1] had great gifts of 113 invention and great precision of language (indeed, some think him too precise), while his judgment and spirit were fully adequate. But he is so far from equalling the polish and charm of Cicero that he might have been born a generation before him. Messala,[2] on the other hand, is polished and transparent and displays his nobility in his utterance, but he fails to do his powers full justice. As 114 for Gaius Caesar, if he had had leisure to devote himself to the courts, he would have been the one orator who could have been considered a serious rival to Cicero. Such are his force, his penetration and his energy that we realise that he was as vigorous in speech as in his conduct of war. And yet all these qualities are enhanced by a marvellous elegance of language, of which he was an exceptionally zealous

115 proprie studiosus fuit, elegantia. Multum ingenii
in Caelio et praecipue in accusando multa urbanitas,
dignusque vir cui et mens melior et vita longior
contigisset. Inveni qui Calvum praeferrent omnibus,
inveni qui Ciceroni crederent, eum nimia contra se
calumnia verum sanguinem perdidisse; sed est et
sancta et gravis oratio et castigata et frequenter
vehemens quoque. Imitator autem est Atticorum,
fecitque illi properata mors iniuriam, si quid adiec-
116 turus fuit.[1] Et Servius Sulpicius insignem non
immerito famam tribus orationibus meruit. Multa,
si cum iudicio legatur, dabit imitatione digna Cassius
Severus, qui si ceteris virtutibus colorem et gravitatem
orationis adiecisset, ponendus inter praecipuos foret.
117 Nam et ingenii plurimum est in eo et acerbitas mira,
et urbanitas et fervor;[2] sed plus stomacho quam consilio dedit. Praeterea ut amari sales, ita frequenter
118 amaritudo ipsa ridicula est. Sunt alii multi diserti, quos
persequi longum est. Eorum quos viderim Domitius
Afer et Iulius Africanus longe praestantissimi. Arte
ille et toto genere dicendi praeferendus et quem in
numero veterum habere non timeas; hic concitatior,

---

[1] adiecturus fuit, *B*: *most later MSS.* add non si quid
detracturus *with slight variations.*
[2] et fervor, *Bursian*: et sermo, *B*.

---

[1] M. Rufus Caelius, defended by Cicero in the *pro Caelio*.
Killed in 48 B.C.   *Cp.* IV. ii. 123.; VIII. vi. 53.
[2] Calvus (Gaius Licinius), a distinguished poet and, with
Brutus, the leading orator of the Attic School.   He died
at the age of 34 in 48 B.C.
[3] Servius Sulpicius Rufus, the greatest jurist of the
Ciceronian age.
[4] Cassius Severus (*d.* A.D 34) banished by Augustus on
account of his scurrilous lampoons.

student. Caelius[1] has much natural talent and much 115
wit, more especially when speaking for the prosecution, and deserved a wiser mind and a longer life.
I have come across some critics who preferred
Calvus[2] to all other orators, and others again who
agreed with Cicero that too severe self-criticism had
robbed him of his natural vigour. But he was the
possessor of a solemn, weighty and chastened style,
which was also capable at times of genuine vehemence. He was an adherent of the Attic school and
an untimely death deprived him of his full meed of
honour, at least if we regard him as likely to have
acquired fresh qualities. Servius Sulpicius[3] acquired 116
a great and well-deserved reputation by his three
speeches. Cassius Severus,[4] if read with discrimination, will provide much that is worthy of imitation:
if to his other merits he had added appropriateness
of tone and dignity of style, he would deserve a 117
place among the greatest. For his natural talents
are great, his gift of bitterness, wit and passion
remarkable, but he allowed the sharpness of his
temper to prevail over his judgment. Moreover,
though his jests are pungent enough, this very
pungency often turned the laugh against himself.
There are many other clever speakers, but it 118
would be a long task to deal with them all. Domitius
Afer[5] and Julius Africanus[6] are by far the most distinguished. The former is superior in art and in
every department of oratory, indeed he may be
ranked with the old orators without fear of contra-

[5] Domitius Afer (d. 59 A D.), the leading orator of the
reigns of Tiberius and his successors.
[6] Iulius Africanus, a Gaul, who flourished in the reign of
Nero.

sed in cura verborum nimius et compositione nonnunquam longior et translationibus parum modicus.

119 Erant clara et nuper ingenia. Nam et Trachalus plerumque sublimis et satis apertus fuit et quem velle
optima crederes, auditus tamen maior ; nam et vocis,
quantam in nullo cognovi, felicitas et pronuntiatio vel
scenis suffectura et decor, omnia denique ei, quae sunt
extra, superfuerunt ; et Vibius Crispus compositus et
iucundus et delectationi natus, privatis tamen causis

120 quam publicis melior. Iulio Secundo, si longior
contigisset aetas, clarissimum profecto nomen oratoris apud posteros foret. Adiecisset enim atque
adiiciebat ceteris virtutibus suis quod desiderari
potest ; id est autem, ut esset multo magis pugnax
et saepius ad curam rerum ab elocutione respiceret.

121 Ceterum interceptus quoque magnum sibi vindicat
locum ; ea est facundia, tanta in explicando quod
velit gratia, tam candidum et leve et speciosum dicendi genus, tanta verborum etiam quae adsumpta
sunt proprietas, tanta in quibusdam ex periculo

122 petitis significantia. Habebunt, qui post nos de
oratoribus scribent, magnam eos, qui nunc vigent,
materiam vere laudandi. Sunt enim summa hodie,
quibus illustratur forum, ingenia. Namque et con-
summati iam patroni veteribus aemulantur et eos

---

[1] M. Galerius Trachalus (cos. 68 A.D.) *Cp* XII. v. 5.

[2] Vibius Crispus, a *delator* under Nero, died about A.D.
90, after acquiring great wealth. *Cp. Juv.* iv. 81-93.

[3] Julius Secundus, a distinguished orator of the reign of
Vespasian. One of the characters in the *Dialogus* of Tacitus.

diction. The latter shows greater energy, but is too great a precisian in the choice of words, prone to tediously long periods and somewhat extravagant in his metaphors. There have been distinguished talents even of more recent date. For example, 119 Trachalus[1] was, as a rule, elevated and sufficiently clear in his language: one realised that his aims were high, but he was better to listen to than to read. For his voice was, in my experience, unique in its beauty of tone, while his delivery would have done credit to an actor, his action was full of grace and he possessed every external advantage in profusion. Vibius Crispus,[2] again, was well-balanced, agreeable and born to charm, though he was better in private than in public cases. Julius Secundus,[3] 120 had he lived longer, would undoubtedly have attained a great and enduring reputation. For he would have acquired, as he was actually acquiring, all that was lacking to his qualities, namely, a far greater pugnacity and a closer attention to substance as well as form. But, in spite of the untimeliness of his end, 121 he occupies a high place, thanks to his fluency, the grace with which he set forth whatever he desired, the lucidity, smoothness and beauty of his speech, the propriety revealed in the use of words, even when employed figuratively, and the point which characterises even his most hazardous expressions. Subsequent writers on the history of oratory will 122 find abundant material for praise among the orators who flourish to-day: for the law courts can boast a glorious wealth of talent. Indeed, the consummate advocates of the present day are serious rivals of the ancients, while enthusiastic effort and lofty ideals lead many a young student

69

iuvenum ad optima tendentium imitatur ac sequitur industria.

123   Supersunt qui de philosophia scripserint, quo in genere paucissimos adhuc eloquentes litterae Romanae tulerunt. Idem igitur M. Tullius, qui ubique, etiam in hoc opere Platonis aemulus exstitit. Egregius vero multoque quam in orationibus praestantior Brutus suffecit ponderi rerum; scias eum
124 sentire quae dicit.   Scripsit non parum multa Cornelius Celsus, Sextios secutus, non sine cultu ac nitore.   Plautus in Stoicis rerum cognitioni utilis. In Epicureis levis quidem, sed non iniucundus tamen
125 auctor est Catius.   Ex industria Senecam in omni genere eloquentiae distuli propter vulgatam falso de me opinionem, qua damnare eum et invisum quoque habere sum creditus.   Quod accidit mihi, dum corruptum et omnibus vitiis fractum dicendi genus revocare
126 ad severiora iudicia contendo.   Tum autem solus hic fere in manibus adolescentium fuit.   Quem non equidem omnino conabar excutere, sed potioribus praeferri non sinebam, quos ille non destiterat incessere, cum diversi sibi conscius generis placere se in dicendo posse iis, quibus illi placent, diffideret.   Ama-

---

¹ Brutus, omitted from Quintilian's list of orators, was a follower of the Stoic and Academic schools. He is known to have written treatises on Virtue, Duty and Patience.
    ² An encyclopædic writer under Augustus and Tiberius. His medical treatises have survived. He wrote on oratory also, and is not infrequently quoted by Quintilian.
    ³ The Sextii, father and son, were Pythagorean philosophers of the Augustan age, with something of a Stoic tendency as well.
    ⁴ Nothing is known of this writer, save what is told us in III. xiv. 2, and III. vi. 23.

to tread in their footsteps and imitate their excellence.

I have still to deal with writers on philosophy, 123 of whom Rome has so far produced but few who are distinguished for their style. But Cicero, who is great in every department of literature, stands out as the rival of Plato in this department as well. Brutus[1] was an admirable writer on such themes, in which he distinguished himself far more than in his speeches: he is equal to the serious nature of his subject, and the reader realises that he feels what he says. Cornelius Celsus,[2] a follower of the Sextii,[3] 124 wrote a number of philosophical works, which have considerable grace and polish. Among the Stoics Plautus[4] is useful as giving a knowledge of the subject. Among the Epicureans Catius[5] is agreeable to read, though lacking in weight. I have 125 deliberately postponed the discussion of Seneca in connexion with the various departments of literature owing to the fact that there is a general, though false, impression that I condemn and even detest him. It is true that I had occasion to pass censure upon him when I was endeavouring to recall students from a depraved style, weakened by every kind of error, to a severer standard of taste. But 126 at that time Seneca's works were in the hands of every young man, and my aim was not to ban his reading altogether, but to prevent his being preferred to authors superior to himself, but whom he was never tired of disparaging; for, being conscious of the fact that his own style was very different

[5] A contemporary of Cicero, who speaks of him somewhat contemptuously. He wrote four books *de rerum natura et de summo bono.*

bant autem eum magis quam imitabantur tantumque
ab eo defluebant, quantum ille ab antiquis descend-
127 erat.   Foret enim optandum pares ac saltem proximos
illi viro fieri.   Sed placebat propter sola vitia et ad
ea se quisque dirigebat effingenda quae poterat;
deinde cum se iactaret eodem modo dicere, Senecam
128 infamabat.   Cuius et multae alioqui et magnae virtutes fuerunt, ingenium facile et copiosum, plurimum
studii, multa rerum cognitio; in qua tamen aliquando ab his, quibus inquirenda quaedam mandabat,
129 deceptus est.   Tractavit etiam omnem fere studiorum
materiam.   Nam et orationes eius et poemata et
epistolae et dialogi feruntur.   In philosophia parum
diligens, egregius tamen vitiorum insectator fuit.
Multae in eo claraeque sententiae, multa etiam
morum gratia legenda; sed in eloquendo corrupta
pleraque atque eo perniciosissima, quod abundant
130 dulcibus vitiis.   Velles eum suo ingenio dixisse,
alieno iudicio.   Nam si obliqua[1] contempsisset, si
parum recta[2] non concupisset, si non omnia sua
amasset, si rerum pondera minutissimis sententiis
non fregisset, consensu potius eruditorum quam

---

[1] obliqua, *E. Wölfflin*: simile quam, *B*: si aliqua, *2nd
hand.*   [2] recta, *added by Peterson.*

from theirs, he was afraid that he would fail to
please those who admired them. But the young
men loved him rather than imitated him, and fell
as far below him as he fell below the ancients. For 127
I only wish they had equalled or at least approached
his level. But he pleased them for his faults alone,
and each individual sought to imitate such of those
faults as lay within his capacity to reproduce : and
then brought reproach on his master by boasting
that he spoke in the genuine Senecan manner.
Seneca had many excellent qualities, a quick and 128
fertile intelligence with great industry and wide
knowledge, though as regards the last quality he
was often led into error by those whom he had
entrusted with the task of investigating certain
subjects on his behalf. He dealt with almost every 129
department of knowledge ; for speeches, poems,
letters and dialogues all circulate under his name.
In philosophy he showed a lack of critical power,
but was none the less quite admirable in his
denunciations of vice. His works contain a number
of striking general reflexions and much that is
worth reading for edification ; but his style is for
the most part corrupt and exceedingly dangerous,
for the very reason that its vices are so many and
attractive. One could wish that, while he relied on 130
his own intelligence, he had allowed himself to be
guided by the taste of others. For if he had only
despised all unnatural expressions and had not been
so passionately fond of all that was incorrect, if he
had not felt such affection for all that was his own,
and had not impaired the solidity of his matter by
striving after epigrammatic brevity, he would have
won the approval of the learned instead of the

131 puerorum amore comprobaretur. Verum sic quoque iam robustis et severiore genere satis firmatis legendus vel ideo quod exercere potest utrinque iudicium. Multa enim, ut dixi, probanda in eo, multa etiam admiranda sunt, eligere modo curae sit; quod utinam ipse fecisset. Digna enim fuit illa natura, quae meliora vellet; quod voluit effecit.

II. Ex his ceterisque lectione dignis auctoribus et verborum sumenda copia est et varietas figurarum et componendi ratio, tum ad exemplum virtutum omnium mens dirigenda. Neque enim dubitari potest, quin artis pars magna contineatur imitatione. Nam ut invenire primum fuit estque praecipuum, sic ea, quae 2 bene inventa sunt, utile sequi. Atque omnis vitae ratio sic constat, ut quae probamus in aliis facere ipsi velimus. Sic litterarum ductus, ut scribendi fiat usus, pueri sequuntur, sic musici vocem docentium, pictores opera priorum, rustici probatam experimento culturam in exemplum intuentur; omnis denique disciplinae initia ad propositum sibi praescriptum 3 formari videmus. Et hercule necesse est aut similes aut dissimiles bonis simus. Similem raro natura praestat, frequenter imitatio. Sed hoc ipsum, quod

enthusiasm of boys. But even as it is, he deserves **131**
to be read by those whose powers have been formed
and firmly moulded on the standards of a severer
taste, if only because he will exercise their critical
faculties in distinguishing between his merits and
his defects. For, as I have said, there is much in
him which we may approve, much even that we may
admire. Only we must be careful in our selection :
would he had been as careful himself. For his
genius deserved to be devoted to better aims, since
what it does actually aim at, it succeeds in achieving.

II. It is from these and other authors worthy of
our study that we must draw our stock of words, the
variety of our figures and our methods of composition,
while we must form our minds on the model of every
excellence. For there can be no doubt that in art
no small portion of our task lies in imitation, since,
although invention came first and is all-important, it
is expedient to imitate whatever has been invented
with success. And it is a universal rule of life that **2**
we should wish to copy what we approve in others.
It is for this reason that boys copy the shapes of
letters that they may learn to write, and that
musicians take the voices of their teachers, painters
the works of their predecessors, and peasants the
principles of agriculture which have been proved in
practice, as models for their imitation. In fact, we
may note that the elementary study of every branch
of learning is directed by reference to some definite
standard that is placed before the learner. We **3**
must, in fact, either be like or unlike those who
have proved their excellence. It is rare for nature
to produce such resemblance, which is more often
the result of imitation. But the very fact that in

tanto faciliorem nobis rationem rerum omnium facit
quam fuit iis, qui nihil quod sequerentur habuerunt,
nisi caute et cum iudicio apprehenditur, nocet.

4   Ante omnia igitur imitatio per se ipsa non sufficit,
vel quia pigri est ingenii contentum esse iis, quae
sint ab aliis inventa.   Quid enim futurum erat
temporibus illis, quae sine exemplo fuerunt, si
homines nihil, nisi quod iam cognovissent, faciendum
sibi aut cogitandum putassent?   Nempe nihil fuisset
5 inventum.   Cur igitur nefas est reperiri aliquid a
nobis, quod ante non fuerit?   An illi rudes sola
mentis natura ducti sunt in hoc ut tam multa gene-
rarent, nos ad quaerendum non eo ipso concitemur,
6 quod certe scimus invenisse eos qui quaesierunt?   Et
cum illi, qui nullum cuiusquam rei habuerunt magistrum, plurima in posteros tradiderunt, nobis usus
aliarum rerum ad eruendas alias non proderit, sed
nihil habebimus nisi beneficii alieni?   Quemadmodum quidam pictores in id solum student, ut de-
7 scribere tabulas mensuris ac lineis sciant.   Turpe
etiam illud est, contentum esse id consequi quod
imiteris.   Nam rursus quid erat futurum, si nemo
plus effecisset eo quem sequebatur?   Nihil in poetis
supra Livium Andronicum, nihil in historiis supra
Pontificum annales haberemus; ratibus adhuc navi-

---

[1] The reference is to copying by dividing the surface of
the picture to be copied, and of the material on which the
copy is to be made, into a number of equal squares.

[2] Livius Andronicus, a slave from Tarentum, was the
founder of Latin poetry.   He translated the *Odyssey*, and
produced the first Latin comedy and tragedy composed in
Greek metres (240 B.C.)

[3] The Annales Maximi kept by the Pontifex Maximus,
containing the list of the consuls and giving a curt summary
of the events of each consulate.

every subject the procedure to be followed is so
much more easy for us than it was for those who
had no model to guide them, is a positive drawback,
unless we use this dubious advantage with caution
and judgment.

The first point, then, that we must realise is that 4
imitation alone is not sufficient, if only for the reason
that a sluggish nature is only too ready to rest
content with the inventions of others. For what
would have happened in the days when models were
not, if men had decided to do and think of nothing
that they did not know already? The answer is
obvious: nothing would ever have been discovered.
Why, then, is it a crime for us to discover something 5
new? Were primitive men led to make so many
discoveries simply by the natural force of their
imagination, and shall we not then be spurred on to
search for novelty by the very knowledge that those
who sought of old were rewarded by success? And 6
seeing that they, who had none to teach them anything, have handed down such store of knowledge
to posterity, shall we refuse to employ the experience
which we possess of some things, to discover yet
other things, and possess nought that is not owed to
the beneficent activity of others? Shall we follow
the example of those painters whose sole aim is to
be able to copy pictures by using the ruler and the
measuring rod?[1] It is a positive disgrace to be 7
content to owe all our achievement to imitation.
For what, I ask again, would have been the result
if no one had done more than his predecessors?
Livius Andronicus[2] would mark our supreme
achievement in poetry and the annals of the *Pontifices*[3] would be our *ne plus ultra* in history. We

garemus; non esset pictura, nisi quae lineas modo
extremas umbrae, quam corpora in sole fecissent,
8 circumscriberet. Ac si omnia percenseas, nulla mansit [1] ars, qualis inventa est, nec intra initium stetit,
nisi forte nostra potissimum tempora damnamus
huius infelicitatis, ut nunc demum nihil crescat.
9 Nihil autem crescit sola imitatione. Quodsi prioribus adiicere fas non est, quomodo sperare possumus
illum oratorem perfectum? cum in his, quos maximos
adhuc novimus, nemo sit inventus, in quo nihil aut
desideretur aut reprehendatur. Sed etiam qui summa
non appetent, contendere potius quam sequi debent.
10 Nam qui hoc agit [2] ut prior sit, forsitan, etiamsi
non transierit, aequabit. Eum vero nemo potest
aequare, cuius vestigiis sibi utique insistendum putat;
necesse est enim semper sit posterior qui sequitur.
Adde quod plerumque facilius est plus facere quam
idem. Tantam enim difficultatem habet similitudo,
ut ne ipsa quidem natura in hoc ita evaluerit, ut non
res quae simillimae, quaeque pares maxime videantur,
11 utique discrimine aliquo discernantur. Adde quod,
quidquid alteri simile est, necesse est minus sit eo,
quod imitatur, ut umbra corpore et imago facie et

---

[1] mansit, *Meister* : sit, *MSS.*
[2] hoc agit, *Halm, om. B* : agit, *later MSS.*

should still be sailing on rafts, and the art of painting would be restricted to tracing a line round a shadow thrown in the sunlight. Cast your eyes over the 8 whole of history; you will find that no art has remained just as it was when it was discovered, nor come to a standstill at its very birth, unless indeed we are ready to pass special condemnation on our own generation on the ground that it is so barren of invention that no further development is possible; and it is undoubtedly true that no development is possible for those who restrict themselves to imitation. But if we are forbidden to add anything to 9 the existing stock of knowledge, how can we ever hope for the birth of our ideal orator? For of all the greatest orators with whom we are as yet acquainted, there is not one who has not some deficiency or blemish. And even those who do not aim at supreme excellence, ought to press toward the mark rather than be content to follow in the tracks of others. For the man whose aim 10 is to prove himself better than another, even if he does not surpass him, may hope to equal him. But he can never hope to equal him, if he thinks it his duty merely to tread in his footsteps: for the mere follower must always lag behind. Further, it is generally easier to make some advance than to repeat what has been done by others, since there is nothing harder than to produce an exact likeness, and nature herself has so far failed in this endeavour that there is always some difference which enables us to distinguish even the things which seem most like and most equal to one another. Again, what- 11 ever is like another object, must necessarily be inferior to the object of its imitation, just as the

actus histrionum veris adfectibus. Quod in orationibus quoque evenit. Namque eis, quae in exemplum adsumimus, subest natura et vera vis; contra omnis imitatio ficta est et ad alienum propositum accommo-

12 datur.[1] Quod facit, ut minus sanguinis ac virium declamationes habeant quam orationes, quod in illis vera, in his adsimilata materia est. Adde quod ea, quae in oratore maxima sunt, imitabilia non sunt, ingenium, inventio, vis, facilitas et quidquid arte non

13 traditur. Ideoque plerique, cum verba quaedam ex orationibus excerpserunt aut aliquos compositionis certos pedes, mire a se, quae legerunt, effingi arbitrantur; cum et verba intercidant invalescantque temporibus, ut quorum certissima sit regula in consuetudine, eaque non sua natura sint bona aut mala (nam per se soni tantum sunt), sed prout opportune proprieque aut secus collocata sunt, et compositio cum rebus accommodata sit, tum ipsa varietate gratissima.

14 Quapropter exactissimo iudicio circa hanc partem studiorum examinanda sunt omnia. Primum, quos imitemur; nam sunt plurimi, qui similitudinem pessimi cuiusque et corruptissimi concupierunt; tum in

[1] accommodatur, *2nd hand of B and later MSS.*: commodatur, *B.*

shadow is inferior to the substance, the portrait to the features which it portrays, and the acting of the player to the feelings which he endeavours to reproduce. The same is true of oratory. For the models which we select for imitation have a genuine and natural force, whereas all imitation is artificial and moulded to a purpose which was not that of the original orator. This is the reason why declamations 12 have less life and vigour than actual speeches, since the subject is fictitious in the one and real in the other. Again, the greatest qualities of the orator are beyond all imitation, by which I mean, talent, invention, force, facility and all the qualities which are independent of art. Consequently, there are 13 many who, after excerpting certain words from published speeches or borrowing certain particular rhythms, think that they have produced a perfect copy of the works which they have read, despite the fact that words become obsolete or current with the lapse of years, the one sure standard being contemporary usage; and they are not good or bad in virtue of their inherent nature (for in themselves they are no more than mere sounds), but solely in virtue of the aptitude and propriety (or the reverse) with which they are arranged, while rhythmical composition must be adapted to the theme in hand and will derive its main charm from its variety.

Consequently the nicest judgment is required in 14 the examination of everything connected with this department of study. First we must consider whom to imitate. For there are many who have shown a passionate desire to imitate the worst and most decadent authors. Secondly, we must consider what

ipsis, quos elegerimus, quid sit, ad quod nos effici-
15 endum comparemus. Nam in magnis quoque auctoribus incidunt aliqua vitiosa et a doctis, inter ipsos
etiam mutuo reprehensa; atque utinam tam bona
imitantes dicerent melius quam mala peius dicunt.
Nec vero saltem iis, quibus ad evitanda vitia iudicii
satis fuit, sufficiat imaginem virtutis effingere et
solam, ut sic dixerim, cutem vel potius illas Epicuri
16 figuras, quas e summis corporibus dicit effluere. Hoc
autem his accidit, qui non introspectis penitus virtutibus ad primum se velut aspectum orationis aptarunt;
et cum iis felicissime cessit imitatio, verbis atque
numeris sunt non multum differentes, vim dicendi
atque inventionis non adsequuntur, sed plerumque
declinant in peius et proxima virtutibus vitia compre-
hendunt fiuntque pro grandibus tumidi, pressis exiles,
fortibus temerarii, laetis corrupti, compositis exult-
17 antes, simplicibus negligentes. Ideoque qui horride
atque incomposite quidlibet illud frigidum et inane
extulerunt, antiquis se pares credunt; qui carent
cultu atque sententiis, Attici scilicet; qui praecisis
conclusionibus obscuri, Sallustium atque Thucydidem

---

[1] Epicurus held that all sense-perception was caused by
the impact of such atomic sloughs : *cp. Lucret.* iv. 42 sqq.

it is that we should set ourselves to imitate in the authors thus chosen. For even great authors have 15 their blemishes, for which they have been censured by competent critics and have even reproached each other. I only wish that imitators were more likely to improve on the good things than to exaggerate the blemishes of the authors whom they seek to copy. And even those who have sufficient critical acumen to avoid the faults of their models will not find it sufficient to produce a copy of their merits, amounting to no more than a superficial resemblance, or rather recalling those sloughs which, according to Epicurus, are continually given off by material things.[1] But this is just what happens to those who mould 16 themselves on the first impressions derived from the style of their model, without devoting themselves to a thorough investigation of its good qualities, and, despite the brilliance of their imitation and the close resemblance of their language and rhythm, not only fail absolutely to attain the force of style and invention possessed by the original, but as a rule degenerate into something worse, and achieve merely those faults which are hardest to distinguish from virtues : they are turgid instead of grand, bald instead of concise, and rash instead of courageous, while extravagance takes the place of wealth, over-emphasis the place of harmony and negligence of simplicity. As a result, 17 those who flaunt tasteless and insipid thoughts, couched in an uncouth and inharmonious form, think that they are the equals of the ancients ; those who lack ornament and epigram, pose as Attic ; those who darken their meaning by the abruptness with which they close their periods, count themselves the superiors of Sallust and Thucydides ; those who are

superant; tristes ac ieiuni Pollionem aemulantur:
otiosi et supini, si quid modo longius circumduxerunt,
18 iurant ita Ciceronem locuturum fuisse. Noveram
quosdam, qui se pulchre expressisse genus illud
caelestis huius in dicendo viri sibi viderentur, si in
clausula posuissent *Esse videatur*. Ergo primum est,
ut quod imitaturus est quisque intelligat et quare
bonum sit sciat.

19 Tum in suscipiendo onere consulat suas vires. Nam
quaedam sunt imitabilia, quibus aut infirmitas naturae
non sufficiat aut diversitas repugnet. Ne, cui tenue
ingenium erit, sola velit fortia et abrupta; cui forte
quidem, sed indomitum, amore subtilitatis et vim
suam perdat et elegantiam quam cupit non perse-
quatur; nihil est enim tam indecens, quam cum
20 mollia dure fiunt. Atque ego illi praeceptori, quem
institueram in libro secundo, credidi non ea sola
docenda esse, ad quae quemque discipulorum natura
compositum videret; nam is et adiuvare debet, quae
in quoque eorum invenit bona, et, quantum fieri
potest, adiicere quae desunt et emendare quaedam et
mutare; rector enim est alienorum ingeniorum atque
21 formator. Difficilius est naturam suam fingere. Sed

---

[1] *cp.* IX. iv. 73. Tac. *Dial.* 23.   [2] Ch. 8.

dreary and jejune, think that they are serious rivals
to Pollio, while those who are tame and listless, if
only they can produce long enough periods, swear
that this is just the manner in which Cicero would
have spoken. I have known some who thought that 18
they had produced a brilliant imitation of the style
of that divine orator, by ending their periods with
the phrase *esse videatur*.[1] Consequently it is of the
first importance that every student should realise
what it is that he is to imitate, and should know
why it is good.

The next step is for each student to consult his 19
own powers when he shoulders his burden. For
there are some things which, though capable of
imitation, may be beyond the capacity of any given
individual, either because his natural gifts are insufficient or of a different character. The man whose
talent is for the plain style should not seek only
what is bold and rugged, nor yet should he who has
vigour without control suffer himself through love of
subtlety at once to waste his natural energy and
fail to attain the elegance at which he aims: for
there is nothing so unbecoming as delicacy wedded
to ruggedness. True, I did express the opinion 20
that the instructor whose portrait I painted in my
second book,[2] should not confine himself to teaching
those things for which he perceived his individual
pupils to have most aptitude. For it is his further
duty to foster whatever good qualities he may per-
ceive in his pupils, to make good their deficiencies
as far as may be, to correct their faults and turn
them to better things. For he is the guide and
director of the minds of others. It is a harder task
to mould one's own nature. But not even our 21

ne ille quidem doctor, quanquam omnia quae recta sunt velit esse in suis auditoribus quam plenissima, in eo tamen, cui naturam obstare viderit, laborabit.

Id quoque vitandum, in quo magna pars errat, ne in oratione poetas nobis et historicos, in illis operibus 22 oratores aut declamatores imitandos putemus.   Sua cuique proposita[1] lex, suus cuique decor est.   Nam nec comoedia in cothurnos adsurgit, nec contra tragoedia socco ingreditur. Habet tamen omnis eloquentia aliquid commune ; id imitemur quod commune est.

23   Etiam hoc solet incommodi accidere iis, qui se uni alicui generi dediderunt, ut, si asperitas iis placuit alicuius, hanc etiam in leni ac remisso causarum genere non exuant; si tenuitas ac iucunditas, in asperis gravibusque causis ponderi rerum parum respondeant: cum sit diversa non causarum modo inter ipsas condicio, sed in singulis etiam causis partium, sintque alia leniter alia aspere, alia concitate alia remisse, alia docendi alia movendi gratia dicenda; quorum omnium dissimilis atque diversa inter se ratio est.   Itaque ne hoc quidem suaserim, uni se

[1] proposita, *most later MSS.* : propositio, *B* : proposito, *Gertz.*

ideal teacher, however much he may desire that
everything that is correct should prevail in his
school to the fullest extent, will waste his labour in
attempting to develop qualities to the attainment of
which he perceives nature's gifts to be opposed.

It is also necessary to avoid the fault to which the
majority of students are so prone, namely, the idea
that in composing speeches we should imitate the
poets and historians, and in writing history or poetry
should copy orators and declaimers. Each branch 22
of literature has its own laws and its own appropriate
character. Comedy does not seek to increase its
height by the buskin and tragedy does not wear
the slipper of comedy. But all forms of eloquence
have something in common, and it is to the imitation
of this common element that our efforts should be
confined.

There is a further fault to which those persons 23
are liable who devote themselves entirely to the
imitation of one particular style: if the rude vigour
of some particular author takes their fancy, they
cling to it even when the case on which they are
engaged calls for an easy and flowing style; if, on
the other hand, it is a simple or agreeable style that
claims their devotion, they fail to meet the heavy
demands of severe and weighty cases. For not only
do cases differ in their general aspect, but one part
of a case may differ from another, and some things
require a gentle and others a violent style, some
require an impetuous and others a calm diction, while
in some cases it is necessary to instruct and in others
to move the audience, in all these instances dis-
similar and different methods being necessary. Con- 24
sequently I should be reluctant even to advise a

alicui proprie, quem per omnia sequatur, addicere.
Longe perfectissimus Graecorum Demosthenes,
aliquid tamen aliquo in loco melius alii, plurima ille.
Sed non qui maxime imitandus, et solus imitandus
25 est. Quid ergo? non est satis omnia sic dicere, quomodo M. Tullius dixit? Mihi quidem satis esset, si
omnia consequi possem. Quid tamen noceret vim
Caesaris, asperitatem Caelii, diligentiam Pollionis,
26 iudicium Calvi quibusdam in locis adsumere? Nam
praeter id quod prudentis est, quod in quoque optimum est, si possit, suum facere, tum in tanta rei
difficultate unum intuentes vix aliqua pars sequitur.
Ideoque cum totum exprimere quem elegeris paene
sit homini inconcessum, plurium bona ponamus ante
oculos, ut aliud ex alio haereat, et quod cuique loco
conveniat aptemus.

27 Imitatio autem (nam saepius idem dicam) non sit
tantum in verbis. Illuc intendenda mens, quantum
fuerit illis viris decoris in rebus atque personis, quod
consilium, quae dispositio, quam omnia, etiam quae

student to select one particular author to follow through thick and thin. Demosthenes is by far the most perfect of Greek orators, yet there are some things which others have said better in some contexts as against the many things which he has said better than others. But it does not follow that because we should select one author for special imitation, he should be our only model. What then? Is it not 25 sufficient to model our every utterance on Cicero? For my own part, I should consider it sufficient, if I could always imitate him successfully. But what harm is there in occasionally borrowing the vigour of Caesar, the vehemence of Caelius, the precision of Pollio or the sound judgment of Calvus? For quite 26 apart from the fact that a wise man should always, if possible, make whatever is best in each individual author his own, we shall find that, in view of the extreme difficulty of our subject, those who fix their eyes on one model only will always find some one quality which it is almost impossible to acquire there-from. Consequently, since it is practically impossible for mortal powers to produce a perfect and complete copy of any one chosen author, we shall do well to keep a number of different excellences before our eyes, so that different qualities from different authors may impress themselves on our minds, to be adopted for use in the place that becomes them best.

But imitation (for I must repeat this point again 27 and again) should not be confined merely to words. We must consider the appropriateness with which those orators handle the circumstances and persons involved in the various cases in which they were engaged, and observe the judgment and powers of arrangement which they reveal, and the manner

delectationi videantur data, ad victoriam spectent;
quid agatur prooemio, quae ratio et quam varia narrandi, quae vis probandi ac refellendi, quanta in
adfectibus omnis generis movendis scientia, quamque
laus ipsa popularis utilitatis gratia adsumpta, quae
tum est pulcherrima, cum sequitur, non cum arcessi-
tur. Haec si perviderimus, tum vere imitabimur.
28 Qui vero etiam propria his bona adiecerit, ut sup-
pleat quae deerant, circumcidat, si quid redundabit,
is erit, quem quaerimus, perfectus orator; quem
nunc consummari potissimum oporteat, cum tanto
plura exempla bene dicendi supersint quam illis, qui
adhuc summi sunt, contigerunt. Nam erit haec
quoque laus eorum, ut priores superasse, posteros
docuisse dicantur.

III. Et haec quidem auxilia extrinsecus adhiben-
tur; in iis autem quae nobis ipsis paranda sunt, ut
laboris sic utilitatis etiam longe plurimum adfert stilus.
Nec immerito M. Tullius hunc *optimum effectorem ac
magistrum dicendi* vocat;[1] cui sententiae personam L.
Crassi in disputationibus quae sunt de oratore adsig-
nando, iudicium suum cum illius auctoritate coniunxit.
2 Scribendum ergo quam diligentissime et quam pluri-

---

[1] *De Or.* i. 150.

in which everything they say, not excepting those portions of their speeches which seem designed merely to delight their audience, is concentrated on securing the victory over their opponents. We must note their procedure in the exordium, the method and variety of their statement of facts, the power displayed in proof and refutation, the skill revealed in their appeal to every kind of emotion, and the manner in which they make use of popular applause to serve their case, applause which is most honourable when it is spontaneous and not deliberately courted. If we have thoroughly appreciated all these points, we shall be able to imitate our models with accuracy. But the man who to these good qualities **28** adds his own, that is to say, who makes good deficiencies and cuts down whatever is redundant, will be the perfect orator of our search; and it is now above all times that such perfection should be attained when there are before us so many more models of oratorical excellence than were available for those who have thus far achieved the highest success. For this glory also shall be theirs, that men shall say of them that while they surpassed their predecessors, they also taught those who came after.

III. Such are the aids which we may derive from external sources; as regards those which we must supply for ourselves, it is the pen which brings at once the most labour and the most profit. Cicero is fully justified in describing it as the best producer and teacher of eloquence, and it may be noted that in the *de Oratore*[1] he supports his own judgment by the authority of Lucius Crassus, in whose mouth he places this remark. We must **2**

mum. Nam ut terra alte refossa generandis alendisque
seminibus fecundior fit, sic profectus non a summo
petitus studiorum fructus effundit uberius et fidelius
continet.   Nam sine hac quidem conscientia ipsa illa
ex tempore dicendi facultas inanem modo loquacita-
3 tem dabit et verba in labris nascentia.   Illic radices,
illic fundamenta sunt, illic opes velut sanctiore quodam aerario conditae, unde ad subitos quoque casus,
cum res exiget, proferantur.   Vires faciamus ante
omnia, quae sufficiant labori certaminum et usu non
4 exhauriantur.   Nihil enim rerum ipsa natura voluit
magnum effici cito praeposuitque pulcherrimo cuique
operi difficultatem; quae nascendi quoque hanc fecerit legem, ut maiora animalia diutius visceribus
parentis continerentur.

Sed cum sit duplex quaestio, quomodo et quae
maxime scribi oporteat, iam hinc ordinem sequar.
5 Sit primo vel tardus dum diligens stilus, quaeramus
optima nec protinus offerentibus se gaudeamus, adhi-
beatur iudicium inventis, dispositio probatis.   Delectus enim rerum verborumque agendus est et

therefore write as much as possible and with the utmost care. For as deep ploughing makes the soil more fertile for the production and support of crops, so, if we improve our minds by something more than mere superficial study, we shall produce a richer growth of knowledge and shall retain it with greater accuracy. For without the consciousness of such preliminary study our powers of speaking extempore will give us nothing but an empty flow of words, springing from the lips and not from the brain. It 3 is in writing that eloquence has its roots and foundations, it is writing that provides that holy of holies where the wealth of oratory is stored, and whence it is produced to meet the demands of sudden emergencies. It is of the first importance that we should develop such strength as will not faint under the toil of forensic strife nor be exhausted by continual use. For it is an ordinance of nature that nothing 4 great can be achieved in a moment, and that all the fairest tasks are attended with difficulty, while on births as well she has imposed this law, that the larger the animal, the longer should be the period of gestation.

There are, however, two questions which present themselves in this connexion, namely, what should be our method and what the subjects on which we write, and I propose to treat them in this order. At first, our pen must be slow yet sure: we 5 must search for what is best and refuse to give a joyful welcome to every thought the moment that it presents itself; we must first criticise the fruits of our imagination, and then, once approved, arrange them with care. For we must select both thoughts and words and weigh them one by one. This done,

pondera singulorum examinanda. Post subeat ratio
collocandi versenturque omni modo numeri, non ut
6 quodque se proferet verbum occupet locum. Quae
quidem ut diligentius exsequamur, repetenda saepius
erunt scriptorum proxima. Nam praeter id quod sic
melius iunguntur prioribus sequentia, calor quoque
ille cogitationis, qui scribendi mora refrixit, recipit
ex integro vires et velut repetito spatio sumit impetum; quod in certamine saliendi fieri videmus, ut
conatum longius petant et ad illud, quo contenditur,
spatium cursu ferantur; utque in iaculando brachia
reducimus et expulsuri tela nervos retro tendimus.
7 Interim tamen, si feret flatus, danda sunt vela, dum
nos indulgentia illa non fallat. Omnia enim nostra,
dum nascuntur, placent; alioqui nec scriberentur.
Sed redeamus ad iudicium et retractemus suspectam
8 facilitatem. Sic scripsisse Sallustium accepimus, et
sane manifestus est etiam ex opere ipso labor. Ver-
gilium quoque paucissimos die composuisse versus
auctor est Varius. Oratoris quidem alia condicio
9 est; itaque hanc moram et sollicitudinem initiis
impero. Nam primum hoc constituendum, hoc obti-

we must consider the order in which they should be placed, and must examine all the possible varieties of rhythm, refusing necessarily to place each word in the order in which it occurs to us. In order to do 6 this with the utmost care, we must frequently revise what we have just written. For beside the fact that thus we secure a better connexion between what follows and what precedes, the warmth of thought which has cooled down while we were writing is revived anew, and gathers fresh impetus from going over the ground again. We may compare this process with what occurs in jumping matches. The competitors take a longer run and go at full speed to clear the distance which they aim at covering; similarly, in throwing the javelin, we draw back our arms, and in archery pull back the bow-string to propel the shaft. At times, however, we may 7 spread our sails before the favouring breeze, but we must beware that this indulgence does not lead us into error. For we love all the offspring of our thought at the moment of their birth; were that not so, we should never commit them to writing. But we must give them a critical revision, and go carefully over any passage where we have reason to regard our fluency with suspicion. It is thus, we 8 are told, that Sallust wrote, and certainly his works give clear evidence of the labour which he expended on them. Again, we learn from Varius that Virgil composed but a very small number of verses every day. It is true that with orators the case is some- 9 what different, and it is for this reason that I enjoin such slowness of speed and such anxious care at the outset. For the first aim which we must fix in our minds and insist on carrying into execution

nendum est, ut quam optime scribamus; celeritatem
dabit consuetudo. Paulatim res facilius se ostendent,
verba respondebunt, compositio sequetur, cuncta
denique ut in familia bene instituta in officio erunt.

10 Summa haec est rei: cito scribendo non fit, ut bene
scribatur; bene scribendo fit, ut cito. Sed tum
maxime, cum facultas illa contigerit, resistamus ut
provideamus et efferentes equos frenis quibusdam
coerceamus; quod non tam moram faciet quam novos
impetus dabit. Neque enim rursus eos, qui robur
aliquod in stilo fecerint, ad infelicem calumniandi

11 se poenam alligandos puto. Nam quomodo sufficere
officiis civilibus possit, qui singulis actionum partibus
insenescat? Sunt autem quibus nihil sit satis; omnia
mutare, omnia aliter dicere quam occurrit velint;
increduli quidam et de ingenio suo pessime meriti,
qui diligentiam putant facere sibi scribendi diffi-

12 cultatem. Nec promptum est dicere, utros peccare
validius putem, quibus omnia sua placent an quibus
nihil. Accidit enim etiam ingeniosis adolescentibus
frequenter, ut labore consumantur et in silentium
usque descendant nimia bene dicendi cupiditate.
Qua de re memini narrasse mihi Iulium Secundum
illum, aequalem meum atque a me, ut notum est,
familiariter amatum, mirae facundiae virum, infinitae

is to write as well as possible; speed will come with
practice. Gradually thoughts will suggest themselves with increasing readiness, the words will
answer to our call and rhythmical arrangement will
follow, till everything will be found fulfilling its
proper function as in a well-ordered household.
The sum of the whole matter is this: write quickly 10
and you will never write well, write well and you
will soon write quickly. But it is just when we
have acquired this facility that we must pause awhile
to look ahead and, if I may use the metaphor, curb
the horses that would run away with us. This will
not delay our progress so much as lend us fresh
vigour. For I do not think that those who have
acquired a certain power in writing should be condemned to the barren pains of false self-criticism.
How can anyone fulfil his duties as an advocate if he 11
wastes his time in putting unnecessary finish on each
portion of his pleadings? There are some who are
never satisfied. They wish to change everything
they have written and to put it in other words.
They are a diffident folk, and deserve but ill of their
own talents, who think it a mark of precision to cast
obstacles in the way of their own writing. Nor is it 12
easy to say which are the most serious offenders, those
who are satisfied with everything or those who are
satisfied with nothing that they write. For it is
of common occurrence with young men, however
talented they may be, to waste their gifts by superfluous elaboration, and to sink into silence through
an excessive desire to speak well. I remember in
this connexion a story that Julius Secundus, my contemporary, and, as is well known, my very dear friend,
a man with remarkable powers of eloquence, but

13 tamen curae, quid esset sibi a patruo suo dictum. Is
fuit Iulius Florus, in eloquentia Galliarum, quoniam
ibi demum exercuit eam, princeps, alioqui inter paucos disertus et dignus illa propinquitate. Is cum
Secundum, scholae adhuc operatum, tristem forte
vidisset, interrogavit, quae causa frontis tam ad-
14 ductae. Nec dissimulavit adolescens, tertium iam
diem esse, quod omni labore materiae ad scribendum
destinatae non inveniret exordium; quo sibi non
praesens tantum dolor, sed etiam desperatio in posterum fieret. Tum Florus arridens, *Numquid tu,* in-
15 quit, *melius dicere vis quam potes ?* Ita se res habet.
Curandum est ut quam optime dicamus; dicendum
tamen pro facultate. Ad profectum enim opus est
studio non indignatione. Ut possimus autem scribere
etiam plura et celerius, non exercitatio modo praestabit, in qua sine dubio multum est, sed etiam ratio;
si non resupini spectantesque tectum et cogitationem
murmure agitantes exspectaverimus quid obveniat;
sed quid res poscat, quid personam deceat, quod sit
tempus, qui iudicis animus intuiti, humano quodam
modo ad scribendum accesserimus. Sic nobis et
initia et quae sequuntur natura ipsa praescribit.
16 Certa sunt enim pleraque et, nisi conniveamus, in

with an infinite passion for precision, told me of the
words once used to him by his uncle, Julius Florus, 13
the leading orator of Gaul, for it was there that he
practised, a man eloquent as but few have ever
been, and worthy of his nephew. He once noticed
that Secundus, who was still a student, was looking
depressed, and asked him the meaning of his frowns.
The youth made no concealment of the reason: he 14
had been working for three days, and had been unable, in spite of all his efforts, to devise an exordium
for the theme which he had been given to write,
with the result that he was not only vexed over
his immediate difficulty, but had lost all hope of
future success. Florus smiled and said, "Do you
really want to speak better than you can?" There 15
lies the truth of the whole matter. We must aim
at speaking as well as we can, but must not try to
speak better than our nature will permit. For to
make any real advance we need study, not self-
accusation. And it is not merely practice that will
enable us to write at greater length and with
increased fluency, although doubtless practice is
most important. We need judgement as well. So
long as we do not lie back with eyes turned up to the
ceiling, trying to fire our imagination by muttering
to ourselves, in the hope that something will present
itself, but turn our thoughts to consider what the
circumstances of the case demand, what suits the
characters involved, what is the nature of the occasion and the temper of the judge, we shall acquire
the power of writing by rational means. It is thus
that nature herself bids us begin and pursue our
studies once well begun. For most points are of a 16
definite character and, if we keep our eyes open,

99

oculos incurrunt; ideoque nec indocti nec rustici diu
quaerunt, unde incipiant; quo pudendum est magis,
si difficultatem facit doctrina. Non ergo semper
putemus optimum esse quod latet; immutescamus
alioqui, si nihil dicendum videatur, nisi quod non
17 invenimus. Diversum est huic eorum vitium, qui
primo decurrere per materiam stilo quam velocissimo
volunt et sequentes calorem atque impetum ex tempore scribunt; hanc silvam vocant. Repetunt deinde
et componunt quae effuderant; sed verba emendan-
tur et numeri, manet in rebus temere congestis quae
18 fuit levitas. Protinus ergo adhibere curam rectius
erit atque ab initio sic opus ducere, ut caelandum,
non ex integro fabricandum sit. Aliquando tamen
adfectus sequemur, in quibus fere plus calor quam
diligentia valet.

Satis apparet ex eo, quod hanc scribentium negligentiam damno, quid de illis dictandi deliciis sentiam.
19 Nam in stilo quidem quamlibet properato dat aliquam cogitationi moram non consequens celeritatem
eius manus; ille cui dictamus urget, atque interim

will spontaneously present themselves. That is the reason why peasants and uneducated persons do not beat about the bush to discover with what they should begin, and our hesitation is all the more shameful if it is simply the result of education. We must not, therefore, persist in thinking that what is hard to find is necessarily best; for, if it seems to us that there is nothing to be said except that which we are unable to find, we must say nothing at all. On the other hand, there is a fault 17 which is precisely the opposite of this, into which those fall who insist on first making a rapid draft of their subject with the utmost speed of which their pen is capable, and write in the heat and impulse of the moment. They call this their rough copy. They then revise what they have written, and arrange their hasty outpourings. But while the words and the rhythm may be corrected, the matter is still marked by the superficiality resulting from the speed with which it was thrown together. The more correct method is, therefore, to exercise 18 care from the very beginning, and to form the work from the outset in such a manner that it merely requires to be chiselled into shape, not fashioned anew. Sometimes, however, we must follow the stream of our emotions, since their warmth will give us more than any diligence can secure.

The condemnation which I have passed on such 19 carelessness in writing will make it pretty clear what my views are on the luxury of dictation which is now so fashionable. For, when we write, however great our speed, the fact that the hand cannot follow the rapidity of our thoughts gives us time to think,

pudet etiam dubitare aut resistere aut mutare quasi
20 conscium infirmitatis nostrae timentes. Quo fit, ut
non rudia tantum et fortuita, sed impropria interim,
dum sola est connectendi sermonis cupiditas, effluant,
quae nec scribentium curam nec dicentium impetum
consequantur.   At idem ille, qui excipit, si tardior in
scribendo aut incertior in intellegendo [1] velut offen-
sator fuit, inhibetur cursus, atque omnis quae erat
concepta mentis intentio mora et interdum ira-
21 cundia excutitur. Tum illa, quae altiorem [2] animi
motum sequuntur quaeque ipsa animum quodammodo concitant, quorum est iactare manum, torquere
vultum, frontem et latus [3] interim obiurgare, quaeque Persius notat, cum leviter dicendi genus
significat,

   Nec pluteum, inquit, *caedit nec demorsos sapit ungues*,

22 etiam ridicula sunt, nisi cum soli sumus.   Denique
ut semel quod est potentissimum dicam, secretum
in [4] dictando perit.   Atque liberum arbitris locum et
quam altissimum silentium scribentibus maxime convenire nemo dubitaverit.   Non tamen protinus audiendi, qui credunt aptissima in hoc nemora silvasque,
quod illa caeli libertas locorumque amoenitas subli-
23 mem animum et beatiorem spiritum parent. Mihi certe

---

[1] intellegendo, *Müller*: legendo, *B*.
[2] altiorem, *later MSS.*: aptiorem, *B*.
[3] frontem et latus, *Peterson*: sintielatus, *B (2nd hand)*:
simul et, *almost all MSS.*
[4] in, *several later MSS.*: quod, *B*.

---

[1] i. 106.

whereas the presence of our amanuensis hurries us on, and at times we feel ashamed to hesitate or pause, or make some alteration, as though we were afraid to display such weakness before a witness. As a result our language tends not merely to be 20 haphazard and formless, but in our desire to produce a continuous flow we let slip positive improprieties of diction, which show neither the precision of the writer nor the impetuosity of the speaker. Again, if the amanuensis is a slow writer, or lacking in intelligence, he becomes a stumbling-block, our speed is checked, and the thread of our ideas is interrupted by the delay or even perhaps by the loss of temper to which it gives rise. Moreover, the 21 gestures which accompany strong feeling, and sometimes even serve to stimulate the mind, the waving of the hand, the contraction of the brow, the occasional striking of forehead or side, and those which Persius[1] notes when he describes a trivial style as one that

"Thumps not the desk nor smacks of bitten nails,"

all these become ridiculous, unless we are alone, Finally, we come to the most important considera- 22 tion of all, that the advantages of privacy are lost when we dictate. Everyone, however, will agree that the absence of company and deep silence are most conducive to writing, though I would not go so far as to concur in the opinion of those who think woods and groves the most suitable localities for the purpose, on the ground that the freedom of the sky and the charm of the surroundings produce sublimity of thought and wealth of inspiration. Personally I regard such an environment as a 23

iucundus hic magis quam studiorum hortator videtur
esse secessus.   Namque illa, quae ipsa delectant,
necesse est avocent ab intentione operis destinati.
Neque enim se bona fide in multa simul intendere
animus totum potest, et quocunque respexit, desinit
24 intueri quod propositum erat.   Quare silvarum amoenitas et praeterlabentia flumina et inspirantes ramis
arborum aurae volucrumque cantus et ipsa late cir-
cumspiciendi libertas ad se trahunt, ut mihi remittere
potius voluptas ista videatur cogitationem quam in-
25 tendere.   Demosthenes melius, qui se in locum, ex
quo nulla exaudiri vox et ex quo nihil prospici posset,
recondebat ne aliud agere mentem cogerent oculi.
Ideoque lucubrantes silentium noctis et clausum
cubiculum et lumen unum velut tectos[1] maxime
26 teneat.   Sed cum in omni studiorum genere tum in
hoc praecipue bona valetudo, quaeque eam maxime
praestat, frugalitas, necessaria est, cum tempora ab
ipsa rerum natura ad quietem refectionemque nobis
data in acerrimum laborem convertimus.   Cui tamen
non plus irrogandum est quam quod somno supererit,
27 haud deerit.   Obstat enim diligentiae scribendi etiam
fatigatio, et abunde, si vacet, lucis spatia sufficiunt ;
occupatos in noctem necessitas agit.   Est tamen lu-
cubratio, quotiens ad eam integri ac refecti venimus,
optimum secreti genus.

[1] tectos, *ed. Leid.* : rectos, *MSS.*

---

[1] An underground room.   See Plut. *Dem.* vii.

pleasant luxury rather than a stimulus to study.
For whatever causes us delight, must necessarily
distract us from the concentration due to our work.
The mind cannot devote its undivided and sincere
attention to a number of things at the same time,
and wherever it turns its gaze it must cease to
contemplate its appointed task. Therefore, the 24
charm of the woods, the gliding of the stream, the
breeze that murmurs in the branches, the song of
birds, and the very freedom with which our eyes
may range, are mere distractions, and in my opinion
the pleasure which they excite is more likely to
relax than to concentrate our attention. Demos- 25
thenes took a wiser view; for he would retire to
a place [1] where no voice was to be heard, and no
prospect greeted the sight, for fear that his eyes
might force his mind to neglect its duty. Therefore, let the burner of the midnight oil seclude
himself in the silence of night, within closed doors,
with but a solitary lamp to light his labours. But 26
for every kind of study, and more especially for
night work, good health and its chief source, simple
living, are essential; for we have fallen into the
habit of devoting to relentless labour the hour which
nature has appointed for rest and relaxation. From
those hours we must take only such time as is superfluous for sleep, and will not be missed. For fatigue 27
will make us careless in writing, and the hours of
daylight are amply sufficient for one who has no
other distractions. It is only the busy man who
is driven to encroach on the hours of darkness.
Nevertheless, night work, so long as we come to it
fresh and untired, provides by far the best form of
privacy.

28 Sed silentium et secessus et undique liber animus ut sunt maxime optanda, ita non semper possunt contingere, ideoque non statim, si quid obstrepet, abiiciendi codices erunt et deplorandus dies; verum incommodis repugnandum et hic faciendus usus, ut omnia quae impedient vincat intentio; quam si tota mente in opus ipsum direxeris, nihil eorum, quae oculis vel auribus in-

29 cursant, ad animum perveniet. An vero frequenter etiam fortuita hoc cogitatio praestat, ut obvios non videamus et itinere deerremus: non consequemur idem, si et voluerimus? Non est indulgendum causis desidiae. Nam si non nisi refecti, non nisi hilares, non nisi omnibus aliis curis vacantes studendum existimarimus, semper erit propter quod

30 nobis ignoscamus. Quare in turba, itinere, conviviis etiam faciat sibi cogitatio ipsa secretum Quid alioqui fiet, cum in medio foro, tot circum stantibus iudiciis, iurgiis, fortuitis etiam clamoribus, erit subito continua oratione dicendum, si particulas quas ceris mandamus nisi in solitudine reperire non possumus? Propter quae idem ille tantus amator secreti Demosthenes in litore, in quo se maximo cum sono fluctus illideret, meditans consuescebat contionum fremitus non expavescere.

31 Illa quoque minora (sed nihil in studiis parvum

But although silence and seclusion and absolute 28
freedom of mind are devoutly to be desired, they
are not always within our power to attain. Consequently we must not fling aside our book at once,
if disturbed by some noise, and lament that we
have lost a day: on the contrary, we must make
a firm stand against such inconveniences, and train
ourselves so to concentrate our thoughts as to rise
superior to all impediments to study. If only you
direct all your attention to the work which you
have in hand, no sight or sound will ever penetrate
to your mind. If even casual thoughts often occupy 29
us to such an extent that we do not see passers-by,
or even stray from our path, surely we can obtain
the same result by the exercise of our will. We
must not give way to pretexts for sloth. For unless
we make up our mind that we must be fresh, cheerful and free from all other care when we approach our
studies, we shall always find some excuse for idleness.
Therefore, whether we be in a crowd, on a journey, 30
or even at some festive gathering, our thoughts should
always have some inner sanctuary of their own to
which they may retire. Otherwise what shall we
do when we are suddenly called upon to deliver
a set speech in the midst of the forum, with lawsuits in progress on every side, and with the sound
of quarrels and even casual outcries in our ears, if
we need absolute privacy to discover the thoughts
which we jot down upon our tablets? It was for
this reason that Demosthenes, the passionate lover
of seclusion, used to study on the seashore amid the
roar of the breakers that they might teach him not
to be unnerved by the uproar of the public assembly.

There are also certain minor details which deserve 31

est) non sunt transeunda: scribi optime ceris, in quibus facillima est ratio delendi, nisi forte visus infirmior membranarum potius usum exiget, quae ut iuvant aciem, ita crebra relatione, quoad intinguuntur, calami morantur manum et cogitationis

32 impetum frangunt. Relinquendae autem in utrolibet genere contra erunt vacuae tabellae, in quibus libera adiiciendo sit excursio. Nam interim pigritiam emendandi augustiae faciunt aut certe novorum interpositione priora confundant. Ne latas quidem ultra modum esse ceras velim, expertus iuvenem studiosum alioqui praelongos habuisse sermones, quia illos numero versuum metiebatur, idque vitium, quod frequenti admonitione corrigi non

33 potuerat, mutatis codicibus esse sublatum. Debet vacare etiam locus, in quo notentur quae scribentibus solent extra ordinem, id est ex aliis, quam qui sunt in manibus loci, occurrere. Irrumpunt enim optimi nonnunquam sensus, quos neque inserere oportet neque differre tutum est, quia interim elabuntur, interim memoriae suae intentos ab alia inventione declinant ideoque optime sunt in deposito.

IV. Sequitur emendatio, pars studiorum longe utilissima. Neque enim sine causa creditum est stilum non minus agere, cum delet. Huius autem

our attention, for there is nothing too minute for the
student. It is best to write on wax owing to the
facility which it offers for erasure, though weak
sight may make it desirable to employ parchment
by preference. The latter, however, although of
assistance to the eye, delays the hand and interrupts
the stream of thought owing to the frequency with
which the pen has to be supplied with ink. But 32
whichever we employ, we must leave blank pages
that we may be free to make additions when we
will. For lack of space at times gives rise to a
reluctance to make corrections, or, at any rate, is
liable to cause confusion when new matter is
inserted. The wax tablets should not be unduly
wide; for I have known a young and over-zealous
student write his compositions at undue length,
because he measured them by the number of lines,
a fault which persisted, in spite of frequent ad-
monition, until his tablets were changed, when it
disappeared. Space must also be left for jotting 33
down the thoughts which occur to the writer out
of due order, that is to say, which refer to subjects
other than those in hand. For sometimes the most
admirable thoughts break in upon us which cannot
be inserted in what we are writing, but which, on
the other hand, it is unsafe to put by, since they are
at times forgotten, and at times cling to the memory
so persistently as to divert us from some other line
of thought. They are, therefore, best kept in
store.

IV. The next point which we have to consider is
the correction of our work, which is by far the most
useful portion of our study: for there is good reason
for the view that erasure is quite as important a

operis est adiicere, detrahere, mutare. Sed facilius in iis simpliciusque iudicium, quae replenda vel deiicienda sunt; premere vero tumentia, humilia extollere, luxuriantia adstringere, inordinata digerere, soluta componere, exultantia coercere, duplicis operae. Nam et damnanda sunt quae placuerunt et invenienda quae fugerant. Nec dubium est optimum esse emendandi genus, si scripta in aliquod tempus reponantur, ut ad ea post intervallum velut nova atque aliena redeamus, ne nobis scripta nostra tanquam recentes fetus blandiantur. Sed neque hoc contingere semper potest praesertim oratori, cui saepius scribere ad praesentes usus necesse est; et ipsa emendatio finem habeat. Sunt enim qui ad omnia scripta tanquam vitiosa redeant et, quasi nihil fas sit rectum esse quod primum est, melius existiment quidquid est aliud, idque faciant, quotiens librum in manus resumpserunt, similes medicis etiam integra secantibus. Accidit itaque ut cicatricosa sint et exsanguis et cura peiora. Sit ergo aliquando quod placeat aut certe quod sufficiat, ut opus poliat lima, non exterat. Temporis quoque

function· of the pen as actual writing. Correction takes the form of addition, excision and alteration. But it is a comparatively simple and easy task to decide what is to be added or excised. On the other hand, to prune what is turgid, to elevate what is mean, to repress exuberance, arrange what is disorderly, introduce rhythm where it is lacking, and modify it where it is too emphatic, involves a twofold labour. For we have to condemn what had previously satisfied us and discover what had escaped our notice. There can be no doubt that the best 2 method of correction is to put aside what we have written for a certain time, so that when we return to it after an interval it will have the air of novelty and of being another's handiwork; for thus we may prevent ourselves from regarding our writings with all the affection that we lavish on a newborn child. But this is not always possible, especially in the case 3 of an orator who most frequently has to write for immediate use, while some limit, after all, must be set to correction. For there are some who return to everything they write with the presumption that it is full of faults and, assuming that a first draft must necessarily be incorrect, think every change an improvement and make some alteration as often as they have the manuscript in their hands: they are, in fact, like doctors who use the knife even where the flesh is perfectly healthy. The result of their critical activities is that the finished work is full of scars, bloodless, and all the worse for their anxious care. No! let there be something in all 4 our writing which, if it does not actually please us, at least passes muster, so that the file may only polish our work, not wear it away. There must

esse debet modus. Nam quod Cinnae Zmyrnam
novem annis accepimus scriptam, et Panegyricum
Isocratis, qui parcissime, decem annis dicunt elabo-
ratium, ad oratorem nihil pertinet, cuius nullum
erit, si tam tardum fuerit, auxilium.

V. Proximum est, ut dicamus, quae praecipue
scribenda sint ἕξιν parantibus. Non est huius[1]
quidem operis, ut explicemus quae sint materiae,
quae prima aut secunda aut deinceps tractanda sint
(nam id factum est etiam primo libro, quo puerorum,
et secundo, quo iam robustorum studiis ordinem
dedimus) sed de quo nunc agitur, unde copia ac
facilitas maxime veniat.

2 Vertere Graeca in Latinum veteres nostri oratores
optimum iudicabant. Id se L. Crassus in illis
Ciceronis de Oratore libris dicit factitasse. Id
Cicero sua ipse persona frequentissime praecipit,
quin etiam libros Platonis atque Xenophontis edidit
hoc genere translatos. Id Messalae placuit, mul-
taeque sunt ab eo scriptae ad hunc modum orationes,
adeo ut etiam cum illa Hyperidis pro Phryne

3 difficillima Romanis subtilitate contenderet. Et
manifesta est exercitationis huiusce ratio. Nam et
rerum copia Graeci auctores abundant et plurimum
artis in eloquentiam intulerunt, et hos transfe-
rentibus verbis uti optimis licet, omnibus enim

---

[1] non est huius, *added by Bursian.*

---

[1] C. Helvius Cinna, the friend of Catullus. The Smyrna
was a short but exceptionally obscure and learned epic.
[2] See x. i. 1. [3] Ch. ix.
[4] Ch. iv. [5] i. 155.
[6] The *Œconomicus* of Xenophon, the *Protagoras* and *Timaeus*
of Plato.

also be a limit to the time which we spend on its revision. For the fact that Cinna[1] took nine years to write his Smyrna, and that Isocrates required ten years, at the lowest estimate, to complete his Panegyric does not concern the orator, whose assistance will be of no use, if it is so long delayed.

V. My next task is to indicate what those should write whose aim is to acquire facility.[2] At this part of my work there is no necessity for me to set forth the subjects which should be selected for writing, or the order in which they should be approached, since I have already done this in the first book,[3] where I prescribed the sequence of studies for boys, and in the second book,[4] where I did the same for young men. The point which concerns me now is to show from what sources copiousness and facility may most easily be derived.

Our earlier orators thought highly of translation from Greek into Latin. In the *de Oratore*[5] of 2 Cicero, Lucius Crassus says that he practised this continually, while Cicero himself advocates it again and again, nay, he actually published translations of Xenophon and Plato,[6] which were the result of this form of exercise. Messala likewise gave it his approval, and we have a number of translations of speeches from his hand; he even succeeded in coping with the delicacy of Hyperides' speech in defence of Phryne, a task of exceeding difficulty for a Roman. The purpose of this form of exercise is 3 obvious. For Greek authors are conspicuous for the variety of their matter, and there is much art in all their eloquence, while, when we translate them, we are at liberty to use the best words available,

utimur nostris.   Figuras vero, quibus maxime ornatur oratio, multas ac varias excogitandi etiam necessitas quaedam est, quia plerumque a Graecis
Romana dissentiunt.

4   Sed et illa ex Latinis conversio multum et ipsa
contulerit.   Ac de carminibus quidem neminem
credo dubitare, quo solo genere exercitationis dicitur
usus esse Sulpicius.   Nam et sublimis spiritus attollere orationem potest, et verba poetica libertate
audaciora non praesumunt eadem proprie dicendi
facultatem.   Sed et ipsis sententiis adiicere licet
oratorium robur et omissa supplere, effusa sub-
5 stringere.   Neque ego paraphrasim esse interpre-
tationem tantum volo, sed circa eosdem sensus
certamen atque aemulationem.   Ideoque ab illis
dissentio, qui vertere orationes Latinas vetant, quia
optimis occupatis, quidquid aliter dixerimus, necesse
sit esse deterius.   Nam neque semper est desperan-
dum, aliquid illis, quae dicta sunt, melius posse
reperiri ; neque adeo ieiunam ac pauperem natura
eloquentiam fecit, ut una de re bene dici nisi semel
6 non possit.   Nisi forte histrionum multa circa voces
easdem variare gestus potest, orandi minor vis, ut

---

[1] *I. e.* we shall not borrow from our models, as we do in
paraphrasing Latin.
[2] *Lit.* "forestall the power of using the language of
ordinary prose."

since all that we use are our very own.[1]   As regards
figures, too, which are the chief ornament of oratory,
it is necessary to think out a great number and variety
for ourselves, since in this respect the Roman idiom
differs largely from the Greek.

But paraphrase from the Latin will also be of 4
much assistance, while I think we shall all agree that
this is specially valuable with regard to poetry ;
indeed, it is said that the paraphrase of poetry was
the sole form of exercise employed by Sulpicius.
For the lofty inspiration of verse serves to elevate
the orator's style and the bold license of poetic
language does not preclude[2] our attempting to
render the same words in the language natural to
prose.   Nay, we may add the vigour of oratory
to the thoughts expressed by the poet, make good
his omissions, and prune his diffuseness.   But I 5
would not have paraphrase restrict itself to the
bare interpretation of the original : its duty is
rather to rival and vie with the original in the
expression of the same thoughts.   Consequently,
I disagree with those who forbid the student to
paraphrase speeches of our own orators, on the
ground that, since all the best expressions have
already been appropriated, whatever we express
differently must necessarily be a change for the
worse.   For it is always possible that we may discover expressions which are an improvement on
those which have already been used, and nature
did not make eloquence such a poor and starveling
thing, that there should be only one adequate
expression for any one theme.   It can hardly be 6
argued that, while the gestures of the actor are
capable of imparting a wealth of varied meaning

dicatur aliquid, post quod in eadem materia nihil
dicendum sit. Sed esto neque melius quod inveni-
7 mus esse neque par: est certe proximis locus. An
vero ipsi non bis ac saepius de eadem re dicimus et
quidem continuas nonnunquam sententias? Nisi
forte contendere nobiscum possumus, cum aliis non
possumus. Nam si uno genere bene diceretur, fas
erat existimari praeclusam nobis a prioribus viam;
nunc vero innumerabiles sunt modi plurimaeque
8 eodem viae ducunt. Sua brevitati gratia, sua copiae,
alia translatis virtus alia propriis, hoc oratio recta
illud figura declinata commendat. Ipsa denique
utilissima est exercitationi difficultas. Quid, quod
auctores maximi sic diligentius cognoscuntur? Non
enim scripta lectione secura transcurrimus, sed
tractamus singula et necessario introspicimus et,
quantum virtutis habeant, vel hoc ipso cognoscimus,
quod imitari non possumus.

9   Nec aliena tantum transferre sed etiam nostra
pluribus modis tractare proderit, ut ex industria

to the same words, the power of oratory is restricted to a narrower scope, so that when a thing has once been said, it is impossible to say anything else on the same theme. Why, even if it be granted that no new expression we discover can be better than or even equal to the old, it may, at any rate, be a good second. Do we not often speak twice, or 7 even more frequently, on the same subject, sometimes even to the extent of a number of sentences in succession? It will scarce be asserted that we must not match ourselves against others when we are permitted to match ourselves against ourselves. For if there were only one way in which anything could be satisfactorily expressed, we should be justified in thinking that the path to success had been sealed to us by our predecessors. But, as a matter of fact, the methods of expression still left us are innumerable, and many roads lead us to the same goal. Brevity and copiousness each 8 have their own peculiar grace, the merits of metaphor are one thing and of literalness another, and, while direct expression is most effective in one case, in another the best result is gained by a use of figures. Further, the exercise is valuable in virtue of its difficulty; and again, there is no better way of acquiring a thorough understanding of the greatest authors. For, instead of hurriedly running a careless eye over their writings, we handle each separate phrase and are forced to give it close examination, and we come to realise the greatness of their excellence from the very fact that we cannot imitate them.

Nor is it only the paraphrase of the works of 9 others that we shall find of advantage: much may

sumamus sententias quasdam easque versemus quam

numerosissime, velut eadem cera aliae aliaeque

10 formae duci solent. Plurimum autem parari facultatis

existimo ex simplicissima quaque materia. Nam illa

multiplici personarum, causarum, temporum, loco-

rum, dictorum, factorum diversitate facile delitescet

infirmitas, tot se undique rebus, ex quibus aliquam

11 apprehendas, offerentibus. Illud virtutis indicium

est fundere quae natura contracta sunt, augere parva,

varietatem similibus, voluptatem expositis dare et

bene dicere multa de paucis.

In hoc optime facient infinitae quaestiones, quas

vocari θέσεις diximus, quibus Cicero iam princeps in

12 re publica exerceri solebat. His confinis est de-

structio et confirmatio sententiarum. Nam cum

sit sententia decretum quoddam atque praeceptum,

quod de re idem de iudicio rei quaeri potest. Tum

loci communes, quos etiam scriptos ab oratoribus

scimus. Nam qui haec recta tantum et in nullos

flexus recedentia copiose tractaverit, utique in illis

---

[1] See III. v. 5 *sqq.* [2] *Ad Att.* IX. iv. 1.
[3] See II. i. 9–11 and iv. 22.

be gained from paraphrasing our own words in a number of different ways: for instance, we may specially select certain thoughts and recast them in the greatest variety of forms, just as a sculptor will fashion a number of different images from the same piece of wax. But it is the simplest subjects 10 which, in my opinion, will serve us best in our attempt to acquire facility. For our lack of talent may easily shelter itself behind the complicated mass of detail presented by persons, cases, circumstances of time and place, words and deeds, since the subjects which present themselves on all sides are so many that it will always be possible to lay hold of some one or other. True merit is revealed 11 by the power to expand what is naturally compressed, to amplify what is small, to lend variety to sameness, charm to the commonplace, and to say a quantity of good things about a very limited number of subjects.

For this purpose *indefinite questions*,[1] of the kind we call *theses*, will be found of the utmost service: in fact, Cicero[2] still exercised himself upon such themes after he had become the leading man in the state. Akin to these are the proof or refuta- 12 tion of general statements. For such statements are a kind of decree or rule, and whatever problem may arise from the thing, may equally arise from the decision passed upon the thing. Then there are commonplaces,[3] which, as we know, have often been written by orators as a form of exercise. The man who has practised himself in giving full treatment to such simple and uncomplicated themes, will assuredly find his fluency increased in those subjects which admit of varied digression, and will be pre-

plures excursus recipientibus magis abundabit eritque
in omnes causas paratus. Omnes enim generalibus
13 quaestionibus constant. Nam quid interest, Cornelius tribunus plebis quod codicem legerit, reus sit,
an quaeramus, violeturne maiestas, si magistratus
rogationem suam populo ipse recitaverit; Milo Clo-
dium rectene occiderit, veniat in iudicium, an,
oporteatne insidiatorem interfici vel perniciosum rei
publicae civem, etiamsi non insidietur; Cato Mar-
ciam honestene tradiderit Hortensio, an, conveniatne
res talis bono viro? De personis iudicatur, sed de
14 rebus contenditur. Declamationes vero, quales in
scholis rhetorum dicuntur, si modo sunt ad veritatem
accommodatae et orationibus similes, non tantum
dum adolescit profectus sunt utilissimae, quia in-
ventionem et dispositionem pariter exercent, sed
etiam cum est consummatus ac iam in foro clarus.
Alitur enim atque enitescit velut pabulo laetiore
facundia et adsidua contentionum asperitate fati-
15 gata renovatur. Quapropter historiae nonnunquam

---

[1] See IV. iv. 8; V. xiii. 26; VI. v. 10; VII. iii. 3, 35.
[2] profectus, *lit.* "progress," abstract for concrete.

pared to deal with any case that may confront him,
since all cases ultimately turn upon general questions.   For what difference is there between the 13
special case where Cornelius,[1] the tribune of the
people, is charged with reading the text of a proposed law, and the general question whether it is
lése-majestè for a magistrate himself to read the
law which he proposes to the people ; what does it
matter whether we have to decide whether Milo was
justified in killing Clodius, or whether it is justifiable to kill a man who has set an ambush for his
slayer, or a citizen whose existence is a danger to
the state, even though he has set no such ambush?
What difference is there between the question
whether it was an honourable act on the part of
Cato to make over Marcia to Hortensius, or whether
such an action is becoming to a virtuous man ?   It is
on the guilt or innocence of specific persons that
judgement is given, but it is on general principles
that the case ultimately rests.   As for declamations 14
of the kind delivered in the schools of the rhetoricians, so long as they are in keeping with actual
life and resemble speeches, they are most profitable
to the student, not merely while he [2] is still immature,
for the reason that they simultaneously exercise the
powers both of invention and arrangement, but even
when he has finished his education and acquired a
reputation in the courts.   For they provide a richer
diet from which eloquence derives nourishment and
brilliance of complexion, and at the same time afford
a refreshing variety after the continuous fatigues
of forensic disputes.   For the same reason, the wealth 15
of language that marks the historian should be from
time to time imported into portions of our written

ubertas in aliqua exercendi stili parte ponenda et
dialogorum libertate gestiendum.   Ne carmine quidem ludere contrarium fuerit, sicut athletae, remissa
quibusdam temporibus ciborum atque exercitationum
certa necessitate, otio et iucundioribus epulis refi-

16 ciuntur.   Ideoque mihi videtur M. Tullius tantum
intulisse eloquentiae lumen, quod in hos quoque
studiorum secessus excurrit.   Nam si nobis sola
materia fuerit ex litibus, necesse est deteratur
fulgor et durescat articulus et ipse ille mucro ingenii
cotidiana pugna retundatur.

17   Sed quemadmodum forensibus certaminibus exer-
citatos et quasi militantes reficit ac reparat haec
velut sagina dicendi, sic adolescentes non debent
nimium in falsa rerum imagine detineri et inanibus
simulacris usque adeo, ut difficilis ab his digressus
sit, assuescere,[1] ne ab illa, in qua prope con-
senuerunt, umbra vera discrimina velut quendam

18 solem reformident.   Quod accidisse etiam M. Porcio
Latroni, qui primus clari nominis professor fuit,
traditur, ut, cum ei summam in scholis opinionem
obtinenti causa in foro esset oranda, impense pe-
tierit, uti subsellia in basilicam transferrentur.   Ita
illi caelum novum fuit, ut omnis eius eloquentia

---

[1] assuescere, *Zumpt* : assuefacere, *MSS.*

exercises, and we should indulge in the easy freedom of dialogue. Nay, it may even be advantageous to amuse ourselves with the writing of verse, just as athletes occasionally drop the severe régime of diet and exercise to which they are subjected and refresh themselves by taking a rest and indulging in more dainty and agreeable viands. Indeed, in my opinion, **16** one of the reasons why Cicero was enabled to shed such glory upon the art of speaking is to be found in his excursions to such bypaths of study. For if all our material was drawn solely from actions at law, our eloquence must needs lose its gloss, our limbs grow stiff, and the keen edge of the intellect be blunted by its daily combats.

But although those who find their practice in the **17** contests of forensic warfare derive fresh strength and repair their forces by means of this rich fare of eloquence, the young should not be kept too long at these false semblances of reality, nor should they be allowed to become so familiar with these empty shadows that it is difficult for them to leave them: otherwise there is always the danger that, owing to the seclusion in which they have almost grown old, they will shrink in terror from the real perils of public life, like men dazzled by the unfamiliar sunlight. Indeed it is recorded that this fate **18** actually befell Marcus Porcius Latro, the first professor of rhetoric to make a name for himself; for when, at the height of his fame in the schools, he was called upon to plead a case in the forum, he put forward the most earnest request that the court should be transferred to some public hall. He was so unaccustomed to speak in the open air that all his eloquence seemed to reside within the compass of a

19 contineri tecto ac parietibus videretur. Quare
iuvenis, qui rationem inveniendi eloquendique a
praeceptoribus diligenter acceperit (quod non est
infiniti operis, si docere sciant et velint), exercitationem quoque modicam fuerit consecutus, oratorem
sibi aliquem, quod apud maiores fieri solebat, deligat,
quem sequatur, quem imitetur ; iudiciis intersit
quam plurimis et sit certaminis, cui destinatur,
20 frequens spectator. Tum causas vel easdem, quas
agi audierit, stilo et ipse componat, vel etiam alias
veras modo et utrinque tractet, et, quod in gla-
diatoribus fieri videmus, decretoriis exerceatur, ut
fecisse Brutum diximus pro Milone. Melius hoc
quam rescribere veteribus orationibus, ut fecit
Cestius contra Ciceronis actionem habitam pro
eodem, cum alteram partem satis nosse non posset
ex sola defensione.

21   Citius autem idoneus erit iuvenis, quem praeceptor
coegerit in declamando quam simillimum esse veritati
et per totas ire materias, quarum nunc facillima et
maxime favorabilia decerpunt. Obstant huic, quod
secundo loco posui, fere turba discipulorum et consuetudo classium certis diebus audiendarum, nonnihil

---

¹ See III. vi. 93 ; x. i. 23.   ² *I.e.* "per totas ire materias."

roof and four walls. For this reason a young man 19
who has acquired a thorough knowledge from his
instructors of the methods of invention and style
(which is not by any means an endless task, if those
instructors have the knowledge and the will to
teach), and who has also managed to obtain a
reasonable amount of practice in the art, should
follow the custom in vogue with our ancestors, and
select some one orator to follow and imitate. He
should attend as many trials as possible and be a
frequent spectator of the conflicts in which he is
destined to take part. Next he should write out 20
speeches of his own dealing either with the cases
which he has actually heard pleaded or with others,
provided always they be actual cases, and should
argue them from both sides, training himself with
the real weapons of his warfare, just as gladiators do
or as Brutus did in that speech in defence of Milo
which I have already mentioned.[1] This is better
than writing replies to old speeches, as Cestius did
to Cicero's defence of Milo in spite of the fact that,
his knowledge being confined to what was said for
the defence, he could not have possessed sufficient
acquaintance with the other side of the case.

The young man, however, whom his instructor has 21
compelled to be as realistic as possible in declamation,
and to deal with every class of subject, instead of
merely selecting the easiest and most attractive cases,
as is done at present, will thus qualify himself much
more rapidly for actual forensic practice. Under existing circumstances the practice of the principle[2] which
I mentioned second is, as a rule, hampered by the
large size of the classes and the practice of allotting
certain days for recitation, to which must be added

etiam persuasio patrum numerantium potius decla-
22 mationes quam aestimantium. Sed, quod dixi primo,
ut arbitror, libro, nec ille se bonus praeceptor maiore
numero quam sustinere possit onerabit et inanem
loquacitatem recidet, ut omnia quae sunt in controversia, non, ut quidem volunt, quae in rerum
natura, dicantur; et vel longiore potius dierum
spatio laxabit dicendi necessitatem vel materias
23 dividere permittet. Una enim diligenter effecta
plus proderit quam plures inchoatae et quasi de-
gustatae. Propter quod accidit, ut nec suo loco
quidque ponatur, nec illa quae prima sunt servent
suam legem, iuvenibus flosculos omnium partium in
ea quae sunt dicturi congerentibus; quo fit, ut
timentes, ne sequentia perdant, priora confundant.

VI. Proxima stilo cogitatio est, quae et ipsa vires
ab hoc accipit, estque inter scribendi laborem ex-
temporalemque fortunam media quaedam et nescio
an usus frequentissimi. Nam scribere non ubique
nec semper possumus; cogitationi temporis ac loci
plurimum est. Haec paucis admodum horis magnas

---

[1] I. ii. 15.

the contributory circumstance that the boys' parents are more interested in the number of their sons' recitations than their quality. But, as I think I said 22 in the first book,[1] the really good teacher will not burden himself with a larger number of pupils than he can manage, and will prune any tendency to excessive loquacity, limiting their remarks to the actual points involved by the subject of the declamation and forbidding them to range, as some would have them do, over every subject in heaven and earth: further, he will either extend the period within which he insists on their speaking, or will permit them to divide their themes into several portions. The thorough treatment of one theme 23 will be more profitable than the sketchy and superficial treatment of a number of subjects. For the latter practice has the result that nothing is put in its proper place and that the opening of the declamation exceeds all reasonable bounds, since the young orator crams all the flowers of eloquence which belong to all the different portions of the theme into that portion which he has to deliver, and fearing to lose what should naturally come later, introduces wild confusion into the earlier portions of his speech.

VI. Having dealt with writing, the next point which claims our attention is premeditation, which itself derives force from the practice of writing and forms an intermediate stage between the labours of the pen and the more precarious fortunes of improvisation; indeed I am not sure that it is not more frequently of use than either. For there are places and occasions where writing is impossible, while both are available in abundance for premeditation. For

etiam causas complectitur; haec, quotiens inter-
missus est somnus, ipsis noctis tenebris adiuvatur;
haec inter medios rerum actus aliquid invenit vacui
2 nec otium patitur. Neque vero rerum ordinem
modo, quod ipsum satis erat, intra se ipsa disponit,
sed verba etiam copulat totamque ita contexit
orationem, ut ei nihil praeter manum desit. Nam
memoriae quoque plerumque inhaerent fidelius,
quae nulla scribendi securitate laxantur.

Sed ne ad hanc quidem vim cogitandi perveniri
3 potest aut subito aut cito. Nam primum facienda
multo stilo forma est, quae nos etiam cogitantes
sequatur; tum adsumendus usus paulatim, ut pauca
primum complectamur animo, quae reddi fideliter
possint; mox per incrementa tam modica, ut onerari
se labor ille non sentiat, augenda vis et exercitatione
multa continenda est, quae quidem maxima ex parte
memoria constat. Ideoque aliqua mihi in illum
4 locum differenda sunt. Eo tandem[1] pervenit, ut is,
cui non refragetur ingenium, acri studio adiutus

---

[1] tandem, *Madvig* : tamen, *MSS.*

---

[1] XI. ii. 1 *sqq.*

but a few hours' thought will suffice to cover all the points even of cases of importance; if we wake at night, the very darkness will assist us, while even in the midst of legal proceedings our mind will find some vacant space for meditation, and will refuse to remain inactive. Again, this practice will not merely 2 secure the proper arrangement of our matter without any recourse to writing, which in itself is no small achievement, but will also set the words which we are going to use in their proper order, and bring the general texture of our speech to such a stage of completion that nothing further is required beyond the finishing touches. And as a rule the memory is more retentive of thoughts when the attention has not been relaxed by the fancied security which results from committing them to writing.

But the concentration which this requires cannot be attained in a moment or even quickly. For, in 3 the first place, we must write much before we can form that ideal of style which must always be present to our minds even when engaged in pre-meditation. Secondly, we must gradually acquire the habit of thought: to begin with, we shall content ourselves with covering but a few details, which our minds are capable of reproducing with accuracy; then by advances so gradual that our labour is not sensibly increased we must develop our powers and confirm them by frequent practice, a task in which the most important part is played by the memory. For this reason I must postpone some of my remarks 4 to the portion of this work reserved for the treatment of that topic.[1] At length, however, our powers will have developed so far that the man who is not hampered by lack of natural ability will by dint of

tantum consequatur, ut ei tam quae cogitarit quam quae scripserit atque edidicerit in dicendo fidem servent. Cicero certe Graecorum Metrodorum Scepsium et Empylum Rhodium nostrorumque Hortensium tradidit, quae cogitaverant, ad verbum in agendo retulisse.

5 Sed si forte aliquis inter dicendum effulserit extemporalis color, non superstitiose cogitatis demum est inhaerendum. Neque enim tantum habent curae, ut non sit dandus et fortunae locus, cum saepe etiam scriptis ea quae subito nata sunt inserantur. Ideoque totum hoc exercitationis genus ita instituendum est, ut et digredi ex eo et redire in id facile 6 possimus. Nam ut primum est domo adferre paratam dicendi copiam et certam, ita refutare temporis munera longe stultissimum est. Quare cogitatio in hoc praeparetur, ut nos fortuna decipere non possit, adiuvare possit. Id autem fiet memoriae viribus, ut illa, quae complexi animo sumus, fluant secura, non sollicitos et respicientes et una spe suspensos recordationis non sinant providere. Alioqui vel extemporalem temeritatem malo quam male cohaerentem 7 cogitationem. Peius enim quaeritur retrorsus, quia, dum illa desideramus, ab aliis avertimur, et ex

---

[1] A philosopher of the Academic school, contemporary with Cicero, *cp. de Or.* ii. 360.
[2] Empylus is not mentioned elsewhere.
[3] *Cp. Brut.* 301.

130

persistent study be enabled, when it comes to speaking, to rely no less on what he has thought out than what he has written out and learnt by heart. At any rate, Cicero records that Metrodorus of Scepsis,[1] Empylus of Rhodes,[2] and our own Hortensius[3] were able to reproduce what they had thought out word for word when it came to actual pleading.

If, however, some brilliant improvisation should 5 occur to us while speaking, we must not cling superstitiously to our premeditated scheme. For premeditation is not so accurate as to leave no room for happy inspiration: even when writing we often insert thoughts which occur to us on the spur of the moment. Consequently this form of preparation must be conceived on such lines that we shall find no difficulty either in departing from it or returning to it at will. For, although it is essential to bring 6 with us into court a supply of eloquence which has been prepared in advance in the study and on which we can confidently rely, there is no greater folly than the rejection of the gifts of the moment. Therefore our premeditation should be such that fortune may never be able to fool us, but may, on the contrary, be able to assist us. This end will be obtained by developing the power of memory so that our conceptions may flow from us without fear of disaster, and that we may be enabled to look ahead without anxious backward glances or the feeling that we are absolutely dependent on what we can call to mind. Otherwise I prefer the rashness of improvisation to the coherence given by premeditation. For such backward glances place us 7 at a disadvantage, because our search for our premeditated ideas makes us miss others, and we draw

memoria potius res petimus quam ex materia. Plura sunt autem, si utrimque[1] quaerendum est, quae inveniri possunt quam quae inventa sunt.

VII. Maximus vero studiorum fructus est et velut praemium quoddam[2] amplissimum longi laboris ex tempore dicendi facultas, quam qui non erit consecutus, mea quidem sententia civilibus officiis renuntiabit et solam scribendi facultatem potius ad alia opera convertet. Vix enim bonae fidei viro convenit auxilium in publicum polliceri, quod praesentissimis quibusque periculis desit, intrare[3] portum ad quem navis accedere nisi lenibus ventis vecta non possit, 2 siquidem innumerabiles accidunt subitae necessitates vel apud magistratus vel repraesentatis iudiciis continuo agendi. Quarum si qua, non dico cuicunque innocentium civium sed amicorum ac propinquorum alicui evenerit, stabitne mutus et salutarem petentibus vocem statimque, si non succurratur, perituris, moras et secessum et silentium quaeret, dum illa verba fabricentur et memoriae insidant et vox 3 ac latus praeparetur? Quae vero patitur hoc ratio,[4] ut quisquam possit orator omittere aliquando casus? Quid, cum adversario respondendum erit, fiet? Nam saepe ea, quae opinati sumus et contra quae scrip-

---

[1] utrimque, *Bonnell*: utrumque, *MSS.*
[2] praemium quoddam, *cod. Harl.* 4995: primus quid, *B.*
[3] intrare portum, *MSS*: instar portus, *Meister.*
[4] ratio, *cod. Harl.* 4995: oratio, *B.* possit, *Frotscher, Bonnell*: sit, *MSS.* omittere, *Bonnell*: mittere, *B.*

our matter from our memory rather than from the
subject on which we are speaking. And even if we
are to rely on our memory and our subject alike,
there are more things that may be discovered than
ever yet have been.

VII. But the crown of all our study and the
highest reward of our long labours is the power of
improvisation. The man who fails to acquire this
had better, in my opinion, abandon the task of
advocacy and devote his powers of writing to other
branches of literature. For it is scarcely decent for
an honourable man to promise assistance to the
public at large which he may be unable to provide in
the most serious emergencies, or to attempt to enter
a harbour which his ship cannot hope to make save
when sailing before a gentle breeze. For there are 2
countless occasions when the sudden necessity may be
imposed upon him of speaking without preparation
before the magistrates or in a trial which comes on
unexpectedly. And if any such sudden emergency
befalls, I will not say any innocent citizen, but some
one of the orator's friends or connexions, is he to
stand tongue-tied and, in answer to those who seek
salvation in his eloquence and are doomed, unless
they secure assistance, to ask for delay of proceedings and time for silent and secluded study, till such
moment as he can piece together the words that fail
him, commit them to memory and prepare his voice
and lungs for the effort? What theory of the duties 3
of an orator is there which permits him to ignore
such sudden issues? What will happen when he
has to reply to his opponent? For often the expected arguments to which we have written a reply
fail us and the whole aspect of the case undergoes

simus, fallunt, ac tota subito causa mutatur; atque
ut gubernatori ad incursus tempestatum, sic agenti
4 ad varietatem causarum ratio mutando est. Quid
porro multus stilus et adsidua lectio et longa studiorum aetas facit, si manet eadem quae fuit incipientibus difficultas? Perisse profecto confitendum est
praeteritum laborem, cui semper idem laborandum
est. Neque ego hoc ago ut ex tempore dicere
malit, sed ut possit. Id autem maxime hoc modo
consequemur.

5 Nota sit primum dicendi via. Neque enim prius
contingere cursus potest quam scierimus, quo sit et
qua perveniendum. Nec satis est non ignorare quae
sunt causarum iudicialium partes, aut quaestionum
ordinem recte disponere, quanquam ista sunt praecipua, sed quid quoque loco primum sit ac secundum
et deinceps; quae ita sunt natura copulata, ut
mutari aut intervelli sine confusione non possint.
6 Quisquis autem via dicet, ducetur[1] ante omnia rerum
ipsa serie velut duce; propter quod homines etiam
modice exercitati facillime tenorem in narrationibus
servant. Deinde, quid quoque loco quaerant, scient.
nec circumspectabunt nec offerentibus se aliunde
sensibus turbabuntur nec confundent ex diversis

---

[1] ducetur dicet, *Eussner.*

---

[1] See III. ix. 1.

a sudden change; consequently the variation to which cases are liable makes it as necessary for us to change our methods as it is for a pilot to change his course before the oncoming storm. Again, what 4 use is much writing, assiduous reading and long years of study, if the difficulty is to remain as great as it was in the beginning? The man who is always faced with the same labour can only confess that his past labour has been spent in vain. I do not ask him to prefer to speak extempore, but merely that he should be able to do so. And this capacity is best acquired by the following method.

In the first place, we must note the direction which 5 the argument is likely to take, since we cannot run our race unless we know the goal and the course. It is not enough to know what are the parts[1] into which forensic pleadings are divided or the principles determining the order of the various questions, important though these points are. We must realise what should come first, second, and so on, in the several parts; for these points are so closely linked together by the very nature of things that they cannot be separated, nor their order changed, without giving rise to confusion. The orator, who speaks 6 methodically, will above all take the actual sequence of the various points as his guide, and it is for this reason that even but moderately trained speakers find it easiest to keep the natural order in the *statement of facts*. Secondly, the orator must know what to look for in each portion of his case: he must not beat about the bush or allow himself to be thrown off the track by thoughts which suggest themselves from irrelevant quarters, or produce a speech which is a confused mass of incongruities,

orationem velut salientes huc illuc nec usquam in-
7 sistentes. Postremo habebunt modum et finem,
qui esse citra divisionem nullus potest. Expletis
pro facultate omnibus quae proposuerint, pervenisse
se ad ultimum sentient.

Et haec quidem ex arte, illa vero ex studio: ut
copiam sermonis optimi, quemadmodum praeceptum
est, comparemus: multo ac fideli stilo sic formetur
oratio, ut scriptorum colorem etiam quae subito
effusa sint reddant, ut, cum multa scripserimus,
8 etiam multa dicamus. Nam consuetudo et exercitatio facilitatem maxime parit; quae si paulum
intermissa fuerit, non velocitas illa modo tardatur,
sed ipsum os [1] coit atque concurrit. Quanquam enim
opus est naturali quadam mobilitate animi ut, dum
proxima dicimus, struere ulteriora possimus semperque nostram vocem provisa et formata cogitatio
9 excipiat, vix tamen aut natura aut ratio in tam
multiplex officium diducere animum queat, ut in-
ventioni, dispositioni, elocutioni, ordini rerum verborumque, tum iis, quae dicit, quae subiuncturus est,
quae ultra spectanda sunt, adhibita vocis, pronuntia-

---

[1] os, *added by Halm.*

owing to his habit of leaping this way and that, and never sticking to any one point. Finally, he must 7 confine himself to certain definite bounds, and for this *division* is absolutely necessary. When to the best of his ability he has dealt fully with all the points which he has advanced, he will know that he has reached his goal.

The precepts just given are dependent on theory. Those to which I now come depend on individual study. We must acquire a store of the best words and phrases on lines that I have already laid down, while our style must be formed by continuous and conscientious practice in writing, so that even our improvisations may reproduce the tone of our writing, and after writing much, we must give ourselves frequent practice in speaking. For facility is mainly 8 the result of habit and exercise and, if it be lost only for a brief time, the result will be not merely that we fall short of the requisite rapidity, but that our lips will become clogged and slow to open. For although we need to possess a certain natural nimbleness of mind to enable us, while we are saying what the instant demands, to build up what is to follow and to secure that there will always be some thought formed and conceived in advance ready to serve our voice, none the less, it is scarcely possible either for natural 9 gifts or for methodic art to enable the mind to grapple simultaneously with such manifold duties, and to be equal at one and the same time to the tasks of invention, arrangement, and style, together with what we are uttering at the moment, what we have got to say next and what we have to look to still further on, not to mention the fact that it

10 tionis, gestus observatione, una sufficiat. Longe
enim praecedat oportet intentio ac prae se res agat,
quantumque dicendo consumitur, tantum ex ultimo
prorogetur; ut, donec perveniamus ad finem, non
minus prospectu procedamus quam gradu, si non
intersistentes offensantesque brevia illa atque con-
cisa singultantium modo eiecturi sumus.

11   Est igitur usus quidam irrationalis, quem Graeci
ἄλογον τριβὴν vocant, qua manus in scribendo de-
currit, qua oculi totos simul in lectione versus flexus-
que eorum et transitus intuentur, et ante sequentia
vident quam priora dixerunt. Quo constant miracula
illa in scenis pilariorum ac ventilatorum, ut ea quae
emiserint ultro venire in manus credas et qua iuben-
12 tur decurrere. Sed hic usus ita proderit, si ea de
qua locuti sumus ars antecesserit, ut ipsum illud,
quod in se rationem non habet, in ratione versetur.
Nam mihi ne dicere quidem videtur nisi qui dis-
13 posite, ornate, copiose dicit, sed tumultuari. Nec
fortuiti sermonis contextum mirabor unquam, quem
iurgantibus etiam mulierculis superfluere video, cum

---

[1] §§ 5-7.

is necessary all the time to give close attention to
voice, delivery and gesture. For our mental activities 10
must range far ahead and pursue the ideas which
are still in front, and in proportion as the speaker
pays out what he has in hand, he must make advances
to himself from his reserve funds, in order that, until
we reach our conclusion, our mind's eye may urge
its gaze forward, keeping time with our advance:
otherwise we shall halt and stumble, and pour forth
short and broken phrases, like persons who can only
gasp out what they have to say.

There is, therefore, a certain mechanical knack, 11
which the Greeks call ἄλογος τριβή, which enables
the hand to go on scribbling, while the eye takes
in whole lines at once as it reads, observes the in-
tonations and the stops, and sees what is coming
before the reader has articulated to himself what
precedes. It is a similar knack which makes possible
those miraculous tricks which we see jugglers and
masters of sleight of hand perform upon the stage,
in such a manner that the spectator can scarcely
help believing that the objects which they throw
into the air come to hand of their own accord, and
run where they are bidden. But this knack will 12
only be of real service if it be preceded by the art
of which we have spoken,[1] so that what is irrational
in itself will nevertheless be founded on reason. For
unless a man speaks in an orderly, ornate and fluent
manner, I refuse to dignify his utterance with the
name of speech, but consider it the merest rant.
Nor again shall I ever be induced to admire a con- 13
tinuous flow of random talk, such as I note streams in
torrents even from the lips of women when they
quarrel, although, if a speaker is swept away by

eo quod, si calor ac spiritus tulit, frequenter accidit
ut successum extemporalem consequi cura non
14 possit. Deum tunc adfuisse, cum id evenisset,
veteres oratores, ut Cicero, dictitabant. Sed ratio
manifesta est. Nam bene concepti adfectus et
recentes rerum imagines continuo impetu feruntur,
quae nonnunquam mora stili refrigescunt et dilatae
non revertuntur. Utique vero, cum infelix illa
verborum cavillatio accessit et cursus ad singula
vestigia restitit, non potest ferri contorta vis, sed,
ut optime vocum singularum cedat electio, non continua, sed composita est.

15 Quare capiendae sunt illae, de quibus dixi, rerum
imagines, quas vocari φαντασίας indicavimus, omnia-
que, de quibus dicturi erimus, personae, quaestiones,
spes, metus habenda in oculis, in adfectus recipienda.
Pectus est enim, quod disertos facit, et vis mentis.
Ideoque imperitis quoque, si modo sint aliquo adfectu
16 concitati, verba non desunt. Tum intendendus
animus, non in aliquam rem unam, sed in plures
simul continuas; ut, si per aliquam rectam viam
mittamus oculos, simul omnia quae sunt in ea
circaque intuemur, non ultimum tantum videmus
sed usque ad ultimum. Addit ad dicendum etiam
pudor stimulos,[1] mirumque videri potest, quod, cum

[1] *after* habet *cod. Monac. gives* et dicendorum exspectata
laus.

---

[1] No such saying is found in Cicero's extant works.
[2] VI. ii. 29.

warmth of feeling and genuine inspiration, it frequently happens that he attains a success from improvisation which would have been beyond the reach of
the most careful preparation. When this occurred, the 14
old orators, such as Cicero,[1] used to say that some god
had inspired the speaker. But the reason is obvious.
For profound emotion and vivid imagination sweep
on with unbroken force, whereas, if retarded by the
slowness of the pen, they are liable to grow cold and,
if put off for the moment, may never return. Above
all, if we add to these obstacles an unhealthy tendency
to quibble over the choice of words, and check our
advance at each step, the vehemence of our onset
loses its impetus; while even though our choice of
individual words may be of the happiest, the style
will be a mere patchwork with no regular pattern.

Consequently those vivid conceptions of which I 15
spoke [2] and which, as I remarked, are called φαντάσιαι,
together with everything that we intend to say,
the persons and questions involved, and the hopes
and fears to which they give rise, must be kept
clearly before our eyes and admitted to our hearts:
for it is feeling and force of imagination that make
us eloquent. It is for this reason that even the uneducated have no difficulty in finding words to express
their meaning, if only they are stirred by some strong
emotion. Further the attention of the mind must be 16
directed not to some one thing, but simultaneously to
a number of things in continuous sequence. The
result will be the same as when we cast our eyes
along some straight road and see at once all that is on
and near it, obtaining a view not merely of its end,
but of the whole way there. Dread of the shame
of failure is also a powerful stimulant to oratory,

stilus secreto gaudeat atque omnes arbitros reformi-
det, extemporalis actio auditorum frequentia, ut miles
17 congestu signorum, excitatur. Namque et difficili-
orem cogitationem exprimit et expellit dicendi
necessitas, et secundos impetus auget placendi
cupido. Adeo pretium omnia spectant, ut eloquentia quoque, quanquam plurimum habeat in se
voluptatis, maxime tamen praesenti fructu laudis
18 opinionisque ducatur. Nec quisquam tantum fidat
ingenio, ut id sibi speret incipienti statim posse
contingere, sed, sicut in cogitatione praecipimus,
ita facilitatem quoque extemporalem a parvis initiis
paulatim perducemus ad summam, quae neque perfici
neque contineri nisi usu potest.

19 Ceterum pervenire eo debet, ut cogitatio non utique melior sit ea sed tutior, cum hanc facilitatem non
prosa modo multi sint consecuti, sed etiam carmine,
ut Antipater Sidonius et Licinius Archias (credendum
enim Ciceroni est), non quia nostris quoque temporibus
non et fecerint quidam hoc et faciant. Quod
tamen non ipsum tam probabile puto, (neque enim
habet aut usum res aut necessitatem) quam exhor-

---

[1] Ch. vi. 3.
[2] *De Or.* iii. 194; *Pro Arch.* viii. 18.

and it may be regarded as a matter for wonder that, whereas when writing we delight in privacy and shrink from the presence of witnesses, in extempore pleading a large audience has an encouraging effect, like that which the sight of the massed standards has on the soldier. For the sheer necessity of speak- 17 ing thrusts forward and forces out our labouring thought, and the desire to win approbation kindles and fosters our efforts. So true is it that there is nothing which does not look for some reward, that eloquence, despite the fact that its activity is in itself productive of a strong feeling of pleasure, is influenced by nothing so much as the immediate acquisition of praise and renown. Nor should any man put such 18 trust in his native ability as to hope that this power will present itself to him at the outset of his career as an orator; for the precepts which I laid down for premeditation [1] apply to improvisation also; we must develop it by gradual stages from small beginnings, until we have reached that perfection which can only be produced and maintained by practice.

Moreover, the orator should reach such a pitch of 19 excellence that, while premeditation may still be the safer method, it will not necessarily be the better, since many have acquired the gift of improvisation not merely in prose, but in verse as well, as, for example, Antipater of Sidon and Licinius Archias (for whose powers we have the unquestionable authority of Cicero [2]), not to mention the fact that there are many, even in our own day, who have done this and are still doing it. I do not, however, regard this accomplishment as being particularly valuable in itself, for it is both unpractical and unnecessary, but mention it as a useful example to encourage students

tandis in hanc spem, qui foro praeparantur, utile
20 exemplum. Neque vero tanta esse unquam debet[1]
fiducia facilitatis, ut non breve saltem tempus, quod
nusquam fere deerit, ad ea quae dicturi simus
dispicienda sumamus, quod quidem in iudiciis ac foro
datur semper. Neque enim quisquam est, qui causam
21 quam non didicerit agat. Declamatores quosdam
perversa ducit ambitio, ut exposita controversia
protinus dicere velint; quin etiam, quod est in
primis frivolum ac scenicum, verbum petant, quo
incipiant. Sed tam contumeliosos in se ridet invicem eloquentia, et qui stultis videri eruditi volunt,
22 stulti eruditis videntur. Si qua tamen fortuna
tam subitam fecerit agendi necessitatem, mobiliore
quodam opus erit ingenio, et vis omnis intendenda
rebus, et in praesentia remittendum aliquid ex cura
verborum, si consequi[2] utrumque non dabitur. Tum
et tardior pronuntiatio moras habet et suspensa ac
velut dubitans oratio, ut tamen deliberare, non
23 haesitare videamur. Hoc, dum egredimur e portu,
si nos nondum aptatis satis armamentis aget ventus;
deinde paulatim simul euntes aptabimus vela et
disponemus rudentes et impleri sinus optabimus.

---

[1] debet, *add'd by Herzog.*
[2] consequi, *added by Spalding*: non sequi, *2nd hand of
cod. Bamb.*

training for the bar, in the hope that they may be able to acquire this accomplishment. Still our con- 20 fidence in our power of speaking extempore should never be so great that we should neglect to devote a few minutes to the consideration of what we are going to say. There will but rarely be occasions when this is impossible, while in the lawsuits of the courts there is always some time allowed for the purpose. For no one can plead a cause with the facts of which he is unacquainted. Some declaimers, 21 it is true, are led by a perverse ambition to attempt to speak the moment their theme has been given them, and even ask for a word with which to start, an affectation which is in the worst and most theatrical taste. But eloquence has, in her turn, nothing but derision for those that insult her thus, and speakers who wish to seem learned to fools are merely regarded as fools by the learned. If, how- 22 ever, chance should impose the necessity upon us of pleading a case at such short notice, we shall require to develop special mental agility, to give all our attention to the subject, and to make a temporary sacrifice of our care for the niceties of language, if we find it impossible to secure both. On such occasions a slower delivery and a style of speaking suggestive of a certain indecision and doubt will secure us time to think, but we must be careful to do this in such a way as to give the impression of thought, not of hesitation. This precaution may be 23 employed while we are clearing harbour, if the wind drive us forward before all our tackle is ready. Afterwards, as we proceed upon our course, we shall trim our sails, arrange our ropes, and pray that the breeze may fill our sails. Such a procedure is

Id potius quam se inani verborum torrenti dare
quasi tempestatibus quo volent auferendum.

24 Sed non minore studio continetur haec facultas
quam paratur. Ars enim semel percepta non labitur,[1]
stilus quoque intermissione paulum admodum de
celeritate deperdit; promptum hoc et in expedito
positum exercitatione sola continetur. Hac uti sic
optimum est, ut cotidie dicamus audientibus pluribus,
maxime de quorum simus iudicio atque opinione
solliciti; rarum est enim ut satis se quisque vereatur.

25 Vel soli tamen dicamus potius quam omnino non
dicamus. Est et[2] illa exercitatio cogitandi totasque
materias vel silentio (dum tamen quasi dicat intra se
ipsum) persequendi, quae nullo non et tempore et
loco, quando non aliud agimus, explicari potest, et

26 est in parte utilior[3] quam haec proxima. Diligentius
enim componitur quam illa, in qua contextum dicendi intermittere veremur. Rursus in alia plus
prior confert, vocis firmitatem, oris facilitatem, motum
corporis, qui et ipse, ut dixi, excitat oratorem et
iactatione manus, pedis supplosione, sicut cauda
leones facere dicuntur, hortatur. Studendum vero

27 semper et ubique. Neque enim fere tam est ullus
dies occupatus, ut nihil lucrativae, ut Cicero Brutum

---

[1] labitur, *ed. Gryph*: capitur, *MSS.*
[2] et, *added by Spalding.*
[3] utilior, *early edd.*: utilitatis, *B.*

---

[1] Ch. iii. 21.
[2] *Or.* 34.

preferable to yielding ourselves to an empty torrent
of words, that the storm may sweep us where it will.

But it requires no less careful study to maintain 24
than to acquire this facility. Theory once mastered
is not forgotten, and the pen loses but little of its
speed by disuse: but this promptitude and readiness
for action can be maintained by practice only. The
best form of exercise is to speak daily before an
audience of several persons, who should, as far as
possible, be selected from those whose judgement
and good opinion we value, since it is rare for anyone to be sufficiently critical of himself. It is even
better to speak alone than not at all. There is yet 25
another method of exercising this faculty: it consists
in going over our subjects in their entirety in silent
thought, although we must all the time formulate
the words to ourselves: such practice is possible at
any moment or place that finds us unoccupied, and
is, in some respects, more useful than that which I
have just mentioned; for we are more careful about 26
our composition than when we are actually speaking
and in momentary fear of interrupting the continuous
flow of our language. On the other hand, the first
method is more valuable for certain purposes, as it
gives strength to our voice, fluency to our tongue
and vigour to our gesture; and the latter, as I have
already remarked,[1] in itself excites the orator and
spurs him on, as he waves his hand or stamps his
foot: he is, in fact, like the lion, that is said to lash
himself to fury with his tail. But we must study
always and everywhere. For there is scarce a single 27
day in our lives that is so full of occupations that we
may not, at some moment or other, snatch a few
precious minutes, as Cicero[2] records that Brutus was

facere tradit, operae ad scribendum aut legendum [1]
aut dicendum rapi aliquo momento temporis possit;
siquidem C. Carbo etiam in tabernaculo solebat hac
28 uti exercitatione dicendi.   Ne id quidem tacendum,
quod eidem Ciceroni placet, nullum nostrum usquam
negligentem esse sermonem; quidquid loquemur
ubicunque, sit pro sua scilicet portione perfectum.
Scribendum certe nunquam est magis, quam cum
multa dicemus ex tempore.   Ita enim servabitur
pondus, et innatans [2] illa verborum facilitas in altum
reducetur; sicut rustici proximas vitis radices ampu-
tant, quae illam in summum solum ducunt, ut inferi-
29 ores penitus descendendo firmentur.   Ac nescio an,
si [3] utrumque cum cura et studio fecerimus, invicem
prosit, ut scribendo dicamus diligentius, dicendo
scribamus facilius.   Scribendum ergo, quotiens licebit; si id non dabitur, cogitandum; ab utroque
exclusi debent tamen sic dicere, [4] ut neque depre-
hensus orator neque litigator destitutus esse videatur.
30   Plerumque autem multa agentibus accidit, ut
maxime necessaria et utique initia scribant, cetera
quae domo adferunt cogitatione complectantur, subi-
tis ex tempore occurrant; quod fecisse M. Tullium
commentariis ipsius apparet.   Sed feruntur aliorum
quoque et inventi forte, ut eos dicturus quisque

---

[1] aut legendum, *2nd hand of cod. Bamb.* : *omitted by B.*
[2] innatans, *Stoer* : unatrans, *B.*
[3] si *added by ed. Camp.*
[4] sic dicere, *Peterson* : inicere, *B.*

---

[1] A supporter of Tib. Gracchus, who went over to the
senatorial party and was consul 120 B.C. Committed suicide
in the following year. Cicero praises his eloquence and
industry ; cp. *Brut.* 103–5, *de Or.* I. § 154.
[2] There is no trace of this.

wont to do, either for writing or reading or speaking ;
Gaius Carbo,[1] for example, was in the habit of indulging in such exercises even in his tent.   I must also 28
mention the precept (which again has the approval
of Cicero [2]) that we should never be careless about
our language.   Whatever we say, under whatever
circumstances, should be perfect in its way.   As regards writing, this is certainly never more necessary
than when we have frequently to speak extempore.
For it maintains the solidity of our speech and gives
depth to superficial facility.   We may compare the
practice of husbandmen who cut away the uppermost
roots of their vines, which run close to the surface of
the soil, that the taproots may strike deeper and gain
in strength.   Indeed I am not sure that, if we prac- 29
tise both with care and assiduity, mutual profit will
not result, and writing will give us greater precision
of speech, while speaking will make us write with
greater facility.   We must write, therefore, whenever possible ; if we cannot write, we must meditate :
if both are out of the question, we must still speak in
such a manner that we shall not seem to be taken
unawares nor our client to be left in the lurch.

It is, however, a common practice with those who 30
have many cases to plead to write out the most
necessary portions, more especially the beginnings of
their speeches, to cover the remainder of that which
they are able to prepare by careful premeditation
and to trust to improvisation in emergency, a practice regularly adopted by Cicero, as is clear from his
note-books.   But the notes of other orators are also
in circulation ; some have been discovered by
chance, just as they were jotted down previous to a
speech, while others have been edited in book form,

composuerat, et in libros digesti, ut causarum quae
sunt actae a Ser. Sulpicio, cuius tres orationes extant;
sed hi de quibus loquor commentarii ita sunt exacti,
ut ab ipso mihi in memoriam posteritatis videantur
31 esse compositi.   Nam Ciceronis ad praesens modo
tempus aptatos libertus Tiro contraxit; quos non
ideo excuso, quia non probem, sed ut sint magis
admirabiles.   In hoc genere prorsus recipio hanc
brevem adnotationem libellosque, qui vel manu tene-
32 antur, et ad quos interim respicere fas sit.   Illud quod
Laenas praecipit displicet mihi, vel in his quae
scripserimus velut[1] summas in commentarium et capita
conferre.   Facit enim ediscendi negligentiam haec
ipsa fiducia et lacerat ac deformat orationem.   Ego
autem ne scribendum quidem puto, quod non[2] simus
memoria persecuturi.   Nam hic quoque accidit, ut
revocet nos cogitatio ad illa elaborata nec sinat
33 praesentem fortunam experiri.   Sic anceps inter
utrumque animus aestuat, cum et scripta perdidit et
non quaerit nova.   Sed de memoria destinatus est
libro proximo locus nec huic parti subiungendus, quia
sunt alia prius nobis dicenda.

[1] vel in his, *Bonnell* : ne in his, *B.* velut, *Halm* : vel in, *B.*
[2] non, *added by Regius.*

---

[1] Or perhaps "abbreviated." Tiro was Cicero's friend,
freedman and secretary.

as in the case of the speeches delivered in the courts by Servius Sulpicius, of whose works only three speeches survive. These memoranda, however, of which I am speaking are so carefully drawn up that they seem to me to have been composed by himself for the benefit of posterity. But Cicero's notes were 31 originally intended merely to meet the requirements of the moment, and were afterwards collected [1] by Tiro. In making this apology I do not mean to imply that I disapprove of them, but merely wish to make them more worthy of admiration. And in this connexion I must state that I admit the use of brief memoranda and note-books, which may even be held in the hand and referred to from time to time. But I disapprove of the advice given by Laenas, that 32 we should set down in our note-books, duly tabulated under the appropriate headings, summaries of what we propose to say, even in cases where we have already written it out in full. For reliance on such notes as these makes us careless in learning what we have written and mutilates and deforms our style. For my own part I think that we should never write out anything which we do not intend to commit to memory. For if we do, our thoughts will run back to what we have elaborated in writing and will not permit us to try the fortune of the moment. Consequently, the mind will waver in doubt between 33 the two alternatives, having forgotten what was committed to writing and being unable to think of anything fresh to say. However, as the topic of memory will be discussed in the next book, I will not introduce it here, as there are other points which require to be dealt with first.

BOOK XI

LIBER XI

I. Parata, sicut superiore libro continetur, facultate scribendi cogitandique et ex tempore etiam, cum res poscet, orandi, proxima est cura, ut dicamus apte; quam virtutem quartam elocutionis Cicero demonstrat, quaeque est meo quidem iudicio maxime

2 necessaria. Nam cum sit ornatus orationis varius et multiplex conveniatque alius alii, nisi fuerit accommodatus rebus atque personis, non modo non illustrabit eam, sed etiam destruet et vim rerum in contrarium vertet. Quid enim prodest, esse verba et Latina et significantia et nitida, figuris etiam numerisque elaborata, nisi cum iis, in quae iudicem

3 duci formarique volumus, consentiant, si genus sublime dicendi parvis in causis, parvum limatumque grandibus, laetum tristibus, lene asperis, minax supplicibus, summissum concitatis, trux atque violentum iucundis adhibeamus? ut monilibus et margaritis ac veste longa, quae sunt ornamenta feminarum, deformentur viri, nec habitus triumphalis, quo nihil

---

¹ *De Or.* III. x. 37.

BOOK XI

I. After acquiring the power of writing and think-ing, as described in the preceding book, and also of pleading extempore, if occasion demand, our next task will be to ensure that appropriateness of speech, which Cicero[1] shows to be the fourth department of style, and which is, in my opinion, highly necessary. For since the ornaments of style are varied and 2 manifold and suited for different purposes, they will, unless adapted to the matter and the persons con-cerned, not merely fail to give our style distinction, but will even destroy its effect and produce a result quite the reverse of that which our matter should produce. For what profit is it that our words should be Latin, significant and graceful, and be further embellished with elaborate figures and rhythms, unless all these qualities are in harmony with the views to which we seek to lead the judge and mould his opinions? What use is it if we employ a lofty 3 tone in cases of trivial import, a slight and refined style in cases of great moment, a cheerful tone when our matter calls for sadness, a gentle tone when it demands vehemence, threatening language when supplication, and submissive when energy is re-quired, or fierceness and violence when our theme is one that asks for charm? Such incongruities are as unbecoming as it is for men to wear necklaces and pearls and flowing raiment which are the natural adornments of women, or for women to robe them-

4 excogitari potest augustius, feminas deceat. Hunc locum Cicero breviter in tertio de Oratore libro perstringit, neque tamen videri potest quidquam omisisse dicendo, *non omni causae neque auditori neque personae neque tempori congruere orationis unum genus.* Nec fere pluribus in Oratore eadem. Sed illic L. Crassus, cum apud summos oratores hominesque eruditissimos dicat, satis habet partem hanc velut 5 notare inter agnoscentes; et hic Cicero adloquens Brutum testatur esse haec ei nota ideoque brevius a se dici, quanquam sit fusus locus tracteturque a philosophis latius. Nos institutionem professi non solum scientibus ista, sed etiam discentibus tradimus, ideoque paulo pluribus verbis debet haberi venia.

6   Quare notum sit nobis ante omnia, quid conciliando, docendo, movendo iudici conveniat, quid quaque parte orationis petamus. Ita nec vetera aut translata aut ficta verba in incipiendo, narrando, argumentando tractabimus neque decurrentes contexto nitore circuitus, ubi dividenda erit causa et in partes suas digerenda, neque humile atque cotidianum sermonis genus et compositione ipsa dissolutum epilogis dabi-

---

[1] III. lv. 210.
[2] Ch. xxi. *sqq.*

selves in the garb of triumph, than which there can
be conceived no more majestic raiment. This topic 4
is discussed by Cicero in the third book of the *de
Oratore*,[1] and, although he touches on it but lightly,
he really covers the whole subject when he says,
*One single style of oratory is not suited to every case, nor
to every audience, nor every speaker, nor every occasion.*
And he says the same at scarcely greater length in
the *Orator*.[2] But in the first of these works Lucius
Crassus, since he is speaking in the presence of men
distinguished alike for their learning and their eloquence, thinks it sufficient merely to indicate this topic
to his audience for their recognition ; while in the 5
latter work Cicero asserts that, as these facts are
familiar to Brutus, to whom that treatise is addressed,
they will be given briefer treatment, despite the fact
that the subject is a wide one and is discussed at
greater length by the philosophers. I, on the other
hand, have undertaken the education of an orator,
and, consequently, am speaking not merely to those
that know, but also to learners ; I shall, therefore,
have some claim to forgiveness if I discuss the topic
in greater detail.

For this reason, it is of the first importance that 6
we should know what style is most suitable for conciliating, instructing or moving the judge, and what
effects we should aim at in different parts of our
speech. Thus we shall eschew antique, metaphori-
cal and newly-coined words in our *exordium, statement of facts* and *arguments,* as we shall avoid flowing
periods woven with elaborate grace, when the case
has to be divided and distinguished under its various
heads, while, on the other hand, we shall not employ
mean or colloquial language, devoid of all artistic

mus, nec iocis lacrimas, ubi opus erit miseratione,
7 siccabimus.   Nam ornatus omnis non tam sua quam
rei, cui adhibetur, condicione constat; nec plus
refert, quid dicas quam quo loco.   Sed totum hoc
apte dicere non elocutionis tantum genere constat,
sed est cum inventione commune.   Nam si tantum
habent etiam verba momentum, quanto res ipsae
magis?   Quarum quae esset observatio, suis locis
subinde subiecimus.

8   Illud est diligentius docendum, eum demum dicere
apte, qui non solum quid expediat, sed etiam quid
deceat inspexerit.   Nec me fugit, plerumque haec
esse coniuncta.   Nam quod decet, fere prodest, neque
alio magis animi iudicum conciliari aut, si res in
9 contrarium tulit, alienari solent.   Aliquando tamen
et haec dissentiunt.   Quotiens autem pugnabunt,
ipsam utilitatem vincet quod decet.   Nam quis nescit,
nihil magis profuturum ad absolutionem Socrati fuisse,
quam si esset usus illo iudiciali genere defensionis
et oratione summissa conciliasset iudicum animos sibi
10 crimenque ipsum sollicite redarguisset?   Verum id
eum minime decebat; ideoque sic egit, ut qui poenam

structure, in the *peroration*, nor, when the theme calls
for compassion, attempt to dry the tears of our audience with jests. For all ornament derives its effect **7**
not from its own qualities so much as from the
circumstances in which it is applied, and the occasion
chosen for saying anything is at least as important a
consideration as what is actually said. But the whole
of this question of appropriate language turns on
something more than our choice of style, for it has
much in common with invention. For if words can
produce such an impression, how much greater must
that be which is created by the facts themselves.
But I have already laid down rules for the treatment
of the latter in various portions of this work.

Too much insistence cannot be laid upon the point **8**
that no one can be said to speak appropriately who
has not considered not merely what it is expedient,
but also what it is becoming to say. I am well
aware that these two considerations generally go
hand in hand. For whatever is becoming is, as a
rule, useful, and there is nothing that does more to
conciliate the good-will of the judge than the
observance or to alienate it than the disregard of
these considerations. Sometimes, however, the two **9**
are at variance. Now, whenever this occurs, expe-
diency must yield to the demands of what is
becoming. Who is there who does not realise that
nothing would have contributed more to secure the
acquittal of Socrates than if he had employed the
ordinary forensic methods of defence and had
conciliated the minds of his judges by adopting a
submissive tone and had devoted his attention to
refuting the actual charge against him? But such **10**
a course would have been unworthy of his character,

suam honoribus summis esset aestimaturus. Maluit
enim vir sapientissimus, quod superesset ex vita, sibi
perire, quam quod praeterisset. Et quando ab
hominibus sui temporis parum intelligebatur, poste-
riorum se iudiciis reservavit, brevi detrimento iam
ultimae senectutis aevum saeculorum omnium con-
11 secutus. Itaque quamvis Lysias, qui tum in dicendo
praestantissimus habebatur, defensionem illi scriptam
obtulisset, uti ea noluit, cum bonam quidem, sed
parum sibi convenientem iudicavisset. Quo vel solo
patet non persuadendi sed bene dicendi finem in
oratore servandum, cum interim persuadere deforme
sit. Non fuit hoc utile absolutioni, sed, quod est
12 maius, homini fuit. Et nos secundum communem
potius loquendi consuetudinem quam ipsam veritatis
regulam divisione hac utimur, ut ab eo, quod deceat,
utilitatem separemus; nisi forte prior ille Africanus,
qui patria cedere quam cum tribuno plebis humillimo
contendere de innocentia sua maluit, inutiliter sibi
videtur consuluisse; aut P. Rutilius, vel cum illo
paene Socratico genere defensionis est usus, vel cum
revocante eum P. Sulla manere in exilio maluit, quid
13 sibi maxime conduceret, nesciebat. Hi vero parva
illa, quae abiectissimus quisque animus utilia credit, si

---

[1] Falsely accused of having taken a bribe from King
Antiochus. See *Livy*, XXXVIII. li. 56.
[2] See *de Or.* I. liii. 227 *sqq.*

and, therefore, he pleaded as one who would account the penalty to which he might be sentenced as the highest of honours. The wisest of men preferred to sacrifice the remnant of his days rather than to cancel all his past life. And since he was but ill understood by the men of his own day, he reserved his case for the approval of posterity and at the cost of a few last declining years achieved through all the ages life everlasting. And so although Lysias, who 11 was accounted the first orator of that time, offered him a written defence, he refused to make use of it, since, though he recognised its excellence, he regarded it as unbecoming to himself. This instance alone shows that the end which the orator must keep in view is not persuasion, but speaking well, since there are occasions when to persuade would be a blot upon his honour. The line adopted by Socrates was useless to secure his acquittal, but was of real service to him as a man; and that is by far the greater consideration. In drawing this dis- 12 tinction between what is expedient and what is becoming, I have followed rather the usage of common speech than the strict law of truth; unless, indeed, the elder Africanus[1] is to be regarded as having failed to consult his true interests, when he retired into exile sooner than wrangle over his own innocence with a contemptible tribune of the people, or unless it be alleged that Publius Rutilius[2] was ignorant of his true advantage both on the occasion when he adopted a defence which may almost be compared with that of Socrates, and when he preferred to remain in exile rather than return at Sulla's bidding. No, these great men regarded all those 13 trifles that the most abject natures regard as advan-

cum virtute conferantur despicienda iudicaverunt,
ideoque perpetua saeculorum admiratione celebrantur.
Neque nos simus tam humiles, ut quae laudamus
14 inutilia credamus. Sed hoc qualecunque discrimen
raro admodum eveniet: idem fere, ut dixi, in omni
genere causarum et proderit et decebit. Est autem,
quod omnes et semper et ubique deceat, facere ac[1]
dicere honeste, contraque neminem unquam ullo in
loco turpiter. Minora vero quaeque sunt ex mediis
plerumque sunt talia, ut aliis sint concedenda, aliis
non sint, aut pro persona, tempore, loco, causa magis
ac minus vel excusata debeant videri vel repre-
15 hendenda. Cum dicamus autem de rebus aut alienis
aut nostris, dividenda ratio est eorum, dum sciamus
pleraque neutro loco convenire.

In primis igitur omnis vitiosa iactatio est, eloquentiae tamen in oratore praecipue, adfertque
audientibus non fastidium modo, sed plerumque
16 etiam odium. Habet enim mens nostra sublime
quiddam et erectum et impatiens superioris; ideoque
abiectos aut summittentes se libenter allevamus, quia

---

[1] deceat facere ac, *2nd hand of cod. Bamb.*: persuadere
ac, *B*: deceat ac, *cod. Mon.*

tageous, as being contemptible if weighed in the balance with virtue, and for this reason they have their reward in the deathless praise of all generations. Let not us, then, be so poor spirited as to regard the acts, which we extol, as being inexpedient. However, it is but rarely that this distinction, such 14 as it is, is called into play. As I have said, the expedient and the becoming will, as a rule, be identical in every kind of case. Still, there are two things which will be becoming to all men at all times and in all places, namely, to act and speak as befits a man of honour, and it will never at any time beseem any man to speak or act dishonourably. On the other hand, things of minor importance and occupying something like a middle position between the two are generally of such a nature that they may be conceded to some, but not to others, while it will depend on the character of the speaker and the circumstances of time, place and motive whether we regard them as more or less excusable or reprehensible. When, however, we are speaking of our 15 own affairs or those of others, we must distinguish between the expedient and the becoming, while recognising that the majority of the points which we have to consider will fall under neither head.

In the first place, then, all kinds of boasting are a mistake, above all, it is an error for an orator to praise his own eloquence, and, further, not merely wearies, but in the majority of cases disgusts the audience. For there is ever in the mind of man a certain 16 element of lofty and unbending pride that will not brook superiority: and for this reason we take delight in raising the humble and submissive to their feet, since such an act gives us a consciousness of our

hoc facere tanquam maiores videmur; et quotiens
discessit aemulatio, succedit humanitas. At qui se
supra modum extollit, premere ac despicere creditur,
nec tam se maiorem quam minores ceteros facere.
17 Inde invident humiliores, (hoc vitium est eorum, qui
nec cedere volunt nec possunt contendere) rident
superiores, improbant boni. Plerumque vere deprehendas arrogantium falsum de se opinionem; sed in
veris quoque sufficit conscientia.

Reprehensus est in hac parte non mediocriter
Cicero, quanquam is quidem rerum a se gestarum
maior quam eloquentiae fuit in orationibus utique
18 iactator. Et plerumque illud quoque non sine aliqua
ratione fecit. Aut enim tuebatur eos, quibus erat
adiutoribus usus in opprimenda coniuratione, aut
respondebat invidiae (cui tamen non fuit par, servatae
patriae poenam passus exilium), ut illorum, quae
egerat in consulatu, frequens commemoratio possit
videri non gloriae magis quam defensioni data.
19 Eloquentiam quidem, cum plenissimam diversae partis
advocatis concederet, sibi nunquam in agendo im-
modice arrogavit. Illius sunt enim: *Si quid est ingenii
in me, quod sentio quam sit exiguum,* et, *Quo ingenio*

superiority, and as soon as all sense of rivalry disappears, its place is taken by a feeling of humanity. But the man who exalts himself beyond reason is looked upon as depreciating and showing a contempt for others and as making them seem small rather than himself seem great. As a result, those who are 17 beneath him feel a grudge against him (for those who are unwilling to yield and yet have not the strength to hold their own are always liable to this failing), while his superiors laugh at him and the good disapprove. Indeed, as a rule, you will find that arrogance implies a false self-esteem, whereas those who possess true merit find satisfaction enough in the consciousness of possession.

Cicero has been severely censured in this connexion, although he was far more given to boasting of his political achievements than of his eloquence, at any rate, in his speeches. And as a rule he had 18 some sound reason for his self-praise. For he was either defending those who had assisted him to crush the conspiracy of Catiline, or was replying to attacks made upon him by those who envied his position; attacks which he was so far unable to withstand that he suffered exile as the penalty for having saved his country. Consequently, we may regard his frequent reference to the deeds accomplished in his consulship as being due quite as much to the necessities of defence as to the promptings of vainglory. As regards his own eloquence, he never 19 made immoderate claims for it in his pleading, while he always paid a handsome tribute to the eloquence of the advocate, who opposed him. For example, there are passages such as the following: "If there be aught of talent in me, and I am only too conscious

20 *minus possum, subsidium mihi diligentia comparavi.* Quin etiam contra Q. Caecilium de accusatore in Verrem constituendo, quamvis multum esset in hoc quoque momenti, uter ad agendum magis idoneus veniret, dicendi tamen facultatem magis illi detraxit quam arrogavit sibi, seque non consecutum, sed *omnia*

21 *fecisse, ut posset eam consequi,* dixit. In epistolis aliquando familiariter apud amicos, nonnunquam in dialogis aliena tamen persona verum de eloquentia sua dicit. Et aperte tamen gloriari nescio an sit magis tolerabile vel ipsa vitii huius simplicitate, quam illa iactatio perversa, si abundans opibus pauperem se neget, nobilis obscurum et potens infirmum et

22 disertus imperitum plane et infantem vocet. Ambitiosissimum gloriandi genus est etiam deridere. Ab aliis ergo laudemur; nam ipsos, ut Demosthenes ait, *erubescere, etiam cum ab aliis laudabimur, decet.* Neque hoc dico, non aliquando de rebus a se gestis oratori esse dicendum, sicut eidem Demostheni pro Ctesiphonte; quod tamen ita emendavit, ut necessitatem id faciendi ostenderet invidiamque omnem in eum

23 regereret, qui hoc se coegisset. Et M. Tullius saepe dicit de oppressa coniuratione Catilinae; sed modo

---

[1] *Pro Arch.* i. 1. [2] *Pro Quint.* i. 4.
[3] *Div. in Caec.* xii. 40. [4] *De Cor.* 128.

how little it is," [1] and, " In default of talent, I turned
to industry for aid." [2]   Again, in his speech against 20
Caecilius on the selection of an accuser for Verres,
despite the fact that the question as to which was
the most capable pleader, was a factor of great
importance, he rather depreciated his opponent's
eloquence than exalted his own, and asserted that
he had done all in his power to make himself an
orator,[3] though he knew he had not succeeded.   In 21
his letters to intimate friends, it is true, and occasionally in his dialogues, he tells the truth of his own
eloquence, though in the latter case he is careful
always to place the remarks in question in the
mouth of some other character.   And yet I am not
sure that open boasting is not more tolerable, owing
to its sheer straightforwardness, than that perverted
form of self-praise, which makes the millionaire say
that he is not a poor man, the man of mark describe
himself as obscure, the powerful pose as weak,
and the eloquent as unskilled and even inarticulate.
But the most ostentatious kind of boasting takes 22
the form of actual self-derision.   Let us therefore
leave it to others to praise us.   For it beseems us,
as Demosthenes says, to blush even when we are
praised by others.   I do not mean to deny that
there are occasions when an orator may speak of
his own achievements, as Demosthenes himself does
in his defence of Ctesiphon.[4]   But on that occasion
he qualified his statements in such a way as to show
that he was compelled by necessity to do so, and to
throw the odium attaching to such a proceeding on
the man who had forced him to it.   Again, Cicero 23
often speaks of his suppression of the Catilinarian
conspiracy, but either attributes his success to the

id virtuti senatus, modo providentiae deorum im-
mortalium adsignat. Plerumque contra inimicos
atque obtrectatores plus vindicat sibi. Erant enim
24 illa tuenda,[1] cum obiicerentur. In carminibus utinam
pepercisset, quae non desierunt carpere maligni :

> *Cedant arma togae, concedat laurea linguae ;* [2]

et

> *O fortunatam natam me consule Romam ;*

et *Iovem illum, a quo in concilium deorum advocatur ;*
et *Minervam, quae artes eum edocuit ;* quae sibi ille
secutus quaedam Graecorum exempla permiserat.

25 Verum eloquentiae ut indecora iactatio, ita nonnunquam concedenda fiducia est. Nam quis repre-
hendat haec : *Quid putem ? contemptumne me ? Non
video nec in vita nec in gratia nec in rebus gestis nec in
hac mea mediocritate ingenii, quid despicere possit*
26 *Antonius ?* Et paulo post apertius : *An decertare
mecum voluit contentione dicendi ? Hoc quidem est
beneficium. Quid enim plenius, quid uberius quam mihi
et pro me et contra Antonium dicere ?*

27 Arrogantes et illi, qui se iudicasse de causa nec

---

[1] illa tuenda, *Halm* : intuenda, *B.*
[2] linguae, *B* : laudi, *vulgo.*

---

[1] From the poem on his consulship.
[2] *Phil.* ii. i. 2.

courage shown by the senate or to the providence of
the immortal gods. If he puts forward stronger claims
to merit, it is generally when speaking against his
enemies and detractors; for he was bound to defend
his actions when they were denounced as discreditable. One could only wish that he had shown 24
greater restraint in his poems, which those who love
him not are never weary of criticising. I refer to
passages such as : [1]

> " Let arms before the peaceful toga yield,
>   Laurels to eloquence resign the field,"

or

> " O happy Rome, born in my consulship ! "

together with that " Jupiter, by whom he is
summoned to the assembly of the gods," and the
" Minerva that taught him her accomplishments " ;
extravagances which he permitted himself in imitation of certain precedents in Greek literature.

But while it is unseemly to make a boast of one's 25
eloquence, it is, however, at times permissible to
express confidence in it. Who, for instance, can
blame the following ? [2] " What, then, am I to think ?
That I am held in contempt ? I see nothing either
in my past life, or my position, or such poor talents
as I may possess, that Antony can afford to despise."
And a little later he speaks yet more openly : 26
" Or did he wish to challenge me to a contest of
eloquence ? I could wish for nothing better. For
what ampler or richer theme could I hope to find
than to speak at once for myself and against
Antony ? "

Another form of arrogance is displayed by those who 27
declare that they have come to a clear conviction of

aliter adfuturos fuisse proponunt. Nam et inviti
iudices audiunt praesumentem partes suas, nec hoc
oratori contingere inter adversarios quod Pytha-
gorae inter discipulos potest *Ipse dixit.* Sed istud
magis minusve vitiosum est pro personis dicentium.

28 Defenditur enim aliquatenus aetate, dignitate,
auctoritate; quae tamen vix in ullo tanta fuerint,
ut non hoc adfirmationis genus temperandum sit
aliqua moderatione sicut omnia, in quibus patronus
argumentum ex se ipso petet. Quid fuisset tumidius,
si accipiendum criminis loco negasset Cicero equitis
Romani esse filium, se defendente? At ille fecit
hoc etiam favorabile coniungendo cum iudicibus
dignitatem suam: *Equitis autem Romani esse filium,
criminis loco poni ab accusatoribus, neque vobis iudicantibus oportuit neque defendentibus nobis.*

29 Impudens, tumultuosa, iracunda actio omnibus
indecora, sed ut quisque aetate, dignitate, usu prae-
cedit, magis in ea reprehendendus. Videas autem
rixatores quosdam neque iudicum reverentia neque
agendi more ac modo contineri, quo ipso mentis

Pro Cael. ii. **4.**

the justice of their cause, which they would not
otherwise have undertaken. For the judges give
but a reluctant hearing to such as presume to
anticipate their verdict, and the orator cannot hope
that his opponents will regard his *ipse dixit* with the
veneration accorded by the Pythagoreans to that of
their master. But this fault will vary in seriousness
according to the character of the orator who uses
such language. For such assertions may to some 28
extent be justified by the age, rank, and authority
of the speaker. But scarcely any orator is possessed
of these advantages to such an extent as to exempt
him from the duty of tempering such assertions by
a certain show of modesty, a remark which also
applies to all passages in which the advocate draws
any of his arguments from his own person. What
could have been more presumptuous than if Cicero
had asserted that the fact that a man was the son
of a Roman knight should never be regarded as a
serious charge, in a case in which *he* was appearing
for the defence? But he succeeded in giving this
very argument a favourable turn by associating his
own rank with that of the judges, and saying,[1]
" The fact of a man being the son of a Roman knight
should never have been put forward as a charge by
the prosecution when these gentlemen were in the
jury-box and I was appearing for the defendant."

An impudent, disorderly, or angry tone is always 29
unseemly, no matter who it be that assumes it; and
it becomes all the more reprehensible in proportion
to the age, rank, and experience of the speaker.
But we are familiar with the sight of certain brawl-
ing advocates who are restrained neither by respect
for the court nor by the recognised methods and

habitu manifestum sit, tam in suscipiendis quam in
30 agendis causis nihil pensi habere.   Profert enim
mores plerumque oratio et animi secreta detegit.
Nec sine causa Graeci prodiderunt, ut vivat, quemque
etiam dicere. Humiliora illa vitia: summissa adulatio,
adfectata scurrilitas, in rebus ac verbis parum modestis
ac pudicis vilis pudor, in omni negotio neglecta
auctoritas; quae fere accidunt iis, qui nimium aut
blandi esse aut ridiculi volunt.

31   Ipsum etiam eloquentiae genus alios aliud decet.
Nam neque tam plenum et erectum et audax et
praecultum senibus convenerit quam pressum et
mite et limatum et quale intelligi vult Cicero, cum
dicit, orationem suam coepisse *canescere;* sicut
vestibus quoque non purpura coccoque fulgentibus
32 illa aetas satis apta sit.   In iuvenibus etiam ube-
riora paulo et paene periclitantia feruntur. At in
iisdem siccum et sollicitum et contractum dicendi
propositum plerumque adfectatione ipsa severitatis
invisum est, quando etiam morum senilis auctoritas
immatura in adolescentibus creditur. Simpliciora
33 militares decent. Philosophiam ex professo, ut
quidam faciunt, ostentantibus parum decori sunt
plerique orationis ornatus maximeque ex adfectibus,
quos illi vitia dicunt. Verba quoque exquisitiora et
34 compositio numerosa tali proposito diversa. Non

---

1 *Brut.* ii. 8.

manners of pleading. The obvious inference from this attitude of mind is that they are utterly reckless both in undertaking cases and in pleading them. For a man's character is generally revealed and the 30 secrets of his heart are laid bare by his manner of speaking, and there is good ground for the Greek aphorism that, " as a man lives, so will he speak." The following vices are of a meaner type : grovelling flattery, affected buffoonery, immodesty in dealing with things or words which are unseemly or obscene, and disregard of authority on all and every occasion. They are faults which, as a rule, are found in those who are over-anxious either to please or amuse.

Again, different kinds of eloquence suit different 31 speakers. For example, a full, haughty, bold and florid style would be less becoming to an old man than that restrained, mild and precise style to which Cicero refers, when he says that his style is beginning to grow grey-haired.[1] It is the same with their style as their clothes ; purple and scarlet raiment goes ill with grey hairs. In the young, however, we can 32 endure a rich and even, perhaps, a risky style. On the other hand, a dry, careful and compressed style is unpleasing in the young as suggesting the affectation of severity, since even the authority of character that goes with age is considered as premature in young men. Soldiers are best suited by a simple style. Those, again, who make ostentatious pro- 33 fession, as some do, of being philosophers, would do well to avoid most of the ornaments of oratory, more especially those which consist in appeals to the passions, which they regard as moral blemishes. So, too, the employment of rare words and of rhythmical structure are incongruous with their profession. For 34

enim sola illa laetiora, qualia a Cicerone dicuntur,
Saxa atque solitudines voci respondent; sed etiam illa,
quanquam plena sanguinis, *Vos enim iam, Albani
tumuli atque luci, vos, inquam, imploro atque testor,
vosque, Albanorum obrutae arae, sacrorum populi
Romani sociae et aequales,* non conveniant barbae illi
35 atque tristitiae.   At vir civilis vereque sapiens, qui
se non otiosis disputationibus, sed administrationi
rei publicae dediderit, a qua longissime isti, qui
philosophi vocantur, recesserunt, omnia, quae ad
efficiendum oratione quod proposuerit valent, libenter
adhibebit, cum prius quid honestum sit efficere in
36 animo suo constituerit.   Est quod principes deceat,
aliis non concesseris.   Imperatorum ac triumphalium
separata est aliqua ex parte ratio eloquentiae, sicut
Pompeius abunde disertus rerum suarum narrator,
et hic, qui bello civili se interfecit, Cato eloquens
37 senator fuit.   Idem dictum saepe in alio liberum, in
alio furiosum, in alio superbum est.   Verba adversus
Agamemnonem a Thersite habita ridentur; da illa
Diomedi aliive cui pari : magnum animum ferre prae
se videbuntur. *Ego te consulem putem,* inquit L.
Crassus Philippo, *cum tu me non putes senatorem?*

---

[1] *Pro Arch.* viii. 19.   [2] *Pro Mil.* xxxi. 85.
[3] *Il.* ii. 225.   [4] *De Or.* iii. 1.

their beards and gloomy brows are ill-suited not merely to luxuriance of style, such as we find in Cicero's "Rocks and solitudes answer to the voice,"[1] but even to full-blooded passages as, "For on you I call, ye hills and groves of Alba; I call you to bear me witness, and ye, too, fallen altars of the Albans, that were once the peers and equals of the holy places of Rome."[2] But the public man, who is truly 35 wise and devotes himself not to idle disputations, but to the administration of the state, from which those who call themselves philosophers have withdrawn themselves afar, will gladly employ every method that may contribute to the end which he seeks to gain by his eloquence, although he will first form a clear conception in his mind as to what aims are honourable and what are not. There is a form 36 of eloquence which is becoming in the greatest men, but inadmissible in others. For example, the methods of eloquence employed by commanders and conquerors in their hour of triumph are to a great extent to be regarded as in a class apart. The comparison of the eloquence of Pompey and Cato the younger, who slew himself in the civil war, will illustrate my meaning. The former was extraordinarily eloquent in the description of his own exploits, while the latter's powers were displayed in debates in the senate. Again, the same remark 37 will seem freedom of speech in one's mouth, madness in another's, and arrogance in a third. We laugh at the words used by Thersites[3] to Agamemnon; but put them in the mouth of Diomede or some other of his peers, and they will seem the expression of a great spirit. "Shall I regard you as consul," said Lucius Crassus[4] to Philippus, "when you refuse to

Vox honestissimae libertatis; non tamen ferres
38 quemcunque dicentem. Negat se magni facere
aliquis poetarum, *utrum Caesar ater an albus homo
sit,* insania; verte, ut idem Caesar de illo dixerit,
arrogantia est. Maior in personis observatio est
apud tragicos comicosque, multis enim utuntur et
variis. Eadem et eorum, qui orationes aliis scribe-
bant, fuit ratio et declamantium est; non enim
semper ut advocati sed plerumque ut litigatores
dicimus.

39 Verum etiam in iis causis, quibus advocamur,
eadem differentia diligenter est custodienda. Utimur
enim fictione personarum et velut ore alieno loquimur, dandique sunt iis, quibus vocem accommodamus,
sui mores. Aliter enim P. Clodius, aliter Appius
Caecus, aliter Caecilianus ille, aliter Terentianus
pater fingitur. Quid asperius lictore Verris: *Ut
40 adeas, tantum dabis?* Quid fortius illo, cuius inter
ipsa verberum supplicia una vox audiebatur: *Civis
Romanus sum?* Quam dignae Milonis in peroratione
ipsa voces eo viro, qui pro re publica seditiosum
civem totiens compescuisset quique insidias virtute
41 superasset? Denique non modo quot in causa

---

[1] *Cat.* 93.   [2] *Cp.* II. xv. 30; III. viii. 51.
[3] Clodius, the unscrupulous enemy of Cicero. Appius
Caecus, his ancestor, the great senator, who secured the
rejection of the terms of Pyrrhus.
[4] See *Pro Cael.* xvi.
[5] *I.e.* to visit a relative in prison, *Verr.* v. xlv. 118; *cp.*
Quint. IX. iv. 71.
[6] *Verr.* v. lxii. 162.   [7] *Cp.* IV. ii. 25; VI. v. 10.

regard me as a senator?" That was honourable
freedom of speech, and yet we should not tolerate
such words from everybody's lips. One of the poets[1] 38
says that he does not care whether Caesar be white
or black. That is madness. But reverse the case.
Suppose that Caesar said it of the poet? That
would be arrogance. The tragic and comic poets
pay special attention to character, since they introduce a great number and variety of persons. Those
who wrote speeches [2] for others paid a like attention
to these points, and so do the declaimers; for we do
not always speak as advocates, but frequently as
actual parties to the suit.

But even in these cases in which we appear as 39
advocates, differences of character require careful
observation. For we introduce fictitious personages
and speak through other's lips, and we must therefore
allot the appropriate character to those to whom
we lend a voice. For example, Publius Clodius will
be represented in one way, Appius Caecus[3] in
another, while Caecilius[4] makes the father in his
comedy speak in quite a different manner from the
father in the comedy of Terence. What can be 40
more brutal than the words of Verres' lictor, "To
see him you will pay so much"?[5] or braver than
those of the man from whom the scourge could
wring but one cry, "I am a Roman citizen!"[6]
Again, read the words which Cicero places in the
mouth of Milo in his peroration: are they not
worthy of the man who to save the state had so
oft repressed a seditious citizen, and had triumphed
by his valour over the ambush that was laid for
him?[7] Further, it is not merely true that the 41
variety required in impersonation will be in

totidem in prosopopoeia sunt varietates, sed hoc
etiam plures, quod in his puerorum, feminarum,
populorum, mutarum etiam rerum assimulamus
42 adfectus, quibus omnibus debetur suus decor. Eadem
in iis, pro quibus agemus, observanda sunt; aliter
enim pro alio saepe dicendum est, ut quisque
honestus, humilis, invidiosus, favorabilis erit, adiecta
propositorum quoque et anteactae vitae differentia.
Iucundissima vero in oratore humanitas, facilitas,
moderatio, benivolentia. Sed illa quoque diversa
bonum virum decent: malos odisse, publica vice
commoveri, ultum ire scelera et iniurias, et omnia,
ut initio dixi, honesta.

43   Nec tantum, quis et pro quo sed etiam apud quem
dicas, interest. Facit enim et fortuna discrimen et
potestas, nec eadem apud principem, magistratum,
senatorem, privatum, tantum liberum ratio est, nec
eodem sono publica iudicia et arbitrorum discepta-
44 tiones aguntur. Nam ut orantem pro capite sollicitudo deceat et cura et omnes ad amplificandam
orationem quasi machinae, ita in parvis rebus

---

[1] See § 14.

proportion to the variety presented by the case, for impersonation demands even greater variety, since it involves the portrayal of the emotions of children, women, nations, and even of voiceless things, all of which require to be represented in character. The same points have to be observed with respect **42** to those for whom we plead: for our tone will vary with the character of our client, according as he is distinguished, or of humble position, popular or the reverse, while we must also take into account the differences in their principles and their past life. As regards the orator himself, the qualities which will most commend him are courtesy, kindliness, moderation and benevolence. But, on the other hand, the opposite of these qualities will sometimes be becoming to a good man. He may hate the bad, be moved to passion in the public interest, seek to avenge crime and wrong, and, in fine, as I said at the beginning,[1] may follow the promptings of every honourable emotion.

The character of the speaker and of the person on **43** whose behalf he speaks are, however, not the only points which it is important to take into account: the character of those before whom we have to speak calls for serious consideration. Their power and rank will make no small difference; we shall employ different methods according as we are speaking before the emperor, a magistrate, a senator, a private citizen, or merely a free man, while a different tone is demanded by trials in the public courts, and in cases submitted to arbitration. For **44** while a display of care and anxiety, and the employment of every device available for the amplification of our style are becoming when we are

iudiciisque vana sint eadem, rideaturque merito,
qui apud disceptatorem de re levissima sedens
dicturus utatur illa Ciceronis confessione, *non modo
se animo commoveri, sed etiam corpore ipso perhorrescere.*

45 Quis vero nesciat, quanto aliud dicendi genus poscat
gravitas senatoria, aliud aura popularis? cum etiam
singulis iudicantibus non idem apud graves viros
quod leviores, non idem apud eruditum quod
militarem ac rusticum deceat, sitque nonnunquam
summittenda et contrahenda oratio, ne iudex eam
vel intelligere vel capere non possit.

46 Tempus quoque ac locus egent observatione
propria. Nam et tempus tum triste, tum laetum,
tum liberum, tum angustum est, atque ad haec
47 omnia componendus orator ; et loco publico privatone,
celebri an secreto, aliena civitate an tua, in castris
denique an foro dicas, interest plurimum, ac suam
quidque formam et proprium quendam modum eloquentiae poscit : cum etiam in ceteris actibus vitae
non idem in foro, curia, campo, theatro, domi facere

---

[1] *Div. in Caec.* xiii. 41

pleading for a client accused on a capital charge, it would be useless to employ the same methods in cases and trials of minor importance, and the speaker who, when speaking from his chair before an arbitrator on some trivial question, should make an admission like that made by Cicero, to the effect that it was not merely his soul that was in a state of commotion, but that his whole body was convulsed with shuddering,[1] would meet with well-deserved ridicule. Again, who does not know what different styles of 45 eloquence are required when speaking before the grave assembly of the senate and before the fickle populace, since even when we are pleading before single judges the same style will not be suitable for use before one of weighty character and another of a more frivolous disposition, while a learned judge must not be addressed in the same tone that we should employ before a soldier or a rustic, and our style must at times be lowered and simplified, for fear that he may be unable to take it in or to understand it.

Again, circumstances of time and place demand 46 special consideration. The occasion may be one for sorrow or for rejoicing, the time at our disposal may be ample or restricted, and the orator must adapt himself to all these circumstances. It, like-47 wise, makes no small difference whether we are speaking in public or in private, before a crowded audience or in comparative seclusion, in another city or our own, in the camp or in the forum: each of these places will require its own style and peculiar form of oratory, since even in other spheres of life the same actions are not equally suited to the forum, the senate-house, the Campus Martius, the theatre

conveniat; et pleraque, quae natura non sunt reprehendenda atque adeo[1] interim sunt necessaria, alibi
48 quam mos permiserit turpia habeantur. Illud iam
diximus, quanto plus nitoris et cultus demonstrativae
materiae, ut ad delectationem audientium compositae,
quam, quae sunt in actu et contentione, suasoriae
iudicialesque permittant.

Hoc adhuc adiiciendum aliquas etiam, quae sunt
egregiae dicendi virtutes, quo minus deceant, effici
49 condicione causarum.   An quisquam tulerit reum in
discrimine capitis, praecipueque si apud victorem et
principem pro se ipse dicat, frequenti translatione,
fictis aut repetitis ex vetustate verbis, compositione
quae sit maxime a vulgari usu remota, decurrentibus
periodis, quam laetissimis locis sententiisque dicentem?   Non perdant haec omnia necessarium
periclitanti sollicitudinis colorem, petendumque etiam
50 innocentibus misericordiae auxilium?   Moveaturne
quisquam eius fortuna, quem tumidum ac sui iactan-
tem et ambitiosum institorem eloquentiae in ancipiti
sorte videat?   Non immo oderit reum verba au-
cupantem et anxium de fama ingenii, et cui esse
51 diserto vacet?   Quod mire M. Caelius in defen-

---

[1] adeo, *Gesner*: ideo, *B.*

---

[1] VIII. iii. 11 *sqq.*

or one's own house, and there is much that is not
in itself reprehensible, and may at times be absolutely necessary, which will be regarded as unseemly
if done in some place where it is not sanctioned by
custom. I have already pointed out[1] how much 48
more elegance and ornament is allowed by the
topics of demonstrative oratory, whose main object
is the delectation of the audience, than is permitted
by deliberative or forensic themes which are concerned with action and argument.

To this must be added the fact that certain
qualities, which are in themselves merits of a high
order, may be rendered unbecoming by the special
circumstances of the case. For example, when a 49
man is accused on a capital charge, and, above all,
if he is defending himself before his conqueror or
his sovereign, it would be quite intolerable for him
to indulge in frequent metaphors, antique or newly-
coined words, rhythms as far removed as possible
from the practice of every-day speech, rounded
periods, florid commonplaces and ornate reflexions.
Would not all these devices destroy the impression
of anxiety which should be created by a man in
such peril, and rob him of the succour of pity, on
which even the innocent are forced to rely? Would 50
any man be moved by the sad plight of one who
revealed himself as a vainglorious boaster, and
ostentatiously flaunted the airs and graces of his
eloquence at a moment when his fate hung in
suspense? Would he not rather hate the man who,
despite his position as accused, hunted for fine
words, showed himself concerned for his reputation
as a clever speaker, and found time at such a
moment to display his eloquence? I consider that 51

sione causae, qua reus de vi fuit, comprehendisse
videtur mihi : *Ne cui vestrum atque etiam omnium, qui
ad rem agendam adsunt, meus aut vultus molestior aut vox
immoderatior aliqua aut denique, quod minimum est,*
52 *iactantior gestus fuisse videatur.* Atqui sunt quaedam
actiones in satisfactione, deprecatione, confessione
positae : sententiolisne flendum erit ? epiphonemata
aut enthymemata exorabunt ? Non, quidquid meris
adiicietur adfectibus, omnes eorum diluet vires et
53 miserationem securitate laxabit ? Age, si de morte
filii sui vel iniuria, quae morte sit gravior, dicendum
patri fuerit, aut in narrando gratiam illam expositionis, quae continget ex sermone puro atque dilucido,
quaeret, breviter ac significanter ordinem rei protulisse contentus, aut argumenta diducet in digitos et
propositionum ac partitionum captabit leporem et,
ut plerumque in hoc genere moris est, intentione
54 omni remissa loquetur ? Quo fugerit interim dolor
ille ? ubi lacrimae substiterint ? unde se in medium
tam secura observatio artium miserit ? Non ab
exordio usque ad ultimam vocem continuus quidam
gemitus et idem tristitiae vultus servabitur, si quidem
volet dolorem suum etiam in audientes transfundere ?
quem si usquam remiserit, in animum iudicantium

---

[1] A form of syllogism. See v. xiv. 1.
[2] See VIII. v. 11. " An exclamation attached to the close
of a statement or a proof by way of climax."

Marcus Caelius, in the speech in which he defended
himself against a charge of breach of the peace, showed
a wonderful grasp of these facts, when he said: "I
trust that none of you gentlemen, or of all those
who have come to plead against me, will find offence
in my mien or insolence in my voice, or, though that
is a comparative trifle, any trace of arrogance in
my gesture." But there are some cases where the 52
success of the pleader depends on apology, entreaties
for mercy, or confession of error. Can sorrow be
expressed in epigram? Or will *enthymemes*[1] or
epiphonemata[2] avail to win the judge's mercy? Will
not all embellishment of pure emotion merely impair its force and dispel compassion by such a display
of apparent unconcern? Or, suppose that a father 53
has to speak of his son's death, or of some wrong
that is worse than death, will he, in making his statement of facts, seek to achieve that grace in exposition which is secured by purity and lucidity of
language, and content himself with setting forth
his case in due order with brevity and meaning?
Or will he count over the heads of his argument
upon his fingers, aim at niceties of division and
proposition, and speak without the least energy of
feeling as is usual in such portions of a speech?
Whither will his grief have fled while he is thus 54
engaged? Where has the fountain of his tears been
stayed? How came this callous attention to the
rules of text-books to obtrude itself? Will he not
rather, from his opening words to the very last he
utters, maintain a continuous voice of lamentation
and a mien of unvaried woe, if he desires to trans-
plant his grief to the hearts of his audience? For
if he once remits aught of his passion of grief, he

55 non reducet.   Quod praecipue declamantibus (neque
enim me paenitet ad hoc quoque opus meum et
curam susceptorum semel adolescentium respicere)
custodiendum est, quo plures in schola finguntur
adfectus, quos non ut advocati, sed ut passi subimus.

56 Cum etiam hoc genus simulari litium soleat, cum ius
mortis a senatu quidam ob aliquam magnam infelici-
tatem vel etiam paenitentiam petunt, in quibus non
solum cantare, quod vitium pervasit, aut lascivire,
sed ne argumentari quidem nisi mixtis, et quidem
ita ut ipsa probatione magis emineant, adfectibus
decet.   Nam qui intermittere in agendo dolorem
potest, videtur posse etiam deponere.

57   Nescio tamen an huius, de quo loquimur, decoris
custodia maxime circa eos, contra quos dicimus,
examinanda sit.   Nam sine dubio in omnibus statim
accusationibus hoc agendum est, ne ad eas libenter
descendisse videamur.   Ideoque mihi illud Cassii
Severi non mediocriter displicet: *Di boni, vivo: et,*

---

[1] VII. iv. 39.   It is said that poison was provided by the
state of Massilia to serve the turn of such unhappy persons,
so soon as they could convince the local senate that their
proposed suicide was justifiable.

[2] *Cp.* I. viii. 2.

[3] *Cp.* X. i. 22.   In 9 B.C. he accused Nonius Asprenas, a
friend of Augustus, of the crime of poisoning.   Asprenas
was defended by Pollio, and supported by Augustus during
his trial.

will never be able to recall it to the hearts of them that hear him. This is a point which declaimers, 55 above all, must be careful to bear in mind: I mention this because I have no compunction in referring to a branch of the art which was once also my own, or in reverting to the consideration of the youthful students such as once were in my charge: the declaimer, I repeat, must bear this in mind, since in the schools we often feign emotions that affect us not as advocates, but as the actual sufferers. For example, we even imagine cases where persons, 56 either because of some overwhelming misfortune or repentance for some sin, demand from the senate the right to make an end of their lives;[1] and in these cases it is obviously unbecoming not merely to adopt a chanting intonation,[2] a fault which has also become almost universal, or to use extravagant language, but even to argue without an admixture of emotional appeal, so managed as to be even more prominent than the proof which is advanced. For the man who can lay aside his grief for a moment while he is pleading, seems capable even of laying it aside altogether

I am not sure, however, that it is not in our 57 attitude towards our opponents that this care for decorum, which we are now discussing, should be most rigorously maintained. For there can be no doubt, that in all accusations our first aim should be to give the impression that it is only with the greatest reluctance that we have consented to undertake the rôle of accuser. Consequently, I strongly disapprove of such remarks as the following which was made by Cassius Severus:[3] "Thank Heaven, I am still alive; and that I may find some savour in

quo me vivere iuvet, Asprenatem reum video. Non enim
iusta ex causa vel necessaria videri potest postulasse
58 eum, sed quadam accusandi voluptate. Praeter hoc
tamen, quod est commune, propriam moderationem
quaedam causae desiderant. Quapropter et, qui
curationem bonorum patris postulabit, doleat eius
valetudinem; et quamlibet gravia filio pater obiec-
turus miserrimam sibi ostendat esse hanc ipsam
necessitatem, nec hoc paucis modo verbis, sed toto
colore actionis, ut id eum non dicere modo, sed
59 etiam vere dicere appareat. Nec causanti pupillo
sic tutor irascatur unquam, ut non remaneant amoris
vestigia et sacra quaedam patris eius memoria. Iam
quomodo contra abdicantem patrem, querentem
uxorem, agi causam oporteret, in libro, ut arbitror,
septimo dixi. Quando etiam ipsos loqui, quando
advocati voce uti deceat, quartus liber, in quo
prooemii praecepta sunt, continet.

60 Esse et in verbis quod deceat aut turpe sit,
nemini dubium est. Unum iam igitur huic loco,
quod est sane summae difficultatis, adiiciendum

---

[1] The imagined case would be as follows. The father disinherits the son for an alleged offence. The son accuses the
father of madness and demands a curator, etc.
[2] VII. iv. 24.   [3] IV. i. 46.

life, I see Asprenas arraigned for his crimes." For, after this, it is impossible to suppose that he had just or necessary reasons for accusing Asprenas, and we cannot help suspecting that his motive was sheer delight in accusation. But, beside this considera- 58 tion, which applies to all cases, there is the further point that certain cases demand special moderation. Therefore, a man who demands the appointment of a curator for his father's property, should express his grief at his father's affliction; and, however grave be the charges that a father may be going to bring against his son, he should emphasize the painful nature of the necessity that is imposed upon him.[1] And this he should do not merely in a few brief words, but his emotion should colour his whole speech, so that it may be felt not merely that he is speaking, but that he is speaking the truth. Again, if a ward make allegations against his 59 guardian, the latter must never give way to such anger that no trace is left of his former love or of a certain reverent regard for the memory of his opponent's father. I have already spoken, in the seventh book, I think,[2] of the way in which a case should be pleaded against a father who disinherits his son, or a wife who brings a charge of ill-treatment against her husband, while the fourth book,[3] in which I prescribed certain rules for the exordium, contains my instructions as to when it is becoming that the parties should speak themselves, and when they should employ an advocate to speak for them.

It will be readily admitted by everyone that 60 words may be becoming or offensive in themselves. There is therefore a further point, which presents the most serious difficulty, that requires notice in

videtur, quibus modis ea, quae sunt natura parum
speciosa quaeque non dicere, si utrumlibet esset
liberum, maluissemus, non tamen sint indecora dicen-
61 tibus.   Quid asperiorem habere frontem potest aut
quid aures hominum magis respuunt, quam cum est
filio filiive advocatis in matrem perorandum? Aliquando tamen necesse est, ut in causa Cluentii
Habiti.   Sed non semper illa via, qua contra Sasiam
Cicero usus est; non quia non ille optime, sed quia
plurimum refert, qua in re et quo modo laedat.
62 Itaque illa, cum filii caput palam impugnaret,
fortiter fuit repellenda.   Duo tamen, quae sola
supererant, divine Cicero servavit, primum, ne obli-
visceretur reverentiae, quae parentibus debetur;
deinde ut, repetitis altius causis, diligentissime ostenderet, quam id, quod erat in matrem dicturus, non
oporteret modo fieri, sed etiam necesse esset.
63 Primaque haec expositio fuit, quanquam ad praesentem quaestionem nihil pertinebat.   Adeo in causa
difficili atque perplexa nihil prius intuendum credidit
quam quid deceret.   Fecit itaque nomen parentis
non filio invidiosum, sed ipsi in quam dicebatur.
64 Potest tamen aliquando mater et in re leviore aut

---

[1] See *pro Clu.* lxi. 169 *sqq.*   Sasia was Cluentius' mother.
[2] *pro Clu.* vi. 17.

this connexion: we must consider by what means things which are naturally unseemly and which, had we been given the choice, we should have preferred not to say, may be uttered without indecorum. What at first sight can be more unpleasing and what 61 more revolting to the ears of men than a case in which a son or his advocate has to speak against his mother? And yet sometimes it is absolutely necessary, as, for example, in the case of Cluentius Habitus.[1] But it is not always desirable to employ the method adopted by Cicero against Sasia, not because he did not make most admirable use of it, but because in such cases it makes the greatest difference what the point may be and what the manner in which the mother seeks to injure her son. In the case of Sasia she had 62 openly sought to procure the destruction of her son, and consequently vigorous methods were justified against her. But there were two points, the only points which remained to be dealt with, that were handled by Cicero with consummate skill: in the first place, he does not forget the reverence that is due to parents, and in the second, after a thorough investigation of the history of the crime, he makes it clear that it was not merely right, but a positive necessity that he should say what he proposed to say against the mother. And he placed this ex- 63 planation in the forefront of his case,[2] although it had really nothing to do with the actual question at issue; a fact which shows that his first consideration in that difficult and complicated case was the consideration of what was becoming for him to say. He therefore made the name of mother cast odium not on the son, but on her who was the object of his denunciations. It is, however, always possible that a 64

minus infeste contra filium stare ; tum lenior atque summissior decebit oratio. Nam et satisfaciendo aut nostram minuemus invidiam aut etiam in diversum eam transferemus ; et si graviter dolere filium palam fuerit, credetur abesse ab eo culpam fietque ultro

65 miserabilis. Avertere quoque in alios crimen decet, ut fraude aliquorum concita credatur, et omnia nos passuros, nihil aspere dicturos testandum, ut, etiamsi non possumus non conviciari, nolle videamur. Etiam, si quid obiiciendum erit, officium est patroni, ut id filio invito, sed fide cogente facere credatur. Ita

66 poterit uterque laudari. Quod de matre dixi, de utroque parente accipiendum est ; nam inter patres etiam filiosque, cum intervenisset emancipatio, litigatum scio. In aliis quoque propinquitatibus custodiendum est, ut inviti et necessario et parce iudicemur dixisse, magis autem aut minus, ut cuique personae debetur reverentia. Eadem pro libertis adversus patronos observantia. Et ut semel plura complectar,

---

[1] *I.e.* from the *patria potestas* by a fictitious form of sale.

mother may be her son's opponent in a case of less
serious import, or at any rate in a way which involves
less deadly hostility. Under such circumstances the
orator must adopt a gentler and more restrained
tone. For example, we may offer apology for the
line which we take, and thus lessen the odium
which we incur or even transfer it to a different
quarter, while if it be obvious that the son is deeply
grieved by the situation, it will be believed that he
is blameless in the matter and he will even become
an object of pity. It will also be desirable to throw 65
the blame on others, so that it may be believed that
the mother's action was instigated by their malice,
and to assert that we will put up with every form of
provocation, and will say nothing harsh in reply, so
that, even although strong language may be absolutely necessary on our part, we may seem to be
driven to use it against our will. Nay, if some
charge has to be made against the mother, it will be
the advocate's task to make it seem that he does so
against the desire of the son and from a sense of
duty to his client. Thus both son and advocate will
win legitimate praise. What I have said about 66
mothers will apply to either parent; for I have
known of litigation taking place between fathers
and sons as well, after the *emancipation*[1] of the son.
And when other relationships are concerned, we
must take care to create the impression that we
have spoken with reluctance and under stress of
necessity and that we have been forbearing in our
language; but the importance of so doing will vary
according to the respect due to the persons concerned. The same courtesy should be observed in
speaking on behalf of freedmen against their patrons.

nunquam decebit sic adversus tales agere personas,
quomodo contra nos agi ab hominibus condicionis
67 eiusdem iniquo animo tulissemus. Praestatur hoc
aliquando etiam dignationibus, ut libertatis nostrae
ratio reddatur, ne quis nos aut petulantes in lae-
dendis eis aut etiam ambitiosos putet. Itaque
Cicero, quanquam erat in Cottam gravissime dicturus,
neque aliter agi P. Oppii causa poterat, longa tamen
68 praefatione excusavit officii sui necessitatem. Aliquando etiam inferioribus praecipueque adolescentulis
parcere aut videri decet. Utitur hac moderatione
Cicero pro Caelio contra Atratinum, ut eum non
inimice corripere, sed paene patrie monere videatur.
Nam et nobilis et iuvenis et non iniusto dolore
venerat ad accusandum.

Sed in his quidem, in quibus vel iudici vel etiam
adsistentibus ratio nostrae moderationis probari
debet, minor est labor; illic plus difficultatis, ubi
69 ipsos, contra quos dicimus, veremur offendere. Duae
simul huiusmodi personae Ciceroni pro Murena di-
centi obstiterunt, M. Catonis Serviique Sulpicii.
Quam decenter tamen Sulpicio, cum omnes con-
cessisset virtutes, scientiam petendi consulatus

---

[1] *Cp.* v. xiii. 20. P. Oppius, quaestor to M. Aurelius
Cotta in Bithynia, was charged by Cotta in a letter to the
Senate with misappropriation of supplies for his troops and
with an attempt on his life. The speech in which Cicero
defended Oppius (69 B.C.) is lost.
[2] See opening sections of *pro Caelio.*

In fact, to sum up, it will never become us to plead against such persons in a tone which we ourselves should have resented in the mouth of men of like condition. The same respect is on occasion due to 67 persons of high rank, and it may be necessary to offer justification for our freedom of speech to avoid giving the impression that we have shown ourselves insolent or ostentatious in our attack upon such persons. Consequently Cicero, although he intended to speak against Cotta[1] with the utmost vehemence, and indeed the case of Publius Oppius was such that he could not do otherwise, prefaced his attack by pleading at some length the necessity imposed upon him by his duty to his client. Sometimes, again, it 68 will beseem us to spare or seem to spare our inferiors, more especially if they be young. Cicero[2] gives an example of such moderation in the way in which he deals with Atratinus in his defence of Caelius: he does not lash him like an enemy, but admonishes him almost like a father. For Atratinus was of noble birth and young, and the grievance which led him to bring the accusation was not unreasonable.

But the task is comparatively easy in those cases in which it is to the judge, or even, it may be, to our audience that we have to indicate the reason for our moderation. The real difficulty arises when we are afraid of offending those against whom we are speaking. The difficulties of Cicero when defending 69 Murena were increased by the fact that he was opposed by two persons of this character, namely Marcus Cato and Servius Sulpicius. And yet in what courteous language, after allowing Sulpicius all the virtues, he refuses to admit that he has any idea of the way to conduct a candidature for the consul-

ademit? Quid enim aliud esset, quo se victum
homo nobilis et iuris antistes magis ferret? Ut
vero rationem defensionis suae reddidit, cum se
studuisse petitioni Sulpicii contra honorem Murenae,
70 non idem debere accusationi contra caput diceret!
Quam molli autem articulo tractavit Catonem!
Cuius naturam summe admiratus non ipsius vitio,
sed Stoicae sectae quibusdam in rebus factam du-
riorem videri volebat; ut inter eos non forensem
contentionem, sed studiosam disputationem crederes
71 incidisse. Haec est profecto ratio et certissimum
praeceptorum genus illius viri observatio, ut, cum
aliquid detrahere salva gratia velis, concedas alia
omnia : in hoc solo vel minus peritum quam in
ceteris, adiecta, si poterit fieri, etiam causa, cur id
ita sit, vel paulo pertinaciorem vel credulum vel
72 iratum vel impulsum ab aliis. Hoc enim commune
remedium est, si in tota actione aequaliter appareat
non honor modo eius, sed etiam caritas. Praeterea
causa sit nobis iusta sic dicendi, neque id moderate
73 tantum faciamus, sed etiam necessario. Diversum ab

---

[1] *Pro Muren.* vii. 15.   [2] *Pro Muren.* xxix. 60.

ship.[1] What else was there in which a man of high
birth and a distinguished lawyer would sooner
admit his inferiority? With what skill he sets forth
his reasons for undertaking the defence of Murena,
when he says that he supported Sulpicius' candidature as opposed to that of Murena, but did not
regard that preference as reason why he should
support him in bringing a capital charge against his
rival! And with what a light touch he deals with 70
Cato![2] He has the highest admiration for his
character and desires to show that the fact that in
certain respects it has become severe and callous is due
not to any personal fault, but to the influence of the
Stoic school of philosophy ; in fact you would imagine
that they were engaged not in a forensic dispute,
but merely in some philosophical discussion. This 71
is undoubtedly the right method, and the safest rule
in such cases will be to follow the practice of Cicero,
namely, that, when we desire to disparage a man
without giving offence, we should allow him to be
the possessor of all other virtues and point out that
it is only in this one respect that he falls short of
his high standard, while we should, if possible, add
some reason why this should be so, such, for example,
as his being too obstinate or credulous or quick to
anger, or acting under the influence of others.
(For we may generally find a way out of such em- 72
barrassments by making it clear throughout our
whole speech that we not merely honour the object
of our criticism, but even regard him with affection.)
Further, we should have good cause for speaking thus
and must do so not merely with moderation, but also
give the impression that our action is due to the
necessities of the case. A different situation arises, 73

hoc sed facilius, cum hominum aut alioqui turpium
aut nobis invisorum quaedam facta laudanda sunt.
Decet enim rem ipsam probare in qualicunque
persona. Dixit Cicero pro Gabinio et P. Vatinio,
inimicissimis antea sibi hominibus et in quos orationes etiam scripserat, verum ait, ut sit iusta causa
sic faciendi,[1] non se de ingenii fama, sed de fide
74 esse sollicitum. Difficilior ei ratio in iudicio Cluenti-
ano fuit, cum Scamandrum necesse haberet dicere
nocentem, cuius egerat causam. Verum id ele-
gantissime cum eorum, a quibus ad se perductus
esset, precibus, tum etiam adolescentia sua excusat,
detracturus alioqui plurimum auctoritatis sibi,[2] in
causa praesertim suspecta, si eum se esse, qui temere
nocentes reos susciperet, fateretur.

75 Apud iudicem vero, qui aut erit inimicus aut
propter aliquod commodum a causa, quam nos
susceperimus, aversus, ut persuadendi ardua ratio,
ita dicendi expeditissima. Fiducia enim iustitiae
eius et nostrae causae nihil nos timere simulabimus.
Ipse erit gloria inflandus, ut tanto clarior eius futura
sit fides ac religio in pronuntiando, quanto minus

---

[1] ait ut sit . . . sic faciendi, *Halm*: et iusta sit
faciendi (*and the like*), *MSS.*
[2] sibi, *Halm*: sicut, *G*: si, *vulgo.*

---

[1] Ch. 17 *sqq.*

but an easier one, when we have to praise the actions
of men who are otherwise disreputable or hateful to
ourselves: for it is only right that we should award
praise where it is deserved, whatever the character
of the person praised may be. Cicero spoke in
defence of Gabinius and Publius Vatinius, both of
them his deadly enemies and men against whom
he had previously spoken and even published his
speeches: but he justifies himself by declaring that
he does so not because he is anxious for his reputation as an accomplished speaker, but because he is
concerned for his honour. He had a more difficult 74
task in his defence of Cluentius,[1] as it was necessary
for him to denounce Scamander's guilt, although he
had previously appeared for him. But he excuses
his action with the utmost grace, alleging the
importunity of those persons who had brought
Scamander to him, and his own youth at the time,
whereas it would have been a serious blot on his
reputation, especially in connexion with a case of the
most dubious character, if he had admitted that he
was one who was ready to undertake the defence of
guilty persons without asking awkward questions.
On the other hand, when we are pleading before 75
a judge, who has special reasons for being hostile to
us or is for some personal motive ill-disposed to the
cause which we have undertaken, although it may
be difficult to persuade him, the method which we
should adopt in speaking is simple enough: we shall
pretend that our confidence in his integrity and in
the justice of our cause is such that we have no
fears. We must play upon his vanity by pointing out
that the less he indulges his own personal enmity
or interest, the greater will be the reputation for

76 vel offensae vel utilitati suae indulserit. Hoc et
apud eos, a quibus appellatum erit, si forte ad
eosdem remittemur; adiicienda ratio vel necessitatis
alicuius, si id causa concedit, vel erroris vel sus-
picionis. Tutissimum ergo paenitentiae confessio
et satisfactio culpae, perducendusque omni modo
77 iudex ad irae pudorem. Accidit etiam nonnunquam
ut eadem de[1] causa, de qua pronuntiarit, cognoscat
iterum. Tum illud quidem commune: apud alium
nos iudicem disputaturos de illius sententia non
fuisse, neque enim emendari ab alio quam ipso fas
esse; ceterum ex causa, ut quaeque permittet, aut
ignorata quaedam aut defuisse testes aut (quod
timidissime et, si nihil aliud plane fuerit, dicendum
78 est) patronos non suffecisse succurret. Etiam, si
apud alios iudices agetur, ut in secunda adsertione
aut in centumviralibus iudiciis duplicibus, parte
victa decentius erit, quotiens contigerit, servare
iudicum pudorem; de qua re latius probationum
loco dictum est.

Potest evenire, ut in aliis reprehendenda sint,

---

[1] ut, *added by Regius*, de *by Halm*.

---

[1] *I. e.* apologise for refusing to accept his original judgement.

[2] v. ii. 1, where, as here, it is indicated that different
portions of a case might be tried by two panels of *centumviri*
sitting separately. The centumviral court dealt mainly with
cases of inheritance.

conscientious rectitude that will accrue to him from
his verdict.   The same method may be adopted if 76
our case should chance to be sent back to the same
judges from whom we have appealed : but we may
further, if the case should permit, plead that we
were forced to take the action which we did or were
led to it by error or suspicion.[1]   The safest course
will therefore be to express our regret, apologise for
our fault and employ every means to induce the
judge to feel compunction for his anger.   It will 77
also sometimes happen that a judge may have to try
the same case on which he has previously given
judgment.   In such circumstances the method
commonly adopted is to say that we should not
have ventured to dispute his sentence before any
other judge, since he alone would be justified in
revising it : but (and in this we must be guided by
the circumstances of the case) we may allege that
certain facts were not known on the previous
occasion or certain witnesses were unavailable, or,
though this must be advanced with the utmost
caution and only in the last resort, that our clients'
advocates were unequal to their task.   And even if 78
we have to plead a case afresh before different
judges, as may occur in a second trial of a claim to
freedom or in cases in the centumviral courts, which
are divided between two different panels, it will be
most seemly, if we have lost our case before the first
panel, to say nothing against the judges who tried
the case on that occasion.   But this is a subject
with which I dealt at some length in the passage
where I discussed *proofs*.[2]

It may happen that we have to censure actions in
others, of which we have been guilty ourselves,

quae ipsi fecerimus, ut obiicit Tubero Ligario, quod
79 in Africa fuerit. Et ambitus quidam damnati re-
cuperandae dignitatis gratia reos eiusdem criminis
detulerunt, ut in scholis luxuriantem patrem luxu-
riosus ipse iuvenis accusat. Id quomodo decenter
fieri possit, equidem non invenio, nisi aliquid repe-
ritur, quod intersit, persona, aetas, tempus, causa,
80 locus, animus. Tubero, iuvenem se patri haesisse,
illum a senatu missum non ad bellum, sed ad fru-
mentum coemendum ait, ut primum licuerit, a
partibus recessisse; Ligarium et perseverasse et non
pro Cn. Pompeio, inter quem et Caesarem dignitatis
fuerit contentio, cum salvam uterque rem publicam
vellet, sed pro Iuba atque Afris inimicissimis populo
81 Romano stetisse. Ceterum vel facillimum est, ibi
alienam culpam incusare, ubi fateris tuam. Verum
id iam indicis est, non actoris. Quodsi nulla contingit excusatio, sola colorem habet paenitentia.
Potest enim videri satis emendatus, qui in odium
82 eorum, in quibus erraverat, ipse conversus est. Sunt
enim casus quidam, qui hoc natura ipsa rei non
indecens faciant: ut cum pater ex meretrice natum,
quod duxerit[1] meretricem in matrimonium, abdicat;

---

[1] meretrice . . . duxerit, *added by ed. Camp.*

---

[1] See v. x. 108 note and with reference to *pro Clu.* xxxvi.
98.

as, for example, when Tubero charges Ligarius with having been in Africa. Again, there have 79 been cases where persons condemned for bribery have indicted others for the same offence with a view to recovering their lost position: [1] for this the schools provide a parallel in the theme where a luxurious youth accuses his father of the same offence. I do not see how this can be done with decorum unless we succeed in discovering some difference between the two cases, such as character, age, motives, circumstances of time and place or intention. Tubero, for example, alleges that he 80 was a young man at the time and went thither in the company of his father, who had been sent by the senate not to take part in the war, but to purchase corn, and further that he left the party as soon as he could, whereas Ligarius clung to the party and gave his support, not to Gnaeus Pompeius, who was engaged with Caesar in a struggle for the supreme power, though both wished to preserve the state, but to Juba and the Africans who were the sworn enemies of Rome. The easiest 81 course, however, is to denounce another's guilt, while admitting our own in the same connexion. However, that is the part of an informer, not of a pleader. But if there is no excuse available, penitence is our only hope. For the man who is converted to the hatred of his own errors, may perhaps be regarded as sufficiently reformed. For 82 there are occasionally circumstances which from the very nature of the case may make such an attitude not unbecoming, as, for example, in the case where the father disinherits a son born of a harlot because that son has married a harlot, a case

scholastica materia sed non quae in foro non possit accidere. Hic igitur multa non deformiter dicet: vel quod omnium sit votum parentum, ut honestiores quam sint ipsi liberos habeant, (nam et si filia nata, meretrix eam mater pudicam esse voluisset) vel quod humilior ipse fuerit, (licet enim huic ducere)[1]

83 vel quod non habuerit patrem qui moneret; quin eo minus id faciendum filio fuisse, ne renovaret domus pudorem et exprobraret patri nuptias, matri prioris vitae necessitatem, ne denique legem quandam suis quoque rursum[2] liberis daret. Credibilis erit etiam propria quaedam in illa meretrice turpitudo, quam nunc hic pater ferre non possit. Alia praetereo; neque enim nunc declamamus, sed ostendimus nonnunquam posse dicentem ipsis incommodis bene uti.

84 Illic maior aestus, ubi quis pudenda queritur, ut stuprum, praecipue in maribus, aut os profanatum. Non dico, si loquatur ipse; nam quid aliud ei quam gemitus ac fletus et exsecratio vitae conveniat, ut iudex intelligat potius dolorem illum quam audiat? Sed patrono quoque per similes adfectus eundum

---

[1] huic ducere, *Spalding*: hoc ducere *or* dicere, *MSS.*
[2] rursum, *Halm*: sum, *G*: subinde, *vulgo.*

---

[1] The *lex Iulex de maritandis ordinibus* (18 B.C.) forbade the marriage of a senator with a prostitute.

which, although it forms a scholastic theme, might
actually arise in a court of law.   There are a number
of pleas which the father may put forward with
becoming effect.   He will say that it is the prayer 83
of all parents that their sons should be better men
than themselves (for example, if a daughter also
had been born to him, the harlot, her mother,
would have wished her to be chaste), or that he
himself was in a humbler position (for a man in
such a position is permitted to marry a harlot),[1] or
that he had no father to warn him; and further
that there was an additional reason against his son's
conduct, namely, that he should not revive the old
family scandal nor reproach his father with his
marriage and his mother with the hard necessity
of her former life, nor give a bad example to his
own children in their turn.   We may also plausibly
suggest that there is some particularly shameful
feature in the character of the harlot married by
the son, which the father cannot under existing
circumstances tolerate.   There are other possible
arguments which I pass by: for I am not now
engaged in declamation, but am merely pointing
out that there are occasions when the speaker may
turn his own drawbacks to good account.

More arduous difficulties confront us when we have 84
to deal with a complaint of some shameful act such
as rape, more especially when this is of an unnatural kind.   I do not refer to cases when the
victim himself is speaking.   For what should he do
but groan and weep and curse his existence, so that
the judge will understand his grief rather than hear
it articulately expressed?   But the victim's advocate
will have to exhibit similar emotions, since the

erit, quia hoc iniuriae genus verecundius est fateri [1]
85 passis quam ausis. Mollienda est in plerisque alio
colore asperitas orationis, ut Cicero de proscriptorum
liberis fecit. Quid enim crudelius quam homines
honestis parentibus ac maioribus natos a re publica
summoveri? Itaque durum id esse summus ille
tractandorum animorum artifex confitetur, sed ita
legibus Sullae cohaerere statum civitatis adfirmat, ut
iis solutis stare ipsa non possit. Adsecutus itaque
est, ut aliquid eorum quoque causa videretur facere
86 contra quos diceret. Illud etiam in iocis monui,
quam turpis esset fortunae insectatio, et ne in totos
ordines aut gentes aut populos petulantia incurreret.
Sed interim fides patrocinii cogit quaedam de universo genere aliquorum hominum dicere, liber-
tinorum vel militum vel publicanorum vel similiter
87 aliorum. In quibus omnibus commune remedium
est, ut ea, quae laedunt, non libenter tractare vi-
dearis nec in omnia impetum facias, sed in id quod
expugnandum est, et reprehendens alia laude com-
88 penses: si cupidos milites dicas, [2] sed non mirum,

---

[1] fateri, *added by Halm.*
[2] cupidos milites dicas, sed, *Spalding*: cupidum dedi-
casset, *G.*

---

[1] Now lost.
[2] Cicero argued that it was better that a few should suffer
unjustly than that the state should be upset by admitting
them to office. But he admitted that their case was hard
and suggested that it was better for them to live in an
orderly state than run the risks in which revolution would
involve them as well as others.   [3] VI. iii. 28.

admission of such wrongs cause more shame to the
sufferer than the criminal. In many cases it is 85
desirable to soften the harshness of our language
by the infusion of a more conciliatory tone, as, for
example, Cicero did in his speech [1] dealing with
the children of the proscribed. What fate could
be more cruel than that the children of men of
good birth and the descendants of distinguished
ancestors should be excluded from participation
in public life? For this reason that supreme artist
in playing on the minds of men admits that it is
hard, but asserts that the constitution is so essenti-
ally dependent on the laws of Sulla, that their
repeal would inevitably involve its destruction.
Thus he succeeded in creating the impression that
he was doing something on behalf of those very
persons against whom he spoke.[2] I have already [3] 86
pointed out, in dealing with the subject of jests,
how unseemly it is to take the position in life of
individuals as the target for our gibes, and also
have urged that we should refrain from insulting
whole classes, races or communities. But at times
our duty toward our client will force us to say
something on the general character of a whole
class of people, such as freedmen, soldiers, tax-
farmers or the like. In all these cases the usual 87
remedy is to create the impression that it is with
reluctance that we introduce topics which must
give pain, while further we shall avoid attacking
everything, and even while using the language
of reproof with regard to the essential point of
attack, shall make up for our censure by praising
our victims in some other connexion. For example, 88
if we charge soldiers with rapacity, we shall

quod periculorum ac sanguinis maiora sibi deberi
praemia putent; eosdem petulantes, sed hoc fieri,
quod bellis magis quam paci consuerint. Libertinis
detrahenda est auctoritas; licet iis testimonium red-
89 dere industriae, per quam exierint de servitute. Quod
ad nationes exteras pertinet, Cicero varie: detracturus Graecis testibus fidem, doctrinam iis
concedit ac litteras, seque eius gentis amatorem
esse profitetur, Sardos contemnit, Allobrogas ut
hostes insectatur; quorum nihil tunc, cum diceretur, parum aptum aut remotum cura decoris
90 fuit. Verborum etiam moderatione detrahi solet,
si qua est rei invidia: si asperum dicas nimium
severum, iniustum persuasione labi, pertinacem ultra
modum tenacem esse propositi; plerumque velut
ipsos coneris ratione vincere, quod est mollissimum.
91   Indecorum est super haec omne nimium, ideoque
etiam quod natura rei satis aptum est, nisi modo
quoque temperatur, gratiam perdit.   Cuius rei

---

[1] *E.g. pro Flacco* xxvi.
[2] In a fragment of *pro Scauro.*
[3] *pro Font.* viii.

qualify our statement by saying that the fact is not
surprising, as they think that they are entitled to
some special reward for the perils they have faced
and the wounds they have sustained. Or, if we
censure them for insolence, we shall add that this
quality is due to the fact that they are more
accustomed to war than to peace. In the case of
freedmen we should disparage their influence: but
we may also give them credit for the industry
which secured their emancipation. With regard 89
to foreign nations, Cicero's practice varies. When
he intends to disparage the credibility of Greek
witnesses he admits their distinction in learning
and literature and professes his admiration for their
nation.[1] On the other hand, he has nothing but
contempt for the Sardinians[2] and attacks the Allo-
broges as the enemies of Rome.[3] In all these cases
none of his remarks, at the time they were made,
were inconsistent with or adverse to the claims of
decorum. ·If there be anything offensive in the 90
subject on which we have to speak, it may be
toned down by a studied moderation in our language; for example, we may describe a brutal character as being unduly severe, an unjust man as led
astray by prejudice, an obstinate man as unreason-
ably tenacious of his opinion. And there are a
large number of cases where we should attempt to
defeat our opponents by reasoning, which forms the
gentlest of all methods of attack.

To these remarks I would add that all extrava- 91
gance of any kind is indecorous, and consequently
statements which are in sufficient harmony with the
facts will none the less lose all their grace unless
they are modified by a certain restraint. It is hard

observatio iudicio magis quodam sentiri quam praeceptis tradi potest, quantum satis sit et quantum
recipiant aures. Non habet res mensuram et quasi
pondus, quia ut in cibis alia aliis magis complent.

92   Adiiciendum etiam breviter videtur, quod fit ut [1]
dicendi virtutes diversissimae non solum suos
amatores habeant, sed ab eisdem saepe laudentur.
Nam Cicero quodam loco scribit, id esse optimum,
quod, cum te facile credideris consequi imitatione,
non possis. Alio vero, non id egisse, ut ita diceret,
quomodo se quilibet posse confideret, sed quomodo
93 nemo. Quod potest pugnare inter se videri. Verum
utrumque ac merito laudatur; causarum enim [2] modo
distat, quia simplicitas illa et velut securitas in-
adfectatae orationis mire tenues causas decet, maioribus illud admirabile dicendi genus magis convenit.
In utroque eminet Cicero; ex quibus alterum
imperiti se posse consequi credent, neutrum, qui
intelligunt.

II. Memoriam quidam naturae modo esse munus
existimaverunt, estque in ea non dubie plurimum,

---

[1] fit ut, *Halm :* fiat, *MSS.*
[2] causarum enim, *Spalding :* causa enim enim, *G.*

---

[1] See *Or.* xxiii. 76. In this and the next passage Quintilian does not quote, but paraphrases.
[2] See *Or.* xxviii. 97.

to give rules as to the exact method in which this precept should be observed, but the problem will easily be solved by following the dictates of our own judgement, which will tell us what it is sufficient to say and how much the ears of our audience will tolerate. We cannot weigh or measure our words by fixed standards : they are like foods, some of which are more satisfying than others.

I think I should also add a few brief words to the effect that not only very different rhetorical virtues have their special admirers, but that they are often praised by the same persons. For instance, there is one passage [1] in Cicero where he writes that the best style is that which we think we can easily acquire by imitation, but which we find is really beyond our powers. But in another passage [2] he says that his aim was not to speak in such a manner that everyone should be confident that he could do the same, but rather in a style that should be the despair of all. These two statements may seem to be inconsistent, but as a matter of fact both alike deserve the praise which they receive. The difference is due to the fact that cases differ in character. Those of minor importance are admirably suited by the simplicity and negligence of unaffected language, whereas cases of greater moment are best suited by the grand style. Cicero is pre-eminent in both. Now while eminence in one of these styles may seem to the inexperienced to be within their grasp, those who understand know that they are capable of eminence in neither.

II. Some regard memory as being no more than one of nature's gifts ; and this view is no doubt true to a great extent ; but, like everything else, memory

sed ipsa excolendo sicut alia omnia augetur; et
totus, de quo diximus adhuc, inanis est labor, nisi
ceterae partes hoc velut spiritu continentur.   Nam
et omnis disciplina memoria constat, frustraque
docemur, si quidquid audimus praeterfluat; et exem-
plorum, legum, responsorum, dictorum denique
factorumque velut quasdam copias, quibus abundare
quasque in promptu semper habere debet orator,
eadem illa vis praesentat.   Neque immerito thesaurus
2 hic eloquentiae dicitur.   Sed non firme tantum
continere, verum etiam cito percipere multa acturos
oportet, nec quae scripseris modo iterata lectione
complecti, sed in cogitatis quoque rerum ac verborum
contextum sequi, et quae sint ab adversa parte dicta
meminisse, nec utique ea, quo dicta sunt ordine,
3 refutare, sed opportunis locis ponere.   Quid? extemporalis oratio non alio mihi videtur mentis vigore
constare.   Nam dum alia dicimus, quae dicturi
sumus intuenda sunt.   Ita, cum semper cogitatio
ultra eat,[1] id quod est longius quaerit, quidquid
autem repperit quodam modo apud memoriam
deponit; quod illa quasi media quaedam manus

---

[1] ultra eat id, *Halm*: ultre ad id, *G*: ultra id, *codd. Mon.
Argentorat.*

may be improved by cultivation. And all the labour of which I have so far spoken will be in vain unless all the other departments be co-ordinated by the animating principle of memory. For our whole education depends upon memory, and we shall receive instruction all in vain if all we hear slips from us, while it is the power of memory alone that brings before us all the store of precedents, laws, rulings, sayings and facts which the orator must possess in abundance and which he must always hold ready for immediate use. Indeed it is not without good reason that memory has been called the treasure-house of eloquence. But **2** pleaders need not only to be able to retain a number of facts in their minds, but also to be quick to take them in; it is not enough to learn what you have written by dint of repeated reading; it is just as necessary to follow the order both of matter and words when you have merely thought out what you are going to say, while you must also remember what has been said by your opponents, and must not be content merely with refuting their arguments in the order in which they were advanced, but must be in a position to deal with each in its appropriate place. Nay, even extempore eloquence, in my **3** opinion, depends on no mental activity so much as memory. For while we are saying one thing, we must be considering something else that we are going to say : consequently, since the mind is always looking ahead, it is continually in search of something which is more remote : on the other hand, whatever it discovers, it deposits by some mysterious process in the safe-keeping of memory, which acts as a transmitting agent and hands on to the delivery

4 acceptum ab inventione tradit elocutioni. Non
arbitror autem mihi in hoc immorandum, quid sit
quod memoriam faciat, quanquam plerique imprimi
quaedam vestigia animo, velut in ceris anulorum
signa serventur, existimant. Neque ero tam credu-
lus, ut, qui [1] habitu tardiorem firmioremque memoriam
fieri videam, ei artem quoque audeam impertire.[2]

5 Magis admirari naturam subit, tot res vetustas tanto ex
intervallo repetitas reddere se et offerre, nec tantum
requirentibus sed etiam sponte interim, nec vigil-

6 antibus sed etiam quiete compositis : eo magis, quod
illa quoque animalia, quae carere intellectu videntur,
meminerunt et agnoscunt et quamlibet longo itinere
deducta ad adsuetas sibi sedes revertuntur. Quid ?
non haec varietas mira est, excidere proxima, vetera
inhaerere ? hesternorum immemores acta pueritiae

7 recordari ? Quid quod quaedam requisita se oc-
cultant et eadem forte succurrunt ? nec manet
semper memoria, sed aliquando etiam redit ? Nesci-
retur tamen, quanta vis esset eius, quanta divinitas
illa, nisi in hoc lumen vim [3] orandi extulisset. Non

8 enim rerum modo sed etiam verborum ordinem

---

[1] qui . . . fieri videam, *Spalding*: quam . . . fieri, *MSS.*
[2] ei artem quoque audeam impertire, *Spalding*: et actem
(*or* autem) quoque ad animum pertire (pertinere *or* partire)
MSS.
[3] vim, *added by Regius.*

what it has received from the imagination. I do 4
not conceive, however, that I need dwell upon the
question of the precise function of memory, although
many hold the view that certain impressions are
made upon the mind, analogous to those which a
signet-ring makes on wax. Nor, again, shall I be so
credulous, in view of the fact that the retentiveness
or slowness of the memory depends upon our
physical condition, as to venture to allot a special
art to memory. My inclination is rather to marvel 5
at its powers of reproducing and presenting a
number of remote facts after so long an interval,
and, what is more, of so doing not merely when we
seek for such facts, but even at times of its own
accord, and not only in our waking moments, but
even when we are sunk in sleep. And my wonder is 6
increased by the fact that even beasts, which seem to
be devoid of reason, yet remember and recognise
things, and will return to their old home, however far
they have been taken from it. Again, is it not an
extraordinary inconsistency that we forget recent and
remember distant events, that we cannot recall what
happened yesterday and yet retain a vivid impression
of the acts of our childhood? And what, again, shall 7
we say of the fact that the things we search for
frequently refuse to present themselves and then
occur to us by chance, or that memory does not
always remain with us, but will even sometimes
return to us after it has been lost? But we should
never have realised the fullness of its power nor its
supernatural capacities, but for the fact that it is
memory which has brought oratory to its present
position of glory. For it provides the orator not 8
merely with the order of his thoughts, but even of

praestat, nec ea pauca contexit, sed durat prope in
infinitum, et in longissimis actionibus prius audiendi
9 patientia quam memoriae fides deficit. Quod et
ipsum argumentum est subesse artem aliquam iu-
varique ratione naturam, cum idem docti facere
illud, indocti inexercitatique non possimus. Quanquam invenio apud Platonem obstare memoriae usum
litterarum, videlicet quoniam illa, quae scriptis
10 reposuimus, velut custodire desinimus et ipsa securitate dimittimus. Nec dubium est quin plurimum
in hac parte valeat mentis intentio et velut acies
luminum a prospectu rerum, quas intuetur, non
aversa. Unde accidit, ut quae per plures dies
scribimus ediscendi causa, cogitatione[1] ipsa contineamus.[2]

11 Artem autem memoriae primus ostendisse dicitur
Simonides. Cuius vulgata fabula est : cum pugili
coronato carmen, quale componi victoribus solet,
mercede pacta scripsisset, abnegatam ei pecuniae
partem, quod more poetis frequentissimo digressus
in laudes Castoris ac Pollucis exierat. Quapropter
partem ab iis petere, quorum facta celebrasset, iube-

---

[1] causa, cogitatione, *early edd.* : sint cogitationes, *MSS.*
[2] contineamus, *Slothouwer* : contineat, *MSS.*

---

[1] *Phaedr.* 275 A.   [2] See x. i. 64.

his words, nor is its power limited to stringing merely a few words together; its capacity for endurance is inexhaustible, and even in the longest pleadings the patience of the audience flags long before the memory of the speaker. This fact may 9 even be advanced as an argument that there must be some art of memory and that the natural gift can be helped by reason, since training enables us to do things which we cannot do before we have had any training or practice. On the other hand, I find that Plato [1] asserts that the use of written characters is a hindrance to memory, on the ground, that is, that once we have committed a thing to writing, we cease to guard it in our memory and lose it out of sheer carelessness. And there can be no doubt that 10 concentration of mind is of the utmost importance in this connexion; it is, in fact, like the eyesight, which turns to, and not away from, the objects which it contemplates. Thus it results that after writing for several days with a view to acquiring by heart what we have written, we find that our mental effort has of itself imprinted it on our memory.

The first person to discover an art of memory is 11 said to have been Simonides,[2] of whom the following well-known story is told. He had written an ode of the kind usually composed in honour of victorious athletes, to celebrate the achievement of one who had gained the crown for boxing. Part of the sum for which he had contracted was refused him on the ground that, following the common practice of poets, he had introduced a digression in praise of Castor and Pollux, and he was told that, in view of what he had done, he had best ask for the rest of the sum due from those whose deeds he had

12 batur. Et persolverunt, ut traditum est. Nam cum esset grande convivium in honorem eiusdem victoriae atque adhibitus ei cenae Simonides, nuntio est excitus, quod eum duo iuvenes equis advecti desiderare maiorem in modum dicebantur. Et illos quidem non invenit, fuisse tamen gratos erga se deos exitu

13 comperit. Nam vix eo ultra limen egresso, triclinium illud supra convivas corruit atque ita confudit,[1] ut non ora modo oppressorum, sed membra etiam omnia requirentes ad sepulturam propinqui nulla nota possent discernere. Tum Simonides dicitur memor ordinis,[2] quo quisque discubuerat, corpora suis reddi-

14 disse. Est autem magna inter auctores dissensio, Glaucone Carystio an Leocrati an Agatharcho an Scopae scriptum sit id carmen; et Pharsali fuerit haec domus, ut ipse quodam loco significare Simonides videtur utque Apollodorus et Eratosthenes et Euphorion et Larissaeus Eurypylus tradiderunt, an Crannone, ut Apollas Callimachus,[3] quem secutus Cicero

15 hanc famam latius fudit. Scopam nobilem Thessalum periisse in eo convivio constat; adiicitur sororis eius filius; putant et ortos plerosque ab alio Scopa, qui

16 maior aetate fuerit. Quanquam mihi totum de Tyndaridis fabulosum videtur, neque omnino huius

---

[1] confudit ut, *Badius* : confunditur, *MSS.*
[2] ordinis, *Regius* : ordine, *MSS.*
[3] Apollas Callimachus *being unknown*, *Bentley conjectured* Apollas et Callimachus (*Schneidewin* Callimachusque). Apollas would then refer to a philosopher and geographer of Cyrene.

---

[1] Cic. *de Or.* ii. lxxxvi. 352.

extolled.   And according to the story they paid
their debt.   For when a great banquet was given 12
in honour of the boxer's success, Simonides was
summoned forth from the feast, to which he had
been invited, by a message to the effect that two
youths who had ridden to the door urgently desired
his presence.   He found no trace of them, but what
followed proved to him that the gods had shown
their gratitude.   For he had scarcely crossed the 13
threshold on his way out, when the banqueting hall
fell in upon the heads of the guests and wrought
such havoc among them that the relatives of the
dead who came to seek the bodies for burial were
unable to distinguish not merely the faces but even
the limbs of the dead.   Then it is said, Simonides,
who remembered the order in which the guests had
been sitting, succeeded in restoring to each man his
own dead.   There is, however, great disagreement 14
among our authorities as to whether this ode was
written in honour of Glaucus of Carystus, Leocrates,
Agatharcus or Scopas, and whether the house was
at Pharsalus, as Simonides himself seems to indicate
in a certain passage, and as is recorded by Apollodorus, Eratosthenes, Euphorion and Eurypylus of
Larissa, or at Crannon, as is stated by Apollas
Callimachus, who is followed by Cicero,[1] to whom
the wide circulation of this story is due.   It is 15
agreed that Scopas, a Thessalian noble, perished at
this banquet, and it is also said that his sister's son
perished with him, while it is thought that a number
of descendants of an elder Scopas met their death
at the same time.   For my own part, however, I 16
regard the portion of the story which concerns
Castor and Pollux as being purely fictitious, since

rei meminit usquam poeta ipse, profecto non taciturus de tanta sua gloria.

17 Ex hoc Simonidis facto notatum videtur, iuvari memoriam signatis animo sedibus, idque credere suo quisque experimento potest.[1] Nam cum in loca aliqua post tempus reversi sumus, non ipsa agnoscimus tantum, sed etiam, quae in his fecerimus, reminiscimur personaeque subeunt, nonnunquam tacitae quoque cogitationes in mentem revertuntur. Nata est igitur, ut in plerisque, ars ab experimento.

18 Loca deligunt[2] quam maxime spatiosa, multa varietate signata, domum forte magnam et in multos diductam recessus. In ea quidquid notabile est, animo diligenter adfigunt, ut sine cunctatione ac mora partes eius omnes cogitatio possit percurrere. Et primus hic labor est non haerere in occursu; plus enim quam firma debet esse memoria, quae aliam memoriam

19 adiuvet. Tum, quae scripserunt vel cogitatione complexi sunt,[3] aliquo signo, quo moneantur, notant; quod esse vel ex re tota potest, ut de navigatione, militia, vel ex verbo aliquo; nam etiam excidentes unius admonitione verbi in memoriam reponuntur.

---

[1] potest, *added by Rollin.*
[2] deligunt, *Spalding*: discunt, *MSS.*
[3] complexi sunt, *Spalding*: complectitur, *G.*

the poet himself has nowhere mentioned the occurrence; and he would scarcely have kept silence on an affair which was so much to his credit.

This achievement of Simonides appears to have 17 given rise to the observation that it is an assistance to the memory if localities are sharply impressed upon the mind, a view the truth of which everyone may realise by practical experiment. For when we return to a place after considerable absence, we not merely recognise the place itself, but remember things that we did there, and recall the persons whom we met and even the unuttered thoughts which passed through our minds when we were there before. Thus, as in most cases, art originates in experiment. Some place is chosen of the 18 largest possible extent and characterised by the utmost possible variety, such as a spacious house divided into a number of rooms. Everything of note therein is carefully committed to the memory, in order that the thought may be enabled to run through all the details without let or hindrance. And undoubtedly the first task is to secure that there shall be no delay in finding any single detail, since an idea which is to lead by association to some other idea requires to be fixed in the mind with more than ordinary certitude. The next step 19 is to distinguish something which has been written down or merely thought of by some particular symbol which will serve to jog the memory; this symbol may have reference to the subject as a whole, it may, for example, be drawn from navigation, warfare, etc., or it may, on the other hand, be found in some particular word. (For even in cases of forgetfulness one single word will serve to

Sit autem signum navigationis ut ancora, militiae
20 ut aliquid ex armis. Haec ita digerunt. Primum
sensum vestibulo quasi adsignant, secundum, puta,
atrio, tum impluvia circumeunt, nec cubiculis modo
aut exedris, sed statuis etiam similibusque per
ordinem committunt. Hoc facto, cum est repetenda
memoria, incipiunt ab initio loca haec recensere, et
quod cuique crediderunt reposcunt, ut eorum imagine
admonentur. Ita, quamlibet multa sint, quorum
meminisse oporteat, fiunt singula conexa quodam
choro,[1] nec errant[2] coniungentes prioribus conse-
21 quentia solo ediscendi labore. Quod de domo dixi,
et in operibus publicis et in itinere longo et urbium
ambitu et picturis fieri potest. Etiam fingere sibi
has imagines licet. Opus est ergo locis, quae vel
finguntur vel sumuntur, et imaginibus vel simulacris,
quae utique fingenda sunt. Imagines voces sunt,
quibus ea quae ediscenda sunt notamus, ut, quomodo
Cicero dicit, locis pro cera, simulacris pro litteris
22 utamur. Illud quoque ad verbum ponere optimum
fuerit: *Locis est utendum multis, illustribus, explicatis,
modicis intervallis, imaginibus autem agentibus, acribus,*

---

[1] choro, *early editors* : coria, corio, *MSS.*
[2] nec errant, *Bonnell* : onerant, *G.*

---

[1] The *impluvium* was the light-well in the centre of the
atrium with a cistern beneath it to catch the rainwater from
the roof, which sloped inwards.
[2] *De Or.* II. lxxxvi. 354.　　　[3] *De Or.* II. lxxxvii. 358.

restore the memory.) However, let us suppose that
the symbol is drawn from navigation, as, for instance,
an anchor; or from warfare, as, for example, some
weapon. These symbols are then arranged as follows. 20
The first thought is placed, as it were, in the forecourt;
the second, let us say, in the living-room; the remainder are placed in due order all round the *impluvium*[1] and entrusted not merely to bedrooms and
parlours, but even to the care of statues and the
like. This done, as soon as the memory of the facts
requires to be revived, all these places are visited in
turn and the various deposits are demanded from
their custodians, as the sight of each recalls the
respective details. Consequently, however large the
number of these which it is required to remember,
all are linked one to the other like dancers
hand in hand, and there can be no mistake since
they join what precedes to what follows, no trouble
being required except the preliminary labour of
committing the various points to memory. What 21
I have spoken of as being done in a house, can
equally well be done in connexion with public
buildings, a long journey, the ramparts of a city,
or even pictures. Or we may even imagine such
places to ourselves. We require, therefore,
places, real or imaginary, and images or symbols,
which we must, of course, invent for ourselves. By
images I mean the words by which we distinguish
the things which we have to learn by heart: in
fact, as Cicero says, we use " places like wax tablets
and symbols in lieu of letters."[2] It will be best to 22
give his words *verbatim:*[3] "We must for this purpose employ a number of remarkable places, clearly
envisaged and separated by short intervals: the

insignitis, quae occurrere celeriterque percutere animum possint. Quo magis miror, quomodo Metrodorus in XII signis, per quae sol meat, trecenos et sexagenos invenerit locos. Vanitas nimirum fuit atque iactatio circa memoriam sua potius arte quam natura gloriantis.

23 Equidem haec ad quaedam prodesse non negaverim, ut si rerum nomina multa per ordinem audita reddenda sint. Namque in iis quae didicerunt locis ponunt res illas: mensam, ut hoc utar, in vestibulo et pulpitum [1] in atrio et sic cetera, deinde relegentes

24 inveniunt, ubi posuerunt. Et forsitan hoc sunt adiuti qui, auctione dimissa, quid cuique vendidissent testibus argentariorum tabulis reddiderunt; quod praestitisse Hortensium dicunt. Minus idem proderit in ediscendis, quae orationis perpetuae erunt. Nam et sensus non eandem imaginem quam res habent, cum alterum fingendum sit, et horum tamen utcunque commonet locus, sicut sermonis alicuius habiti.

At [2] verborum contextus eadem arte quomodo com-

25 prehendetur? Mitto quod quaedam nullis simulacris

---

[1] pulpitum, *Bonnell*: populum, *G*: pulvinum, *early editors.*
[2] At, *added by Halm.*

---

[1] Of Scepsis, the favourite of Mithradates Eupator. See *de Or.* II. lxxxviii. 360. He used the signs of the Zodiac as aids to the memory, subdividing each into thirty compartments. Quintilian wonders on what principle he can have made such a division, necessarily purely artificial in nature.

images which we use must be active, sharply-cut and distinctive, such as may occur to the mind and strike it with rapidity." This makes me wonder all the more, how Metrodorus[1] should have found three hundred and sixty different localities in the twelve signs of the Zodiac through which the sun passes. It was doubtless due to the vanity and boastfulness of a man who was inclined to vaunt his memory as being the result of art rather than of natural gifts.

I am far from denying that those devices may be 23 useful for certain purposes, as, for example, if we have to reproduce a number of names in the order in which we heard them. For those who use such aids place the things which have to be remembered in localities which they have previously fixed in the memory; they put a table, for instance, in the fore-court, a platform in the hall and so on with the rest, and then, when they retrace their steps, they find the objects where they had placed them. Such 24 a practice may perhaps have been of use to those who, after an auction, have succeeded in stating what object they had sold to each buyer, their state-ments being checked by the books of the money-takers; a feat which it is alleged was performed by Hortensius. It will, however, be of less service in learning the various parts of a set speech. For thoughts do not call up the same images as material things, and a symbol requires to be specially invented for them, although even here a particular place may serve to remind us, as, for example, of some conver-sation that may have been held there. But how can such a method grasp a whole series of con-nected words? I pass by the fact that there are 25 certain things which it is impossible to represent by

significari possunt, ut certe coniunctiones. Habeamus enim sane, ut qui notis scribunt, certas imagines omnium et loca scilicet infinita, per quae verba, quot sunt in quinque contra Verrem secundae actionis libris, explicentur, meminerimus etiam omnium quasi depositorum: nonne impediri quoque dicendi cursum[1] necesse est duplici memoriae cura? Nam

26 quomodo poterunt copulata fluere, si propter singula verba ad singulas formas respiciendum erit? Quare et Charmadas et Scepsius, de quo modo dixi, Metrodorus, quos Cicero dicit usos hac exercitatione, sibi habeant sua; nos simpliciora tradamus.

27 Si longior complectenda memoria fuerit oratio, proderit per partes ediscere; laborat enim maxime onere; et hae partes non sint perexiguae, alioqui rursus multae erunt et eam distinguent atque concident. Nec utique certum imperaverim modum, sed maxime ut quisque finietur locus, ni forte tam

28 numerosus, ut ipse quoque dividi debeat. Dandi sunt certi quidam termini, ut contextum verborum, qui est difficillimus, continua et crebra meditatio, partes deinceps ipsas repetitus ordo coniungat. Non est inutile, iis quae difficilius haereant aliquas

---

[1] quoque dicendi cursum, *Spalding*: quodque dicit dicursum, *G.*

---

[1] *de Or.* II. lxxxvii. 360. Charmadas or Charmides, an elder contemporary of Cicero.

symbols, as, for example, conjunctions. We may, it is true, like shorthand writers, have definite symbols for everything, and may select an infinite number of places to recall all the words contained in the five books of the second pleading against Verres, and we may even remember them all as if they were deposits placed in safe-keeping. But will not the flow of our speech inevitably be impeded by the double task imposed upon our memory? For how 26 can our words be expected to flow in connected speech, if we have to look back at separate symbols for each individual word? Therefore the experts mentioned by Cicero[1] as having trained their memory by methods of this kind, namely Charmadas, and Metrodorus of Scepsis, to whom I have just referred, may keep their systems for their own use. My precepts on the subject shall be of a simpler kind.

If a speech of some length has to be committed 27 to memory, it will be well to learn it piecemeal, since there is nothing so bad for the memory as being overburdened. But the sections into which we divide it for this purpose should not be very short: otherwise they will be too many in number, and will break up and distract the memory. I am not, however, prepared to recommend any definite length; it will depend on the natural limits of the passage concerned, unless, indeed, it be so long as itself to require subdivision. But some limits must be fixed to enable us, 28 by dint of frequent and continuous practice, to connect the words in their proper order, which is a task of no small difficulty, and subsequently to unite the various sections into a whole when we go over them in order. If certain portions prove especially difficult to

apponere notas, quarum recordatio commoneat et
29 quasi excitet memoriam; nemo etiam fere tam
infelix, ut, quod cuique loco signum destinaverit,
nesciat. At, si tardus[1] ad hoc, eo quoque adhuc
remedio utetur[2] ut ipsae notae (hoc enim est ex illa
arte non inutile) aptentur[3] ad eos qui excidunt
sensus: ancora[4] ut supra pro posui, si de nave dicen-
30 dum est,[5] spiculum, si de proelio. Multum enim
signa faciunt, et ex alia memoria venit alia: ut cum
translatus anulus vel alligatus commoneat nos, cur
id fecerimus. Haec magis adhuc adstringunt, qui
memoriam ab aliquo simili transferunt ad id quod
continendum est: ut in nominibus, si Fabius forte
sit tenendus, referamus ad illum Cunctatorem, qui
excidere non potest, aut ad aliquem amicum, qui
31 idem vocetur. Quod est facilius in Apris et in Ursis
et Nasone aut Crispo, ut id memoriae adfigatur unde
sunt nomina. Origo quoque aliquando declinatorum
tenendi magis causa est, ut in Cicerone, Verrio,
Aurelio. Sed hoc miserim.[6]
32   Illud neminem non iuvabit, iisdem quibus scripserit[7]
ceris ediscere. Sequitur enim vestigiis quibusdam

[1] at, *Halm*: ut, *G.*: tardus, *an early emendation*: trandus,
G: tradendus, late *MSS*.
[2] utetur, *Halm*: utitur, *MSS*.
[3] aptentur, *Hiecke*: adtentus. *MSS*.
[4] ancora, *Hiecke*: ancoram, *MSS*.
[5] est, *Halm*: esset, *MSS*.
[6] miserim, *Halm*: misceri, *G*.
[7] scripserit, *early edd.*: ceteris, *MSS*.

---

[1] Sects. 18-23.
[2] Boar, Bear, Long-nose, and Curly respectively.
[3] Cicero, a sower of chickpea (*cicer*), according to Pliny
(xviii. 10). Aurelius = Auselius, child of the sun (*a sole*)
according to Festus. Verrius unknown.

remember, it will be found advantageous to indicate
them by certain marks, the remembrance of which
will refresh and stimulate the memory. For there can **29**
be but few whose memory is so barren that they will
fail to recognise the symbols with which they have
marked different passages. But if anyone is slow to
recognise his own signs, he should employ the following additional remedy, which, though drawn from the
mnemonic system discussed above,[1] is not without its
uses: he will adapt his symbols to the nature of the
thoughts which tend to slip from his memory, using
an anchor, as I suggested above, if he has to speak
of a ship, or a spear, if he has to speak of a battle.
For symbols are highly efficacious, and one idea **30**
suggests another: for example, if we change a ring
from one finger to another or tie a thread round it,
it will serve to remind us of our reason for so doing.
Specially effective are those devices which lead the
memory from one thing to another similar thing which
we have got to remember; for example, in the case of
names, if we desire to remember the name Fabius,
we should think of the famous Cunctator, whom we
are certain not to forget, or of some friend bearing
the same name. This is specially easy with names **31**
such as Aper, Ursus, Naso, or Crispus,[2] since in
these cases we can fix their origin in our memory.
Origin again may assist us to a better remembrance of derivative names, such as Cicero, Verrius,
or Aurelius.[3] However, I will say no more on this
point.

There is one thing which will be of assistance to **32**
everyone, namely, to learn a passage by heart from
the same tablets on which he has committed it to
writing. For he will have certain tracks to guide

memoriam, et velut oculis intuetur non paginas modo, sed versus prope ipsos, estque cum[1] dicit similis legenti. Iam vero si litura aut adiectio aliqua atque mutatio interveniat, signa sunt quaedam, quae in-
33 tuentes deerrare non possumus. Haec ratio, ut est illi, de qua primum locutus sum, arti non dissimilis, ita, si quid me experimenta docuerunt, et expeditior et potentior. Ediscere tacite (nam id quoque est quaesitum) erat optimum, si non subirent velut otiosum animum plerumque aliae cogitationes; pro-pter quas excitandus est voce, ut duplici motu iuvetur memoria dicendi et audiendi. Sed haec vox sit
34 modica et magis murmur. Qui autem legente alio ediscit, in parte tardatur, quod acrior est oculorum quam aurium sensus; in parte iuvari potest, quod, cum semel aut bis audierit, continuo illi memoriam suam experiri licet et cum legente contendere. Nam et alioqui id maxime faciendum est, ut nos subinde temptemus, quia continua lectio et quae magis et
35 quae minus haerent aequaliter transit. In experiendo

---

[1] estque cum, *Meister*: quae cum, *G.*

him in his pursuit of memory, and the mind's eye will be fixed not merely on the pages on which the words were written, but on individual lines, and at times he will speak as though he were reading aloud. Further, if the writing should be interrupted by some erasure, addition or alteration, there are certain symbols available, the sight of which will prevent us from wandering from the track. This device bears 33 some resemblance to the mnemonic system which I mentioned above, but if my experience is worth anything, is at once more expeditious and more effective. The question has been raised as to whether we should learn by heart in silence; it would be best to do so, save for the fact that under such circumstances the mind is apt to become indolent, with the result that other thoughts break in. For this reason the mind should be kept alert by the sound of the voice, so that the memory may derive assistance from the double effort of speaking and listening. But our voice should be subdued, rising scarcely above a murmur. On the other hand, if we 34 attempt to learn by heart from another reading aloud, we shall find that there is both loss and gain; on the one hand, the process of learning will be slower, because the perception of the eye is quicker than that of the ear, while, on the other hand, when we have heard a passage once or twice, we shall be in a position to test our memory and match it against the voice of the reader. It is, indeed, important for other reasons to test ourselves thus from time to time, since continuous reading has this drawback, that it passes over the passages which we find hard to remember at the same speed as those which we find less difficulty in retaining. By testing ourselves to see 35

teneasne, et maior intentio est et et nihil supervacui
temporis perit, quo etiam quae tenemus repeti solent;
ita sola, quae exciderunt, retractantur, ut crebra
iteratione firmentur, quanquam solent hoc ipso
maxime haerere, quod exciderunt. Illud ediscendo
scribendoque commune est, utrique plurimum conferre bonam valetudinem, digestum cibum, animum
36 cogitationibus aliis liberum. Verum et in iis quae
scripsimus complectendis multum valent, et in iis
quae cogitamus continendis prope solae (excepta,
quae potentissima est, exercitatione) divisio et compositio. Nam qui recte diviserit, nunquam poterit in
37 rerum ordine errare. Certa sunt enim non solum in
digerendis quaestionibus, sed etiam in exsequendis,
si modo recte dicimus, prima ac secunda et deinceps;
cohaeretque omnis rerum copulatio, ut ei nihil neque
subtrahi sine manifesto intellectu neque inseri possit.
38 An vero Scaevola in lusu duodecim scriptorum, cum
prior calculum promovisset essetque victus, dum rus
tendit, repetito totius certaminis ordine, quo dato
errasset recordatus, rediit ad eum, quocum luserat,
isque ita factum esse confessus est? Minus idem

whether we remember a passage, we develop greater
concentration without waste of time over the repetition of passages which we already know by heart.
Thus, only those passages which tend to slip from
the memory are repeated with a view to fixing them
in the mind by frequent rehearsal, although as a rule
the mere fact that they once slipped our memory
makes us ultimately remember them with special
accuracy. Both learning by heart and writing have
this feature in common: namely, that good health,
sound digestion, and freedom from other preoccupa-
tions of mind contribute largely to the success of
both. But for the purpose of getting a real grasp 36
of what we have written under the various heads,
division and artistic structure will be found of great
value, while, with the exception of practice, which
is the most powerful aid of all, they are practically
the only means of ensuring an accurate remembrance
of what we have merely thought out. For correct
division will be an absolute safeguard against error in
the order of our speech, since there are certain points 37
not merely in the distribution of the various questions
in our speech, but also in their development (provided we speak as we ought), which naturally come
first, second, and third, and so on, while the connexion
will be so perfect that nothing can be omitted or
inserted without the fact of the omission or insertion being obvious. We are told that Scaevola, 38
after a game of draughts in which he made the first
move and was defeated, went over the whole game
again in his mind on his way into the country, and
on recalling the move which had cost him the game,
returned to tell the man with whom he had been
playing, and the latter acknowledged that he was

ordo valebit in oratione, praesertim totus nostro
arbitrio constitutus, cum tantum ille valeat alternus?

39 Etiam quae bene composita erunt, memoriam serie
sua ducent. Nam sicut facilius versus ediscimus
quam prosam orationem, ita prosae vincta quam
dissoluta. Sic contingit, ut etiam quae ex tempore
videbantur effusa, ad verbum repetita reddantur.
Quod meae quoque memoriae mediocritatem sequebatur, si quando interventus aliquorum, qui hunc
honorem mererentur, iterare declamationis partem
coegisset. Nec est mendacio locus, salvis qui inter-
fuerunt.

40 Si quis tamen unam maximamque a me artem
memoriae quaerat, exercitatio est et labor; multa
ediscere, multa cogitare, et si fieri potest cotidie,
potentissimum est. Nihil aeque vel augetur cura vel
41 negligentia intercidit. Quare et pueri statim, ut
praecepi, quam plurima ediscant, et, quaecunque
aetas operam iuvandae studio memoriae dabit, de-
voret initio taedium illud et scripta et lecta saepius
revolvendi et quasi eundem cibum remandendi.
Quod ipsum hoc fieri potest levius, si pauca primum
et quae odium non adferant coeperimus ediscere,

---

right. Is order, then, I ask you, to be accounted of less importance in a speech, in which it depends entirely on ourselves, whereas in a game our opponent has an equal share in its development? Again, if 39 our structure be what it should, the artistic sequence will serve to guide the memory. For just as it is easier to learn verse than prose, so it is easier to learn prose when it is artistically constructed than when it has no such organisation. If these points receive attention, it will be possible to repeat *verbatim* even such psssages as gave the impression of being delivered extempore. My own memory is of a very ordinary kind, but I found that I could do this with success on occasions when the interruption of a declamation by persons who had a claim to such a courtesy forced me to repeat part of what I had said. There are persons still living, who were then present to witness if I lie.

However, if anyone asks me what is the one 40 supreme method of memory, I shall reply, practice and industry. The most important thing is to learn much by heart and to think much, and, if possible, to do this daily, since there is nothing that is more increased by practice or impaired by neglect than memory. Therefore boys should, as I have already 41 urged,[1] learn as much as possible by heart at the earliest stage, while all who, whatever their age, desire to cultivate the power of memory, should endeavour to swallow the initial tedium of reading and re-reading what they have written or read, a process which we may compare to chewing the cud. This task will be rendered less tiresome if we begin by confining ourselves to learning only a little at a time, in amounts not sufficient to create disgust : we

tum cotidie adiicere singulos versus, quorum accessio labori sensum incrementi non adferat, in summam ad infinitum usque perveniat, et poetica prius, tum oratorum, novissime etiam solutiora numeris et magis ab usu dicendi remota, qualia sunt iurisconsultorum.

42 Difficiliora enim debent esse, quae exercent, quo sit levius ipsum illud, in quod exercent, ut athletae ponderibus plumbeis adsuefaciunt manus, quibus vacuis et nudis in certamine utendum est. Non omittam etiam, quod cotidianis experimentis deprehenditur, minime fidelem esse paulo tardioribus in-

43 geniis recentem memoriam. Mirum dictu est nec in promptu ratio, quantum nox interposita adferat firmitatis, sive requiescit labor ille, cuius sibi ipsa fatigatio obstabat, sive maturatur atque concoquitur, quae firmissima eius pars est, recordatio; quae statim referri non poterant, contexuntur postera die, confirmatque memoriam illud tempus, quod esse in causa

44 solet oblivionis. Etiam illa praevelox fere cito effluit, et, velut praesenti officio functa nihil in posterum

may then proceed to increase the amount by a line a day, an addition which will not sensibly increase the labour of learning, until at last the amount we can attack will know no limits. We should begin with poetry and then go on to oratory, while finally we may attempt passages still freer in rhythm and less akin to ordinary speech, such, for example, as passages from legal writers. For passages intended 42 as an exercise should be somewhat difficult in character if they are to make it easy to achieve the end for which the exercise is designed; just as athletes train the muscles of their hands by carrying weights of lead, although in the actual contests their hands will be empty and free. Further, I must not omit the fact, the truth of which our daily practice will teach us, that in the case of the slower type of mind the memory of recent events is far from being exact. It is 43 a curious fact, of which the reason is not obvious, that the interval of a single night will greatly increase the strength of the memory, whether this be due to the fact that it has rested from the labour, the fatigue of which constituted the obstacle to success, or whether it be that the power of recollection, which is the most important element of memory, undergoes a process of ripening and maturing during the time which intervenes. Whatever the cause, things which could not be recalled on the spot are easily co-ordinated the next day, and time itself, which is generally accounted one of the causes of forgetfulness, actually serves to strengthen the memory. On the other hand, the abnormally rapid 44 memory fails as a rule to last and takes its leave as though, its immediate task accomplished, it had no further duties to perform. And indeed there is

debeat, tanquam dimissa discedit. Nec est mirum,
magis haerere animo quae diutius adfixa sint.

Ex hac ingeniorum diversitate nata dubitatio est,
ad verbum sit ediscendum dicturis, an vim modo rerum atque ordinem complecti satis sit; de quo sine
45 dubio non potest in universum pronuntiari. Nam si
memoria suffragatur, tempus non defuit, nulla me
velim syllaba effugiat; alioqui etiam scribere sit
supervacuum. Idque praecipue a pueris obtinendum,
atque in hanc consuetudinem memoria exercitatione
redigenda, ne nobis discamus ignoscere. Ideoque
et admoneri et ad libellum respicere vitiosum, quod
libertatem negligentiae facit, nec quisquam se parum
tenere iudicat, quod, ne sibi excidat, non timet.
46 Inde interruptus actionis impetus et resistens ac
salebrosa oratio; et qui dicit ediscenti similis, etiam
omnem bene scriptorum gratiam perdit vel hoc ipso,
quod scripsisse se confitetur. Memoria autem facit
etiam prompti ingenii famam, ut illa, quae dicimus,
non domo attulisse sed ibi protinus sumpsisse videamur; quod et oratori et ipsi causae plurimum con-
47 fert. Nam et magis miratur et minus timet iudex,

nothing surprising in the fact that things which have been implanted in the memory for some time should have a greater tendency to stay there.

The difference between the powers of one mind and another, to which I have just referred, gives rise to the question whether those who are intending to speak should learn their speeches *verbatim* or whether it is sufficient to get a good grasp of the essence and the order of what they have got to say. To this problem no answer is possible that will be of universal application. Give me a reliable memory and 45 plenty of time, and I should prefer not to permit a single syllable to escape me: otherwise writing would be superfluous. It is specially important to train the young to such precision, and the memory should be continually practised to this end, that we may never learn to become indulgent to its failure. For this reason I regard it as a mistake to permit the student to be prompted or to consult his manuscript, since such practices merely encourage carelessness, and no one will ever realise that he has not got his theme by heart, if he has no fear of forgetting it. It is this which causes interruptions in the flow of 46 speech and makes the orator's language halting and jerky, while he seems as though he were learning what he says by heart and loses all the grace that a well-written speech can give, simply by the fact that he makes it obvious that he has written it. On the other hand, a good memory will give us credit for quickness of wit as well, by creating the impression that our words have not been prepared in the seclusion of the study, but are due to the inspiration of the moment, an impression which is of the utmost assistance both to the orator and to his cause. For 47

quae non putat adversus se praeparata. Idque in actionibus inter praecipua servandum est, ut quaedam etiam, quae optime vinximus, velut soluta enuntiemus et cogitantibus nonnunquam et dubitantibus similes quaerere videamur quae attulimus.

48   Ergo quid sit optimum, neminem fugit. Si vero aut memoria natura durior erit aut non suffragabitur tempus, etiam inutile erit ad omnia se verba adligare, cum oblivio unius eorum cuiuslibet aut deformem haesitationem aut etiam silentium inducat, tutiusque multo comprehensis animo rebus ipsis libertatem sibi elo-
49 quendi relinquere. Nam et invitus perdit quisque id quod elegerat verbum, nec facile reponit aliud, dum id, quod scripserat, quaerit. Sed ne hoc quidem infirmae memoriae remedium est nisi in iis, qui sibi facultatem aliquam dicendi ex tempore paraverunt. Quodsi cui utrumque defuerit, huic omittere omnino totum actionum laborem ac, si quid in litteris valet, ad scribendum potius suadebo convertere. Sed haec rara infelicitas erit.

50   Ceterum quantum natura studioque valeat memoria, vel Themistocles testis, quem unum intra annum optime locutum esse Persice constat ; vel Mithri-

the judge admires those words more and fears them less which he does not suspect of having been specially prepared beforehand to outwit him. Further, we must make it one of our chief aims in pleading to deliver passages which have been constructed with the utmost care, in such manner as to make it appear that they are but casually strung together, and to suggest that we are thinking out and hesitating over words which we have, as a matter of fact, carefully prepared in advance.

48 It should now be clear to all what is the best course to adopt for the cultivation of memory. If, however, our memory be naturally somewhat dull or time presses, it will be useless to tie ourselves down rigidly to every word, since if we forget any one of them, the result may be awkward hesitation or even a tongue-tied silence. It is, therefore, far safer to secure a good grasp of the facts themselves and to leave ourselves free to speak as we will. For the loss of even a single word that we 49 have chosen is always a matter for regret, and it is hard to supply a substitute when we are searching for the word that we had written. But even this is no remedy for a weak memory, except for those who have acquired the art of speaking extempore. But if both memory and this gift be lacking, I should advise the would-be orator to abandon the toil of pleading altogether and, if he has any literary capacity, to betake himself by preference to writing. But such a misfortune will be of but rare occurrence.

For the rest there are many historical examples 50 of the power to which memory may be developed by natural aptitude and application. Themistocles is said to have spoken excellently in Persian after a

dates, cui duas et viginti linguas, quot nationibus
imperabat, traditur notas fuisse; vel Crassus ille
Dives, qui, cum Asiae praeesset, quinque Graeci
sermonis differentias sic tenuit ut, qua quisque apud
eum lingua postulasset, eadem ius sibi redditum
ferret; vel Cyrus, quem omnium militum tenuisse
51 creditum est nomina. Quin semel auditos quamlibet
multos versus protinus dicitur reddidisse Theodectes.
Dicebantur etiam nunc esse, qui facerent, sed mihi
nunquam, ut ipse interessem, contigit; habenda
tamen fides est vel in hoc ut, qui crediderit, et
speret.

III. Pronuntiatio a plerisque actio dicitur, sed
prius nomen a voce, sequens a gestu videtur accipere. Namque actionem Cicero alias *quasi sermonem*
alias *eloquentiam quandam corporis* dicit. Idem tamen
duas eius partes facit, quae sunt eaedem pronuntia-
2 tionis, vocem atque motum. Qua propter utraque
appellatione indifferenter uti licet. Habet autem
res ipsa miram quandam in orationibus vim ac potes-
tatem; neque enim tam refert, qualia sint, quae intra
nosmet ipsos composuimus, quam quo modo effe-
rantur; nam ita quisque, ut audit, movetur. Quare
neque probatio ulla, quae modo venit ab oratore,
tam firma est, ut non perdat vires suas, nisi adiuvatur

---

[1] King of Pontus.
[2] Consul, 131 B.C. Commanded in the war against Aris-
tonicus of Pergamum, was defeated and killed.
[3] Rhetorician of first half of fourth century B.C.
[4] *de Or.* III. lix. 222.   [5] *Or.* xvii. 55.

year's study; Mithridates is recorded to have known
twenty-two languages, that being the number of
the different nations included in his empire;[1] Crassus,
surnamed the Rich,[2] when commanding in Asia had
such a complete mastery of five different Greek
dialects, that he would give judgement in the dialect
employed by the plaintiff in putting forward his
suit; Cyrus is believed to have known the name
of every soldier in his army, while Theodectes[3] is 51
actually said to have been able to repeat any number
of verses after only a single hearing. I remember
that it used to be alleged that there were persons
still living who could do the same, though I never
had the good fortune to be present at such a performance. Still, we shall do well to have faith in
such miracles, if only that he who believes may also
hope to achieve the like.

III. *Delivery* is often styled *action*. But the first
name is derived from the voice, the second from the
gesture. For Cicero in one passage[4] speaks of *action*
as being a *form of speech*, and in another[5] as being
a *kind of physical eloquence*. None the less, he
divides action into two elements, which are the
same as the elements of delivery, namely, voice and
movement. Therefore, it matters not which term
we employ. But the thing itself has an extra- 2
ordinarily powerful effect in oratory. For the
nature of the speech that we have composed within
our minds is not so important as the manner in
which we produce it, since the emotion of each
member of our audience will depend on the impression made upon his hearing. Consequently, no
proof, at least if it be one devised by the orator
himself, will ever be so secure as not to lose its force

adseveratione dicentis.   Adfectus omnes languescant necesse est, nisi voce, vultu, totius prope habitu
3 corporis inardescunt.   Nam cum haec omnia fecerimus, felices tamen, si nostrum illum ignem iudex conceperit ; nedum eum supini securique moveamus,
4 ac non et ipse nostra oscitatione solvatur.   Documento sunt vel scenici actores, qui et optimis poetarum tantum adiiciunt gratiae, ut nos infinito magis eadem illa audita quam lecta delectent ; et vilissimis etiam quibusdam impetrant aures, ut, quibus nullus est in bibliothecis locus, sit etiam frequens in theatris.
5 Quodsi in rebus, quas fictas esse scimus et inanes, tantum pronuntiatio potest, ut iram, lacrimas, sollicitudinem adferat, quanto plus valeat necesse est, ubi et credimus ?   Equidem vel mediocrem orationem commendatam viribus actionis adfirmarim plus habituram esse momenti quam optimam eadem illa destitu-
6 tam.   Siquidem et Demosthenes, quid esset in toto dicendi opere primum, interrogatus pronuntiationi palmam dedit eidemque secundum ac tertium locum, donec ab eo quaeri desineret, ut eam videri posset
7 non praecipuam, sed solam iudicasse ; ideoque ipse

if the speaker fails to produce it in tones that drive it home. All emotional appeals will inevitably fall flat, unless they are given the fire that voice, look, and the whole carriage of the body can give them. For when we have done all this, we may still 3 account ourselves only too fortunate if we have succeeded in communicating the fire of our passion to the judge: consequently, we can have no hope of moving him if we speak with languor and indifference, nor of preventing him from yielding to the narcotic influence of our own yawns. A proof of this 4 is given by actors in the theatre. For they add so much to the charm even of the greatest poets, that the verse moves us far more when heard than when read, while they succeed in securing a hearing even for the most worthless authors, with the result that they repeatedly win a welcome on the stage that is denied them in the library. Now 5 if delivery can count for so much in themes which we know to be fictitious and devoid of reality, as to arouse our anger, our tears or our anxiety, how much greater must its effect be when we actually believe what we hear? For my own part I would not hesitate to assert that a mediocre speech supported by all the power of delivery will be more impressive than the best speech unaccompanied by such power. It was for this reason that Demos- 6 thenes, when asked what was the most important thing in oratory, gave the palm to delivery and assigned it second and third place as well, until his questioner ceased to trouble him. We are therefore almost justified in concluding that he regarded it not merely as the first, but as the only virtue of oratory. This explains why he studied 7

tam diligenter apud Andronicum hypocriten studuit,
ut admirantibus eius orationem Rhodiis non immerito
Aeschines dixisse videatur : *Quid si ipsum audissetis ?*
Et M. Cicero unam in dicendo actionem dominari
8 putat. Hac Cn. Lentulum plus opinionis consecutum
quam eloquentia tradit, eadem C. Gracchum in de-
flenda fratris nece totius populi Romani lacrimas
concitasse, Antonium et Crassum multum valuisse,
plurimum vero Q. Hortensium. Cuius rei fides est,
quod eius scripta tantum intra famam sunt, qua diu
princeps oratorum, aliquando aemulus Ciceronis existi-
matus est, novissime, quoad vixit, secundus, ut appareat placuisse aliquid eo dicente, quod legentes
9 non invenimus. Et hercule cum valeant multum
verba per se, et vox propriam vim adiiciat rebus, et
gestus motusque significet aliquid, profecto perfectum
quiddam fieri, cum omnia coierunt, necesse est.

10 Sunt tamen qui rudem illam, et qualem impetus
cuiusque animi tulit, actionem iudicent fortiorem et
solam viris dignam, sed non alii fere quam qui etiam

---

[1] *de Or.* III. lvi. 213. Aeschines in exile at Rhodes first
recited his own speech against Ctesiphon, and then by special
request read Demosthenes' reply, the famous *De Corona*.
[2] *Brut.* lxvi., lxxxix., xxxviii., xliii., lxxxviii.

under the instruction of the actor Andronicus with
such diligence and success as thoroughly to justify
the remark made by Aeschines to the Rhodians when
they expressed their admiration of the speech of
Demosthenes on behalf of Ctesiphon, "What would
you have said if you had heard him yourselves?"[1]
Cicero likewise regards *action* as the supreme element
of oratory. He records that Gnaeus Lentulus ac- 8
quired a greater reputation by his delivery than
by his actual eloquence, and that Gaius Gracchus
by the same means stirred the whole Roman people
to tears when he bewailed his brother's death,
while Antonius and Crassus produced a great impression by their command of this quality, though
the greatest of all was that produced by Quintus
Hortensius.[2] This statement is strongly supported
by the fact that the latter's writings fall so far
short of the reputation which for so long secured
him the first place among orators, then for a
while caused him to be regarded as Cicero's rival,
and finally, for the remainder of his life assigned
him a position second only to that of Cicero, that
his speaking must clearly have possessed some
charm which we fail to find when we read him.
And, indeed, since words in themselves count for 9
much and the voice adds a force of its own to the
matter of which it speaks, while gesture and motion
are full of significance, we may be sure of finding
something like perfection when all these qualities
are combined.

There are some, however, who consider that de- 10
livery which owes nothing to art and everything to
natural impulse is more forcible, and in fact the only
form of delivery which is worthy of a manly speaker.

in dicendo curam et artem et nitorem, et quidquid studio paratur, ut adfectata et parum naturalia solent improbare, vel qui verborum atque ipsius etiam soni rusticitate, ut L. Cottam dicit Cicero fecisse, imita-

11 tionem antiquitatis adfectant. Verum illi persuasione sua fruantur, qui hominibus, ut sint oratores, satis putant nasci; nostro labori dent veniam, qui nihil credimus esse perfectum, nisi ubi natura cura iuvetur. In hoc igitur non contumaciter consentio

12 primas partes esse naturae. Nam certe bene pronuntiare non poterit, cui aut in scriptis memoria aut in iis, quae subito dicenda erunt, facilitas prompta defuerit, nec si inemendabilia oris incommoda obstabunt. Corporis etiam potest esse aliqua tanta

13 deformitas, ut nulla arte vincatur. Sed ne vox quidem exilis actionem habere optimam potest. Bona enim firmaque, ut volumus, uti licet; mala vel imbecilla et inhibet multa, ut insurgere et exclamare, et aliqua cogit, ut intermittere et deflectere et rasas fauces ac latus fatigatum deformi cantico reficere. Sed nos de eo nunc loquamur, cui non frustra praecipitur.

14 Cum sit autem omnis actio, ut dixi, in duas divisa partes, vocem gestumque, quorum alter oculos, altera

---

[1] de Or. III. xi. 42. Brut. lxxiv. 259.

But these persons are as a rule identical, either with those who are in the habit of disapproving of care, art, polish and every form of premeditation in actual speaking, as being affected and unnatural, or else with those who (like Lucius Cotta, according to Cicero)[1] affect the imitation of ancient writers both in their choice of words and even in the rudeness of their intonation and rhythm. Those, however, who 11 think it sufficient for men to be born to enable them to become orators, are welcome to their opinion, and I must ask them to be indulgent to the efforts to which I am committed by my belief that we cannot hope to attain perfection unless nature is assisted by study. But I will not be so obstinate as to deny that to nature must be assigned the first place. For 12 a good delivery is undoubtedly impossible for one who cannot remember what he has written, or lacks the quick facility of speech required by sudden emergencies, or is hampered by incurable impediments of speech. Again, physical uncouthness may be such that no art can remedy it, while a weak 13 voice is incompatible with first-rate excellence in delivery. For we may employ a good, strong voice as we will; whereas one that is ugly or feeble not only prevents us from producing a number of effects, such as a *crescendo* or a sudden *fortissimo*, but at times forces faults upon us, making us drop the voice, alter its pitch and refresh the hoarseness of the throat and fatigue of the lungs by a hideous chanting intonation. However, let me now turn to consider the speaker on whom my precepts will not be wasted.

All delivery, as I have already said, is concerned 14 with two different things, namely, voice and gesture,

aures movet, per quos duos sensus omnis ad animum penetrat adfectus, prius est de voce dicere, cui etiam gestus accommodatur.

In ea prima observatio est, qualem habeas ; secunda, quomodo utaris. Natura vocis spectatur quantitate 15 et qualitate. Quantitas simplicior ; in summa enim grandis aut exigua est, sed inter has extremitates mediae sunt species, et ab ima ad summam ac retro sunt multi gradus. Qualitas magis varia. Nam est et candida et fusca, et plena et exilis, et lenis et aspera, et contracta et fusa, et dura et flexibilis, et clara et obtusa. Spiritus etiam longior breviorque. 16 Nec causas, cur quidque eorum accidat, persequi proposito operi necessarium est: eorumne sit differentia, in quibus aura illa concipitur, an eorum, per quae velut organa meat; ipsi propria natura, an prout movetur; lateris pectorisve firmitas an capitis etiam plus adiuvet. Nam opus est omnibus sicut non oris modo suavitate, sed narium quoque, per quas quod superest vocis egeritur. Dulcis esse 17 tamen debet non exprobrans sonus. Utendi voce

of which the one appeals to the eye and the other to the ear, the two senses by which all emotion reaches the soul. But the voice has the first claim on our attention, since even our gesture is adapted to suit it.

The first point which calls for consideration is the nature of the voice, the second the manner in which it is used. The nature of the voice depends on its quantity and quality. The question of quantity is 15 the simpler of the two, since as a rule it is either strong or weak, although there are certain kinds of voice which fall between these extremes, and there are a number of gradations from the highest notes to the lowest and from the lowest to the highest. Quality, on the other hand, presents more variations; for the voice may be clear or husky, full or thin, smooth or harsh, of wide or narrow compass, rigid or flexible, and sharp or flat, while lung-power may be great or small. It is not necessary for my purpose 16 to enquire into the causes which give rise to these peculiarities. I need not raise the question whether the difference lies in those organs by which the breath is produced, or in those which form the channels for the voice itself; whether the voice has a character of its own or depends on the motions which produce it; whether it be the strength of the lungs, chest or the vocal organs themselves that affords it most assistance, since the co-operation of all these organs is required. For example, it is not the mouth only that produces sweetness of tone; it requires the assistance of the nostrils as well, which carry off what I may describe as the overflow of the voice. The important fact is that the tone must be agreeable and not harsh. The methods of using the 17

multiplex ratio. Nam praeter illam differentiam,
quae est tripertita, acutae, gravis, flexae, tum in-
tentis, tum remissis, tum elatis, tum inferioribus modis opus est, spatiis quoque lentioribus aut citatioribus.

18 Sed his ipsis media interiacent multa, et ut facies,
quanquam ex paucissimis constat, infinitam habet
differentiam, ita vox, etsi paucas, quae nominari possint, continet species, propria cuique est, et non
haec minus auribus quam oculis illa dinoscitur.

19 Augentur autem sicut omnium, ita vocis quoque
bona cura, negligentia minuuntur. Sed cura non
eadem oratoribus quae phonascis convenit; tamen
multa sunt utrisque communia, firmitas corporis, ne
ad spadonum et mulierum et aegrorum exilitatem
vox nostra tenuetur; quod ambulatio, unctio, veneris
abstinentia, facilis ciborum digestio, id est frugalitas,

20 praestat. Praeterea ut sint fauces integrae, id est
molles ac leves, quarum vitio et frangitur et obscura-
tur et exasperatur et scinditur vox. Nam ut tibiae
eodem spiritu accepto alium clausis, alium apertis
foraminibus, alium non satis purgatae, alium quassae
sonum reddunt, ita fauces tumentes strangulant

voice present great variety. For in addition to the triple division of accents into sharp, grave and circumflex, there are many other forms of intonation which are required: it may be intense or relaxed, high or low, and may move in slow or quick time. But here again there are many intermediate 18 gradations between the two extremes, and just as the face, although it consists of a limited number of features, yet possesses infinite variety of expression, so it is with the voice: for though it possesses but few varieties to which we can give a name, yet every human being possesses a distinctive voice of his own, which is as easily distinguished by the ear as are facial characteristics by the eye.

The good qualities of the voice, like everything 19 else, are improved by training and impaired by neglect. But the training required by the orator is not the same as that which is practised by the singing-master, although the two methods have many points in common. In both cases physical robustness is essential to save the voice from dwindling to the feeble shrillness that characterises the voices of eunuchs, women and invalids, and the means for creating such robustness are to be found in walking, rubbing-down with oil, abstinence from sexual intercourse, an easy digestion, and, in a word, in the simple life. Further, the throat must be sound, 20 that is to say, soft and smooth; for if the throat be unsound, the voice is broken or dulled or becomes harsh or squeaky. For just as the sound produced in the pipe by the same volume of breath varies according as the stops are closed or open, or the instrument is clogged or cracked, so the voice is strangled if the throat be swollen, and muffled if it

vocem, obtusae obscurant, rasae exasperant, convulsae
21 fractis sunt organis similes. Finditur etiam spiritus
obiectu aliquo sicut lapillo tenues aquae, quarum
cursus [1] etiamsi ultra paulum coit, aliquid tamen cavi
relinquit post id ipsum quod offenderat. Humor
quoque vocem ut nimius impedit, ita consumptus
destituit. Nam fatigatio, ut corpora, non ad praesens
22 modo tempus, sed etiam in futurum adficit. Sed ut
communiter et phonascis et oratoribus necessaria est
exercitatio, qua omnia convalescunt, ita curae non
idem genus est. Nam neque certa tempora ad
spatiandum dari possunt tot civilibus officiis occu-
pato, nec praeparare ab imis sonis vocem ad summos
nec semper a contentione condere licet, cum pluribus
23 iudiciis saepe dicendum sit. Ne ciborum quidem est
eadem observatio. Non enim tam molli teneraque
voce quam forti ac durabili opus est, cum illi omnes
etiam altissimos sonos leniant cantu oris, nobis pleraque aspere sint concitateque dicenda et vigilandae
noctes et fuligo lucubrationum bibenda et in sudata
24 veste durandum. Quare vocem deliciis non mollia-
mus, nec imbuatur ea consuetudine, quam desidera-
tura sit; sed exercitatio eius talis sit qualis usus, ne

----

[1] cursus, *Spalding* : spiritus, *MSS.*

is obstructed, while it becomes rasping if the throat
is inflamed, and may be compared to an organ with
broken pipes in cases where the throat is subject to
spasms. Again, the presence of some obstacle may 21
divide the breath just as a pebble will divide shallow
waters, which, although their currents unite again
soon after the obstruction is past, still leave a hollow
space in rear of the object struck. An excess of
moisture also impedes the voice, while a deficiency
weakens it. As regards fatigue, its effect is the same
as upon the body : it affects the voice not merely at
the moment of speaking, but for some time afterwards. But while exercise, which gives strength in 22
all cases, is equally necessary both for orators and
singing-masters, it is a different kind of exercise
which they require. For the orator is too much
occupied by civil affairs to be able to allot fixed
times for taking a walk, and he cannot tune his
voice through all the notes of the scale nor spare
it exertion, since it is frequently necessary for him
to speak in several cases in succession. Nor is the 23
same régime suitable as regards food : for the orator
needs a strong and enduring voice rather than one
which is soft and sweet, while the singer mellows all
sounds, even the highest, by the modulation of his
voice, whereas we have often to speak in harsh and
agitated tones, must pass wakeful nights, swallow
the soot that is produced by the midnight oil and
stick to our work though our clothes be dripping
with sweat. Consequently, we must not attempt to 24
mellow our voice by coddling it nor accustom it to
the conditions which it would like to enjoy, but
rather give it exercise suited to the tasks on which
it will be employed, never allowing it to be impaired

silentio subsidat, sed firmetur consuetudine, qua diffi-
25 cultas omnis levatur. Ediscere autem, quo exer-
cearis, erit optimum (nam ex tempore dicentes
avocat a cura vocis ille, qui ex rebus ipsis concipitur, adfectus) et ediscere quam maxime varia,
quae et clamorem et disputationem et sermonem et
flexus habeant, ut simul in omnia paremur. Hoc
26 satis est; alioqui nitida illa et curata vox insolitum
laborem recusabit, ut assueta gymnasiis et oleo corpora, quamlibet sint in suis certaminibus speciosa
atque robusta, si militare iter fascemque et vigilias
imperes, deficiant et quaerant unctores suos nudum-
27 que sudorem. Illa quidem in hoc opere praecipi
quis ferat vitandos soles atque ventos et nubila etiam
ac siccitates? Ita, si dicendum in sole aut ventoso,
humido, calido die fuerit, reos deseremus? Nam
crudum quidem aut saturum aut ebrium aut eiecto
modo vomitu, quae cavenda quidam monent, decla-
28 mare neminem, qui sit mentis compos, puto. Illud
non sine causa est ab omnibus praeceptum, ut parca-
tur maxime voci in illo a pueritia in adolescentiam
transitu, quia naturaliter impeditur, non, ut arbitror,
propter calorem, quod quidam putaverunt (nam est

by silence, but strengthening it by practice, which removes all difficulties. The best method for secur- 25 ing such exercise is to learn passages by heart (for if we have to speak extempore, the passion inspired by our theme will distract us from all care for our voice), while the passages selected for the purpose should be as varied as possible, involving a combination of loud, argumentative, colloquial and modulated utterance, so that we may prepare ourselves for all exigencies simultaneously. This will be sufficient. 26 Otherwise your delicate, overtrained voice will succumb before any unusual exertion, like bodies accustomed to the oil of the training school, which for all the imposing robustness which they display in their own contests, yet, if ordered to make a day's march with the troops, to carry burdens and mount guard at night, would faint beneath the task and long for their trainers to rub them down with oil and for the free perspiration of the naked limbs. Who 27 would tolerate me if in a work such as this I were to prescribe avoidance of exposure to sun, wind, rain or parching heat? If we are called upon to speak in the sun or on a windy, wet or warm day, is that a reason for deserting the client whom we have under- taken to defend? While as for the warning given by some that the orator should not speak when dyspeptic, replete or drunk, or immediately after vomiting, I think that no sane person would dream of declaiming under such circumstances. There is, 28 however, good reason for the rule prescribed by all authorities, that the voice should not be overstrained in the years of transition between boyhood and man- hood, since at that period it is naturally weak, not, I think, on account of heat, as some allege (for there

maior alias), sed propter humorem potius ; nam hoc
29 aetas illa turgescit. Itaque nares etiam ac pectus eo
tempore tument, atque omnia velut germinant eoque
sunt tenera et iniuriae obnoxia. Sed, ut ad propositum redeam, iam confirmatae constitutaeque voci
genus exercitationis optimum duco, quod est operi
simillimum, dicere cotidie sicut agimus. Namque
hoc modo non vox tantum confirmatur et latus, sed
etiam corporis decens et accommodatus orationi
motus componitur.

30　Non alia est autem ratio pronuntiationis quam
ipsius orationis. Nam ut illa emendata, dilucida,
ornata, apta esse debet, ita haec quoque emendata
erit, id est, vitio carebit, si fuerit os facile, explana-
tum, iucundum, urbanum, id est, in quo nulla neque
31 rusticitas neque peregrinitas resonet. Non enim
sine causa dicitur *barbarum Graecumve*. Nam sonis
homines ut aera tinnitu dinoscimus. Ita fiet illud,
quod Ennius probat, cum dicit *suaviloquenti ore* Cethe-
gum fuisse, non quod Cicero in his reprehendit, quos
ait *latrare non agere*. Sunt enim multa vitia, de
quibus dixi, cum in quadam primi libri parte puerorum ora formarem, opportunius ratus, in ea aetate
facere illorum mentionem, in qua emendari possunt.
32 Itemque si ipsa vox primum fuerit, ut sic dicam, sana,

---

　　¹ *Ann.* ix. 305 (Vahlen).　　　² *Brut.* xv. 58.
　　　　³ *i.* i. 37 ; v. 32 ; viii. 1 and xi. 1 *sqq.*

is more heat in the body at other periods), but rather on account of moisture, of which at that age there is a superabundance. For this reason the nostrils and 29 the breast swell at this stage, and all the organs develop new growth, with the result that they are tender and liable to injury. However, to return to the point, the best and most realistic form of exercise for the voice, once it has become firm and set, is, in my opinion, the practice of speaking daily just as we plead in the courts. For thus, not merely do the voice and lungs gain in strength, but we acquire a becoming deportment of the body and develop grace of movement suited to our style of speaking.

The rules for delivery are identical with those for the 30 language of oratory itself. For, as our language must be correct, clear, ornate and appropriate, so with our delivery; it will be correct, that is, free from fault, if our utterance be fluent, clear, pleasant and "urbane," that is to say, free from all traces of a rustic or a foreign accent. For there is good reason for the saying we so 31 often hear, "He must be a barbarian or a Greek": since we may discern a man's nationality from the sound of his voice as easily as we test a coin by its ring. If these qualities be present, we shall have those harmonious accents of which Ennius[1] expresses his approval when he describes Cethegus as one whose "words rang sweetly," and avoid the opposite effect, of which Cicero[2] expresses his disapproval by saying, "They bark, not plead." For there are many faults of which I spoke in the first book[3] when I discussed the method in which the speech of children should be formed, since I thought it more appropriate to mention them in connexion with a period of life when it is still possible to correct them. Again, the 32

id est, nullum eorum, de quibus modo rettuli, patietur
incommodum; deinde non subsurda, rudis, immanis,
dura, rigida, rava,[1] praepinguis, aut tenuis, inanis,
acerba, pusilla, mollis, effeminata, spiritus nec brevis
nec parum durabilis nec in receptu difficilis.

33 Dilucida vero erit pronuntiatio primum, si verba tota
exierint, quorum pars devorari, pars destitui solet,
plerisque extremas syllabas non perferentibus, dum
priorum sono indulgent. Ut est autem necessaria
verborum explanatio, ita omnes imputare et velut
34 adnumerare litteras molestum et odiosum. Nam et
vocales frequentissime coeunt, et consonantium quaedam insequente vocali dissimulantur. Utriusque
exemplum posuimus:

Multum ille et terris —.

35 Vitatur etiam duriorum inter se congressus, unde
pellexit et *collegit*, et quae alio loco dicta sunt; ideoque
laudatur in Catulo suavis appellatio litterarum. Secundum est, ut sit oratio distincta, id est, qui dicit,
et incipiat ubi oportet et desinat. Observandum
etiam, quo loco sustinendus et quasi suspendendus
sermo sit, quod Graeci ὑποδιαστολὴν vel ὑποστιγμὴν
36 vocant, quo deponendus. Suspenditur *Arma virumque cano,* quia illud *virum* ad sequentia pertinet, ut

---

[1] rava, *Burman*: vana, *MSS.*

---

[1] IX. iv. 40.   [2] *Aen.* i. 3.   [3] IX. iv. 37.
[4] *Brut.* lxxiv. 259. "suavitas vocis et lenis appellatio
literarum" ("the sweetness of his voice and the delicacy
with which he pronounced the various letters.")
[5] "A slight stop," corresponding to our "comma."
[6] *Aen.* i. 1.

delivery may be described as correct if the voice be sound, that is to say, exempt from any of the defects of which I have just spoken, and if it is not dull, coarse, exaggerated, hard, stiff, hoarse or thick, or again, thin, hollow, sharp, feeble, soft or effeminate, and if the breath is neither too short nor difficult to sustain or recover.

The delivery will be clear if, in the first place, the 33 words are uttered in their entirety, instead of being swallowed or clipped, as is so often the case, since too many people fail to complete the final syllables through over-emphasising the first. But although words must be given their full phonetic value, it is a tiresome and offensive trick to pronounce every letter as if we were entering them in an inventory. For 34 vowels frequently coalesce and some consonants disappear when followed by a vowel. I have already [1] given an example of both these occurrences:— *multum ille et terris.*[2] Further, we avoid placing two 35 consonants near each other when their juxtaposition would cause a harsh sound; thus, we say *pellexit* and *collegit* and employ other like forms of which I have spoken elsewhere.[3] It is with this in mind that Cicero [4] praises Catulus for the sweetness with which he pronounced the various letters. The second essential for clearness of delivery is that our language should be properly punctuated, that is to say, the speaker must begin and end at the proper place. It is also necessary to note at what point our speech should pause and be momentarily suspended (which the Greeks term ὑποδιαστολή and ὑποστιγμή)[5] and when it should come to a full stop. After the words *arma virumque cano*[6] there is a mo- 36 mentary suspension, because *virum* is connected with

sit *virum Troiae qui primus ab oris,* et hic iterum.
Nam etiamsi aliud est, unde venit quam quo venit,
non distinguendum tamen, quia utrumque eodem
37 verbo continetur *venit.* Tertio *Italiam,* quia interiectio
est *fato profugus* et continuum sermonem, qui faciebat
Italiam Lavinaque, dividit. Ob eandemque causam
quarto *profugus,* deinde *Lavinaque venit litora,* ubi
iam erit distinctio, quia inde alius incipit sensus.
Sed in ipsis etiam distinctionibus tempus alias
brevius, alias longius dabimus; interest enim, ser-
38 monem finiant an sensum. Itaque illam distinctionem
Litora protinus altero spiritus initio insequar; cum
illuc venero *Atque altae moenia Romae,* deponam et
39 morabor et novum rursus exordium faciam. Sunt
aliquando et sine respiratione quaedam morae etiam
in periodis. Ut enim [1] illa *In coetu vero populi Romani,
negotium publicum gerens, magister equitum,* etc., multa
membra habent (sensus enim sunt alii atque alii), sed
unam circumductionem, ita paulum morandum in his
intervallis, non interrumpendus est contextus. Et e
contrario spiritum interim recipere sine intellectu
morae necesse est, quo loco quasi surripiendus est;
alioqui si inscite recipiatur, non minus adferat ob-
scuritatis quam vitiosa distinctio. Virtus autem
distinguendi fortasse sit parva; sine qua tamen esse
nulla alia in agendo potest.

[1] enim, *Obrecht*: in, *MSS.*

---

[1] *Phil.* II. xxv. 63. See *Quint.* VIII. iv. 8.
[2] See IX. iv. 22, 67, 123. The name *colon* is applied to the
longer clauses contained in a period, as opposed to the shorter,
which are styled *commata.*

what follows, the full sense being given by *virum Troiae qui primus ab oris*, after which there is a similar suspension. For although the mention of the hero's destination introduces an idea different from that of the place whence he came, the difference does not call for the insertion of a stop, since both ideas are expressed by the same verb *venit*. After *Italiam* 37 comes a third pause, since *fato profugus* is parenthetic and breaks up the continuity of the phrase *Italiam Lavinaque*. For the same reason there is a fourth pause after *profugus*. Then follows *Lavinaque venit litora*, where a stop must be placed, as at this point a new sentence begins. But stops themselves vary in length, according as they mark the conclusion of a phrase or a sentence. Thus after *litora* I shall 38 pause and continue after taking breath. But when I come to *atque altae moenia Romae* I shall make a full stop, halt and start again with the opening of a fresh sentence. There are also occasionally, even in 39 periods, pauses which do not require a fresh breath. For although the sentence *in coetu vero populi Romani, negotium publicum gerens, magister equitum,*[1] etc., contains a number of different *cola,*[2] expressing a number of different thoughts, all these *cola* are embraced by a single period: consequently, although short pauses are required at the appropriate intervals, the flow of the period as a whole must not be broken. On the other hand, it is at times necessary to take breath without any perceptible pause: in such cases we must do so surreptitiously, since if we take breath unskilfully, it will cause as much obscurity as would have resulted from faulty punctuation. Correctness of punctuation may seem to be but a trivial merit, but without it all the other merits of oratory are nothing worth.

40 Ornata est pronuntiatio, cui suffragatur vox facilis, magna, beata, flexibilis, firma, dulcis, durabilis, clara, pura, secans aëra et auribus sedens (est enim quaedam ad auditum accommodata non magnitudine, sed proprietate), ad hoc velut tractabilis, utique habens omnes in se qui desiderantur sinus intentionesque et toto, ut aiunt, organo instructa; cui aderit lateris firmitas, spiritus cum spatio pertinax, tum labori non

41 facile cessurus. Neque gravissimus autem in musica sonus nec acutissimus orationibus convenit. Nam et hic parum clarus nimiumque plenus nullum adferre animis motum potest, et ille praetenuis et immodicae claritatis, cum est ultra verum, tum neque pronuntiatione flecti neque diutius ferre intentionem potest.

42 Nam vox ut nervi, quo remissior, hoc gravior et plenior, quo tensior, hoc tenuis et acuta magis est. Sic ima vim non habet, summa rumpi periclitatur. Mediis ergo utendum sonis, hique tum augenda intentione excitandi, tum summittenda sunt temperandi.

43 Nam prima est observatio recte pronuntiandi aequalitas, ne sermo subsultet imparibus spatiis ac sonis, miscens longa brevibus, gravia acutis, elata summissis, et inaequalitate horum omnium sicut

Delivery will be ornate when it is supported by 40
a voice that is easy, strong, rich, flexible, firm, sweet,
enduring, resonant, pure, carrying far and penetrat-
ing the ear (for there is a type of voice which
impresses the hearing not by its volume, but by its
peculiar quality): in addition, the voice must be
easily managed and must possess all the necessary
inflexions and modulations, in fact it must, as the
saying is, be a perfect instrument, equipped with
every stop: further, it must have strong lungs to
sustain it, and ample breathing power that will be
equal to all demands upon it, however fatiguing. The 41
deepest bass and the highest treble notes are un-
suited to oratory: for the former lack clearness and,
owing to their excessive fullness, have no emotional
power, while the latter are too thin and, owing to
excess of clearness, give an impression of extravagance and are incompatible with the inflexions
demanded by delivery and place too great a strain
upon the voice. For the voice is like the strings of 42
a musical instrument; the slacker it is the deeper
and fuller the note produced, whereas if it be
tightened, the sound becomes thinner and shriller.
Consequently, the deepest notes lack force, and the
higher run the risk of cracking the voice. The orator
will, therefore, employ the intermediate notes, which
must be raised when we speak with energy and
lowered when we adopt a more subdued tone.

For the first essential of a good delivery is even- 43
ness. The voice must not run joltingly, with
irregularity of rhythm and sound, mixing long and
short syllables, grave accents and acute, tones loud
and low, without discrimination, the result being that
this universal unevenness produces the impression of

pedum claudicet; secunda varietas, quod solum est
44 pronuntiatio. Ac ne quis pugnare inter se putet
aequalitatem et varietatem, cum illi virtuti contrarium vitium sit inaequalitas, huic, quod dicitur
μονοείδεια, quasi quidam unus aspectus. Ars porro
variandi cum gratiam praebet ac renovat aures, tum
dicentem ipsa laboris mutatione reficit, ut standi,
45 ambulandi, sedendi, iacendi vices sunt, nihilque
eorum pati unum diu possumus. Illud vero maximum (sed id paulo post tractabimus), quod secundum
rationem rerum, de quibus dicimus, animorumque
habitus conformanda vox est, ne ab oratione dis-
cordet. Vitemus igitur illam, quae Graece μονοτονία
vocatur, una quaedam spiritus ac soni intentio; non
solum ne dicamus omnia clamose, quod insanum est,
aut intra loquendi modum, quod motu caret, aut
summisso murmure, quo etiam debilitatur omnis
46 intentio; sed ut in iisdem partibus iisdemque adfectibus sint tamen quaedam non ita magnae vocis
declinationes, prout aut verborum dignitas aut
sententiarum natura aut depositio aut inceptio aut
transitus postulabit: ut, qui singulis pinxerunt
coloribus, alia tamen eminentiora alia reductiora

a limping gait. The second essential is variety of
tone, and it is in this alone that delivery really consists. I must warn my readers not to fall into the **44**
error of supposing that evenness and variety are incompatible with one another, since the fault opposed
to evenness is unevenness, while the opposite of
variety is that which the Greeks term μονοείδεια, or
uniformity of aspect. The art of producing variety
not merely charms and refreshes the ear, but, by the
very fact that it involves a change of effort, revives
the speaker's flagging energies. It is like the relief
caused by changes in position, such as are involved
by standing, walking, sitting and lying, none of
which can be endured for a long time together.
But the most important point (which I shall proceed **45**
to discuss a little later) is the necessity of adapting
the voice to suit the nature of the various subjects
on which we are speaking and the moods that they
demand : otherwise our voice will be at variance with
our language. We must, therefore, avoid that which
the Greeks call *monotony*, that is to say, the unvary-
ing exertion both of lungs and voice. By this I do
not simply mean that we must avoid saying everything in a loud tone, a fault which amounts to
madness, or in a colloquial tone, which creates an
impression of lifelessness, or in a subdued murmur,
which is utterly destructive of all vigour. What I **46**
mean is this : within the limits of one passage and the
compass of one emotion we may vary our tone to a
certain, though not a very great extent, according
as the dignity of the language, the nature of the
thought, the conclusion and opening of our sentences or transitions from one point to another, may
demand. Thus, those who paint in monochrome

fecerunt, sine quo ne membris quidem suas lineas
47 dedissent. Proponamus enim nobis illud Ciceronis
in oratione nobilissima pro Milone principium ; nonne
ad singulas paene distinctiones quamvis in eadem
facie tamen quasi vultus mutandus est ? *Etsi vereor,
iudices, ne turpe sit, pro fortissimo viro dicere incipientem*
48 *timere.* Etiamsi est toto proposito contractum atque
summissum, quia et exordium est et solliciti exordium,
tamen fuerit necesse est aliquid plenius et erectius,
dum dicit *Pro fortissimo viro,* quam cum *Etsi vereor* et
49 *Turpe sit* et *Timere.* Iam secunda respiratio increscat
oportet et naturali quodam conatu, quo minus pavide
dicimus quae sequuntur, et quod magnitudo animi
Milonis ostenditur : *Minimeque deceat, cum T. Annius
ipse magis de rei publicae salute quam de sua perturbetur.*
Deinde quasi obiurgatio sui est : *Me ad eius causam
50 parem animi magnitudinem adferre non posse.* Tum
invidiosiora : *Tamen haec novi iudicii nova forma terret
oculos.* Illa vero iam paene apertis, ut aiunt, tibiis :
*Qui, quocunque inciderunt, consuetudinem fori et pristinum
morem iudiciorum requirunt.* Nam sequens latum etiam
atque fusum est : *Non enim corona consessus vester
51 cinctus est, ut solebat.* Quod notavi, ut appareret, non
solum in membris causae, sed etiam in articulis esse

---

[1] *pro Mil.* i. 1 *sqq.* "Although I fear, gentlemen, that it
may be discreditable that I should feel afraid on rising to
defend the bravest of men, and though it is far from becoming
that, whereas Titus Annius is more concerned for the safety
of the State than for his own, I should be unable to bring a
like degree of courage to aid me in pleading his cause ; still,
the strange appearance of this novel tribunal dismays my
eyes, which, whithersoever they turn, look in vain for the

still represent their objects in different planes, since
otherwise it would have been impossible to depict
even the limbs of their figures. Let us take as an 47
example the opening of Cicero's magnificent speech
in defence of Milo. Is it not clear that the orator
has to change his tone almost at every stop? it is the
same face, but the expression is changed. *Etsi vereor,
iudices, ne turpe sit, pro fortissimo viro dicere incipientem* 48
timere.[1] Although the general tone of the passage is
restrained and subdued, since it is not merely an
exordium, but the *exordium* of a man suffering from
serious anxiety, still something fuller and bolder is
required in the tone, when he says *pro fortissimo viro,*
than when he says *etsi vereor* and *turpe sit* and *timere.*
But his second breath must be more vigorous, partly 49
owing to the natural increase of effort, since we
always speak our second sentence with less timidity,
and partly because he indicates the high courage of
Milo: *minimeque deceat, cum T. Annius ipse magis de
rei publicae salute quam de sua perturbetur.* Then he
proceeds to something like a reproof of himself: *me
ad eius causam parem animi magnitudinem adferre non
posse.* The next clause suggests a reflexion on the 50
conduct of others: *tamen haec novi iudicii nova forma
terret oculos.* And then in what follows he opens
every stop, as the saying is: *qui, quocunque inciderunt,
consuetudinem fori et pristinum morem iudiciorum requirunt:* while the next clause is even fuller and freer:
non enim corona consessus vester cinctus est, ut solebat.
I have called attention to these points to make it 51
clear that there is a certain variety, not merely in

customary aspect of the forum and the time-honoured usage
of the courts. For your bench is not surrounded, as it used
to be, by a ring of spectators," etc.

aliquam pronuntiandi varietatem, sine qua nihil neque maius neque minus est.

Vox autem ultra vires urgenda non est. Nam et suffocatur saepe et maiore nisu minus clara est et interim elisa in illum sonum erumpit, cui Graeci 52 nomen a gallorum immaturo cantu dederunt. Nec volubilitate nimia confundenda quae dicimus, qua et distinctio perit et adfectus, et nonnunquam etiam verba aliqua sui parte fraudantur. Cui contrarium est vitium nimiae tarditatis; nam et difficultatem inveniendi fatetur et segnitia solvit animos et, in quo est aliquid, temporibus praefinitis aquam perdit. Promptum sit os, non praeceps, moderatum, non 53 lentum; spiritus quoque nec crebro receptus concidat sententiam, nec eo usque trahatur, donec deficiat. Nam et deformis est consumpti illius sonus et respiratio sub aqua diu pressi similis et receptus longior et non opportunus, ut qui fiat non ubi volumus, sed ubi necesse est. Quare longiorem dicturis periodum colligendus est spiritus, ita tamen, ut id neque diu neque cum sono faciamus, neque omnino ut manifestum sit; reliquis partibus optime 54 inter iuncturas sermonis revocabitur. Exercendus autem est, ut sit quam longissimus; quod Demosthenes ut efficeret, scandens in adversum continuabat

---

[1] What this word was is not known. Perhaps merely κοκκυσμός.

[2] *aquam perdit.* Lit. wastes water. The reference is to the clepsydra or water-clock employed for the measurement of time.

the delivery of *cola*, but even in that of phrases consisting of one word, a variety the lack of which would make every word seem of equal importance.

The voice, however, must not be pressed beyond its powers, for it is liable to be choked and to become less and less clear in proportion to the increase of effort, while at times it will break altogether and produce the sound to which the Greeks have given a name derived from the crowing of cocks before the voice is developed.[1] We must also beware of con-52 fusing our utterance by excessive volubility, which results in disregard of punctuation, loss of emotional power, and sometimes in the clipping of words. The opposite fault is excessive slowness of speech, which is a sign of lack of readiness in invention, tends by its sluggishness to render our hearers inattentive, and, further, wastes the time allotted to us for speaking,[2] a consideration which is of some importance. Our speech must be ready, but not precipitate, under control, but not slow, while we must not take breath 53 so often as to break up our sentence, nor, on the other hand, sustain it until it fails us from exhaustion. For the sound produced by loss of breath is disagreeable; we gasp like a drowning man and fill our lungs with long-drawn inhalations at inappropriate moments, giving the impression that our action is due not to choice, but to compulsion. Therefore, in attacking a period of abnormal length, we should collect our breath, but quickly, noiselessly and imperceptibly. On other occasions we shall be able to take breath at the natural breaks in the substance of our speech. But we must exercise our breathing capacity to make 54 it as great as possible. To produce this result Demosthenes used to recite as many successive lines as

quam posset plurimos versus. Idem, quo facilius
verba ore libero exprimeret, calculos lingua volvens
55 dicere domi solebat. Est interim et longus et plenus
et clarus satis spiritus, non tamen firmae intentionis
ideoque tremulus, ut corpora, quae aspectu integra
nervis parum sustinentur; id βρασμὸν[1] Graeci vocant.
Sunt qui spiritum cum stridore per raritatem dentium
non recipiunt, sed resorbent. Sunt qui crebro
anhelitu et introrsum etiam clare sonante imitentur
56 iumenta onere et iugo laborantia. Quod adfectant
quoque, tanquam inventionis copia urgeantur maior-
que vis eloquentiae ingruat, quam quae emitti
faucibus possit. Est aliis concursus oris et cum verbis
suis colluctatio. Iam tussire et exspuere crebro
et ab imo pulmone pituitam trochleis[2] adducere et
oris humore proximos spargere et maiorem partem
spiritus in loquendo per nares effundere, etiamsi non
utique vocis sunt vitia, quia tamen propter vocem
57 accidunt, potissimum huic loco subiiciantur. Sed
quodcunque ex his vitium magis tulerim quam, quo
nunc maxime laboratur in causis omnibus scholisque,

---

[1] βρασμὸν, *Butler*: ΒΓΑΜΟΝ, *cod. Bern.*: ΒΡΑΜΟΝ, *cod.
Bamb.*: βράγχον, *Gesner and ed. Tarvis.*

---

[1] βράγχος is generally read, but the word is used in the
sense of "hoarseness," which is not what Quintilian describes.
I would read βρασμός, a word meaning "effervescence,"
"shaking," "shivering." Here = *tremolo*.
[2] *trochlea* is a windlass used for raising water from a
well.

possible, while he was climbing a hill. He also, with
a view to securing fluency free from impediment,
used to roll pebbles under his tongue when speaking
in the privacy of his study. Sometimes the breath, 55
although capable of sustained effort and sufficiently
full and clear, lacks firmness when exerted, and for
that reason is liable to become tremulous, like bodies
which, although to all appearances sound, receive
insufficient support from the sinews. This the Greeks
call βρασμός.[1] There are some too who, owing to
the loss of teeth, do not draw in the breath naturally,
but suck it in with a hissing sound. There are
others who pant incessantly and so loudly that it
is perfectly audible within them: they remind one
of heavily-laden beasts of burden straining against
the yoke. Some indeed actually affect this man- 56
nerism, as though to suggest that they are struggling
with the host of ideas that crowd themselves upon
them and oppressed by a greater flood of eloquence
than their throats are capable of uttering. Others,
again, find a difficulty in opening their mouths, and
seem to struggle with their words; and, further,
although they are not actually faults of the voice,
yet since they arise out of the use of the voice,
I think this is the most appropriate place for
referring to the habit of coughing and spitting with
frequency while speaking, of hawking up phlegm
from the depths of the lungs, like water from a
well,[2] sprinkling the nearest of the bystanders with
saliva, and expelling the greater portion of the
breath through the nostrils. But any of these faults 57
are tolerable compared with the practice of chanting
instead of speaking, which is the worst feature of
our modern oratory, whether in the courts or in the

cantandi, quod inutilius sit an foedius, nescio. Quid
enim minus oratori convenit quam modulatio scenica
et nonnunquam ebriorum aut comissantium licentiae
58 similis? Quid vero movendis adfectibus contrarium
magis quam, cum dolendum,[1] irascendum, indig-
nandum, commiserandum sit, non solum ab his
adfectibus, in quos inducendus est iudex, recedere,
sed ipsam fori sanctitatem Lyciorum et Carum[2]
licentia solvere? Nam Cicero *illos ex Lycia et Caria*[3]
rhetoras paene cantare in epilogis dixit. Nos etiam
59 cantandi severiorem paulo modum excessimus. Quis-
quamne, non dico de homicidio, sacrilegio, parricidio,
sed de calculis certe atque rationibus, quisquam
denique, ut semel finiam, in lite cantat? Quod si
omnino recipiendum est, nihil causae est, cur non
illam vocis modulationem fidibus ac tibiis, immo me
hercule, quod est huic deformitati propius, cymbalis
60 adiuvemus. Facimus tamen hoc libenter; nam nec
cuiquam sunt iniucunda quae cantant ipsi, et laboris
in hoc quam in agendo minus est. Et sunt quidam,
qui secundum alia vitae vitia etiam hac ubique
audiendi, quod aures mulceat, voluptate ducantur.

---

[1] dolendum, *Regius*: docendum, *B. and Iul. Victor.*
[2] Lyciorum et Carum, *Daniel*: ludorum talarium, *MSS.*
[3] Phrygia, *MSS. of Cicero.*

---

[1] *Or.* xviii. 57.

schools, and of which I can only say that I do not
know whether it is more useless or more repugnant
to good taste. For what can be less becoming to
an orator than modulations that recall the stage and
a sing-song utterance which at times resembles the
maudlin utterance of drunken revellers? What can 58
be more fatal to any emotional appeal than that the
speaker should, when the situation calls for grief,
anger, indignation or pity, not merely avoid the
expression of those emotions which require to be
kindled in the judge, but outrage the dignity of
the courts with noises such as are dear to the
Lycians and Carians? For Cicero [1] has told us that
the rhetoricians of Lycia and Caria come near to
singing in their perorations. But, as a matter of fact,
we have somewhat overstepped the limits imposed by
the more restrained style of singing. I ask you, 59
does anyone sing, I will not say when his theme is
murder, sacrilege or parricide, but at any rate when
he deals with figures or accounts, or, to cut a long
story short, when he is pleading in any kind of
lawsuit whatever? And if such a form of intonation
is to be permitted at all, there is really no reason
why the modulations of the voice should not be
accompanied by harps and flutes, or even by cymbals,
which would be more appropriate to the revolting
exhibitions of which I am speaking. And yet we 60
show no reluctance in indulging this vicious practice.
For no one thinks his own singing hideous, and it
involves less trouble than genuine pleading. There
are, moreover, some persons who, in thorough conformity with their other vices, are possessed with a
perpetual passion for hearing something that will
soothe their ears. But, it may be urged, does not

Quid ergo? non et Cicero dicit esse aliquem in oratione *cantum obscuriorem*? et hoc quodam naturali initio venit? Ostendam non multo post, ubi et quatenus recipiendus sit hic flexus et cantus quidem sed, quod plerique intelligere nolunt, obscurior.

61 Iam enim tempus est dicendi, quae sit apta pronuntiatio. Quae certe ea est, quae iis, de quibus dicimus, accommodatur. Quod quidem maxima ex parte praestant ipsi motus animorum, sonatque vox, ut feritur; sed cum sint alii veri adfectus, alii ficti et imitati, veri naturaliter erumpunt, ut dolentium, irascentium, indignantium, sed carent arte, ideoque 62 sunt disciplina et ratione formandi. Contra qui effinguntur imitatione, artem habent; sed hi carent natura, ideoque in iis primum est bene adfici et concipere imagines rerum et tanquam veris moveri. Sic velut media vox, quem habitum a nobis acceperit, hunc iudicum animis dabit. Est enim mentis index 63 ac totidem, quot illa, mutationes habet. Itaque laetis in rebus plena et simplex et ipsa quodammodo hilaris fluit; at in certamine erecta totis viribus et velut omnibus nervis intenditur. Atrox in ira et aspera

---

[1] *Or.* xviii. 57.

Cicero[1] himself say that there is a suggestion of singing in the utterance of an orator? And is not this the outcome of a natural impulse? I shall shortly proceed to show to what extent such musical modulations are permissible: but if we are to call it singing, it must be no more than a suggestion of singing, a fact which too many refuse to realise.

But it is now high time for me to explain what I 61 mean by appropriate delivery. Such appropriateness obviously lies in the adaptation of the delivery to the subjects on which we are speaking. This quality is, in the main, supplied by the emotions themselves, and the voice will ring as passion strikes its chords. But there is a difference between true emotion on the one hand, and false and fictitious emotion on the other. The former breaks out naturally, as in the case of grief, anger or indignation, but lacks art, and therefore requires to be formed by methodical training. The latter, on the other hand, does imply 62 art, but lacks the sincerity of nature: consequently in such cases the main thing is to excite the appropriate feeling in oneself, to form a mental picture of the facts, and to exhibit an emotion that cannot be distinguished from the truth. The voice, which is the intermediary between ourselves and our hearers, will then produce precisely the same emotion in the judge that we have put into it. For it is the index of the mind, and is capable of expressing all its varieties of feeling. Therefore when we 63 deal with a lively theme, the flow of the voice is characterised by fullness, simplicity and cheerfulness; but when it is roused to battle, it puts forth all its strength and strains every nerve. In anger

ac densa et respiratione crebra; neque enim potest
esse longus spiritus, cum immoderate effunditur.
Paulum in invidia facienda lentior, quia non fere ad
hanc nisi inferiores confugiunt; at in blandiendo,
fatendo, satisfaciendo, rogando, lenis et summissa.

64 Suadentium et monentium et pollicentium et conso-
lantium gravis, in metu et verecundia contracta,
adhortationibus fortis, disputationibus teres, miseratione flexa et flebilis et consulto quasi obscurior; at
in egressionibus fusa et securae claritatis, in expositione ac sermonibus recta et inter acutum sonum

65 et gravem media.   Attollitur autem concitatis
adfectibus, compositis descendit pro utriusque rei
modo altius vel inferius.

Quid autem quisque in dicendo postulet locus,
paulum differam, ut de gestu prius dicam, qui et
ipse voci consentit et animo cum ea simul paret.   Is
quantum habeat in oratore momenti, satis vel ex eo
patet quod pleraque etiam citra verba significat.

66 Quippe non manus solum, sed nutus etiam declarant
nostram voluntatem et in mutis pro sermone sunt,
et saltatio frequenter sine voce intelligitur atque
adficit, et ex vultu ingressuque perspicitur habitus

it is fierce, harsh and intense, and calls for frequent filling of the lungs, since the breath cannot be sustained for long when it is poured forth without restraint. When it is desired to throw odium upon our opponents, it will be somewhat slower, since, as a rule, it is none save the weaker party takes refuge in such tactics. On the other hand, in flattery, admission, apology or question it will be gentle and subdued. If we advise, warn, promise or console, 64 it will be grave and dignified, modest if we express fear or shame, bold in exhortation, precise in argument, full of modulations, suggestive of tears and designedly muffled in appeals for pity, whereas in digression it will be full and flowing, and will have all the resonance that is characteristic of confidence; in exposition of facts or conversations it will be even and pitched half-way betwixt high and low. But it will be raised to express violent emotion, and 65 sink when our words are of a calmer nature, rising and falling according to the demands of its theme.

However, for the moment I will defer speaking of the variations in tone required by different topics, and will proceed first to the discussion of gesture which conforms to the voice, and like it, obeys the impulse of the mind. Its importance in oratory is sufficiently clear from the fact that there are many things which it can express without the assistance of words. For we can indicate our will not merely 66 by a gesture of the hands, but also with a nod from the head: signs take the place of language in the dumb, and the movements of the dance are frequently full of meaning, and appeal to the emotions without any aid from words. The temper of the mind can be inferred from the glance and gait,

animorum; et animalium quoque sermone carentium
ira, laetitia, adulatio et oculis et quibusdam aliis
67 corporis signis deprehenditur. Nec mirum, si ista,
quae tamen in aliquo posita sunt motu, tantum in
animis valent, cum pictura, tacens opus et habitus
semper eiusdem, sic in intimos penetret adfectus,
ut ipsam vim dicendi nonnunquam superare videatur.
Contra si gestus ac vultus ab oratione dissentiat,
tristia dicamus hilares, adfirmemus aliqua renuentes
non auctoritas modo verbis, sed etiam fides desit.
68 Decor quoque a gestu atque motu venit; ideoque
Demosthenes grande quoddam intuens speculum
componere actionem solebat; adeo, quamvis fulgor
ille sinistras imagines reddat, suis demum oculis
credidit, quod efficeret.

Praecipuum vero in actione sicut in corpore ipso
caput est cum ad illum, de quo dixi, decorem, tum
69 etiam ad significationem. Decoris illa sunt, ut sit
primo rectum et secundum naturam. Nam et de-
iecto humilitas et supino arrogantia et in latus
inclinato languor et praeduro ac rigente barbaria
quaedam mentis ostenditur. Tum accipiat aptos ex
ipsa actione motus, ut cum gestu concordet et
70 manibus ac lateribus obsequatur. Aspectus enim
semper eodem vertitur quo gestus, exceptis quae aut

and even speechless animals show anger, joy, or the
desire to please by means of the eye and other
physical indications.   Nor is it wonderful that ges- 67
ture which depends on various forms of movement
should have such power, when pictures, which are
silent and motionless, penetrate into our innermost
feelings with such power that at times they seem
more eloquent than language itself.   On the other
hand, if gesture and the expression of the face are
out of harmony with the speech, if we look cheerful
when our words are sad, or shake our heads when
making a positive assertion, our words will not only
lack weight, but will fail to carry conviction.   Ges- 68
ture and movement are also productive of grace.
It was for this reason that Demosthenes used to
practise his delivery in front of a large mirror, since,
in spite of the fact that its reflexions are reversed,
he trusted his eyes to enable him to judge accurately
the effect produced.

The head, being the chief member of the body,
has a corresponding importance in delivery, serving
not merely to produce graceful effect, but to illustrate our meaning as well.   To secure grace it is 69
essential that the head should be carried naturally
and erect.   For a droop suggests humility, while if
it be thrown back it seems to express arrogance, if
inclined to one side it gives an impression of languor,
while if it is held too stiffly and rigidly it appears
to indicate a rude and savage temper.   Further, it
should derive appropriate motion from the subject
of our pleading, maintaining harmony with the gesture and following the movement of the hands and
side.   For the eyes are always turned in the same 70
direction as the gesture, except when we are called

damnare aut concedere aut a nobis removere opor-
tebit, ut idem illud vultu videamur aversari, manu
repellere :

  — *Di talem avertite pestem.*

  — *Haud equidem tali me dignor honore.*

71 Significat vero plurimis modis. Nam praeter adnuendi, renuendi confirmandique motus sunt et verecundiae et dubitationis et admirationis et indigna-
tionis noti et communes omnibus. Solo tamen eo
facere gestum scenici quoque doctores vitiosum
putaverunt. Etiam frequens eius nutus non caret
vitio; adeo iactare id et comas excutientem rotare
fanaticum est.

72   Dominatur autem maxime vultus. Hoc supplices,
hoc minaces, hoc blandi, hoc tristes, hoc hilares, hoc
erecti, hoc summissi sumus; hoc pendent homines,
hunc intuentur, hic spectatur, etiam antequam
dicimus; hoc quosdam amamus, hoc odimus, hoc
plurima intelligimus, hic est saepe pro omnibus
73 verbis. Itaque in iis, quae ad scenam componuntur,
fabulis artifices pronuntiandi a personis quoque adfectus mutuantur, ut sit Aerope in tragoedia tristis,

---

   [1] *Aen.* iii. 620.   [2] *Aen.* i. 335.

upon to condemn or concede something or to express abhorrence, when we shall show our aversion by turning away the face and by thrusting out our hands as though to repel the thought, as in the lines :

> "Ye gods, such dread calamity avert!"[1]

or

> "Not for me
> To claim such honour!"[2]

The methods by which the head may express our 71 meaning are manifold. For in addition to those movements which indicate consent, refusal and affirmation, there are those expressive of modesty, hesitation, wonder or indignation, which are well known and common to all. But to confine the gesture to the movement of the head alone is regarded as a fault by those who teach acting as well as by professors of rhetoric. Even the frequent nodding of the head is not free from fault, while to toss or roll it till our hair flies free is suggestive of a fanatic.

By far the greatest influence is exercised by the 72 glance. For it is by this that we express supplication, threats, flattery, sorrow, joy, pride or submission. It is on this that our audience hang, on this that they rivet their attention and their gaze, even before we begin to speak. It is this that inspires the hearer with affection or dislike, this that conveys a world of meaning and is often more eloquent than all our words. Consequently in plays 73 destined for the stage, the masters of the art of delivery design even their masks to enhance the emotional effect. Thus, in tragedy, Aerope will be

atrox Medea, attonitus Aiax, truculentus Hercules.
74 In comoediis vero praeter aliam observationem, qua
servi, lenones, parasiti, rustici, milites, meretriculae,
ancillae, senes austeri ac mites, iuvenes severi ac
luxuriosi, matronae, puellae inter se discernuntur,
pater ille, cuius praecipuae partes sunt, quia interim
concitatus, interim lenis est, altero erecto, altero
composito est supercilio; atque id ostendere maxime
latus actoribus moris est, quod cum iis, quas agunt,
75 partibus congruat.   Sed in ipso vultu plurimum
valent oculi, per quos maxime animus eminet,[1] ut
citra motum quoque et hilaritate enitescant et
tristitiae quoddam nubilum ducant.   Quin etiam
lacrimas iis natura mentis indices dedit, quae aut
erumpunt dolore aut laetitia manant.   Motu vero
intenti, remissi, superbi, torvi, mites, asperi fiunt,
76 quae, ut actus poposcerit, fingentur.   Rigidi vero et
extenti, aut languidi et torpentes, aut stupentes, aut
lascivi et mobiles, et natantes et quadam voluptate
suffusi, aut limi et, ut sic dicam, venerei, aut pos-
centes aliquid pollicentesve nunquam esse debebunt.
Nam opertos compressosve eos in dicendo quis nisi
77 plane rudis aut stultus habeat?   Et ad haec omnia
exprimenda in palpebris etiam et in genis est quoddam
78 deserviens iis ministerium.   Multum et superciliis
agitur.   Nam et oculos formant aliquatenus et fronti

---

[1] animus eminet, *Spalding*: anima se manat, *B.*

sad, Medea fierce, Ajax bewildered, Hercules trucu-
lent. In comedy, on the other hand, over and 74
above the methods adopted to distinguish between
slaves, pimps, parasites, rustics, soldiers, harlots,
maidservants, old men stern and mild, youths moral
or luxurious, married women and girls, we have
the important rôle of the father who, because at
times he is excited and at others calm, has one
eyebrow raised and the other normal, the custom
among actors being to turn that side of the face to
the audience which best suits the rôle. But of the 75
various elements that go to form the expression,
the eyes are the most important, since they, more
than anything else, reveal the temper of the mind,
and without actual movement will twinkle with
merriment or be clouded with grief. And further,
nature has given them tears to serve as interpreters
of our feelings, tears that will break forth for sorrow
or stream for very joy. But, when the eyes move,
they become intent, indifferent, proud, fierce, mild,
or angry; and they will assume all these characters
according as the pleading may demand. But they 76
must never be fixed or protruding, languid or sluggish, lifeless, lascivious, restless, nor swim with a
moist voluptuous glance, nor look aslant nor leer
in amorous fashion, nor yet must they seem to
promise or ask a boon. As for keeping them fully
or partially closed while speaking, surely none save
an uneducated man or a fool would dream of doing
such a thing. And in addition to all these forms of 77
expression, the upper and lower eyelids can render
service in support of the eyes. The eyebrows also 78
may be used with great effect. For to some extent
they mould the expression of the eyes and deter-

imperant. His contrahitur, attollitur, remittitur, ut
una res in ea plus valeat, sanguis ille, qui mentis
habitu movetur et, cum infirmam verecundia cutem
accipit, effunditur in ruborem, cum metu refugit,
abit omnis et pallore frigescit; temperatus medium
79 quoddam serenum efficit. Vitium in superciliis, si
aut immota sunt omnino aut nimium mobilia aut
inaequalitate, ut modo de persona comica dixeram,
dissident aut contra id quod dicimus finguntur.
Ira enim contractis, tristitia deductis, hilaritas remissis ostenditur. Adnuendi quoque et renuendi
80 ratione demittuntur aut allevantur. Naribus labrisque
non fere quidquam decenter ostendimus, tametsi
derisus iis,[1] contemptus, fastidium significari solet.
Nam et *corrugare nares,* ut Horatius ait, et inflare et
movere et digito inquietare et impulso subito spiritu
excutere et diducere saepius et plana manu resu-
pinare indecorum est, cum emunctio etiam fre-
81 quentior non sine causa reprehendatur. Labra et
porriguntur male et scinduntur et adstringuntur et
diducuntur et dentes nudant et in latus ac paene ad
aurem trahuntur et velut quodam fastidio replican-
tur et pendent et vocem tantum altera parte dimit-

---

[1] derisus iis, *Obrecht*: derisui, *B.*

---

[1] *Ep.* i. v. 23.
[2] It is hard to distinguish between *scindere* and *diducere.*
I have adopted a suggestion of Spalding's.

mine that of the forehead. It is by means of the
eyebrows that we contract, raise or smooth the
latter: in fact, the only thing which has greater
influence over it is the blood, which moves in conformity with the emotions that control the mind,
causing a blush on a skin that is sensitive to shame,
and giving place to an icy pallor under the influence
of fear, whereas, when it is under control, it produces a peaceful complexion, intermediate between
the two. Complete immobility in the eyebrows is 79
a fault, as also is excess of mobility or the tendency
to raise one and lower the other, as in the comic
mask which I mentioned just now: while it is a
further blemish if they express a feeling out of
keeping with the words we utter. For they show
anger by contraction, grief by depression and cheerfulness by their expansion. They are also dropped
or raised to express consent or refusal respectively.
It is not often that the lips or nostrils can be 80
becomingly employed to express our feelings, although they are often used to indicate derision,
contempt or loathing. For to " wrinkle the nostrils ''
(as Horace says),[1] or blow them out, or twitch them,
or fret them with our finger, or snort through them
with a sudden expulsion of the breath, or stretch
them wide or push them up with the flat of the
hand are all indecorous, since it is not without reason
that censure is passed even on blowing the nose too
frequently. It is also an ugly habit to protrude the 81
lips, open them with a sudden smack,[2] compress
them, draw them apart and bare the teeth, or twist
them awry to one side till they almost reach the
ear, or to curl them in scorn, or let them droop, or
allow the voice to escape only on one side. It is

tunt. Lambere quoque ea et mordere deforme est,
cum etiam in efficiendis verbis modicus eorum esse
debeat motus; ore enim magis quam labris loquendum est.

82 Cervicem rectam oportet esse, non rigidam aut
supinam. Collum diversa quidem, sed pari deformi-
tate et contrahitur et tenditur, sed tenso subest et
labor, tenuaturque vox ac fatigatur; adfixum pectori
mentum minus claram et quasi latiorem presso gut-
83 ture facit. Humerorum raro decens adlevatio atque
contractio est; breviatur enim cervix et gestum
quendam humilem atque servilem et quasi frauda-
lentum facit, cum se in habitum adulationis, admira-
84 tionis, metus fingunt. Brachii moderata proiectio,
remissis humeris atque explicantibus se in proferenda
manu digitis, continuos et decurrentes locos maxime
decet. At cum speciosius quid uberiusque dicendum
est, ut illud *Saxa atque solitudines voci respondent,*[1]
exspatiatur in latus et ipsa quodammodo se cum
85 gestu fundit oratio. Manus vero, sine quibus trunca
esset actio ac debilis, vix dici potest, quot motus
habeant, cum paene ipsam verborum copiam consequantur. Nam ceterae partes loquentem adiuvant,
86 hae, prope est ut dicam, ipsae loquuntur. Annon
his poscimus, pollicemur, vocamus, dimittimùs, mina-
mur, supplicamus, abominamur, timemus, interro-
gamus, negamus; gaudium, tristitiam, dubitationem,

---

[1] *pro Arch.* viii. 19. See VIII. iii. 75 and IX. iv. 44.
"Rocks and solitude make answer to the voice."

also unbecoming to lick or bite them, since their
motion should be but slight even when they are
employed in forming words. For we must speak
with the mouth rather than the lips.

The neck must be straight, not stiff or bent 82
backward. As regards the throat, contraction and
stretching are equally unbecoming, though in different ways. If it be stretched, it causes strain
as well, and weakens and fatigues the voice,
while if the chin be pressed down into the chest
it makes the voice less distinct and coarsens it,
owing to the pressure on the windpipe. It is, as a 83
rule, unbecoming to raise or contract the shoulders.
For it shortens the neck and produces a mean and
servile gesture, which is even suggestive of dis-
honesty when men assume an attitude of flattery,
admiration or fear. In continuous and flowing pas- 84
sages a most becoming gesture is slightly to extend
the arm with shoulders well thrown back and the
fingers opening as the hand moves forward. But
when we have to speak in specially rich or impressive style, as, for example, in the passage *saxa atque
solitudines voci respondent*,[1] the arm will be thrown out
in a stately sidelong sweep and the words will, as
it were, expand in unison with the gesture. As 85
for the hands, without which all action would be
crippled and enfeebled, it is scarcely possible to
describe the variety of their motions, since they are
almost as expressive as words. For other portions
of the body merely help the speaker, whereas the
hands may almost be said to speak. Do we not 86
use them to demand, promise, summon, dismiss,
threaten, supplicate, express aversion or fear, question
or deny? Do we not employ them to indicate joy,

confessionem, paenitentiam, modum, copiam, nu-
87 merum, tempus ostendimus? Non eaedem concitant, inhibent,[1] probant, admirantur, verecundantur?
Non in demonstrandis locis ac personis adverbiorum
atque pronominum obtinent vicem? Ut in tanta
per omnes gentes nationesque linguae diversitate hic
mihi omnium hominum communis sermo videatur.

88 Et hi quidem, de quibus sum locutus, cum ipsis
vocibus naturaliter exeunt gestus; alii sunt, qui res
imitatione significant, ut si aegrum temptantis venas
medici similitudine aut citharoedum formatis ad
modum percutientis nervos manibus ostendas; quod
est genus quam longissime in actione fugiendum.

89 Abesse enim plurimum a saltatore debet orator, ut
sit gestus ad sensus magis quam ad verba accommodatus; quod etiam histrionibus paulo gravioribus
facere moris fuit. Ergo ut ad se manum referre,
cum de se ipso loquatur, et in eum quem demonstret
intendere et aliqua his similia permiserim, ita non
effingere status quosdam et quidquid dicet osten-

90 dere. Neque id in manibus solum, sed in omni
gestu ac voce servandum est. Non enim aut in illa
periodo, *Stetit soleatus praetor populi Romani*, incli-
natio incumbentis in mulierculam Verris effingenda
est; aut in illa, *Caedebatur in medio foro Messanae*,

---

[1] *After* inhibent *the MSS. add* supplicant, *rightly deleted by*
Slothouwer.

---

[1] There in his slippers stood the praetor of the Roman
people." *Verr.* v. xxxiii. 86 : see VIII. iii. 64.

sorrow, hesitation, confession, penitence, measure, quantity, number and time? Have they not power 87 to excite and prohibit, to express approval, wonder or shame? Do they not take the place of adverbs and pronouns when we point at places and things? In fact, though the peoples and nations of the earth speak a multitude of tongues, they share in common the universal language of the hands.

The gestures of which I have thus far spoken are 88 such as naturally proceed from us simultaneously with our words. But there are others which indicate things by means of mimicry. For example, you may suggest a sick man by mimicking the gesture of a doctor feeling the pulse, or a harpist by a movement of the hands as though they were plucking the strings. But this is a type of gesture which should be rigorously avoided in pleading. For 89 the orator should be as unlike a dancer as possible, and his gesture should be adapted rather to his thought than to his actual words, a practice which was indeed once upon a time even adopted by the more dignified performers on the stage. I should, therefore, permit him to direct his hand towards his body to indicate that he is speaking of himself, or to point it at some one else to whom he is alluding, together with other similar gestures which I need not mention. But, on the other hand, I would not allow him to use his hands to imitate attitudes or to illustrate anything he may chance to say. And this 90 rule applies not merely to the hands, but to all gesture and to the voice as well. For in delivering the period *stetit soleatus praetor populi Romani*,[1] it would be wrong to imitate Verres leaning on his mistress, or in uttering the phrase *caedebatur in medio*

motus laterum, qualis esse ad verbera solet, torquendus, aut vox, qualis dolore exprimitur, eruenda;
91 cum mihi comoedi quoque pessime facere videantur, quod, etiamsi iuvenem agant, cum tamen in expositione aut senis sermo, ut in Hydriae prologo, aut mulieris, ut in Georgo, incidit, tremula vel effeminata voce pronuntiant. Adeo in illis quoque est aliqua vitiosa imitatio, quorum ars omnis constat imitatione.

92 Est autem gestus ille maxime communis, quo medius digitus in pollicem contrahitur explicitis tribus, et principiis utilis cum leni in utramque partem motu modice prolatus, simul capite atque humeris sensim ad id, quo manus feratur, obsecundantibus, et in narrando certus, sed tum paulo productior, et in exprobrando et coarguendo acer atque instans, longius enim partibus his et liberius exeritur.

93 Vitiose vero idem sinistrum quasi humerum petens in latus agi solet, quanquam adhuc peius aliqui transversum brachium proferunt et cubito pronuntiant. Duo quoque medii sub pollicem veniunt, et est hic adhuc priore gestus instantior, principio et

---

[1] *Verr.* v. lxii. 162. "He was scourged in the midst of the market-place of Messina."
[2] Plays of Menander.

foro Messanae [1] to make the side writhe, as it does
when quivering beneath the lash, or to utter shrieks,
such as are extorted by pain. For even comic actors 91
seem to me to commit a gross offence against the
canons of their art when, if they have in the course
of some narrative to quote either the words of an old
man (as, for example, in the prologue to the *Hydria*),[2]
or of a woman (as in the *Georgus* [2]), they utter them
in a tremulous or a treble voice, notwithstanding the
fact that they are playing the part of a young man.
So true is it that certain forms of imitation may be
a blemish even in those whose whole art consists in
imitation.

One of the commonest of all the gestures consists 92
in placing the middle finger against the thumb and
extending the remaining three: it is suitable to the
exordium, the hand being moved forward with an
easy motion a little distance both to right and left,
while the head and shoulders gradually follow the
direction of the gesture. It is also useful in the
statement of facts, but in that case the hand must be
moved with firmness and a little further forward,
while, if we are reproaching or refuting our adversary, the same movement may be employed with
some vehemence and energy, since such passages
permit of greater freedom of extension. On the 93
other hand, this same gesture is often directed side-
ways towards the left shoulder: this is a mistake,
although it is a still worse fault to thrust the arm
across the chest and gesticulate with the elbow.
The middle and third fingers are also sometimes
turned under the thumb, producing a still more
forcible effect than the gesture previously described,
but not well adapted for use in the *exordium* or *state-*

94 narrationi non commodatus. At cum tres contracti
pollice premuntur, tum digitus ille, quo usum optime
Crassum Cicero dicit, explicari solet. Is in exprobrando et indicando, unde ei nomen est, valet,
et adlevata ac spectante humerum manu paulum
inclinatus adfirmat, versus in terram et quasi pronus
95 urget; et aliquando pro numero est. Idem summo
articulo utrinque leviter apprehenso, duobus modice
curvatis, minus tamen minimo, aptus ad disputandum
est. Acrius tamen argumentari videntur, qui medium articulum potius tenent, tanto contractioribus
96 ultimis digitis, quanto priores descenderunt. Est
et ille verecundae orationi aptissimus, quo, quattuor
primis leviter in summum coeuntibus digitis, non
procul ab ore aut pectore fertur ad nos manus et
97 deinde prona ac paulum prolata laxatur. Hoc modo
coepisse Demosthenen credo in illo pro Ctesiphonte
timido summissoque principio, sic formatam Ciceronis
manum, cum diceret: *Si quid est ingenii in me, quod
sentio quam sit exiguum.* Eadem aliquatenus liberius
deorsum spectantibus digitis colligitur in nos et
fusius paulo in diversum resolvitur, ut quodammodo
98 sermonen ipsum proferre videatur. Binos interim

---

[1] *de Or.* II. xlv. 188.   [2] *pro Arch.* i. 1.

ment of facts. But when three fingers are doubled 94
under the thumb, the finger, which Cicero [1] says
that Crassus used to such effect, is extended. It is
used in denunciation and in indication (whence its
name of index finger), while if it be slightly dropped
after the hand has been raised toward the shoulder,
it signifies affirmation, and if pointed as it were
face downwards toward the ground, it expresses
insistence. It is sometimes also used to indicate
number. Again, if its top joint is lightly gripped on 95
either side, with the two outer fingers slightly
curved, the little finger rather less than the third,
we shall have a gesture well suited for argument.
But for this purpose the same gesture is rendered
more emphatic by holding the middle joint of the
finger and contracting the last two fingers still
further to match the lower position of the middle
finger and thumb. The following gesture is admir- 96
ably adapted to accompany modest language: the
thumb and the next three fingers are gently con-
verged to a point and the hand is carried to the
neighbourhood of the mouth or chest, then relaxed
palm downwards and slightly advanced. It was 97
with this gesture that I believe Demosthenes to
have commenced the timid and subdued exordium
of his speech in defence of Ctesiphon, and it was,
I think, in such a position that Cicero [2] held his
hand, when he said, "If I have any talent, though
I am conscious how little it is." Slightly greater
freedom may be given to the gesture by pointing
the fingers down and drawing the hand in towards
the body and then opening it somewhat more rapidly
in the opposite direction, so that it seems as though
it were delivering our words to the audience. Some- 98

digitos distinguimus, sed non inserto pollice, paulum
tamen inferioribus intra spectantibus, sed ne illis
99 quidem tensis, qui supra sunt.   Interim extremi
palmam circa ima pollicis premunt, ipse prioribus
ad medios articulos iungitur; interim quartus oblique
reponitur; interim quattuor remissis magis quam
tensis, pollice intus inclinato, habilem demonstrando
in latus aut distinguendis, quae dicimus, manum
facimus, cum supina in sinistrum latus, prona in alterum
100 fertur. Sunt et illi breves gestus, cum manus leviter
pandata, qualis voventium est, parvis intervallis et
subadsentientibus humeris movetur, maxime apta
parce et quasi timide loquentibus.   Est admirationi
conveniens ille gestus, quo manus modice supinata
ac per singulos a minimo collecta digitos redeunte
101 flexu simul explicatur atque convertitur. Nec uno
modo interrogantes gestum componimus, plerumque
tamen vertentes manum, utcunque composita est.
Pollici proximus digitus mediumque, qua dexter est,
unguem pollicis summo suo iungens, remissis ceteris,
est et approbantibus et narrantibus et distinguentibus
102 decorus.   Cui non dissimilis, sed complicitis tribus

times we may hold the first two fingers apart without, however, inserting the thumb between them, the remaining two pointing inwards, while even the two former must not be fully extended. Sometimes, **99** again, the third and little finger may be pressed in to the palm near the base of the thumb, which in its turn is pressed against the middle joints of the first and middle fingers; at others the little finger is sometimes drooped obliquely, or the four fingers may be relaxed rather than extended and the thumb slanted inwards: this last gesture is well adapted to pointing to one side or marking the different points which we are making, the hand being carried palm-upwards to the left and swept back to the right face-downwards. The following short gestures are **100** also employed: the hand may be slightly hollowed as it is when persons are making a vow, and then moved slightly to and fro, the shoulders swaying gently in unison: this is adapted to passages where we speak with restraint and almost with timidity. Wonder is best expressed as follows: the hand turns slightly upwards and the fingers are brought in to the palm, one after the other, beginning with the little finger; the hand is then opened and turned round by a reversal of this motion. There are various **101** methods of expressing interrogation; but, as a rule, we do so by a turn of the hand, the arrangement of the fingers being indifferent. If the first finger touch the middle of the right-hand edge of the thumb-nail with its extremity, the other fingers being relaxed, we shall have a graceful gesture well suited to express approval or to accompany *statements of facts*, and to mark the distinction between our different points. There is another gesture not unlike **102**

digitis, quo nunc Graeci plurimum utuntur, etiam
utraque manu, quotiens enthymemata sua gestu
corrotundant velut caesim. Manus lenior promittit
et adsentatur, citatior hortatur, interim laudat. Est
et ille urgentis orationem gestus vulgaris magis
quam ex arte, qui contrahit alterno celerique motu
103 et explicat manum. Est et illa cava et rara et supra
humeri altitudinem elata cum quodam motu velut
hortatrix manus; a peregrinis scholis tamen prope
recepta tremula scenica est. Digitos, cum summi
coierunt, ad os referre, cur quibusdam displicuerit,
nescio. Nam id et leviter admirantes et interim
subita indignatione velut pavescentes et deprecantes
104 facimus. Quin compressam etiam manum in paenitentia vel ira pectori admovemus, ubi vox vel inter
dentes expressa non dedecet: *Quid nunc agam?
Quid facias?* Averso pollice demonstrare aliquid,
105 receptum magis puto quam oratori decorum. Sed
cum omnis motus sex partes habeat, septimus sit ille,
qui in se redit, orbis. Vitiosa est una circumversio:
reliqui ante nos et dextra laevaque et sursum et
deorsum aliquid ostendunt; in posteriora gestus non

---

[1] Rhetorical or incomplete syllogisms. But see v. x. 2.
xiv. 1.

the preceding, in which the remaining three fingers
are folded : it is much employed by the Greeks both
for the left hand and the right, in rounding off their
enthymemes,[1] detail by detail.   A gentle movement of
the hand expresses promise or assent, a more violent
movement suggests exhortation or sometimes praise.
There is also that familiar gesture by which we drive
home our words, consisting in the rapid opening
and shutting of the hand : but this is a common
rather than an artistic gesture.   Again, there is the 103
somewhat unusual gesture in which the hand is
hollowed and raised well above the shoulder with a
motion suggestive of exhortation.   The tremulous
motion now generally adopted by foreign schools is,
however, fit only for the stage.   I do not know why
some persons disapprove of the movement of the
fingers, with their tops converging, towards the
mouth.   For we do this when we are slightly surprised, and at times also employ it to express fear or
entreaty when we are seized with sudden indignation.
Further, we sometimes clench the hand and press 104
it to our breast when we are expressing regret or
anger, an occasion when it is not unbecoming even
to force the voice through the teeth in phrases such
as "What shall I do now ?" "What would you do?"
To point at something with the thumb turned back
is a gesture which is in general use, but is not, in my
opinion, becoming to an orator.   Motion is generally 105
divided into six kinds, but circular motion must be
regarded as a seventh.   The latter alone is faulty
when applied to gesture.   The remaining motions—
that is, forward, to right or left and up or down—all
have their significance, but the gesture is never
directed to what lies behind us, though we do at

106 dirigitur. Interim tamen velut reiici solet. Optime
autem manus a sinistra parte incipit, in dextra
deponitur, sed ut ponere non ut ferire videatur;
quanquam et in fine interim cadit, ut cito tamen
redeat, et nonnunquam resilit vel negantibus nobis
vel admirantibus.

Hic veteres artifices illud recte adiecerunt, ut
manus cum sensu et inciperet et deponeretur.
Alioqui enim aut ante vocem erit gestus aut post
107 vocem, quod est utrumque deforme. In illo lapsi
nimia subtilitate sunt, quod intervallum motus tria
verba esse voluerunt; quod neque observatur neque
fieri potest, sed illi quasi mensuram tarditatis celeri-
tatisque aliquam esse voluerunt, neque immerito,
ne aut diu otiosa esset manus aut, quod multi
108 faciunt, actionem continuo motu concideret. Aliud
est, quod et fit frequentius et magis fallit. Sunt
quaedam latentes sermonis percussiones et quasi
aliqui pedes, ad quos plurimorum gestus cadit, ut
sit unus motus *Novum crimen,* alter *C. Caesar,* tertius
et ante hanc diem, quartus *non auditum,* deinde *propinquus meus,* et *ad te,* et *Quintus Tubero,* et *detulit.*
109 Unde id quoque fluit vitium, ut iuvenes, cum scri-

---

1 *pro Lig.* i. 1. "It is a new charge, Gaius Caesar, a
charge hitherto unheard of, that my kinsman, Quintus Tubero,
has brought to your notice."

times throw the hand back.   The best effect is pro- 106
duced by letting the motion of the hand start from
the left and end on the right, but this must be done
gently, the hand sinking to rest and avoiding all
appearance of giving a blow, although at the end of
a sentence it may sometimes be allowed to drop, but
must quickly be raised again : or it may occasionally,
when we desire to express wonder or dissent, spring
back with a rapid motion.

In this connexion the earlier instructors in the art
of gesture rightly added that the movement of the
hand should begin and end with the thought that is
expressed.   Otherwise the gesture will anticipate or
lag behind the voice, both of which produce an
unpleasing effect.   Some, through excess of subtlety, 107
have erroneously prescribed that there should be an
interval of three words between each movement ;
but this rule is never observed, nor can it be.   These
persons, however, were desirous that there should be
some standard of speed or slowness (a most rational
desire), with a view to avoid prolonged inactivity on
the part of the hands as well as the opposite fault,
into which so many fall, of breaking up the natural
flow of their delivery by continual motion.   There is 108
another still more common error, which is less easy
of detection.   Language possesses certain imper-
ceptible stresses, indeed we might almost call them
feet, to which the gesture of most speakers conforms.
Thus there will be one movement at *novum crimen*,
another at *Gai Caesar*, a third at *et ante hanc diem*,
a fourth at *non auditum*, a fifth at *propinquus meus*, a
sixth at *ad te* and others at *Quintus Tubero* and
detulit.[1]   From this springs a further error, namely, 109
that young men, when writing out their speeches,

bunt, gestum praemodulati cogitatione sic componant,
quomodo casura manus est. Inde et illud vitium, ut
gestus, qui in fine dexter esse debet, in sinistrum
110 frequenter desinat. Melius illud, cum sint in sermone omni brevia quaedam membra, ad quae, si necesse
sit, recipere spiritum liceat, ad haec gestum disponere: ut puta *Novum crimen, C. Caesar,* habet per se
finem quendam suum, quia sequitur coniunctio;
deinde *et ante hanc diem non auditum* satis circum-
scriptum est. Ad haec commodanda manus est,
111 idque dum erit prima et composita actio. At ubi
eam calor concitaverit; etiam gestus cum ipsa
orationis celeritate crebrescet. Aliis locis citata,
aliis pressa conveniet pronuntiatio. Illa transcurrimus, congerimus,[1] festinamus; hac instamus, in-
culcamus, infigimus. Plus autem adfectus habent
lentiora; ideoque Roscius citatior, Aesopus gravior
112 fuit, quod ille comoedias, hic tragoedias egit. Eadem
motus quoque observatio est. Itaque in fabulis
iuvenum, senum, militum, matronarum gravior
ingressus est; servi, ancillulae, parasiti, piscatores
citatius moventur. Tolli autem manum artifices
supra oculos, demitti infra pectus vetant; adeo a

---

[1] *After* congerimus *B. gives* abundamus, *which is omitted by
one late MS. and expunged by Halm.*

devise all their gestures in advance and consider as they compose how the hand is to fall at each particular point. A further unfortunate result is that the movement of the hand, which should end on the right, frequently finishes on the left. It is 110 therefore better, in view of the fact that all speech falls into a number of brief clauses, at the end of which we can take breath, if necessary, to arrange our gesture to suit these sections. For example, the words *novum crimen, Gai Caesar,* in a sense form a phrase complete in itself, since they are followed by a conjunction, while the next words, *et ante hanc diem non auditum,* are also sufficiently self-contained. To these phrases the motions of the hand must be conformed, before the speech has passed beyond the calmness of tone on which it opens. But when in- 111 creasing warmth of feeling has fired the orator, the gesture will become more frequent, in keeping with the impetus of the speech. Some places are best suited by a rapid, and others by a restrained delivery. In the one case we pass rapidly on, fire a volley of arguments and hurry upon our way; in the other, we drive home our points, force them on the hearer and implant them in his mind. But the slower the delivery, the greater its emotional power: thus, Roscius was rapid and Aesopus weighty in his delivery, because the former was a comic and the latter a tragic actor. The same rule applies to the move- 112 ments. Consequently on the stage young men and old, soldiers and married women all walk sedately, while slaves, maidservants, parasites and fishermen are more lively in their movements. But instructors in the art of gesture will not permit the hand to be raised above the level of the eyes or lowered beneath

capite eum petere [1] aut ad imum ventrem deducere,
113 vitiosum habetur. In sinistrum intra humerum pro-
movetur; ultra non decet. Sed cum aversantes in
laevam partem velut propellemus manum, sinister
humerus proferendus, ut cum capite ad dextram
114 ferente consentiat. Manus sinistra nuuquam sola
gestum recte facit; dextrae se frequenter accom-
modat, sive in digitos argumenta digerimus sive
aversis in sinistrum palmis abominamur sive obiicimus
115 adversas sive in latus utramque distendimus, sive
satisfacientes aut supplicantes (diversi autem sunt
hi gestus) summittimus sive adorantes atollimus sive
aliqua demonstratione aut invocatione protendimus:
Vos Albani tumuli atque luci, aut Gracchanum illud:
Quo me miser conferam? in Capitolium? at fratris
116 *sanguine madet: an domum?* Plus enim adfectus in his
iunctae exhibent manus; in rebus parvis, mitibus,
tristibus breves; magnis, laetis, atrocibus exertiores. [2]
117 Vitia quoque earum subiicienda sunt, quae quidem
accidere etiam exercitatis actoribus solent. Nam
gestum poculum poscentis aut verbera minantis aut
numerum quingentorum flexo pollice efficientis, quae
sunt a quibusdam scriptoribus notata, ne in rusticis

---

[1] a capite eum petere *is almost certainly corrupt:* gestum
for eum *is the least improbable correction that has been suggested.*
[2] exertiores, *Spalding:* exteriores, *B.*

---

[1] The general sense is clear, though the text is unsatis-
factory and scarcely translateable.
[2] *pro Mil.* xxxi. 85.   [3] See Cic. *de Or.* iii. lvi. 214.
[4] *I.e.* crooking the thumb against the forefinger to
represent the symbol **D.**

that of the breast; since it is thought a grave blemish to lift it to the top of the head[1] or lower it to the lower portions of the belly. It may be moved to the left 113 within the limits of the shoulder, but no further without loss of decorum. On the other hand, when, to express our aversion, we thrust our hand out to the left, the left shoulder must be brought forward in unison with the head, which will incline to the right. It is never correct to employ the left hand 114 alone in gesture, though it will often conform its motion to that of the right, as, for example, when we are counting our arguments on the fingers, or turn the palms of the hands to the left to express our horror of something, or thrust them out in front 115 or spread them out to right and left, or lower them in apology or supplication (though the gesture is not the same in these two cases), or raise them in adoration, or stretch them out in demonstration or invocation, as in the passage, "Ye hills and groves of Alba,[2]" or in the passage from Gracchus[3]: "Whither, alas! shall I turn me? To the Capitol? Nay, it is wet with my brother's blood. To my home?" etc. For 116 in such passages greater emotional effect is produced if both hands co-operate, short gestures being best adapted to matters of small importance and themes of a gentle or melancholy character, and longer gestures to subjects of importance or themes calling for joy or horror.

It is desirable also that I should mention the faults 117 in the use of the hands, into which even experienced pleaders are liable to fall. As for the gesture of demanding a cup, threatening a flogging, or indicating the number 500 by crooking the thumb,[4] all of which are recorded by writers on the subject, I have never

118 quidem vidi. At ut brachio exerto introspiciatur
latus, ut manum alius ultra sinum proferre non
audeat, alius, in quantum patet longitudo, protendat
aut ad tectum erigat aut repetito ultra laevum
humerum gestu ita in tergum flagellet, ut consistere
post eum parum tutum sit, aut sinistrum ducat
orbem aut temere sparsa manu in proximos offendat
aut cubitum utrumque in diversum latus ventilet,
119 saepe scio evenire. Solet esse et pigra et trepida et
secanti similis; interim etiam uncis digitis, ut[1] aut a
capite deiiciatur aut eadem manu supinata in superiora
iactetur. Fit et ille gestus,[2] qui, inclinato in humerum dextrum capite, brachio ab aure protenso,
manum infesto pollice extendit; qui quidem maxime
placet iis, qui se dicere sublata manu iactant.
120 Adiicias licet eos, qui sententias vibrantes digitis
iaculantur aut manu sublata denuntiant aut, quod
per se interim recipiendum est, quotiens aliquid
ipsis placuit, in ungues eriguntur; sed vitiosum id
faciunt, aut digito, quantum plurimum possunt,
erecto aut etiam duobus, aut utraque manu ad
121 modum aliquid portantium composita. His accedunt
vitia non naturae sed trepidationis, cum ore con-

[1] ut *added by Spalding.*
[2] gestus *suggested by Halm. The second hand of cod. Bamb.
reads* habitus, qui esse in statuis pacificator solet : *pre-
sumably an interpolation.*

---

[1] *I.e.* with exaggerated violence. See II. xii. 9.

seen them employed even by uneducated rustics. But I know that it is of frequent occurrence for a 118 speaker to expose his side by stretching his arm too far, to be afraid in one case of extending his hand beyond the folds of his cloak, and in another to stretch it as far as it will go, to raise it to the roof, or by swinging it repeatedly over his left shoulder to deliver such a rain of blows to the rear that it is scarcely safe to stand behind him, or to make a circular sweep to the left, or by casting out his hand at random to strike the standers-by or to flap both elbows against his sides. There are others, again, 119 whose hands are sluggish or tremulous or inclined to saw the air; sometimes, too, the fingers are crooked and brought down with a run from the top of the head, or tossed up into the air with the hand turned palm upwards. There is also a gesture, which consists in inclining the head to the right shoulder, stretching out the arm from the ear and extending the hand with the thumb turned down. This is a special favourite with those who boast that they speak "with uplifted hand." [1] To these latter we may 120 add those speakers who hurl quivering epigrams with their fingers or denounce with the hand upraised, or rise on tiptoe, whenever they say something of which they are specially proud. This last proceeding may at times be adopted by itself, but they convert it into a blemish by simultaneously raising one or even two fingers as high as they can reach, or heaving up both hands as if they were carrying something. In addition to these faults, there are those 121 which spring not from nature, but from nervousness, such as struggling desperately with our lips when they refuse to open, making inarticulate sounds, as

currente rixari, si memoria fefellerit aut cogitatio
non suffragetur, quasi faucibus aliquid obstiterit,
insonare, in adversum tergere nares, obambulare
sermone imperfecto, resistere subito et laudem
silentio poscere; quae omnia persequi prope in-
122 finitum est; sua enim cuique sunt vitia. Pectus
ac venter ne proiiciantur, observandum; pandant
enim posteriora, et est odiosa omnis supinitas.
Latera cum gestu consentiant. Facit enim aliquid
et totius corporis motus, adeo ut Cicero plus illo agi
quam manibus ipsis putet. Ita enim dicit in
Oratore : *Nullae argutiae digitorum, non ad numerum
articulus cadens, trunco magis toto se ipse moderans et*
123 *virili laterum flexione.* Femur ferire, quod Athenis
primus fecisse creditur Cleon, et usitatum est et
indignantes decet et excitat auditorem. Idque in
Calidio Cicero desiderat; *Non frons,* inquit, *percussa,
non femur.* Quanquam, si licet, de fronte dissentio.
Nam etiam complodere manus scenicum est et pectus
124 caedere. Illud quoque raro decebit cava manu
summis digitis pectus appetere, si quando nosmet
ipsos alloquimur, cohortantes, obiurgantes, mise-
rantes; quod si quando fiet, togam quoque inde
removeri non dedecebit. In pedibus observantur

---

[1] xviii. 59.   [2] *Brut.* lxxx. 278.

though something were sticking in our throat, when
our memory fails us, or our thoughts will not come
at our call; rubbing the end of our nose, walking up
and down in the midst of an unfinished sentence,
stopping suddenly and courting applause by silence,
with many other tricks which it would take too long
to detail, since everybody has his own particular
faults.   We must take care not to protrude the chest 122
or stomach, since such an attitude arches the back,
and all bending backwards is unsightly.   The flanks
must conform to the gesture; for the motion of the
entire body contributes to the effect: indeed, Cicero
holds that the body is more expressive than even the
hands.   For in the *de Orator* [1] he says, "There must
be no quick movements of the fingers, no marking
time with the finger-tips, but the orator should
control himself by the poise of the whole trunk and
by a manly inclination of the side."   Slapping the 123
thigh, which Cleon is said to have been the first to
introduce at Athens, is in general use and is becoming
as a mark of indignation, while it also excites the
audience.   Cicero [2] regrets its absence in Calidius,
"There was no striking of the forehead," he com-
plains, "nor of the thigh."   With regard to the
forehead I must beg leave to differ from him: for it
is a purely theatrical trick even to clap the hands or
beat the breast.   It is only on rare occasions, too, 124
that it is becoming to touch the breast with the
finger-tips of the hollowed hand, when, for example,
we address ourselves or speak words of exhortation,
reproach or commiseration.   But if ever we do employ
this gesture, it will not be unbecoming to pull back
the toga at the same time.   As regards the feet, we
need to be careful about our gait and the attitudes

status et incessus. Prolato dextro stare et eandem
125 manum ac pedem proferre, deforme est. In dextrum
incumbere interim datur sed aequo pectore, qui
tamen comicus magis quam oratorius gestus est.
Male etiam in sinistrum pedem insistentium dexter
aut tollitur aut summis digitis suspenditur. Varicare
supra modum et in stando deforme est et, accedente
motu, prope obscenum. Procursio opportuna brevis,
126 moderata, rara. Conveniet etiam ambulatio quaedam
propter immodicas laudationum moras, quanquam
Cicero rarum incessum neque ita longum probat.[1]
Discursare vero et, quod Domitius Afer de Sura
Manlio dixit, satagere, ineptissimum, urbaneque
Flavus Verginius interrogavit de quodam suo anti-
127 sophiste, quot milia passuum declamasset.[2] Praecipi
et illud scio, ne ambulantes avertamur a iudicibus,
sed sint obliqui pedes ad consilium nobis respici-
entibus. Id fieri iudiciis privatis non potest.[3] Verum
et breviora sunt spatia, nec aversi diu sumus. Interim tamen recedere sensim datur. Quidam et
128 resiliunt, quod est plane ridiculum. Pedis supplosio
ut loco est opportuna, ut ait Cicero, in contentionibus
aut incipiendis aut finiendis,[4] ita crebra et inepti est

---

[1] *Orat.* xviii. 59.   [2] See vi. iii. 54.
[3] The normal arrangement was for the president of the
court and judges to sit on a *tribunal* or dais. The advocates
and parties to the suit were on the ground in front. When
pleading before a large jury the orator could walk diagonally,
half-facing the jury, without at any rate turning his back on
too many at a time. When, however, there was but a single
judge, as in a private trial, the feat would be more difficult,
But apparently the court took up less room in such cases,
and the orator's peregrinations would be but small. See
§ 134 note.
[4] *de Or.* iii. lix. 220.

in which we stand. To stand with the right foot advanced or to thrust forward the same foot and hand are alike unsightly. At times we may rest our 125 weight on the right foot, but without any corresponding inclination of the chest, while, in any case, the gesture is better suited to the comic actor than to the orator. It is also a mistake, when resting on the left foot, to lift the right or poise it on tiptoe. To straddle the feet is ugly if we are standing still, and almost indecent if we are actually moving. To start forward may be effective, provided that we move but a short distance and do so but rarely and without violence. It will also at times be found convenient 126 to walk to and fro, owing to the extravagant pauses imposed by the plaudits of the audience ; Cicero,[1] however, says that this should be done only on rare occasions, and that we should take not more than a few steps. On the other hand, to run up and down, which, in the case of Manlius Sura,[2] Domitius Afer called overdoing it, is sheer folly, and there was no little wit in the question put by Verginius Flavus to a rival professor, when he asked how many miles he had declaimed. I know, too, that some authorities 127 warn us not to walk with our backs turned to the judges, but to move diagonally and keep our eyes fixed on the panel. This cannot be done in private trials, but in such cases the space available is small and the time during which our backs are turned is of the briefest.[3] On the other hand, we are permitted at times to walk backwards gradually. Some even jump backwards, which is merely ludicrous. Stamp- 128 ing the foot is, as Cicero[4] says, effective when done on suitable occasions, that is to say, at the commence- ment or close of a lively argument, but if it be

hominis et desinit iudicem in se convertere. Est et
illa indecora in dextrum ac laevum latus vacillatio
alternis pedibus insistentium. Longissime fugienda
mollis actio, qualem in Titio Cicero dicit fuisse, unde
etiam saltationis quoddam genus Titius sit appel-
129 latum. Reprehendenda et illa frequens et concitata
in utramque partem nutatio, quam in Curione patre
irrisit et Iulius, quaerens, quis in lintre loqueretur, et
Sicinius; nam cum, adsidente collega, qui erat
propter valetudinem et deligatus et plurimis medica-
mentis delibutus, multum se Curio ex more iactasset,
Nunquam, inquit, *Octavi, collegae tuo gratiam referes,*
130 *qui nisi fuisset, hodie te istic muscae comedissent.* Iac-
tantur et humeri; quod vitium Demosthenes ita
dicitur emendasse ut, cum in angusto quodam pulpito
stans diceret, hasta humero dependens immineret,
ut, si calore dicendi vitare id excidisset, offen-
satione illa commoneretur. Ambulantem loqui ita
demum oportet, si in causis publicis, in quibus
multi sunt iudices, quod dicimus quasi singulis
131 inculcare peculiariter velimus. Illud non ferendum,
quod quidam, reiecta in humerum toga, cum dextra
sinum usque ad lumbos reduxerunt, sinistra gestum

---

[1] *Brut.* lxii.   [2] *cp.* Cic. *Brut.* lx.

frequently indulged in, it brands the speaker as a
fool and ceases to attract the attention of the judge.
There is also the unsightly habit of swaying to right
and left, and shifting the weight from one foot to
the other. Above all, we must avoid effeminate
movements, such as Cicero[1] ascribes to Titius, a circumstance which led to a certain kind of dance being
nicknamed Titius. Another reprehensible practice 129
is that of nodding frequently and rapidly to either
side, a mannerism for which the elder Curio[2] was de-
rided by Julius, who asked who it was who was speaking in a boat, while on another occasion, when Curio
had been tossing himself about in his usual manner,
while Octavius, his colleague, was sitting beside him
bandaged and reeking with medicaments on account
of ill-health, Sicinius remarked, "Octavius, you can
never be sufficiently grateful to your colleague : for
if he wasn't there, the flies would have devoured you
this very day where you sit." The shoulders also 130
are apt to be jerked to and fro, a fault of which
Demosthenes is said to have cured himself by
speaking on a narrow platform with a spear hanging
immediately above his shoulder, in order that, if in
the heat of his eloquence he failed to avoid this
fault, he might have his attention called to the
fact by a prick from the spear. The only condition
that justifies our walking about while speaking is
if we are pleading in a public trial before a large
number of judges and desire specially to impress our
arguments upon them individually. The practice 131
adopted by some of throwing the toga back over the
shoulder, while they draw up the fold to their waist
with the right hand, and use the left for gesticulation
as they walk up and down and discourse, is not to

facientes spatiantur et fabulantur, cum etiam laevam
restringere prolata longius dextra sit odiosum. Unde
moneor, (ut ne id quidem transeam) ineptissime fieri,
cum inter moras laudationum aut in aurem alicuius
loquuntur aut cum sodalibus iocantur aut nonnunquam ad librarios suos ita respiciunt, ut sportulam
132 dictare videantur. Inclinari ad iudicem, cum doceas,
utique si id de quo loquaris sit obscurius, decet.
Incumbere advocato adversis subselliis sedenti con-
tumeliosum. Reclinari etiam ad suos et manibus
sustineri, nisi plane iusta fatigatio est, delicatum,
133 sicut palam moneri excidentis aut legere. Namque
in his omnibus et vis illa dicendi solvitur et frigescit
adfectus et iudex parum sibi praestari reverentiae
credit. Transire in diversa subsellia parum vere-
cundum est. Nam et Cassius Severus urbane
adversus hoc facientem lineas poposcit. Et si
aliquando concitate itur, nunquam non frigide
134 reditur. Multum ex iis, quae praecepimus, mutari
necesse est ab iis, qui dicunt apud tribunalia. Nam

---

[1] Asconius (in a note on the *Divinatio* of Cicero) explains
that in minor cases tried by *tribuni, triumviri, quaestores*
and other minor officials, the judges sat on ordinary benches,
not on a raised *tribunal.*

be tolerated; for even to draw back the left hand
while extending the right is an objectionable habit.
This reminds me of an extremely foolish trick, which
I think I ought to mention, that some speakers have
of employing the intervals when the audience are
applauding by whispering in someone's ear or jesting
with their friends or looking back at their clerks, as
if telling them to make a note of some gratuity to
be dispensed to their supporters. On the other 132
hand, when we are making some explanation to the
judge, more especially if the point be somewhat
obscure, a slight inclination in his direction will be
not unbecoming. But to lean forward towards the
advocate seated on the benches of our opponent is
offensive, while, unless we are genuinely fatigued, it
is a piece of affectation to lean back among our own
friends and to be supported in their arms; the same
remark also applies to the practice of being prompted
aloud or reading from manuscript as though uncertain of our memory. For all these manner- 133
isms impair the force of our speaking, chill the
effect of emotional appeals and make the judge
think that he is not being treated with sufficient
respect. To cross over to the seats of our opponents
borders on impudence, and Cassius Severus showed
a neat turn of wit when he demanded that a barrier
might be erected between himself and an opponent
who behaved in this fashion. Moreover, though to
advance towards our opponent may at times produce
an impression of passionate energy, the return to
our former position will always prove correspondingly
tame. Many of the rules which I have given will 134
require modification by those who have to plead
before judges seated on a dais.[1] For in such

et vultus erectior, ut eum, apud quem dicitur,
spectet; et gestus ut ad eundem tendens elatior
sit, necesse est; et alia, quae occurrere etiam me
tacente omnibus possunt. Itemque ab iis, qui
sedentes agent. Nam et fere fit hoc in rebus minoribus, et iidem impetus actionis esse non possunt,
135 et quaedam vitia fiunt necessaria. Nam et dexter
pes a laeva iudicis sedenti proferendus est, et ex
altera parte multi gestus necesse est in sinistrum
eant, ut ad iudicem spectent. Equidem plerosque
et ad singulas clausulas sententiarum video ad-
surgentes et nonnullos subinde aliquid etiam spati-
antes, quod an deceat, ipsi viderint; cum id faciunt,
136 non sedentes agunt. Bibere aut etiam esse inter
agendum, quod multis moris fuit et est quibusdam,
ab oratore meo procul absit. Nam si quis aliter
dicendi onera perferre non possit, non ita miserum
est non agere potiusque multo quam et operis et
hominum contemptum fateri.

137 Cultus non est proprius oratoris aliquis sed magis
in oratore conspicitur. Quare sit, ut in omnibus
honestis debet esse, splendidus et virilis. Nam et

---

[1] *Cp.* XI. i. 44, which shows that the cases in question are
those submitted to arbitration.

cases the face must be raised somewhat higher, so
that the speaker's eyes may be fixed on the president
of the court: for the same reason his gestures must
also be carried a little higher, while there are other
details which will readily occur to my reader without
any mention from me. Similar modifications will
be likewise necessary for those who plead sitting.[1]
For this is done, as a rule, only in cases of minor
importance, where delivery will necessarily be more
restrained, and certain defects are inevitable. For 135
example, when the speaker sits on the left side of the
judge, he will have to advance his right foot, while
if he be seated on the right, many of his gestures
must be made from right to left, in order that they
may be addressed to the judge. Personally, I note
that many speakers start up at the conclusion of
individual periods, while some proceed to walk to
and fro for a little: it is for them to decide whether
this is becoming or not: I will merely remark that,
when they do this, they are not pleading seated.
It was a common custom, which has not entirely 136
disappeared, to drink or even to eat while pleading;
but I shall not permit my ideal orator to do anything
of the kind. For if a man cannot endure the
burdens imposed by oratory without having recourse
to such remedies, he should not find it a serious
hardship to give up pleading altogether, a course
which is far preferable to acknowledging his contempt
both for his profession and his audience.

With regard to dress, there is no special garb 137
peculiar to the orator, but his dress comes more
under the public eye than that of other men. It
should, therefore, be distinguished and manly, as,
indeed, it ought to be with all men of position. For

toga et calceus et capillus tam nimia cura quam
negligentia sunt reprehendenda. Est aliquid in
amictu, quod ipsum aliquatenus temporum condicione mutatum est. Nam veteribus nulli sinus,
138 perquam breves post illos fuerunt. Itaque etiam
gestu necesse est usos esse in principiis eos alio,
quorum brachium, sicut Graecorum, veste con-
tinebatur. Sed nos de praesentibus loquimur. Cui
lati clavi ius non erit, ita cingatur, ut tunicae
prioribus oris infra genua paulum, posterioribus ad
medios poplites usque perveniant. Nam infra
139 mulierum est, supra centurionum. Ut purpura recte
descendat, levis cura est; notatur interim negligentia.
Latum habentium clavum modus est, ut sit paulum
cinctis summissior. Ipsam togam rotundam esse et apte
caesam velim, aliter enim multis modis fiet enormis.
Pars eius prior mediis cruribus optime terminatur,

---

¹ In putting on the toga, it was thrown first over the left
shoulder, so that about 6 feet hung in front and about 12
behind. This longer portion was then carried round under
the right arm and then diagonally across the chest (like a
balteus, or belt) and over the left shoulder again. A fold of
this portion hanging in front formed the *sinus*. The original
6 feet hanging in front from the left shoulder now hung
below the rest. A portion was pulled up from above and
allowed to hang over the edge of that portion of the toga
which Quintilian compares to a *balteus*. This was known
as the *umbo*, and is described by Quintilian as *pars quae
ultima imponitur*. He recommends that a considerable
portion should be thus pulled up and allowed to hang fairly
low in front over the edge of the *balteus*, that the weight
of the hanging portion might balance the remainder of the
original 6 feet of toga hanging from the left shoulder, keep

excessive care with regard to the cut of the toga,[1] the style of the shoes, or the arrangement of the hair, is just as reprehensible as excessive carelessness. There are also details of dress which are altered to some extent by successive changes in fashion. The ancients, for example, wore no folds, and their successors wore them very short. Conse- 138 quently it follows that in view of the fact that their arms were, like those of the Greeks, covered by the garment, they must have employed a different form of gesture in the exordium from that which is now in use. However, I am speaking of our own day. The speaker who has not the right to wear the broad stripe,[2] will wear his girdle in such a way that the front edges of the tunic fall a little below his knees, while the edges in rear reach to the middle of his hams. For only women draw them lower and only centurions higher. If we wear the purple stripe, it 139 requires but little care to see that it falls becomingly; negligence in this respect sometimes excites criticism. Among those who wear the broad stripe, it is the fashion to let it hang somewhat lower than in garments that are retained by the girdle. The toga itself should, in my opinion, be round, and cut to fit, otherwise there are a number of ways in which it may be unshapely. Its front edge should by preference reach to the middle of the shin, while the back should be higher in proportion as the girdle is higher

---

[1] it in place and prevent it from slipping back into its original position. The toga was very nearly semicircular in shape, which explains Quintilian's statement that it should be round. For further details see *Companion to Latin Studies*, Camb. Univ. Press, p. 191.

[2] Worn by senators.

140 posterior eadem portione altius qua cinctura. Sinus decentissimus, si aliquanto supra imam tunicam[1] fuerit; nunquam certe sit inferior. Ille, qui sub humero dextro ad sinistrum oblique ducitur velut balteus, nec strangulet nec fluat. Pars togae, quae postea imponitur, sit inferior; nam ita et sedet melius et continetur. Subducenda etiam pars aliqua tunicae, ne ad lacertum in actu redeat; tum sinus iniiciendus humero, cuius extremam oram reiecisse
141 non dedecet. Operiri autem humerum cum toto iugulo non oportet, alioqui amictus fiet angustus et dignitatem, quae est in latitudine pectoris, perdet. Sinistrum brachium eo usque adlevandum est, ut quasi normalem illum angulum faciat, super quod
142 ora ex toga duplex aequaliter sedeat. Manus non impleatur anulis, praecipue medios articulos non transeuntibus; cuius erit habitus optimus adlevato pollice et digitis leviter inflexis, nisi si libellum tenebit. Quod non utique captandum est; videtur enim fateri memoriae diffidentiam et ad multos
143 gestus est impedimento. Togam veteres ad calceos usque demittebant ut Graeci pallium; idque ut fiat, qui de gestu scripserunt circa tempora illa, Plotius Nigidiusque praecipiunt. Quo magis miror Plinii

---

[1] tunicam, *Spalding*: togam, *MSS.*

---

[1] Plotius Gallus, a rhetorician, and Nigidius Figulus, an encyclopaedic writer, both contemporaries of Cicero.

behind than in front. The fold is most becoming, 140
if it fall to a point a little above the lower edge of
the tunic, and should certainly never fall below it.
The other fold which passes obliquely like a belt
under the right shoulder and over the left, should
neither be too tight nor too loose. The portion of
the toga which is last to be arranged should fall
rather low, since it will sit better thus and be
kept in its place. A portion of the tunic also should
be drawn back in order that it may not fall over the
arm when we are pleading, and the fold should be
thrown over the shoulder, while it will not be
unbecoming if the edge be turned back. On the 141
other hand, we should not cover the shoulder and
the whole of the throat, otherwise our dress will be
unduly narrowed and will lose the impressive effect
produced by breadth at the chest. The left arm
should only be raised so far as to form a right angle
at the elbow, while the edge of the toga should fall
in equal lengths on either side. The hand should 142
not be overloaded with rings, which should under no
circumstances encroach upon the middle joint of
the finger. The most becoming attitude for the
hand is produced by raising the thumb and slightly
curving the fingers, unless it is occupied with holding manuscript. But we should not go out of our
way to carry the latter, for it suggests an acknow-
ledgement that we do not trust our memory, and is
a hindrance to a number of gestures. The ancients 143
used to let the toga fall to the heels, as the Greeks
are in the habit of doing with the cloak : Plotius
and Nigidius[1] both recommend this in the books
which they wrote about gesture as practised in
their own day. I am consequently all the more

Secúndi docti hominis et in hoc utique libro paene
etiam nimium curiosi persuasionem, qui solitum id
facere Ciceronem velandorum varicum gratia tradit;
cum hoc amictus genus in statuis eorum quoque, qui
144 post Ciceronem fuerunt, appareat. Palliolum sicut
fascias, quibus crura vestiuntur, et focalia et aurium
ligamenta sola excusare potest valetudo.

Sed haec amictus observatio, dum incipimus;
procedente vero actu, iam paene ab initio narrationis,
sinus ab humero recte velut sponte delabitur, et,
cum ad argumenta ac locos ventum est, reiicere a
sinistro togam, deiicere etiam, si haereat, sinum
145 conveniet. Laeva a faucibus ac summo pectore
abducere licet: ardent enim iam omnia. Et ut vox
vehementior ac magis varia est, sic amictus quoque
146 habet actum quendam velut proeliantem. Itaque
ut laevam involvere toga et incingi paene furiosum
est, sinum vero in dextrum humerum ab imo reiicere
solutum ac delicatum, fiuntque adhuc peius aliqua,
ita cur laxiorem sinum sinistro brachio non subiici-

---

[1] This work of the elder Pliny was called *Studiosus*.

surprised at the view expressed by so learned a man as Plinius Secundus, especially since it occurs in a book which carries minute research almost to excess:[1] for he asserts that Cicero was in the habit of wearing his toga in such a fashion to conceal his varicose veins, despite the fact that this fashion is to be seen in the statues of persons who lived after Cicero's day. As regards the short cloak, 144 bandages used to protect the legs, mufflers and coverings for the ears, nothing short of ill-health can excuse their use.

But such attention to our dress is only possible at the beginning of a speech, since, as the pleading develops, in fact, almost from the beginning of the *statement of facts,* the fold will slip down from the shoulder quite naturally and as it were of its own accord, while when we come to arguments and commonplaces, it will be found convenient to throw back the toga from the left shoulder, and even to throw down the fold if it should stick. The left 145 hand may be employed to pluck the toga from the throat and the upper portion of the chest, for by now the whole body will be hot. And just as at this point the voice becomes more vehement and more varied in its utterance, so the clothing begins to assume something of a combative pose. Conse- 146 quently, although to wrap the toga round the left hand or to pull it about us as a girdle would be almost a symptom of madness, while to throw back the fold from its bottom over the right shoulder would be a foppish and effeminate gesture, and there are yet worse effects than these, there is, at any rate, no reason why we should not place the looser portions of the fold under the left arm, since

amus? Habet enim acre quiddam atque expeditum
147 et calori concitationique non inhabile. Cum vero
magna pars est exhausta orationis, utique adflante
fortuna, paene omnia decent, sudor ipse et fatigatio
et negligentior amictus et soluta ac velut labens
148 undique toga. Quo magis miror hanc quoque suc-
currisse Plinio curam, ut ita sudario frontem siccari
iuberet, ne comae turbarentur, quas componi post
paulum, sicuti dignum erat, graviter et severe
vetuit. Mihi vero illae quoque turbatae prae se
ferre aliquid adfectus et ipsa oblivione curae huius
149 commendari videntur. At si incipientibus aut
paulum progressis decidat toga, non reponere eam
prorsus negligentis aut pigri aut quomodo debeat
amiciri nescientis est.

Haec sunt vel illustramenta pronuntiationis vel
vitia, quibus propositis multa cogitare debet orator.
150 Primum, quis, apud quos, quibus praesentibus sit
acturus. Nam ut dicere alia aliis et apud alios magis
concessum est, sic etiam facere. Neque eadem in
voce, gestu, incessu, apud principem, senatum
populum, magistratus, privato, publico iudicio,

it gives an air of vigour and freedom not ill-suited
to the warmth and energy of our action. When, 147
however, our speech draws near its close, more
especially if fortune shows herself kind, practically
everything is becoming ; we may stream with sweat,
show signs of fatigue, and let our dress fall in careless disorder and the toga slip loose from us on
every side. This fact makes me all the more sur- 148
prised that Pliny should think it worth while to
enjoin the orator to dry his brow with a hand-
kerchief in such a way as not to disorder the hair,
although a little later he most properly, and with a
certain gravity and sternness of language, forbids
us to rearrange it. For my own part, I feel that
dishevelled locks make an additional appeal to the
emotions, and that neglect of such precautions
creates a pleasing impression. On the other hand, 149
if the toga falls down at the beginning of our
speech, or when we have only proceeded but a little
way, the failure to replace it is a sign of indifference,
or sloth, or sheer ignorance of the way in which
clothes should be worn.

The above are the chief adornments and faults
of delivery. But there are a number of further
considerations which the orator must bear in mind.
In the first place there is the question as to the 150
character of speaker, judges and audience. For
just as the methods of speaking may justifiably be
varied to suit the characteristics of different orators
and different judges, so it is with delivery. The
same characteristics of voice, gesture and gait are
not equally becoming in the presence of the
emperor, the senate, the people, and magistrates,
or in private and public trials, or in making a

postulatione, actione similiter decent. Quam differentiam subiicere sibi quisque, qui animum intenderit, potest; tum qua de re dicat, et efficere 151 quid velit. Rei quadruplex observatio est. Una in tota causa. Sunt enim tristes, hilares, sollicitae, securae, grandes, pusillae, ut vix unquam ita sollicitari partibus earum debeamus, ut non summae 152 meminerimus. Altera, quae est in differentia partium, ut in prooemio, narratione, argumentatione, epilogo. Tertia in sententiis ipsis, in quibus secundum res et adfectus variantur omnia. Quarta in verbis, quorum ut est vitiosa, si efficere omnia velimus, imitatio, ita quibusdam nisi sua natura redditur, vis omnis 153 aufertur. Igitur in laudationibus, nisi si funebres erunt, gratiarum actione, exhortatione, similibus laeta et magnifica et sublimis est actio. Funebres contiones, consolationes, plerumque causae reorum tristes atque summissae. In senatu conservanda auctoritas, apud populum dignitas, in privatis modus.

request to the praetor for the appointment of a judge to hear our case, and in actual pleading. Anyone who will reflect upon the matter will realise the nature of the differences involved, as he will also be able to realise the nature of the subject on which he is speaking and the effect which he desires to produce. The considerations with regard to the 151 subject are four in number, of which the first has reference to the case as a whole. For the case may be of a gloomy or a cheerful nature, an anxious business, or one that calls for no alarm, and may involve issues of great or trivial importance. We ought, therefore, never to be so preoccupied over particular portions of a case as to forget to consider the case as a whole. The second point is concerned 152 with the different aspects of the various portions of the speech, that is, the *exordium, statement of facts, arguments* and *peroration*. The third concerns the thoughts, which will vary according to the subject matter and the emotions which we require to awaken. The fourth has reference to the words, which must be given appropriate expression, unless their force is to be entirely wasted, although it is an error to attempt to make our delivery reproduce the sense of every single word. Consequently, in pane- 153 gyric, funeral orations excepted, in returning thanks, exhortations and the like, the delivery must be luxuriant, magnificent, and grand. On the other hand, in funeral or consolatory speeches, together with most of those in defence of accused persons, the delivery will be melancholy and subdued. When we speak in the senate, it will be authoritative, when we address the people, dignified, and when we are pleading in private cases, restrained.

De partibus causae et sententiis verbisque, quae
sunt multiplicia, pluribus dicendum.

154   Tria autem praestare debet pronuntiatio : conciliet,
persuadeat, moveat, quibus natura cohaeret, ut etiam
delectet. Conciliatio fere aut commendatione morum,
qui nescio quomodo ex voce etiam atque actione
pellucent, aut orationis suavitate constat; persuadendi vis adfirmatione, quae interim plus ipsis
155 probationibus valet. *An ista,* inquit Calidio Cicero,
si vera essent, sic a te dicerentur? et, *Tantum abfuit,
ut inflammares nostros animos; somnum isto loco vix
tenebamus.* Fiducia igitur appareat et constantia,
156 utique si auctoritas subest. Movendi autem ratio
aut in repraesentandis est aut imitandis adfectibus.
Ergo cum iudex in privatis aut praeco in publicis
dicere de causa iusserit, leniter consurgendum; tum
in componenda toga vel, si necesse erit, etiam ex
integro iniicienda, dumtaxat in iudiciis (apud principem enim et magistratus ac tribunalia non licebit),
paulum est commorandum, ut et amictus sit decentior
157 et protinus aliquid spatii ad cogitandum. Etiam

---

[1] *Brut.* lxxx. 278.

As regards the respective portions of speeches, thoughts and words, I must speak at somewhat greater length, as the problems involved are manifold.

There are three qualities which delivery should 154 possess. It should be conciliatory, persuasive and moving, and the possession of these three qualities involves charm as a further requisite. A conciliatory effect may be secured either by charm of style or by producing an impression of excellence of character, which is in some mysterious way clearly revealed both by voice and gesture. A persuasive effect, on the other hand, is produced by the power of assertion, which is sometimes more convincing even than actual proof. "Would those statements," says Cicero[1] to 155 Calidius, "have been delivered by you in such a manner if they had been true?" And again, "You were far from kindling our emotions. Indeed, at that point of your speech we could scarcely keep ourselves awake." We must therefore reveal both confidence and firmness, above all, if we have the requisite authority to back them. The method of 156 arousing the emotions depends on our power to represent or imitate the passions. Therefore when the judge in private, or the usher in public cases, calls upon us to speak, we must rise with deliberation. We shall then, to make our garb the more becoming, and to secure a moment for reflexion, devote a brief space to the arrangement of our toga or even, if necessary, to throwing it on afresh; but it must be borne in mind that this injunction applies only to cases in the courts; for we must not do this if we are speaking before the emperor or a magistrate, or in cases where the judge sits in a position of superior authority. Even when we turn to the judge, 157

cum ad iudicem nos converterimus, et consultus
praetor permiserit dicere, non protinus est erum-
pendum, sed danda brevis cogitationi mora. Mire
enim auditurum dicturi cura delectat, et iudex se
158 ipse componit. Hoc praecipit Homerus Ulixis
exemplo, quem stetisse oculis in terram defixis
immotoque sceptro, priusquam illam eloquentiae
procellam effunderet, dicit. In hac cunctatione
sunt quaedam non indecentes, ut appellant scenici,
morae, caput mulcere, manum intueri, infringere
articulos, simulare conatum, suspiratione sollicitudinem fateri, aut quod quemque magis decet,
eaque diutius, si iudex nondum intendet animum.
159 Status sit rectus, aequi et diducti paulum pedes
vel procedens minimo momento sinister; genua
recta, sic tamen, ut non extendantur; humeri
remissi, vultus severus, non maestus nec stupens
nec languidus; brachia a latere modice remota;
manus sinistra, qualem supra demonstravi; dextra,
cum iam incipiendum erit, paulum prolata ultra
sinum gestu quam modestissimo, velut spectans
160 quando incipiendum sit. Vitiosa enim sunt illa,
intueri lacunaria, perfricare faciem et quasi improbam
facere, tendere confidentia vultum aut, quo sit magis

---

[1] *Il.* iii. 217.   [2] Sect. 142.

and have requested and received the praetor's permission to address the court, we must not break forth at once into speech, but should allow ourselves a few moments for reflexion. For the display of such care on the part of one who is about to speak attracts the audience and gives the judge time to settle down. Homer[1] inculcates this practice by placing before 158 us the example of Ulysses, whom he describes as having stood for a while with eyes fixed on the ground and staff held motionless, before he poured forth his whirlwind of eloquence. In this preliminary delay there are certain pauses, as the actors call them, which are not unbecoming. We may stroke our head, look at our hand, wring the fingers, pretend to summon all our energies for the effort, confess to nervousness by a deep sigh, or may adopt any other method suited to our individual character, while these proceedings may be extended over some time, if we find that the judge is not yet giving us his attention. Our attitude should be upright, our 159 feet level and a slight distance apart, or the left may be very slightly advanced. The knees should be upright, but not stiff, the shoulders relaxed, the face stern, but not sad, expressionless or languid: the arms should be held slightly away from the side, the left hand being in the position described above,[2] while the right, at the moment when our speech begins, should be slightly extended beyond the fold of the toga with the most modest of gestures, as though waiting for the commencement. For it is 160 a mistake to look at the ceiling, to rub the face and give it a flush of impudence, to crane it boldly forward, to frown in order to secure a fierce expression, or brush back the hair from the forehead against its

torvus, superciliis adstringere, capillos a fronte
contra naturam retroagere, ut sit horror ille ter-
ribilis; tum, id quod Graeci frequentissime faciunt,
crebro digitorum labiorumque motu commentari,
clare excreare, pedem alterum longe proferre,
partem togae sinistra tenere, stare diductum vel
rigidum vel supinum vel incurvum vel humeris, ut
luctaturi solent, ad occipitium ductis.

161   Prooemio frequentissime lenis convenit pronuntiatio.   Nihil enim est ad conciliandum gratius verecundia, non tamen semper; neque enim uno modo
dicuntur exordia, ut docui.   Plerumque tamen et
vox temperata et gestus modestus et sedens humero
toga et laterum lenis in utramque partem motus,
162 eodem spectantibus oculis, decebit.   Narratio magis
prolatam manum, amictum recidentem, gestum dis-
tinctum, vocem sermoni proximam et tantum acri-
orem, sonum simplicem frequentissime postulabit in
his dumtaxat: *Q. enim Ligarius, cum esset in Africa
nulla belli suspicio,* et *A. Cluentius Habitus pater huiusce.*
Aliud in eadem poscent adfectus, vel concitati *Nubit*

---

[1] IV. i. 40.   [2] *pro Lig.* i. 2.
[3] *pro Cluent.* v. 11.   [4] *pro Cluent.* v. 14.

natural direction in order to produce a terrifying effect by making it stand on end. Again, there are other unseemly tricks, such as that so dear to the Greeks of twitching our fingers and lips as though studying what to say, clearing the throat with a loud noise, thrusting out one foot to a considerable distance, grasping a portion of the toga in the left hand, standing with feet wide apart, holding ourselves stiffly, leaning backwards, stooping, or hunching our shoulders toward the back of the head, as wrestlers do when about to engage.

A gentle delivery is most often best suited to the 161 *exordium.* For there is nothing better calculated than modesty to win the good-will of the judge, although there are exceptions to the rule, since, as I have already pointed out,[1] all *exordia* are not delivered in the same manner. But, generally speaking, a quiet voice, a modest gesture, a toga sitting well upon the shoulder, and a gentle motion of the sides to right and left, accompanied by a corresponding movement of the eyes, will all be found to produce a becoming effect. In the *statement of facts* the hand 162 should on most occasions be further extended, the toga allowed to slip back, the gestures sharply distinguished and the voice colloquial, but slightly more emphatic, while there should also be uniformity of tone. Such, at any rate, should be the delivery of a passage such as the following:[2] "For Quintus Ligarius, since there was no hint of the likelihood of the war in Africa," or[3] "Aulus Cluentius Habitus, this man's father." But different methods may be called for in this same portion of the speech, in passionate utterances such as, "The mother-in-law weds her son-in-law,"[4] or in pathetic passages such

genero socrus, vel flebiles *Constituitur in foro Laodiceae*
spectaculum acerbum et miserum toti Asiae provinciae.
163 Maxime varia et multiplex actio est probationum.
Nam et proponere, partiri, interrogare sermoni sunt
proxima, et contradictionem sumere : nam ea quoque
diversa propositio est. Sed haec tamen aliquando
164 irridentes, aliquando imitantes pronuntiamus. Argu-
mentatio plerumque agilior et acrior et instantior
consentientem orationi postulat etiam gestum, id est
fortem celeritatem. Instandum quibusdam in partibus
et densanda oratio. Egressiones fere lenes et dulces
et remissae, raptus Proserpinae, Siciliae descriptio,
Cn. Pompeii laus. Neque enim mirum minus habere
165 contentionis ea quae sunt extra quaestionem. Mollior
nonnunquam cum reprehensione diversae partis imitatio : *Videbar videre alios intrantes, alios autem exeuntes,*
quosdam ex vino vacillantes. Ubi non dissidens a voce
permittitur gestus quoque, in utramque partem tenera
quaedam, sed intra manus tamen et sine motu laterum
166 translatio. Accendendi iudicis plures sunt gradus.

---

[1] *Verr.* I. xxx. 76   [2] *cp.* IV. iii. 13.
[3] In the lost *pro Cornelio*: *cp.* IV. iii. 13.
[4] From the lost *pro Gallio.*

as, " There in the market-place of Laodicea was displayed a grievous and afflicting spectacle for all the province of Asia to behold." [1]   The *proofs,* however, 163 require the utmost variety of delivery.   For to state them and distinguish between their various points, and to examine witnesses, we employ something not far removed from a colloquial tone, as is also the case in anticipating objections, which is really another form of statement.   But in all these cases we sometimes deride, and sometimes mimic our opponents. *Argument,* being as a rule of a livelier, more energetic 164 and aggressive character, demands a type of gesture adapted to its style, that is to say, it should be bold and rapid.   There are certain portions of our arguments that require to be pressed home with energy, and in these our style must be compact and concentrated.   *Digressions,* as a rule, are characterised by gentleness, calm and placidity, as, for example, in Cicero's description of the Rape of Proserpine,[2] his picture of Sicily,[2] or his panegyric of Pompey.[3]   For naturally passages which deal with subjects lying outside the main question in dispute demand a less combative tone.   There are occasions on which we 165 may adopt a gentle manner in depreciating our opponents by giving a picture of their character, as in the following passage : [4] " I seemed to see some persons entering the room and others leaving it, while others were staggering to and fro under the influence of wine."   Under such circumstances we may even allow the gesture to match the voice, and may employ a gentle movement from side to side : but this motion should be confined to the hands, and there should be no movement of the flanks.   There 166 are a number of gradations of tone which may be

Summus ille et quo nullus est in oratore acutior:
Suscepto bello, Caesar, gesto iam etiam ex parte magna.
Praedixit enim: *Quantum potero voce contendam, ut
populus hoc Romanus exaudiat.* Paulum inferior et
habens aliquid iam iucunditatis: *Quid enim tuus ille,*
167 *Tubero, in acie Pharsalica gladius agebat?* Plenius
adhuc et lentius ideoque dulcius: *In coetu vero populi
Romani negotium publicum gerens.* Producenda omnia
trahendaeque tum vocales aperiendaeque sunt fauces.
Pleniore tamen haec canali fluunt: *Vos, Albani tumuli
atque luci.* Iam cantici quiddam habent sensimque
resupina sunt: *Saxa atque solitudines voci respondent.*
168 Tales sunt illae inclinationes vocis, quas invicem
Demosthenes atque Aeschines exprobrant, non ideo
improbandae; cum enim uterque alteri obiiciat, palam
est utrumque fecisse. Nam neque ille per Marathonis
et Plataearum et Salaminis propugnatores recto sono
169 iuravit, nec ille Thebas sermone deflevit. Est his
diversa vox et paene extra organum, cui Graeci

---

[1] *pro Lig.* iii. 7 and 6. [2] *pro Lig.* iii. 9.
[3] *Phil.* II. xxv. 63. [4] *pro Mil.* xxxi. 85.
[5] *pro Arch.* viii. 19. [6] *de Cor.* 90. [7] *In Ctes.* 72.
[8] *De Cor.* 60. [9] *In Ctes.* 49.

employed to kindle the feeling of the judges. The most vehement tones that an orator is ever called upon to use will be employed in passages such as the following : [1] " When the war was begun, Caesar, and was, in fact, well on its way to a conclusion." For he has just said : " I will use my voice to its fullest power, that all the Roman people may hear me." On the other hand, a lower tone, not devoid of a certain charm, should be employed in passages such as : [2] " What was that sword of yours doing, Tubero, that sword that was drawn on the field of Pharsalus?" But the utterance must be fuller, 167 slower, and consequently sweeter, when the orator says,[3] " But in an assembly of the Roman people, and when he was performing his official functions." In this passage every sound should be drawn out, we should dwell upon the vowel-sounds and speak full-throated. Still fuller should be the stream of our voice in the invocation,[4] " You, hills and groves of Alba"; while a tone not far removed from chanting, and dying away to a cadence, should be employed in delivering the phrase,[5] " Rocks and solitudes answer to the voice." These are the modulations denounced 168 by Demosthenes [6] and Aeschines,[7] but they do not necessarily for that reason merit our disapprobation. For as each of these orators taunts the other with making use of them, it is clear that they were employed by both. We may be sure that Demosthenes did not restrict himself to his ordinary simplicity of tone when he swore by those that fought for their country at Marathon, Plataea and Salamis,[8] nor did Aeschines employ a colloquial utterance when he lamented for the fate of Thebes.[9] There is also an entirely different 169 tone, which might be described as lying almost

nomen amaritudinis dederunt, super modum ac paene
naturam vocis humanae acerba : *Quin compescitis vocem
istam, indicem stultitiae, testem paucitatis ?* Sed id, quod
excedere modum dixi, in illa parte prima est : *Quin
compescitis.*

170   Epilogus, si enumerationem rerum habet, desiderat
quandam concisorum continuationem ; si ad conci-
tandos iudices est accommodatus, aliquid ex iis, quae
supra dixi ; si placandos, inclinatam quandam leni-
tatem ; si misericordia commovendos, flexum vocis
et flebilem suavitatem, qua praecipue franguntur
animi, quaeque est maxime naturalis. Nam etiam
orbos viduasque videas in ipsis funeribus canoro quo-
171 dam modo proclamantes. Hic etiam fusca illa vox,
qualem Cicero fuisse in Antonio dicit, mire faciet ;
habet enim in se, quod imitamur. Duplex est tamen
miseratio, altera cum invidia, qualis modo dicta de
damnatione Philodami, altera cum deprecatione
172 demissior. Quare, etiamsi est in illis quoque cantus
obscurior, *In coetu vero populi Romani* (non enim haec

---

¹ *pro Rab. perd.* vi. 18.   ² *Brut.* xxxviii. 141.
                           ³ § 162.

outside the range of the instrument. The Greeks call it bitterness, and it consists in an extravagant acerbity almost beyond the compass of the human voice. It is employed in passages such as,[1] "Why do you not restrain those cries, the proof of your folly and the evidence of your small numbers?" But the extravagance of which I spoke will come in at the opening, where the orator cries, "Why do you not restrain?"

The *peroration*, if it involves a recapitulation, 170 requires an even utterance of short, clear-cut clauses. If, on the other hand, it is designed to stir the emotions of the judges, it will demand some of the qualities already mentioned. If it aims at soothing them, it should flow softly; if it is to rouse them to pity, the voice must be delicately modulated to a melancholy sweetness, which is at once most natural and specially adapted to touch the heart. For it may be noted that even orphans and widows have a certain musical quality in the lamentations which they utter at funerals. A 171 muffled voice, such as Cicero[2] says was possessed by Antonius, will also be exceedingly effective under such circumstances, since it has just the natural tone which we seek to imitate. Appeals to pity are, however, of two kinds: they may be marked by an admixture of indignation, as in the passage just quoted[3] describing the condemnation of Philodamus, or they may be coupled with appeals for mercy, in which case their tone will be more subdued. Therefore although there is a suggestion of 172 the chanting tone in the delivery of such passages as "In an assembly of the Roman people" (for he did not utter these words in a contentious tone), or in

rixantis modo dixit); et *Vos, Albani tumuli* (non enim,
quasi inclamaret aut testaretur, locutus est), tamen
infinito magis illa flexa et circumducta sunt: *Me
miserum, me infelicem,* et *Quid respondebo liberis meis ?*
et *Revocare tu me in patriam potuisti, Milo, per hos ;
ego te in eadem patria per eosdem retinere non potero ?*
et cum bona C. Rabirii nummo[1] sestertio addicit:

173 *O meum miserum acerbumque praeconium.*   Illa quoque
mire facit in peroratione velut deficientis dolore et
fatigatione confessio, ut pro eodem Milone, *Sed finis
sit ; neque enim prae lacrimis iam loqui possum.*   Quae
similem verbis habere debent etiam pronuntiationem.

174 Possunt videri alia quoque huius partis atque officii,
reos excitare, pueros attollere, propinquos producere,
vestes laniare ; sed suo loco dicta sunt.

Et quia in partibus causae talis[2] est varietas, satis
apparet, accommodandam sententiis ipsis pronuntiationem, sicut ostendimus, sed verbis quoque, quod

175 novissime dixeram, non semper, sed aliquando.   An
non hoc *misellus et pauperculus* summissa atque contracta, *fortis et vehemens et latro* erecta et concitata

---

[1] nummo, *Bentley* : uno, *MSS.*
[2] causa talis, *ed. Camp* : causa et aliis, *B.*

---

[1] *pro Mil.* xxxvii. 102.
[2] *pro Rab. Post,* xvii. 46.   *addicit,* lit. "knocks down":
praeconium, lit. "the task of the public crier."
[3] *pro Mil.* xxxviii. 105.   [4] vi. i. 30.   [5] § 173.

" Ye hills and groves of Alba " (for he did not say this
as though he were appealing to them or calling them
to witness), the ensuing phrases [1] require infinitely
greater modulation and longer-drawn harmonies:
" Ah, woe is me, unhappy that I am ! " and " What
shall I reply to my children ? " and " You, Milo, had
the power to recall me to my country with the aid of
these men, and shall I be powerless by their aid to
keep you in that same country, your native land
and mine ? " or when he offers to sell the property of
Gaius Rabirius at one sesterce, " Ah, what a sad and
bitter task my voice is called on to perform ! " [2] Again, 173
it is a most effective device to confess in the peroration
that the strain of grief and fatigue is overpowering,
and that our strength is sinking beneath them, as
Cicero does in his defence of Milo : [3] " But here I must
make an end : I can no longer speak for tears." And
in such passages our delivery must conform to our
words. It may be thought that there are other points 174
which should be mentioned in connexion with the
duties of the orator in this portion of his speech, such
as calling forward the accused, lifting up his children
for the court to see, producing his kinsfolk, and
rending his garments ; but they have been dealt
with in their proper place. [4]

Such being the variety entailed by the different
portions of our pleading, it is sufficiently clear that
our delivery must be adapted to our matter, as I
have already shown, and sometimes also, though
not always conform to our actual words, as I have
just remarked. [5] For instance, must not the words, 175
" This poor wretched, poverty-stricken man," be
uttered in a low, subdued tone, whereas, " A bold
and violent fellow and a robber," is a phrase

voce dicendum est? Accedit enim vis et proprietas rebus tali adstipulatione, quae nisi adsit, aliud vox, 176 aliud animus ostendat. Quid? quod eadem verba mutata pronuntiatione indicant, adfirmant, exprobrant, negant, mirantur, indignantur, interrogant, irrident, elevant? Aliter enim dicitur: *Tu mihi quodcunque hoc regni* et *Cantando tu illum?* et *Tune ille Aeneas?* et *Meque timoris Argue tu, Drance.* Et ne morer, intra se quisque vel hoc vel aliud, quod volet, per omnes adfectus verset, verum esse quod dicimus sciet.

177 Unum iam his adiiciendum est, cum praecipue in actione spectetur decorum, saepe aliud alios decere. Est enim latens quaedam in hoc ratio et inenarrabilis; et ut vere hoc dictum est, caput esse artis decere quod facias, ita id neque sine arte esse neque

---

[1] *Aen.* i. 78. [2] *Ecl.* iii. 25. [3] *Aen.* i. 617.
[4] *Aen.* xi. 383. [5] *de Or.* I. xxix. 132

requiring a strong and energetic utterance? For such conformity gives a force and appropriateness to our matter, and without it the expression of the voice will be out of harmony with our thought. Again, what of the fact that a change of delivery 176 may make precisely the same words either demonstrate or affirm, express reproach, denial, wonder or indignation, interrogation, mockery or depreciation? For the word "thou" is given a different expression in each of the following passages:

"Thou this poor kingdom dost on me bestow."[1]

and

"Thou vanquish him in song?"[2]

and

"Art thou, then, that Aeneas?"[3]

and

"And of fear,
Do thou accuse me, Drances!"[4]

To cut a long matter short, if my reader will take this or any other word he chooses and run it through the whole gamut of emotional expression, he will realise the truth of what I say.

There is one further remark which I must add, 177 namely, that while what is becoming is the main consideration in delivery, different methods will often suit different speakers. For this is determined by a principle which, though it is obscure and can hardly be expressed in words, none the less exists: and, though it is a true saying[5] that "the main secret of artistic success is that whatever we do should become us well," none the less, despite the fact that such success cannot be

178 totum arte tradi potest. In quibusdam virtutes non
habent gratiam, in quibusdam vitia ipsa delectant.
Maximos actores comoediarum, Demetrium et Strato-
clea, placere diversis virtutibus vidimus. Sed illud
minus mirum, quod alter deos et iuvenes et bonos
patres servosque et matronas et graves anus optime,
alter acres senes, callidos servos, parasitos, lenones
et omnia agitatiora melius : fuit enim natura diversa.
Nam vox quoque Demetrii iucundior, illius acrior

179 erat. Adnotandae magis proprietates, quae transferri non poterant, manus iactare et dulces excla-
mationes theatri causa producere et ingrediendo
ventum concipere veste et nonnunquam dextro latere
facere gestus, quod neminem alium nisi Demetrium
decuit ; namque in haec omnia statura et mira specie

180 adiuvabatur ; illum cursus et agilitas et vel parum
conveniens personae risus, quem non ignarus rationis
populo dabat, et contracta etiam cervicula. Quidquid horum alter fecisset, foedissimum videretur.

attained without art, it is impossible entirely to com-
municate the secret by the rules of art. There are 178
some persons in whom positive excellences have no
charm, while there are others whose very faults give
pleasure. We have seen the greatest of comic actors,
Demetrius and Stratocles, win their success by
entirely different merits. But that is the less
surprising owing to the fact that the one was at his
best in the rôles of gods, young men, good fathers
and slaves, matrons and respectable old women,
while the other excelled in the portrayal of sharp-
tempered old men, cunning slaves, parasites, pimps
and all the more lively characters of comedy. For
their natural gifts differed. For Demetrius' voice,
like his other qualities, had greater charm, while
that of Stratocles was the more powerful. But 179
yet more noticeable were the incommunicable
peculiarities of their action. Demetrius showed
unique gifts in the movements of his hands, in
his power to charm his audience by the long-
drawn sweetness of his exclamations, the skill with
which he would make his dress seem to puff out
with wind as he walked, and the expressive movements of the right side which he sometimes introduced with effect, in all of which things he was
helped by his stature and personal beauty. On the 180
other hand, Stratocles' *forte* lay in his nimbleness
and rapidity of movement, in his laugh (which,
though not always in keeping with the character
he represented, he deliberately employed to awaken
answering laughter in his audience), and finally, even
in the way in which he sank his neck into his
shoulders. If either of these actors had attempted
any of his rival's tricks, he would have produced a

Quare norit se quisque, nec tantum ex communibus praeceptis, sed etiam ex natura sua capiat consilium 181 formandae actionis. Neque illud tamen est nefas, ut aliquem vel omnia vel plura deceant. Huius quoque loci clausula sit eadem necesse est, quae ceterorum est, regnare maxime modum. Non enim comoedum esse, sed oratorem volo. Quare neque in gestu persequemur omnes argutias nec in loquendo distinctionibus, temporibus, adfectionibus moleste 182 utemur. Ut si sit in scena dicendum:

> *Quid igitur faciam? non eam, ne nunc quidem,*
> *Cum arcessor ultro? an potius ita me comparem,*
> *Non perpeti meretricum contumelias?*

Hic enim dubitationis moras, vocis flexus, varias manus, diversos nutus actor adhibebit. Aliud oratio sapit nec vult nimium esse condita; actione enim 183 constat, non imitatione. Quare non immerito reprehenditur pronuntiatio vultuosa et gesticulationibus molesta et vocis mutationibus resultans. Nec inutiliter ex Graecis veteres transtulerunt, quod ab iis sumptum Laenas Popilius posuit, esse hanc negotiosam[1] actio- 184 nem. Optime igitur idem, qui omnia, Cicero prae-

---

[1] negotiosam, *Halm:* mocosam, *B.*

---

[1] Ter. *Eun.* I. i. 1.

most unbecoming effect. Consequently, every man must get to know his own peculiarities and must consult not merely the general rules of technique, but his own nature as well with a view to forming his delivery. But there is no law of heaven which 181 prohibits the possession of all or at any rate the majority of styles by one and the same person. I must conclude this topic with a remark which applies to all my other topics as well, that the prime essential is a sense of proportion. For I am not trying to form a comic actor, but an orator. Consequently, we need not study all the details of gesture nor, as regards our speaking, be pedantic in the use we make of the rules governing punctuation, rhythm and appeals to the emotions. For example, if an 182 actor has to speak the following lines on the stage :[1]

"What shall I do then? Not go, even now,
Now when she calls me? Or shall I steel my soul
No longer to endure a harlot's insults?"

he will hesitate as in doubt, will vary the modulations of his voice, together with the movements of hand and head. But oratory has a different flavour and objects to elaborate condiments, since it consists in serious pleading, not in mimicry. There is, there- 183 fore, good reason for the condemnation passed on a delivery which entails the continual alteration of facial expression, annoying restlessness of gesture and gusty changes of tone. And it was a wise saying that the ancient orators borrowed from the Greeks, as is recorded by Popilius Laenas, to the effect that there is too much "business" in such delivery. The 184 instructions given by Cicero on this subject, as on all others, are quite admirable ; I allude to the passages

ceperat, quae supra ex Oratore posui ; quibus similia
in Bruto de M. Antonio dicit. Sed iam recepta est
actio paulo agitatior et exigitur et quibusdam partibus
convenit, ita tamen temperanda, ne, dum actoris
captamus elegantiam, perdamus viri boni et gravis
auctoritatem.

which I have already quoted from his *Orator*,[1] while there are similar observations in the *Brutus*[2] with reference to Marcus Antonius. But to-day a rather more violent form of delivery has come into fashion and is demanded of our orators: it is well adapted to certain portions of a speech, but requires to be kept under control. Otherwise, in our attempt to ape the elegances of the stage, we shall lose the authority which should characterise the man of dignity and virtue.

[1] § 122.   [2] *Brut.* xxxviii. 141.

BOOK XII

LIBER XII

Ventum est ad partem operis destinati longe gra-
vissimam. Cuius equidem onus si tantum opinione
prima concipere potuissem, quanto me premi ferens
sentio, maturius consuluissem vires meas. Sed initio
pudor omittendi, quae promiseram, tenuit; mox,
quanquam per singulas prope partes labor cresceret,
ne perderem, quae iam effecta erant, per omnes
2 difficultates animo me sustentavi. Quare nunc quoque, licet maior quam unquam moles premat, tamen
prospicienti finem mihi constitutum est vel deficere
potius quam desperare. Fefellit autem quod initium
a parvis ceperamus. Mox velut aura sollicitante
provecti longius, dum tamen nota illa et plerisque
artium scriptoribus tractata praecipimus, nec adhuc
a litore procul videbamur et multos circa velut iisdem
3 se ventis credere ausos habebamus. Iam cum eloquendi rationem novissime repertam paucissimisque

BOOK XII

I now come to what is by far the most arduous portion of the task which I have set myself to perform. Indeed had I fully realised the difficulties when I first designed this work, I should have considered betimes whether my strength was sufficient to support the load that now weighs upon me so heavily. But to begin with, I felt how shameful it would be to fail to perform what I had promised, and later, despite the fact that my labour became more and more arduous at almost every stage, the fear of stultifying what I had already written sustained my courage through every difficulty. Consequently 2 even now, though the burden that oppresses me is greater than ever, the end is in sight and I am resolved to faint by the wayside rather than despair. But the fact that I began with comparatively trivial details deceived me. Subsequently I was lured still further on my voyage by the temptations of the favouring breeze that filled my sails; but the rules which I was then concerned to give were still of a familiar kind and had been already treated by most writers of rhetorical textbooks: thus far I seemed to myself to be still in sight of shore and I had the company of many who had ventured to entrust themselves to the self-same winds. But presently when 3 I entered on the task of setting forth a theory of

temptatam ingressi sumus, rarus, qui tam procul a
portu recessisset, reperiebatur. Postquam vero nobis
ille, quem instituebamus, orator a dicendi magistris
dimissus aut suo iam impetu fertur aut maiora sibi
auxilia ex ipsis sapientiae penetralibus petit, quam
4 in altum simus ablati sentire coepimus. Nunc *caelum
undique et undique pontus*. Unum modo in illa im-
mensa vastitate cernere videmur M. Tullium, qui
tamen ipse, quamvis tanta atque ita instructa nave
hoc mare ingressus, contrahit vela inhibetque remos
et de ipso demum genere dicendi, quo sit usurus
perfectus orator, satis habet dicere. At nostra
temeritas etiam mores ei conabitur dare et adsignabit
officia. Ita nec antecedentem consequi possumus,
et longius eundum est, ut res feret. Probabilis tamen
cupiditas honestorum et velut tutioris[1] audentiae
est temptare, quibus paratior venia est.

I. Sit ergo nobis orator, quem constituimus, is,
qui a M. Catone finitur, *vir bonus dicendi peritus;*
verum, id quod et ille posuit prius et ipsa natura
potius ac maius est, utique vir bonus. Id non eo
tantum, quod, si vis illa dicendi malitiam instruxerit,
nihil sit publicis privatisque rebus perniciosius elo-

---

[1] velut tutioris, *Obrecht:* velutioris, *B.*

---

[1] *Aen.* iii. 193.   [2] *cp.* I. *Pr.* 9.

eloquence which had been but newly discovered and rarely essayed, I found but few that had ventured so far from harbour. And finally now that the ideal orator, whom it was my design to mould, has been dismissed by his masters and is either proceeding on his way borne onward by his own impetus, or seeking still mightier assistance from the innermost shrine of wisdom, I begin to feel how far I have been swept into the great deep. Now there is   **4**

> "Nothing before and nothing behind but the sky and the Ocean."[1]

One only can I discern in all the boundless waste of waters, Marcus Tullius Cicero, and even he, though the ship in which he entered these seas is of such size and so well found, begins to lessen sail and to row a slower stroke, and is content to speak merely of the kind of speech to be employed by the perfect orator. But my temerity is such that I shall essay to form my orator's character and to teach him his duties. Thus I have no predecessor to guide my steps and must press far, far on, as my theme may demand. Still an honourable ambition is always deserving of approval, and it is all the less hazardous to dare greatly, when forgiveness is assured us if we fail.

I. The orator then, whom I am concerned to form, shall be the orator as defined by Marcus Cato, "a good man, skilled in speaking."[2] But above all he must possess the quality which Cato places first and which is in the very nature of things the greatest and most important, that is, he must be a good man. This is essential not merely on account of the fact that, if the powers of eloquence serve only to lend arms to crime, there can be nothing more pernicious than

quentia, nosque ipsi, qui pro virili parte conferre
aliquid ad facultatem dicendi conati sumus, pessime
mereamur de rebus humanis, si latroni comparamus
2 haec arma, non militi.   Quid de nobis loquor?
Rerum ipsa natura in eo, quod praecipue indulsisse
homini videtur quoque nos a ceteris animalibus se-
parasse, non parens, sed noverca fuerit, si facultatem
dicendi, sociam scelerum, adversam innocentiae,
hostem veritatis invenit. Mutos enim nasci et egere
omni ratione satius fuisset quam providentiae mu-
3 nera in mutuam perniciem convertere.   Longius
tendit hoc iudicium meum.   Neque enim tantum
id dico, eum, qui sit orator, virum bonum esse
oportere, sed ne futurum quidem oratorem nisi virum
bonum. Nam certe neque intelligentiam concesseris
iis qui, proposita honestorum ac turpium via, peiorem
sequi malent, neque prudentiam, cum in gravissimas
frequenter legum, semper vero malae conscientiae
poenas a semet ipsis improviso rerum exitu induantur.
4 Quodsi neminem malum esse nisi stultum eundem
non modo a sapientibus dicitur, sed vulgo quoque
semper est creditum, certe non fiet unquam stultus
orator. Adde quod ne studio quidem operis pulcherrimi vacare mens nisi omnibus vitiis libera potest:
primum quod in eodem pectore nullum est honestorum turpiumque consortium, et cogitare optima
simul ac deterrima non magis est unius animi quam

eloquence to public and private welfare alike, while
I myself, who have laboured to the best of my ability
to contribute something of value to oratory, shall have
rendered the worst of services to mankind, if I forge
these weapons not for a soldier, but for a robber.
But why speak of myself? Nature herself will have 2
proved not a mother, but a stepmother with regard
to what we deem her greatest gift to man, the gift
that distinguishes us from other living things, if she
devised the power of speech to be the accomplice of
crime, the foe to innocency and the enemy of truth.
For it had been better for men to be born dumb and
devoid of reason than to turn the gifts of providence
to their mutual destruction. But this conviction of 3
mine goes further. For I do not merely assert that
the ideal orator should be a good man, but I affirm
that no man can be an orator unless he is a good man.
For it is impossible to regard those men as gifted
with intelligence who on being offered the choice
between the two paths of virtue and of vice choose
the latter, nor can we allow them prudence, when
by the unforeseen issue of their own actions they
render themselves liable not merely to the heaviest
penalties of the laws, but to the inevitable torment
of an evil conscience. But if the view that a bad 4
man is necessarily a fool is not merely held by philosophers, but is the universal belief of ordinary men,
the fool will most assuredly never become an orator.
To this must be added the fact that the mind will
not find leisure even for the study of the noblest of
tasks, unless it first be free from vice. The reasons for
this are, first, that vileness and virtue cannot jointly
inhabit in the selfsame heart and that it is as impossible for one and the same mind to harbour good

357

5 eiusdem hominis bonum esse ac malum; tum illa quoque ex causa, quod mentem tantae rei intentam vacare omnibus aliis etiam culpa carentibus curis oportet. Ita demum enim libera ac tota, nulla distringente atque alio ducente causa, spectabit id 6 solum ad quod accingitur. Quodsi agrorum nimia cura et sollicitior rei familiaris diligentia et venandi voluptas et dati spectaculis dies multum studiis auferunt (huic enim rei perit tempus, quodcunque alteri datur), quid putamus facturas cupiditatem, avaritiam, invidiam, quarum impotentissimae cogitationes somnos etiam ipsos et illa per quietem visa perturbent? 7 Nihil est enim tam occupatum, tam multiforme, tot ac tam variis adfectibus concisum atque laceratum quam mala mens. Nam et cum insidiatur, spe, curis, labore distringitur; et etiam cum sceleris compos fuit, sollicitudine, paenitentia, poenarum omnium exspectatione torquetur. Quis inter haec litteris aut ulli bonae arti locus? Non hercule magis quam frugibus in terra sentibus ac rubis occupata. 8 Age, non ad perferendos studiorum labores necessaria frugalitas? Quid ergo ex libidine ac luxuria spei? Non praecipue acuit ad cupiditatem litterarum amor

and evil thoughts as it is for one man to be at once
both good and evil : and secondly, that if the intelli- 5
gence is to be concentrated on such a vast subject as
eloquence it must be free from all other distractions,
among which must be included even those preoccu-
pations which are free from blame.　For it is only
when it is free and self-possessed, with nothing to
divert it or lure it elsewhere, that it will fix its
attention solely on that goal, the attainment of which
is the object of its preparations.　If on the other 6
hand inordinate care for the development of our
estates, excess of anxiety over household affairs,
passionate devotion to hunting or the sacrifice of
whole days to the shows of the theatre, rob our
studies of much of the time that is their due (for
every moment that is given to other things involves
a loss of time for study), what, think you, will be the
results of desire, avarice, and envy, which waken such
violent thoughts within our souls that they disturb
our very slumbers and our dreams?　There is nothing 7
so preoccupied, so distracted, so rent and torn by so
many and such varied passions as an evil mind.　For
when it cherishes some dark design, it is tormented
with hope, care and anguish of spirit, and even when
it has accomplished its criminal purpose, it is racked
by anxiety, remorse and the fear of all manner of
punishments.　Amid such passions as these what
room is there for literature or any virtuous pursuit ?
You might as well look for fruit in land that is choked
with thorns and brambles.　Well then, I ask you, is 8
not simplicity of life essential if we are to be able to
endure the toil entailed by study ?　What can we
hope to get from lust or luxury ?　Is not the desire
to win praise one of the strongest stimulants to a

laudis? Num igitur malis esse laudem curae putamus? Iam hoc quis non videt, maximam partem orationis in tractatu aequi bonique consistere? Dicetne de his secundum debitam rerum dignitatem malus atque

9 iniquus? Denique, ut maximam partem quaestionis eximam, demus, id quod nullo modo fieri potest, idem ingenii, studii, doctrinae, pessimo atque optimo viro: uter melior dicetur orator? Nimirum qui homo quoque melior. Non igitur unquam malus idem

10 homo et perfectus orator. Non enim perfectum est quidquam, quo melius est aliud. Sed, ne more Socraticorum nobismet ipsi responsum finxisse videamur, sit aliquis adeo contra veritatem obstinatus, ut audeat dicere, eodem ingenio, studio, doctrina praeditum nihilo deteriorem futurum oratorem malum virum quam bonum: convincamus huius quoque

11 amentiam. Nam hoc certe nemo dubitabit, omnem orationem id agere, ut iudici, quae proposita fuerint, vera et honesta videantur. Utrum igitur hoc facilius bonus vir persuadebit an malus? Bonus quidem et

12 dicet saepius vera atque honesta. Sed etiam si quando aliquo ductus officio (quod accidere, ut mox docebimus, potest) falso haec adfirmare conabitur,

passion for literature? But does that mean that we
are to suppose that praise is an object of concern to
bad men? Surely every one of my readers must by
now have realised that oratory is in the main concerned with the treatment of what is just and
honourable? Can a bad and unjust man speak on
such themes as the dignity of the subject demands?
Nay, even if we exclude the most important aspects 9
of the question now before us, and make the impossible concession that the best and worst of men
may have the same talent, industry and learning, we
are still confronted by the question as to which of
the two is entitled to be called the better orator. The
answer is surely clear enough: it will be he who is
the better man. Consequently, the bad man and the
perfect orator can never be identical. For nothing 10
is perfect, if there exists something else that is
better. However, as I do not wish to appear to
adopt the practice dear to the Socratics of framing
answers to my own questions, let me assume the
existence of a man so obstinately blind to the truth
as to venture to maintain that a bad man equipped
with the same talents, industry and learning will
be not a whit inferior to the good man as an
orator; and let me show that he too is mad.
There is one point at any rate which no one will 11
question, namely, that the aim of every speech is to
convince the judge that the case which it puts forward is true and honourable. Well then, which will
do this best, the good man or the bad? The good
man will without doubt more often say what is true
and honourable. But even supposing that his duty 12
should, as I shall show may sometimes happen, lead
him to make statements which are false, his words

maiore cum fide necesse est audiatur. At malis
hominibus ex contemptu opinionis et ignorantia recti
nonnunquam excidit ipsa simulatio. Inde immodeste
13 proponunt, sine pudore adfirmant. Sequitur in iis,
quae certum est effici non posse, deformis pertinacia
et irritus labor. Nam sicut in vita, ita in causis
quoque spes improbas habent. Frequenter autem
accidit, ut iis etiam vera dicentibus fides desit,
videaturque talis advocatus malae causae argumentum.
14   Nunc de iis dicendum est, quae mihi quasi con-
spiratione quadam vulgi reclamari videntur. Orator
ergo Demosthenes non fuit? atqui malum virum
accepimus. Non Cicero? atqui huius quoque mores
multi reprehenderunt. Quid agam? magna responsi
invidia subeunda est, mitigandae sunt prius aures.
15 Mihi enim nec Demosthenes tam gravi morum dignus videtur invidia, ut omnia, quae in eum ab
inimicis congesta sunt, credam, cum et pulcherrima
eius in re publica consilia et finem vitae clarum
16 legam, nec Marco Tullio defuisse video in ulla parte
civis optimi voluntatem. Testimonio est actus nobi-
lissime consulatus, integerrime provincia administrata
et repudiatus vigintiviratus, et civilibus bellis, quae

are still certain to carry greater weight with his
audience. On the other hand bad men, in their
contempt for public opinion and their ignorance of
what is right, sometimes drop their mask unawares,
and are impudent in the statement of their case and
shameless in their assertions. Further, in their 13
attempt to achieve the impossible they display an
unseemly persistency and unavailing energy. For
in lawsuits no less than in the ordinary paths of
life, they cherish depraved expectations. But it
often happens that even when they tell the truth
they fail to win belief, and the mere fact that such
a man is its advocate is regarded as an indication of
the badness of the case.

I must now proceed to deal with the objections 14
which common opinion is practically unanimous in
bringing against this view. Was not Demosthenes
an orator? And yet we are told that he was a bad
man. Was not Cicero an orator? And yet there
are many who have found fault with his character as
well. What am I to answer? My reply will be
highly unpopular and I must first attempt to conciliate my audience. I do not consider that 15
Demosthenes deserves the serious reflexions that
have been made upon his character to such an
extent that I am bound to believe all the charges
amassed against him by his enemies; for my reading
tells me that his public policy was of the noblest and
his end most glorious. Again, I cannot see that the 16
aims of Cicero were in any portion of his career other
than such as may become an excellent citizen. As
evidence I would cite the fact that his behaviour as
consul was magnificent and his administration of his
province a model of integrity, while he refused to

in aetatem eius gravissima inciderunt, neque spe
neque metu declinatus animus, quo minus optimis
17 se partibus, id est rei publicae, iungeret. Parum
fortis videtur quibusdam, quibus optime respondit
ipse, *non se timidum in suscipiendis, sed in providendis
periculis;* quod probavit morte quoque ipsa, quam
18 praestantissimo suscepit animo. Quodsi defuit his
viris summa virtus, sic quaerentibus, an oratores
fuerint, respondebo, quomodo Stoici, si interrogentur
an sapiens Zeno, an Cleanthes, an Chrysippus ipse,
respondeant, magnos quidem illos ac venerabiles,
non tamen id, quod natura hominis summum habet,
19 consecutos. Nam et Pythagoras non sapientem se,
ut qui ante eum fuerunt, sed studiosum sapientiae
vocari voluit. Ego tamen secundum communem
loquendi consuetudinem saepe dixi dicamque, perfectum oratorem esse Ciceronem; ut amicos et bonos
viros et prudentissimos dicimus vulgo, quorum nihil
nisi perfecte sapienti datur. Sed cum proprie et ad
legem ipsam veritatis loquendum erit, eum quaeram
20 oratorem, quem et ille quaerebat. Quanquam enim
stetisse ipsum in fastigio eloquentiae fateor, ac vix,
quid adiici potuerit, invenio, fortasse inventurus,

---

[1] For the distribution of the Campanian lands.
[2] *i. e.* φιλόσοφος, a term of which he was reputed the
inventor.

become one of the twenty commissioners,[1] and in the
grievous civil wars which afflicted his generation
beyond all others, neither hope nor fear ever deterred
him from giving his support to the better party, that
is to say, to the interests of the common weal.
Some, it is true, regard him as lacking in courage. 17
The best answer to these critics is to be found in his
own words, to the effect that he was timid not in
confronting peril, but in anticipating it. And this
he proved also by the manner of his death, in meeting
which he displayed a singular fortitude. But even 18
if these two men lacked the perfection of virtue, I
will reply to those who ask if they were orators, in
the manner in which the Stoics would reply, if asked
whether Zeno, Cleanthes or Chrysippus himself were
wise men. I shall say that they were great men
deserving our veneration, but that they did not
attain to that which is the highest perfection
of man's nature. For did not Pythagoras desire 19
that he should not be called a wise man, like the
sages who preceded him, but rather a student of
wisdom?[2] But for my own part, conforming to the
language of every day, I have said time and again,
and shall continue to say, that Cicero was a perfect
orator, just as in ordinary speech we call our friends
good and sensible men, although neither of these
titles can really be given to any save to him that
has attained to perfect wisdom. But if I am called
upon to speak strictly and in accordance with the
most rigid laws of truth, I shall proclaim that I seek
to find that same perfect orator whom Cicero also
sought to discover. For while I admit that he stood 20
on the loftiest pinnacle of eloquence, and can discover scarcely a single deficiency in him, although I

quod adhuc abscisurum putem fuisse (nam fere
sic docti iudicaverunt, plurimum in eo virtutum,
nonnihil fuisse vitiorum, et se ipse multa ex illa iuve-
nili abundantia coercuisse testatur), tamen, quando
nec sapientis sibi nomen, minime sui contemptor,
asseruit et melius dicere, certe data longiore vita et
tempore [1] ad componendum securiore, potuisset, non
maligne crediderim defuisse ei summam illam, ad
21 quam nemo propius accessit. Et licebat, si aliter
sentirem, fortius id liberiusque defendere. An vero
M. Antonius neminem a se visum eloquentem, quod
tanto minus erat, professus est; ipse etiam M. Tullius
quaerit adhuc eum et tantum imaginatur ac fingit,
ego non audeam dicere, aliquid in hac, quae superest, aeternitate inveniri posse eo, quod fuerit, per-
22 fectius? Transeo illos, qui Ciceroni ac Demostheni
ne in eloquentia quidem satis tribuunt; quanquam
neque ipsi Ciceroni Demosthenes videatur satis esse
perfectus, quem dormitare interim dicit, nec Cicero
Bruto Calvoque, qui certe compositionem illius etiam
apud ipsum reprehendunt, nec Asinio utrique, qui
vitia orationis eius etiam inimice pluribus locis
insequuntur.

[1] tempore, *Burman:* te, *B.*

---

[1] *Brut.* xci. 316. *Orat.* xxx. 107.
[2] Quintilian's reverence for Cicero is such that he feels
hampered in maintaining his thesis.
[3] See x. i. 24.

might perhaps discover certain superfluities which I
think he would have pruned away (for the general
view of the learned is that he possessed many virtues
and a few faults, and he himself[1] states that he has
succeeded in suppressing much of his youthful
exuberance), none the less, in view of the fact that,
although he had by no means a low opinion of himself, he never claimed to be the perfect sage, and,
had he been granted longer life and less troubled conditions for the composition of his works, would doubtless have spoken better still, I shall not lay myself
open to the charge of ungenerous criticism, if I say
that I believe that he failed actually to achieve that
perfection to the attainment of which none have
approached more nearly, and indeed had I felt other- 21
wise in this connexion, I might have defended my
point with greater boldness and freedom.[2] Marcus
Antonius declared that he had seen no man who was
genuinely eloquent (and to be eloquent is a far less
achievement than to be an orator), while Cicero himself has failed to find his orator in actual life and
merely imagines and strives to depict the ideal. Shall
I then be afraid to say that in the eternity of time
that is yet to be, something more perfect may be found
than has yet existed? I say nothing of those critics 22
who will not allow sufficient credit even for eloquence
to Cicero and Demosthenes, although Cicero himself
does not regard Demosthenes as flawless, but asserts
that he sometimes nods,[3] while even Cicero fails to
satisfy Brutus and Calvus (at any rate they criticised
his style to his face), or to win the complete approval
of either of the Asinii, who in various passages attack
the faults of his oratory in language which is positively
hostile.

23 Concedamus sane, quod minime natura patitur,
repertum esse aliquem malum virum summe diser-
tum : nihilo tamen minus oratorem eum negabo.
Nam nec omnibus, qui fuerint manu prompti, viri
fortis nomen concesserim, quia sine virtute intelligi
24 non potest fortitudo. An ei, qui ad defendendas
causas advocatur, non est opus fide, quam nec cupiditas corrumpat nec gratia avertat nec metus frangat ;
sed proditorem, transfugam, praevaricatorem dona-
bimus oratoris illo sacro nomine ? Quodsi medio-
cribus etiam patronis convenit haec, quae vulgo
dicitur, bonitas, cur non orator ille, qui nondum fuit,
sed potest esse, tam sit moribus quam dicendi virtute
25 perfectus ? Non enim forensem quandam instituimus
operam nec mercennariam vocem nec, ut asperi-
oribus verbis parcamus, non inutilem sane litium
advocatum, quem denique causidicum vulgo vocant,
sed virum cum ingenii natura praestantem tum vero
tot pulcherrimas artes penitus mente complexum,
datum tandem rebus humanis, qualem nulla antea
vetustas cognoverit, singularem perfectumque undi-
26 que, optima sentientem optimeque dicentem. In
hoc quota pars erit, quod aut innocentes tuebitur
aut improborum scelera compescet, aut in pecuni-
ariis quaestionibus veritati contra calumniam aderit ?
Summus ille quidem in his quoque operibus fuerit,
sed maioribus clarius elucebit, cum regenda senatus

However, let us fly in the face of nature and 23
assume that a bad man has been discovered who is
endowed with the highest eloquence. I shall none
the less deny that he is an orator. For I should not
allow that every man who has shown himself ready
with his hands was necessarily a brave man, because
true courage cannot be conceived of without the
accompaniment of virtue. Surely the advocate who 24
is called to defend the accused requires to be a man
of honour, honour which greed cannot corrupt, influence seduce, or fear dismay. Shall we then dignify the traitor, the deserter, the turncoat with the
sacred name of orator? But if the quality which is
usually termed goodness is to be found even in quite
ordinary advocates, why should not the orator, who
has not yet existed, but may still be born, be no less
perfect in character than in excellence of speech?
It is no hack-advocate, no hireling pleader, nor yet, 25
to use no harsher term, a serviceable attorney of the
class generally known as *causidici*, that I am seeking to
form, but rather a man who to extraordinary natural
gifts has added a thorough mastery of all the fairest
branches of knowledge, a man sent by heaven to be
the blessing of mankind, one to whom all history
can find no parallel, uniquely perfect in every detail
and utterly noble alike in thought and speech. How 26
small a portion of all these abilities will be required
for the defence of the innocent, the repression of
crime or the support of truth against falsehood in
suits involving questions of money? It is true that
our supreme orator will bear his part in such tasks,
but his powers will be displayed with brighter splendour in greater matters than these, when he is
called upon to direct the counsels of the senate and

27 consilia et popularis error ad meliora ducendus. An non talem quendam videtur finxisse Vergilius, quem in seditione vulgi iam faces et saxa iaculantis moderatorem dedit:

> *Tum pietate gravem ac meritis si forte virum quem*
> *Conspexere, silent arrectisque auribus adstant?*

Habemus igitur ante omnia virum bonum, post haec adiiciet dicendi peritum:

> *Ille regit dictis animos et pectora mulcet.*

28 Quid? non in bellis quoque idem ille vir, quem instituimus, si sit ad proelium miles cohortandus, ex mediis sapientiae praeceptis orationem trahet? Nam quomodo pugnam ineuntibus tot simul metus laboris, dolorum, postremo mortis ipsius exciderint, nisi in eorum locum pietas et fortitudo et honesti
29 praesens imago successerit? Quae certe melius persuadebit aliis qui prius persuaserit sibi. Prodit enim se, quamlibet custodiatur, simulatio, nec unquam tanta fuerit loquendi facultas, ut non titubet atque haereat,[1] quotiens ab animo verba dissentiunt. Vir autem malus aliud dicat necesse est quam sentit.
30 Bonos nunquam honestus sermo deficiet, nunquam rerum optimarum (nam iidem etiam prudentes erunt)

---

[1] atque haereat, *Buttmann:* adhaereat, *B.*

---

[1] *Aen.* i. 151 *sqq.*

guide the people from the paths of error to better
things. Was not this the man conceived by Virgil 27
and described as quelling a riot when torches and
stones have begun to fly :[1]

" Then, if before their eyes some statesman grave
    Stand forth, with virtue and high service crowned,
    Straight are they dumb and stand intent to hear."

Here then we have one who is before all else a
good man, and it is only after this that the poet adds
that he is skilled in speaking :

"His words their minds control, their passions soothe."

Again, will not this same man, whom we are striving 28
to form, if in time of war he be called upon to inspire
his soldiers with courage for the fray, draw for his
eloquence on the innermost precepts of philosophy ?
For how can men who stand upon the verge of battle
banish all the crowding fears of hardship, pain and
death from their minds, unless those fears be re-
placed by the sense of the duty that they owe
their country, by courage and the lively image of a
soldier's honour ? And assuredly the man who will 29
best inspire such feelings in others is he who has
first inspired them in himself. For however we strive
to conceal it, insincerity will always betray itself, and
there was never in any man so great eloquence as
would not begin to stumble and hesitate so soon as
his words ran counter to his inmost thoughts. Now 30
a bad man cannot help speaking things other than
he feels. On the other hand, the good will never be
at a loss for honourable words or fail to find matter
full of virtue for utterance, since among his virtues
practical wisdom will be one. And even though his

inventio; quae etiamsi lenociniis destituta sit, satis
tamen natura sua ornatur nec quidquam non diserte,
31 quod honeste, dicitur.   Quare, iuventus, immo omnes
aetates, (neque enim rectae voluntati serum est
tempus ullum) totis mentibus huc tendamus, in hoc
elaboremus; forsan et consummare contingat.   Nam
si natura non prohibet et esse virum bonum et esse
dicendi peritum, cur non aliquis etiam unus utrumque
consequi possit? cur autem non se quisque speret
32 fore illum aliquem?   Ad quod si vires ingenii non
suffecerint, tamen ad quem usque modum processe-
rimus, meliores erimus ex utroque.   Hoc certe procul
eximatur animo, rerum [1] pulcherrimam eloquentiam
cum vitiis mentis posse misceri.   Facultas dicendi,
si in malos incidit, et ipsa iudicanda est malum;
peiores enim illos facit, quibus contigit.
33   Videor mihi audire quosdam (neque enim deerunt
unquam, qui diserti esse quam boni malint) illa
dicentes: Quid ergo tantum est artis in eloquentia?
cur tu de coloribus et difficilium causarum defensione, nonnihil etiam de confessione locutus es, nisi
aliquando vis ac facultas dicendi expugnat ipsam
veritatem?   Bonus enim vir non agit nisi bonas
causas, eas porro etiam sine doctrina satis per se
34 tuetur veritas ipsa.   Quibus ego, cum de meo pri-

---

[1] rerum, *Regius:* rem, *B.*

---

[1] *color* is a technical term for "the particular aspect given
to a case by skilful manipulation of the facts—the 'gloss'
or 'varnish' put on them by the accused or accuser."—Peterson *on Quint.* **x.** i. 116.

imagination lacks artifice to lend it charm, its own nature will be ornament enough, for if honour dictate the words, we shall find eloquence there as well. Therefore, let those that are young, or rather let all 31 of us, whatever our age, since it is never too late to resolve to follow what is right, strive with all our hearts and devote all our efforts to the pursuit of virtue and eloquence; and perchance it may be granted to us to attain to the perfection that we seek. For since nature does not forbid the attainment of either, why should not someone succeed in attaining both together? And why should not each of us hope to be that happy man? But if our powers are inadequate 32 to such achievement, we shall still be the better for the double effort in proportion to the distance which we have advanced toward either goal. At any rate let us banish from our hearts the delusion that eloquence, the fairest of all things, can be combined with vice. The power of speaking is even to be accounted an evil when it is found in evil men; for it makes its possessors yet worse than they were before.

I think I hear certain persons (for there will 33 always be some who had rather be eloquent than good) asking, "Why then is there so much art in connexion with eloquence? Why have you talked so much of 'glosses,'[1] the methods of defence to be employed in difficult cases, and sometimes even of actual confession of guilt, unless it is the case that the power and force of speech at times triumphs over truth itself? For a good man will only plead good cases, and those might safely be left to truth to support without the aid of learning." Now, though 34 my reply to these critics will in the first place be a defence of my own work, it will also explain what

mum opere respondero, etiam pro boni viri officio,
si quando eum ad defensionem nocentium ratio
duxerit, satisfaciam. Pertractare enim, quomodo
aut pro falsis aut etiam pro iniustis aliquando dicatur,
non est inutile, vel propter hoc solum, ut ea facilius
et deprehendamus et refellamus; quemadmodum
remedia melius adhibebit, cui nota quae nocent
35 fuerint. Neque enim Academici, cum in utramque
disserunt partem, non secundum alteram vivunt, nec
Carneades ille, qui Romae audiente Censorio Catone
non minoribus viribus contra iustitiam dicitur disse-
ruisse quam pridie pro iustitia dixerat, iniustus ipse
vir fuit. Verum et virtus quid sit, adversa ei malitia
detegit, et aequitas fit ex iniqui contemplatione
manifestior, et plurima contrariis probantur. Debent
ergo oratori sic esse adversariorum nota consilia ut
36 hostium imperatori. Verum et illud, quod prima
propositione durum videtur, potest adferre ratio, ut
vir bonus in defensione causae velit auferre aliquando iudici veritatem. Quod si quis a me pro-
poni mirabitur, (quanquam non est haec mea proprie
sententia, sed eorum, quos gravissimos sapientiae
magistros aetas vetus credidit) sic iudicet, pleraque

374

I consider to be the duty of a good man on occasions when circumstances have caused him to undertake the defence of the guilty. For it is by no means useless to consider how at times we should speak in defence of falsehood or even of injustice, if only for this reason, that such an investigation will enable us to detect and defeat them with the greater ease, just as the physician who has a thorough knowledge of all that can injure the health will be all the more skilful in the prescription of remedies. For the Academicians, although they will argue on 35 either side of a question, do not thereby commit themselves to taking one of these two views as their guide in life to the exclusion of the other, while the famous Carneades, who is said to have spoken at Rome in the presence of Cato the Censor, and to have argued against justice with no less vigour than he had argued for justice on the preceding day, was not himself an unjust man. But the nature of virtue is revealed by vice, its opposite, justice becomes yet more manifest from the contemplation of injustice, and there are many other things that are proved by their contraries. Consequently the schemes of his adversaries should be no less well known to the orator than those of the enemy to a commander in the field. But it is even true, although at first sight 36 it seems hard to believe, that there may be sound reason why at times a good man who is appearing for the defence should attempt to conceal the truth from the judge. If any of my readers is surprised at my making such a statement (although this opinion is not of my own invention, but is derived from those whom antiquity regarded as the greatest teachers of wisdom), I would have him reflect that

esse, quae non tam factis quam causis eorum vel
37 honesta fiant vel turpia. Nam si hominem occidere
saepe virtus, liberos necare nonnunquam pulcherri-
mum est, asperiora quaedam adhuc dictu, si communis utilitas exegerit, facere conceditur, ne hoc
quidem nudum est intuendum, qualem causam vir
38 bonus, sed etiam quare et qua mente defendat. Ac
primum concedant mihi omnes oportet, quod Stoicorum quoque asperrimi confitentur, facturum aliquando virum bonum ut mendacium dicat, et quidem
nonnunquam levioribus causis, ut in pueris aegro-
tantibus utilitatis eorum gratia multa fingimus,
39 multa non facturi promittimus; nedum si ab homine
occidendo grassator avertendus sit aut hostis pro
salute patriae fallendus; ut hoc, quod alias in servis
quoque reprehendendum est, sit alias in ipso sapiente
laudandum. Id si constiterit, multa iam video posse
evenire, propter quae orator bene suscipiat tale
causae genus, quale remota ratione honesta non
40 recepisset. Nec hoc dico (quia severiores sequi
placet leges) pro patre, fratre, amico periclitantibus,
tametsi non mediocris haesitatio est, hinc iustitiae
376

there are many things which are made honourable
or the reverse not by the nature of the facts, but by
the causes from which they spring. For if to slay 37
a man is often a virtue and to put one's own children
to death is at times the noblest of deeds, and if it
is permissible in the public interest to do deeds
yet more horrible to relate than these, we should
assuredly take into consideration not solely and
simply what is the nature of the case which the
good man undertakes to defend, but what is his
reason and what his purpose in so doing. And first 38
of all everyone must allow, what even the sternest
of the Stoics admit, that the good man will sometimes tell a lie, and further that he will sometimes do
so for comparatively trivial reasons; for example we
tell countless lies to sick children for their good and
make many promises to them which we do not intend
to perform. And there is clearly far more justifica- 39
tion for lying when it is a question of diverting
an assassin from his victim or deceiving an enemy
to save our country. Consequently a practice which
is at times reprehensible even in slaves, may on
other occasions be praiseworthy even in a wise man.
If this be granted, I can see that there will be many
possible emergencies such as to justify an orator in
undertaking cases of a kind which, in the absence of
any honourable reason, he would have refused to
touch. In saying this I do not mean that we should 40
be ready under any circumstances to defend our
father, brother or friend when in peril (since I
hold that we should be guided by stricter rules in
such matters), although such contingencies may
well cause us no little perplexity, when we have to
decide between the rival claims of justice and natural

proposita imagine, inde pietatis. Nihil dubii relin-
quamus. Sit aliquis insidiatus tyranno atque ob id
reus: utrumne salvum eum nolet is, qui a nobis
finitur, orator? an, si tuendum susceperit, non tam
falsis defendet, quam qui apud iudices malam causam
41 tuetur? Quid si quaedam bene facta damnaturus
est iudex, nisi ea non esse facta convicerimus, non
vel hoc modo servabit orator non innocentem modo,
sed etiam laudabilem civem? Quid si quaedam
iusta natura, sed condicione temporum inutilia civi-
tati sciemus, nonne utemur arte dicendi bona qui-
42 dem, sed malis artibus simili? Ad hoc nemo
dubitabit, quin, si nocentes mutari in bonam mentem
aliquo modo possint, sicut posse conceditur, salvos
esse eos magis e re publica sit quam puniri. Si
liqueat igitur oratori futurum bonum virum, cui vera
43 obiicientur, non id aget, ut salvus sit? Da nunc,
ut crimine manifesto prematur dux bonus et sine
quo vincere hostem[1] civitas non possit: nonne ei
communis utilitas oratorem advocabit? Certe Fabricius Cornelium Rufinum, et alioqui malum civem

---

[1] hostem, *Obrecht*: honestem, *B*.

affection. But let us put the problem beyond all
question of doubt. Suppose a man to have plotted
against a tyrant and to be accused of having done so.
Which of the two will the orator, as defined by us,
desire to save? And if he undertakes the defence
of the accused, will he not employ falsehood with
no less readiness than the advocate who is defending
a bad case before a jury? Again, suppose that the 41
judge is likely to condemn acts which were rightly
done, unless we can convince him that they were
never done. Is not this another case where the
orator will not shrink even from lies, if so he may
save one who is not merely innocent, but a praiseworthy citizen? Again, suppose that we realise that
certain acts are just in themselves, though prejudicial
to the state under existing circumstances. Shall we
not then employ methods of speaking which, despite
the excellence of their intention, bear a close resemblance to fraud. Further, no one will hesitate 42
for a moment to hold the view that it is in the
interests of the commonwealth that guilty persons
should be acquitted rather than punished, if it be
possible thereby to convert them to a better state of
mind, a possibility which is generally conceded. If
then it is clear to an orator that a man who is guilty
of the offences laid to his charge will become a good
man, will he not strive to secure his acquittal?
Imagine for example that a skilful commander, with- 43
out whose aid the state cannot hope to crush its
enemies, is labouring under a charge which is obviously true : will not the common interest irresistibly
summon our orator to defend him? We know at
any rate that Fabricius publicly voted for and secured
the election to the consulate of Cornelius Rufinus,

et sibi inimicum, tamen, quia utilem sciebat ducem,
imminente bello, palam consulem suffragio suo fecit
atque id mirantibus quibusdam respondit, a cive se
spoliari malle quam ab hoste venire. Ita, si fuisset
orator, non defendisset eundem Rufinum vel mani-
44 festi peculatus reum? Multa dici possunt similia,
sed vel unum ex iis quodlibet sufficit. Non enim
hoc agimus, ut istud illi, quem formamus, viro saepe
sit faciendum; sed ut, si talis coegerit ratio, sit
tamen vera finitio, *oratorem esse virum bonum dicendi*
45 *peritum.* Praecipere vero ac discere, quomodo etiam
probatione difficilia tractentur, necessarium est.
Nam frequenter etiam optimae causae similes sunt
malis, et innocens reus multis verisimilibus pre-
mitur; quo fit, ut eadem actionis ratione defendendus
sit, qua si nocens esset. Iam innumerabilia sunt
bonis causis malisque communia, testes, litterae, sus-
piciones, opiniones. Non aliter autem verisimilia
quam vera et confirmantur et refelluntur. Quapropter, ut res feret, flectetur oratio manente honesta
voluntate.

II. Quando igitur orator est vir bonus, is autem
citra virtutem intelligi non potest, virtus, etiamsi

---

[1] The date is uncertain, but the reference must be either to
the Samnite war of 290 or the war with Pyrrhus.

despite the fact that he was a bad citizen and his personal enemy, merely because he knew that he was a capable general and the state was threatened with war.[1] And when certain persons expressed their surprise at his conduct, he replied that he had rather be robbed by a fellow-citizen than be sold as a slave by the enemy. Well then, had Fabricius been an orator, would he not have defended Rufinus against a charge of peculation, even though his guilt were as clear as day? I might produce many 44 other similar examples, but one of them taken at random is enough. For my purpose is not to assert that such tasks will often be incumbent on the orator whom I desire to form, but merely to show that, in the event of his being compelled to take such action, it will not invalidate our definition of an orator as a "good man, skilled in speaking." And it is necessary also both to teach and learn how 45 to establish difficult cases by proof. For often even the best cases have a resemblance to bad and, the charges which tell heavily against an innocent person frequently have a strong resemblance to the truth. Consequently, the same methods of defence have to be employed that would be used if he were guilty. Further, there are countless elements which are common to both good cases and bad, such as oral and documentary evidence, suspicions and opinions, all of which have to be established or disposed of in the same way, whether they be true or merely resemble the truth. Therefore, while maintaining his integrity of purpose, the orator will modify his pleading to suit the circumstances.

II. Since then the orator is a good man, and such goodness cannot be conceived as existing apart from

quosdam impetus ex natura sumit, tamen perficienda doctrina est: mores ante omnia oratori studiis erunt excolendi atque omnis honesti iustique disciplina pertractanda, sine qua nemo nec vir bonus esse nec

2 dicendi peritus potest. Nisi forte accedemus iis, qui natura constare mores et nihil adiuvari disciplina putant; scilicet ut ea quidem, quae manu fiunt, atque eorum etiam contemptissima confiteantur egere doctoribus, virtutem vero, qua nihil homini, quo ad deos immortales propius accederet, datum est, obviam et illaboratam, tantum quia nati simus, habeamus. Abstinens erit qui id ipsum, quid sit abstinentia,

3 ignoret? Et fortis qui metus doloris, mortis, superstitionis nulla ratione purgaverit? Et iustus qui aequi bonique tractatum, qui leges, quaeque natura sunt omnibus datae quaeque propriae populis et gentibus constitutae, nunquam eruditiore aliquo sermone tractarit? O quam istud parvum [1] putant,

4 quibus tam facile videtur! Sed hoc transeo, de quo neminem, qui litteras vel primis, ut aiunt, labris degustarit, dubitaturum puto. Ad illud sequens praevertar, ne dicendi quidem satis peritum fore, qui non et naturae vim omnem penitus perspexerit

5 et mores praeceptis ac ratione formarit. Neque

---

[1] parvum, *Spalding*: parum, *B.*

virtue, virtue, despite the fact that it is in part derived from certain natural impulses, will require to be perfected by instruction.   The orator must above all things devote his attention to the formation of moral character and must acquire a complete knowledge of all that is just and honourable.   For without this knowledge no one can be either a good man or skilled in speaking, unless indeed we agree with 2 those who regard morality as intuitive and as owing nothing to instruction : indeed they go so far as to acknowledge that handicrafts, not excluding even those which are most despised among them, can only be acquired by the result of teaching, whereas virtue, which of all gifts to man is that which makes him most near akin to the immortal gods, comes to him without search or effort, as a natural concomitant of birth.   But can the man who does not know what abstinence is, claim to be truly abstinent ? or brave, if 3 he has never purged his soul of the fears of pain, death and superstition ? or just, if he has never, in language approaching that of philosophy, discussed the nature of virtue and justice, or of the laws that have been given to mankind by nature or established among individual peoples and nations ?   What a contempt it argues for such themes to regard them as being so easy of comprehension !   However, I pass this by ; 4 for I am sure that no one with the least smattering of literary culture will have the slightest hesitation in agreeing with me.   I will proceed to my next point, that no one will achieve sufficient skill even in speaking, unless he makes a thorough study of all the workings of nature and forms his character on the precepts of philosophy and the dictates of reason. For it is with good cause that Lucius Crassus, in the 5

enim frustra in tertio de Oratore libro L. Crassus
cuncta, quae de aequo, iusto, vero, bono deque iis,
quae sunt contra posita, dicantur, propria esse oratoris adfirmat, ac philosophos, cum ea dicendi viribus
tuentur, uti rhetorum armis, non suis. Idem tamen
confitetur, ea iam esse a philosophia petenda, videlicet quia magis haec illi videtur in possessione earum
6 rerum fuisse. Hinc etiam illud est, quod Cicero
pluribus libris et epistolis testatur dicendi facultatem
ex intimis sapientiae fontibus fluere, ideoque ali-
quamdiu praeceptores eosdem fuisse morum atque
dicendi. Quapropter haec exhortatio mea non eo
pertinet ut esse oratorem philosophum velim, quando
non alia vitae secta longius a civilibus officiis atque
7 ab omni munere oratoris recessit. Nam quis philosophorum aut in iudiciis frequens aut clarus in contionibus fuit? Quis denique in ipsa, quam maxime
plerique praecipiunt, rei publicae administratione
versatus est? Atqui ego illum, quem instituo, Roma-
num quendam velim esse sapientem, qui non secretis
disputationibus, sed rerum experimentis atque operi-
8 bus vere civilem virum exhibeat. Sed quia deserta
ab his, qui se ad eloquentiam contulerunt, studia
sapientiae non iam in actu suo atque in hac fori luce
versantur, sed in porticus et in gymnasia primum,

---

[1] Chs. xx. xxvii. and xxxi.

third book of the *de Oratore*,[1] affirms that all that is said concerning equity, justice, truth and the good, and their opposites, forms part of the studies of an orator, and that the philosophers, when they exert their powers of speaking to defend these virtues, are using the weapons of rhetoric, not their own. But he also confesses that the knowledge of these subjects must be sought from the philosophers for the reason that, in his opinion, philosophy has more effective possession of them. And it is for the same 6 reason that Cicero in several of his books and letters proclaims that eloquence has its fountain-head in the most secret springs of wisdom, and that consequently for a considerable time the instructors of morals and of eloquence were identical. Accordingly this exhortation of mine must not be taken to mean that I wish the orator to be a philosopher, since there is no other way of life that is further removed from the duties of a statesman and the tasks of an orator. For what philosopher has ever been a frequent 7 speaker in the courts or won renown in public assemblies? Nay, what philosopher has ever taken a prominent part in the government of the state, which forms the most frequent theme of their instructions? None the less I desire that he, whose character I am seeking to mould, should be a "wise man" in the Roman sense, that is, one who reveals himself as a true statesman, not in the discussions of the study, but in the actual practice and experience of life. But 8 inasmuch as the study of philosophy has been deserted by those who have turned to the pursuit of eloquence, and since philosophy no longer moves in its true sphere of action and in the broad daylight of the forum, but has retired first to porches and gym-

mox in conventus scholarum recesserunt: id, quod
est oratori necessarium nec a dicendi praeceptoribus
traditur, ab iis petere nimirum necesse est, apud
quos remansit, evolvendi penitus auctores, qui de
virtute praecipiunt, ut oratoris vita cum scientia
9 divinarum rerum sit humanarumque coniuncta. Quae
ipsae quanto maiores ac pulchriores viderentur, si
illas ii docerent, qui etiam eloqui praestantissime
possent? Utinamque sit tempus unquam, quo perfectus aliquis, qualem optamus, orator hanc artem
superbo nomine et vitiis quorundam bona eius cor-
rumpentium invisam vindicet sibi ac, velut rebus
10 repetitis, in corpus eloquentiae adducat. Quae
quidem cum sit in tris divisa partes, naturalem,
moralem, rationalem, qua tandem non est cum
oratoris opere coniuncta?

Nam ut ordinem retro agamus, de ultima illa,
quae tota versatur in verbis, nemo dubitaverit, si
et proprietates vocis cuiusque nosse et ambigua
aperire et perplexa discernere et de falsis iudicare
et colligere ac resolvere quae velis oratorum est.
11 Quanquam ea non tam est minute atque concise
in actionibus utendum quam in disputationibus, quia

nasia and finally to the gatherings of the schools, all
that is essential for an orator, and yet is not taught
by the professors of eloquence, must undoubtedly be
sought from those persons in whose possession it
has remained. The authors who have discoursed on
the nature of virtue must be read through and
through, that the life of the orator may be wedded
to the knowledge of things human and divine. But 9
how much greater and fairer would such subjects
appear if those who taught them were also those
who could give them most eloquent expression! O
that the day may dawn when the perfect orator of
our heart's desire shall claim for his own possession
that science that has lost the affection of mankind
through the arrogance of its claims and the vices of
some that have brought disgrace upon its virtues,
and shall restore it to its place in the domain of
eloquence, as though he had been victorious in a
trial for the restoration of stolen goods! And since 10
philosophy falls into three divisions, physics, ethics
and dialectic, which, I ask you, of these departments is not closely connected with the task of the
orator?

Let us reverse the order just given and deal first
with the third department which is entirely concerned with words. If it be true that to know the
properties of each word, to clear away ambiguities,
to unravel perplexities, to distinguish between truth
and falsehood, to prove or to refute as may be
desired, all form part of the functions of an orator,
who is there that can doubt the truth of my contention? I grant that we shall not have to employ 11
dialectic with such minute attention to detail when
we are pleading in the courts as when we are

non docere modo, sed movere etiam ac delectare
audientes debet orator, ad quod impetu quoque ac
viribus et decore est opus; ut vis amnium maior est
altis ripis multoque gurgitis tractu fluentium quam
12 tenuis aquae et obiectu lapillorum resultantis. Et
ut palaestrici doctores illos, quos numeros vocant,
non idcirco discentibus tradunt, ut iis omnibus ii, qui
didicerint, in ipso luctandi certamine utantur (plus
enim pondere et firmitate et spiritu agitur), sed ut
subsit copia illa, ex qua unum aut alterum, cuius se
13 occasio dederit, efficiant, ita haec pars dialectica, sive
illam dicere malumus disputatricem, ut est utilis
saepe et finitionibus et comprehensionibus et se-
parandis quae sunt differentia, et resolvenda ambiguitate, distinguendo, dividendo, illiciendo, implicando,
ita, si totum sibi vindicaverit in foro certamen, obstabit
melioribus et sectas ad tenuitatem suam vires ipsa
14 subtilitate consumet. Itaque reperias quosdam in
disputando mire callidos, cum ab illa cavillatione
discesserint, non magis sufficere in aliquo graviore
actu quam parva quaedam animalia, quae in angustiis
mobilia campo deprehenduntur.
15 Iam quidem pars illa moralis, quae dicitur Ethice,
certe tota oratori est accommodata. Nam in tanta

engaged in philosophical debate, since the orator's
duty is not merely to instruct, but also to move and
delight his audience; and to succeed in doing this
he needs a strength, impetuosity and grace as well.
For oratory is like a river: the current is stronger
when it flows within deep banks and with a mighty
flood, than when the waters are shallow and broken
by the pebbles that bar their way. And just as 12
the trainers of the wrestling school do not impart
the various *throws* to their pupils that those who
have learnt them may make use of all of them in
actual wrestling matches (for weight and strength
and wind count for more than these), but that they
may have a store from which to draw one or two
of such tricks, as occasion may offer; even so the 13
science of dialectic, or if you prefer it of disputa-
tion, while it is often useful in definition, inference,
differentiation, resolution of ambiguity, distinction
and classification, as also in luring on or entangling
our opponents, yet if it claim to assume the entire
direction of the struggles of the forum, will merely
stand in the way of arts superior to itself and by its
very subtlety will exhaust the strength that has
been pared down to suit its limitations. As a 14
result you will find that certain persons who show
astonishing skill in philosophical debate, as soon as
they quit the sphere of their quibbles, are as helpless in any case that demands more serious pleading
as those small animals which, though nimble enough
in a confined space, are easily captured in an open
field.

Proceeding to moral philosophy or ethics, we may 15
note that it at any rate is entirely suited to the
orator. For vast as is the variety of cases (since in

causarum, sicut superioribus libris diximus, varietate,
cum alia coniectura quaerantur, alia finitionibus con-
cludantur, alia iure summoveantur vel transferantur,
alia colligantur vel ipsa inter se concurrant vel in
diversum ambiguitate ducantur, nulla fere dici potest,
cuius non parte in aliqua tractatus aequi ac boni
reperiatur, plerasque vero esse quis nescit, quae
16 totae in sola qualitate consistant? In consiliis vero
quae ratio suadendi est ab honesti quaestione se-
posita? Quin illa etiam pars tertia, quae laudandi
ac vituperandi officiis continetur, nempe in tractatu
17 recti pravique versatur. An de iustitia, fortitudine,
abstinentia, temperantia, pietate non plurima dicet
orator? Sed ille vir bonus, qui haec non vocibus
tantum sibi nota atque nominibus aurium tenus in
usum linguae perceperit, sed qui virtutes ipsas mente
complexus ita sentiat, nec in cogitando ita laborabit
18 sed, quod sciet, vere dicet. Cum sit autem omnis generalis quaestio speciali potentior, quia universo pars
continetur, non utique accedit parti quod universum
est, profecto nemo dubitabit, generales quaestiones
19 in illo maxime studiorum more versatas. Iam vero
cum sint multa propriis brevibusque comprehen-

---

[1] See III. vi. 45.   [2] See III. vi. 23.   [3] See III. vi. 15.
[4] Probably an allusion to contradictory laws. See VII. vii.
[5] See VII. ix.

them, as I have pointed out in previous books, we seek
to discover certain points by conjecture,[1] reach our
conclusions in others by means of definition,[1] dispose
of others on legal grounds[1] or by raising the question of competence,[2] while other points are established by syllogism[3] and others involve contradic-
tions[4] or are diversely interpreted owing to some
ambiguity of language[5]), there is scarcely a single
one which does not at some point or another involve
the discussion of equity and virtue, while there are
also, as everyone knows, not a few which turn
entirely on questions of quality. Again in delib- 16
erative assemblies how can we advise a policy without
raising the question of what is honourable? Nay,
even the third department of oratory, which is
concerned with the tasks of praise and denunciation,
must without a doubt deal with questions of right
and wrong. For the orator will assuredly have 17
much to say on such topics as justice, fortitude,
abstinence, self-control and piety. But the good
man, who has come to the knowledge of these things
not by mere hearsay, as though they were just words
and names for his tongue to employ, but has grasped
the meaning of virtue and acquired a true feeling for
it, will never be perplexed when he has to think out
a problem, but will speak out truly what he
knows. Since, however, *general* questions are always 18
more important than special (for the particular is
contained in the universal, while the universal is
never to be regarded as something superimposed on
the particular), everyone will readily admit that the
studies of which we are speaking are pre-eminently
concerned with general questions. Further, since 19
there are numerous points which require to be

sionibus finienda (unde etiam status causarum dicitur
finitivus), nonne ad id quoque instrui ab iis, qui plus
in hoc studii dederunt, oportet? Quid? non quaestio iuris omnis aut verborum proprietate aut aequi
disputatione aut voluntatis coniectura continetur?
quorum pars ad rationalem, pars ad moralem tracta-
20 tum redundat. Ergo natura permixta est omnibus
istis oratio, quae quidem oratio est vere. Nam
ignara quidem huiusce doctrinae loquacitas erret
necesse est, ut quae vel nullos vel falsos duces
habeat.

Pars vero naturalis, cum est ad exercitationem
dicendi tanto ceteris uberior, quanto maiore spiritu
de divinis rebus quam humanis eloquendum est,
tum illam etiam moralem, sine qua nulla esse, ut
21 docuimus, oratio potest, totam complectitur. Nam
si regitur providentia mundus, administranda certe
bonis viris erit res publica; si divina nostris animis
origo, tendendum ad virtutem nec voluptatibus ter-
reni corporis serviendum. An haec non frequenter
tractabit orator? Iam de auguriis, responsis, religione
denique omni, de quibus maxima saepe in senatu
consilia versata sunt, non erit ei disserendum, si

---

[1] See III. vi. 31.
[2] *i e.* natural philosophy in the widest sense.
[3] § 15.

determined by appropriate and concise definitions (hence the *definitive basis*[1] of cases), it is surely desirable that the orator should be instructed in such things by those who have devoted special attention to the subject. Again, does not every question of law turn either on the precise meaning of words, the discussion of equity, or conjecture as to the intention—subjects which in part encroach on the domain of dialectic and in part on that of ethics? Consequently all oratory involves a natural admixture 20 of all these philosophic elements—at least, that is to say, all oratory that is worthy of the name. For mere garrulity that is ignorant of all such learning must needs go astray, since its guides are either non-existent or false.

Physics[2] on the other hand is far richer than the other branches of philosophy, if viewed from the standpoint of providing exercise in speaking, in proportion as a loftier inspiration is required to speak of things divine than of things human; and further it includes within its scope the whole of ethics, which as we have shown[3] are essential to the very existence of oratory. For, if the world is 21 governed by providence, it will certainly be the duty of all good men to bear their part in the administration of the state. If the origin of our souls be divine, we must win our way towards virtue and abjure the service of the lusts of our earthly body. Are not these themes which the orator will frequently be called upon to handle? Again there are questions concerned with auguries and oracles or any other religious topic (all of them subjects that have often given rise to the most important debates in the senate) on which the orator will have to

quidem, ut nobis placet, futurus est vir civilis idem?
Quae denique intelligi saltem potest eloquentia
22 hominis optima nescientis? Haec si ratione manifesta non essent, exemplis tamen crederemus. Siquidem et Periclem, cuius eloquentiae, etiamsi nulla
ad nos monumenta venerunt, vim tamen quandam
incredibilem cum historici, tum etiam, liberrimum
hominum genus, comici veteres tradunt, Anaxagorae
physici constat auditorem fuisse, et Demosthenem,
principem omnium Graeciae oratorum, dedisse ope-
23 ram Platoni. Nam M. Tullius, non tantum se debere
scholis rhetorum, quantum Academiae spatiis, frequenter ipse testatus est; neque se tanta in eo
unquam fudisset [1] ubertas, si ingenium suum consepto
fori, non ipsius rerum naturae finibus terminasset.

Verum ex hoc alia mihi quaestio exoritur, quae
secta conferre plurimum eloquentiae possit, quanquam ea non inter multas potest esse contentio.
24 Nam in primis nos Epicurus a se ipse dimittit, qui
fugere omnem disciplinam navigatione quam velo-
cissima iubet. Neque vero Aristippus, summum in
voluptate corporis bonum ponens, ad hunc nos laborem
hortetur. Pyrrhon quidem quas in hoc opere habere
partes potest? cui iudices esse, apud quos verba
faciat, et reum, pro quo loquatur, et senatum, in

---

[1] fudisset, *Badius* : fuisset, *MSS*.

---

[1] *Or.* iii. 12.
[2] παιδείαν πᾶσαν ἀκάτιον ἀράμενος φεῦγε.

discourse, if he is also to be the statesman we would have him be. And finally, how can we conceive of any real eloquence at all proceeding from a man who is ignorant of all that is best in the world? If our reason did not make these facts 22 obvious, we should still be led by historical examples to believe their truth. For Pericles, whose eloquence, despite the fact that it has left no visible record for posterity, was none the less, if we may believe the historians and that free-speaking tribe, the old comic poets, endowed with almost incredible force, is known to have been a pupil of the physicist Anaxagoras, while Demosthenes, greatest of all the orators of Greece, sat at the feet of Plato. As for 23 Cicero, he has often proclaimed[1] the fact that he owed less to the schools of rhetoric than to the walks of Academe : nor would he ever have developed such amazing fertility of talent, had he bounded his genius by the limits of the forum and not by the frontiers of nature herself.

But this leads me to another question as to which school of philosophy is like to prove of most service to oratory, although there are only a few that can be said to contend for this honour. For in the first 24 place Epicurus banishes us from his presence without more ado, since he bids all his followers to fly from learning in the swiftest ship that they can find.[2] Nor would Aristippus, who regards the highest good as consisting in physical pleasure, be likely to exhort us to the toils entailed by our study. And what part can Pyrrho have in the work that is before us? For he will have doubts as to whether there exist judges to address, accused to defend, or a senate where he can be called upon to speak his opinion.

25 quo sit dicenda sententia, non liquebit.   Academiam
quidam utilissimam credunt, quod mos in utramque
partem disserendi ad exercitationem forensium causarum proxime accedat.   Adiiciunt loco probationis,
quod ea praestantissimos in eloquentia viros ediderit.
Peripatetici studio quoque se quodam oratorio iactant ;
nam theses dicere exercitationis gratia fere est ab
iis institutum.   Stoici, sicut copiam nitoremque eloquentiae fere praeceptoribus suis defuisse concedant
necesse est, ita nullos aut probare acrius aut con-
26 cludere subtilius contendunt.   Sed haec inter ipsos,
qui velut sacramento rogati vel etiam superstitione
constricti nefas ducunt a suscepta semel persuasione
discedere.   Oratori vero nihil est necesse in cuius-
27 quam iurare leges.   Maius enim est opus atque
praestantius, ad quod ipse tendit, et cuius est velut
candidatus, si quidem est futurus cum vitae, tum
etiam eloquentiae laude perfectus.   Quare in exemplum bene dicendi facundissimum quemque pro-
ponet sibi ad imitandum, moribus vero formandis
quam honestissima praecepta rectissimamque ad
virtutem viam deliget.   Exercitatione quidem utetur
omni, sed tamen erit plurimus in maximis quibusque
28 ac natura pulcherrimis.   Nam quae potest materia

---

[1] See II. i. 9. III. v. 5. and 10.

Some authorities hold that the Academy will be the 25
most useful school, on the ground that its habit of
disputing on both sides of a question approaches
most nearly to the actual practice of the courts.
And by way of proof they add the fact that this
school has produced speakers highly renowned for
their eloquence.   The Peripatetics also make it their
boast that they have a form of study which is near
akin to oratory.   For it was with them in the main
that originated the practice of declaiming on general
questions [1] by way of exercise.   The Stoics, though
driven to admit that, generally speaking, their teachers
have been deficient both in fullness and charm of
eloquence, still contend that no men can prove more
acutely or draw conclusions with greater subtlety
than themselves.   But all these arguments take 26
place within their own circle, for, as though they
were tied by some solemn oath or held fast in the
bonds of some superstitious belief, they consider that
it is a crime to abandon a conviction once formed.
On the other hand, there is no need for an orator to
swear allegiance to any one philosophic code.   For 27
he has a greater and nobler aim, to which he directs
all his efforts with as much zeal as if he were a
candidate for office, since he is to be made perfect
not only in the glory of a virtuous life, but in that of
eloquence as well.   He will consequently select as
his models of eloquence all the greatest masters of
oratory, and will choose the noblest precepts and
the most direct road to virtue as the means for
the formation of an upright character.   He will
neglect no form of exercise, but will devote special
attention to those which are of the highest and
fairest nature.   For what subject can be found more 28

reperiri ad graviter copioseque dicendum magis abundans quam de virtute, de re publica, de providentia, de origine animorum, de amicitia? Haec sunt, quibus mens pariter atque oratio insurgat, quae vere bona, quid mitiget metus, coerceat cupiditates, eximat nos opinionibus vulgi animumque caelestem erigat.[1]

29 Neque ea solum, quae talibus disciplinis continentur, sed magis etiam, quae sunt tradita antiquitus dicta ac facta praeclare, et nosse et animo semper agitare conveniet. Quae profecto nusquam plura maioraque quam in nostrae civitatis monumentis 30 reperientur. An fortitudinem, iustitiam, fidem, continentiam, frugalitatem, contemptum doloris ac mortis melius alii docebunt quam Fabricii, Curii, Reguli, Decii, Mucii aliique innumerabiles? Quantum enim Graeci praeceptis valent, tantum Romani, 31 quod est maius, exemplis. Tantum quod non cognitis ille rebus adquieverit,[2] qui non modo proximum tempus lucemque praesentem intueri satis credat, sed omnem posteritatis memoriam spatium vitae honestae et curriculum laudis existimet. Hinc mihi ille iustitiae haustus bibat, hinc sumptam libertatem in causis atque consiliis praestet. Neque erit per-

---

[1] erigat *added by Meister.*
[2] cognitis ille rebus adquieverit, *Halm, Bonnell*: cognatis ide rebus admoveri, *B.*

fully adapted to a rich and weighty eloquence than the topics of virtue, politics, providence, the origin of the soul and friendship? The themes which tend to elevate mind and language alike are questions such as what things are truly good, what means there are of assuaging fear, restraining the passions and lifting us and the soul that came from heaven clear of the delusions of the common herd.

But it is desirable that we should not restrict our 29 study to the precepts of philosophy alone. It is still more important that we should know and ponder continually all the noblest sayings and deeds that have been handed down to us from ancient times. And assuredly we shall nowhere find a larger or more remarkable store of these than in the records of our own country. Who will teach courage, justice, 30 loyalty, self-control, simplicity, and contempt of grief and pain better than men like Fabricius, Curius, Regulus, Decius, Mucius and countless others? For if the Greeks bear away the palm for moral precepts, Rome can produce more striking examples of moral performance, which is a far greater thing. But the 31 man who does not believe that it is enough to fix his eyes merely on his own age and his own transitory life, but regards the space allotted for an honourable life and the course in which glory's race is run as conditioned solely by the memory of posterity, will not rest content with a mere knowledge of the events of history. No, it is from the thought of posterity that he must inspire his soul with justice and derive that freedom of spirit which it is his duty to display when he pleads in the courts or gives counsel in the senate. No man will ever be the consummate orator of whom we are in quest unless

fectus orator, nisi qui honeste dicere et sciet et
audebit.

III. Iuris quoque civilis necessaria huic viro
scientia est et morum ac religionum eius rei publicae,
quam capesset. Nam qualis esse suasor in consiliis
publicis privativse poterit tot rerum, quibus praecipue
civitas continetur, ignarus? Quo autem modo patro-
num se causarum non falso dixerit, qui, quod est in
causis potentissimum, sit ab altero petiturus, paene
non dissimilis iis, qui poetarum scripta pronuntiant?
2 Nam quodammodo mandata perferet, et ea, quae sibi
a iudice credi postulaturus est, aliena fide dicet, et
ipse litigantium auxiliator egebit auxilio. Quod ut
fieri nonnunquam minore incommodo possit, cum
domi praecepta et composita et sicut cetera, quae
in causa sunt, inde[1] discendo cognita ad iudicem
perfert, quid fiet in iis quaestionibus, quae subito
inter ipsas actiones nasci solent? non deformiter
respectet et inter subsellia minores advocatos in-
3 terroget? Potest autem satis diligenter accipere,
quae tum audiet, cum ei dicenda sunt, aut fortiter
adfirmare aut ingenue pro suis dicere? Possit in
actionibus: quid fiet in altercatione, ubi occurren-
dum continuo, nec libera ad discendum mora est?

---

[1] inde, *Halm* : in, *MSS.*

he has both the knowledge and the courage to speak in accordance with the promptings of honour.

III. Our orator will also require a knowledge of civil law and of the custom and religion of the state in whose life he is to bear his part. For how will he be able to advise either in public or in private, if he is ignorant of all the main elements that go to make the state? How can he truthfully call himself an advocate if he has to go to others to acquire that knowledge which is all-important in the courts? He will be little better than if he were a reciter of the poets. For he will be a mere transmitter of the 2 instructions that others have given him, it will be on the authority of others that he propounds what he asks the judge to believe, and he whose duty it is to succour the litigant will himself be in need of succour. It is true that at times this may be effected with but little inconvenience, if what he advances for the edification of the judge has been taught him and composed in the seclusion of his study and learnt by heart there like other elements of the case. But what will he do, when he is confronted by unexpected problems such as frequently arise in the actual course of pleading? Will he not disgrace himself by looking round and asking the junior counsel who sit on the benches behind him for advice? Can 3 he hope to get a thorough grasp of such information at the very moment when he is required to produce it in his speech? Can he make his assertions with confidence or speak with native simplicity as though his arguments were his own? Grant that he may do so in his actual speech. But what will he do in a debate, when he has continually to meet fresh points raised by his opponent and is given no time to learn

Quid, si forte peritus iuris ille non aderit? Quid,
si quis non satis in ea re doctus falsum aliquid sub-
iecerit? Hoc enim est maximum ignorantiae malum,
4 quod credit eum scire qui moneat.   Neque ego sum
nostri moris ignarus oblitusve eorum, qui velut ad
arculas sedent et tela agentibus subministrant, neque
idem Graecos quoque nescio factitasse, unde nomen
his pragmaticorum datum est.   Sed loquor de oratore, qui non clamorem modo suum causis, sed omnia,
5 quae profutura sunt, debet.   Itaque eum nec inutilem, si ad horam forte constiterit, neque in testa-
tionibus faciendis esse imperitum velim.   Quis enim
potius praeparabit ea quae, cum aget, esse in causa
velit?   Nisi forte imperatorem quis idoneum credit
in proeliis quidem strenuum et fortem et omnium,
quae pugna poscit, artificem, sed neque delectus
agere nec copias contrahere atque instruere nec
prospicere commeatus nec locum capere castris scientem; prius est enim certe parare bella quam gerere.
6 Atqui simillimus huic sit advocatus, si plura, quae
ad vincendum valent, aliis reliquerit, cum praesertim

---

1 *Ad horam constare* appears to be a technical term for
"appearance at the preliminary hour," the purpose of which
is indicated in the paraphrase given above.

up his case? What will he do, if he has no legal expert to advise him or if his prompter through insufficient knowledge of the subject provides him with information that is false? It is the most serious drawback of such ignorance, that he will always believe that his adviser knows what he is talking about.   I am not ignorant of the generally prevail- 4 ing custom, nor have I forgotten those who sit by our store-chests and provide weapons for the pleader: I know too that the Greeks did likewise: hence the name of *pragmaticus* which was bestowed on such persons.   But I am speaking of an orator, who owes it as a duty to his case to serve it not merely by the loudness of his voice, but by all other means that may be of assistance to it.   Consequently I do 5 not wish my orator to be helpless, if it so chance that he puts in an appearance for the preliminary proceedings to which the hour before the commencement of the trial[1] is allotted, or to be unskilful in the preparation and production of evidence.   For who, sooner than himself, should prepare the points which he wishes to be brought out when he is pleading?   You might as well suppose that the qualifications of a successful general consist merely in courage and energy in the field of battle and skill in meeting all the demands of actual conflict, while suffering him to be ignorant of the methods of levying troops, mustering and equipping his forces, arranging for supplies or selecting a suitable position for his camp, despite the fact that preparation for war is an essential preliminary for its successful conduct.   And yet such a general would bear a 6 very close resemblance to the advocate who leaves much of the detail that is necessary for success to

hoc, quod est maxime necessarium, nec tam sit
arduum, quam procul intuentibus fortasse videatur.
Namque omne ius, quod est certum, aut scripto aut
moribus constat; dubium aequitatis regula exami-
7 nandum est. Quae scripta sunt aut posita in more
civitatis, nullam habent difficultatem, cognitionis
sunt enim, non inventionis; at quae consultorum
responsis explicantur, aut in verborum interpretatione
sunt posita aut in recti pravique discrimine. Vim
cuiusque vocis intelligere aut commune prudentium
est aut proprium oratoris; aequitas optimo cuique
8 notissima. Nos porro et bonum virum et prudentem
in primis oratorem putamus, qui cum se ad id, quod
est optimum natura, direxerit, non magnopere com-
movebitur, si quis ab eo consultus dissentiet; cum
ipsis illis diversas inter se opiniones tueri concessum
sit. Sed etiam, si nosse, quid quisque senserit, volet,
lectionis opus est, qua nihil est in studiis minus
9 laboriosum. Quodsi plerique, desperata facultate
agendi, ad discendum ius declinaverunt, quam id
scire facile est oratori, quod discunt qui sua quoque
confessione oratores esse non possunt? Verum et
M. Cato cum in dicendo praestantissimus, tum iuris
idem fuit peritissimus, et Scaevolae Servioque Sul-

the care of others, more especially in view of the
fact that this, the most necessary element in the
management of a case, is not as difficult as it may
perhaps seem to outside observers.   For every point
of law, which is certain, is based either on written
law or accepted custom: if, on the other hand, the
point is doubtful, it must be examined in the light
of equity. Laws which are either written or founded 7
on accepted custom present no difficulty, since they
call merely for knowledge and make no demand on
the imagination.   On the other hand, the points ex-
plained in the rulings of the legal experts turn either
on the interpretation of words or on the distinction
between right and wrong. To understand the meaning of each word is either common to all sensible
men or the special possession of the orator, while
the demands of equity are known to every good
man.   Now I regard the orator above all as being 8
a man of virtue and good sense, who will not be
seriously troubled, after having devoted himself to
the study of that which is excellent by nature, if
some legal expert disagrees with him; for even they
are allowed to disagree among themselves.   But if
he further wishes to know the views of everyone,
he will require to read, and reading is the least
laborious of all the tasks that fall to the student's
lot.   Moreover, if the class of legal experts is as a rule 9
drawn from those who, in despair of making successful pleaders, have taken refuge with the law,
how easy it must be for an orator to know what
those succeed in learning, who by their own confession are incapable of becoming orators!   But
Marcus Cato was at once a great orator and an
expert lawyer, while Scaevola and Servius Sulpicius

10 picio concessa est etiam facundiae virtus. Et M.
Tullius non modo inter agendum nunquam est destitutus scientia iuris, sed etiam componere aliqua de
eo coeperat, ut appareat posse oratorem non discendo tantum iuri vacare, sed etiam docendo.

11 Verum ea, quae de moribus excolendis studioque
iuris praecipimus, ne quis eo credat reprehendenda,
quod multos cognovimus, qui taedio laboris, quem ferre
tendentibus ad eloquentiam necesse est, confugerint
ad haec deverticula desidiae. Quorum alii se ad
album ac rubricas transtulerunt et formularii vel, ut
Cicero ait, leguleii quidam esse maluerunt, tanquam
utiliora eligentes ea, quorum solam facilitatem seque-

12 bantur; alii pigritiae arrogantioris, qui subito fronte
conficta immissaque barba, veluti despexissent oratoria praecepta, paulum aliquid sederunt in scholis
philosophorum, ut deinde in publico tristes, domi
dissoluti captarent auctoritatem contemptu ceterorum. Philosophia enim simulari potest, eloquentia
non potest.

IV. In primis vero abundare debet orator exemplo-
rum copia cum veterum, tum etiam novorum, adeo
ut non ea modo, quae conscripta sunt historiis aut
sermonibus velut per manus tradita, quaeque cotidie
aguntur, debeat nosse, verum ne ea quidem, quae

---

¹ *i. e.* as well as experts on the law.
² The praetor's edicts were displayed on a whitened board
(*in albo*), while the headings of the civil law were written in
red. ³ *de Or.* I. lv. 236.

were universally allowed to be eloquent as well.[1]
And Cicero not merely possessed a sufficient supply of 10
legal knowledge to serve his needs when pleading,
but actually began to write on the subject, so that
it is clear that an orator has not merely time to
learn, but even to teach the law.

Let no one, however, regard the advice I have 11
given as to the attention due to the development
of character and the study of the law as being
impugned by the fact that we are familiar with
many who, because they were weary of the toil
entailed on those who seek to scale the heights
of eloquence, have betaken themselves to the study
of law as a refuge for their indolence. Some of
these transfer their attention to the praetor's edicts
or the civil law,[2] and have preferred to become
specialists in *formulae*, or legalists, as Cicero[3] calls
them, on the pretext of choosing a more useful
branch of study, whereas their real motive was its
comparative easiness. Others are the victims of a 12
more arrogant form of sloth; they assume a stern
air and let their beards grow, and, as though de-
spising the precepts of oratory, sit for a while in
the schools of the philosophers, that, by an assump-
tion of a severe mien before the public gaze and by
an affected contempt of others they may assert their
moral superiority, while leading a life of debauchery
at home. For philosophy may be counterfeited, but
eloquence never.

IV. Above all, our orator should be equipped
with a rich store of examples both old and new:
and he ought not merely to know those which are
recorded in history or transmitted by oral tradition
or occur from day to day, but should not neglect

2 sunt a clarioribus poetis ficta, negligere. Nam illa
quidem priora aut testimoniorum aut etiam iudica-
torum obtinent locum, sed haec quoque aut vetustatis
fide tuta sunt aut ab hominibus magnis praeceptorum
loco ficta creduntur. Sciat ergo quam plurima;
unde etiam senibus auctoritas maior est, quod plura
nosse et vidisse creduntur, quod Homerus frequentissime testatur. Sed non est exspectanda ultima aetas,
cum studia praestent ut, quantum ad cognitionem
pertinet rerum, etiam praeteritis saeculis vixisse
videamur.

V. Haec sunt, quae me redditurum promiseram,
instrumenta non artis, ut quidam putaverunt, sed
ipsius oratoris. Haec arma habere ad manum,
horum scientia debet esse succinctus, accedente
verborum figurarumque facili copia et inventionis
ratione et disponendi usu et memoriae firmitate et
actionis gratia. Sed plurimum ex his valet animi
praestantia, quam nec metus frangat nec adclamatio
terreat nec audientium auctoritas ultra debitam
2 reverentiam tardet. Nam ut abominanda sunt contraria his vitia confidentiae, temeritatis, improbitatis,
arrogantiae, ita citra constantiam, fiduciam, fortitudinem nihil ars, nihil studium, nihil profectus ipse
profuerit, ut si des arma timidis et imbellibus. Invitus mehercule dico, quoniam et aliter accipi potest,

---

[1] I *Pr.* 22 and xii. *Pr.* 4.

even those fictitious examples invented by the great
poets. For while the former have the authority of 2
evidence or even of legal decisions, the latter also
either have the warrant of antiquity or are regarded
as having been invented by great men to serve as
lessons to the world. He should therefore be acquainted with as many examples as possible. It is
this which gives old age so much authority, since
the old are believed to have a larger store of knowledge and experience, as Homer so frequently bears
witness. But we must not wait till the evening of
our days, since study has this advantage that, as far
as knowledge of facts is concerned, it is capable of
giving the impression that we have lived in ages
long gone by.

V. Such are the instruments of which I promised 1
to give account, the instruments, that is, not merely
of the art, as some have held, but of the orator himself. These are the weapons that he should have
ready to his hand, this the knowledge with which he
must be equipped, while it must be supplemented by
a ready store of words and figures, power of imagination, skill in arrangement, retentiveness of memory
and grace of delivery. But of all these qualities the
highest is that loftiness of soul which fear cannot
dismay nor uproar terrify nor the authority of the
audience fetter further than the respect which is
their due. For although the vices which are its 2
opposites, such as arrogance, temerity, impudence
and presumption, are all positively obnoxious, still
without constancy, confidence and courage, art, study
and proficiency will be of no avail. You might as
well put weapons into the hands of the unwarlike
and the coward. It is indeed with some reluctance,

ipsam verecundiam, vitium quidem, sed amabile et
quae virtutes facillime generet, esse interim adversam, multisque in causa fuisse, ut bona ingenii
studiique in lucem non prolata situ quodam secreti
3 consumerentur. Sciat autem, si quis haec forte
minus adhuc peritus distinguendi vim cuiusque verbi
leget, non probitatem a me reprehendi, sed verecundiam, quae est timor quidam reducens animum
ab iis quae facienda sunt; inde confusio et coepti
paenitentia et subitum silentium. Quis porro dubitet
vitiis adscribere adfectum, propter quem facere
4 honeste pudet? Neque ego rursus nolo eum, qui sit
dicturus, et sollicitum surgere et colore mutari et
periculum intelligere; quae si non accident, etiam
simulanda erunt. Sed intellectus hic sit operis, non
metus, moveamurque, non concidamus. Optima est
autem emendatio verecundiae fiducia, et quamlibet
imbecilla frons magna conscientia sustinetur.
5 Sunt et naturalia, ut supra dixi, quae tamen et
cura iuvantur, instrumenta, vox, latus, decor; quae

---

[1] I Pr. 27.

as it may give rise to misunderstanding, that I say
that even modesty (which, though a fault in itself, is
an amiable failing which may easily be the mother of
virtues) is on occasion an impediment and has
frequently caused the fruits of genius and study to
consume away in the mildew of obscurity merely
because they have never been displayed to the public
day. But in case any of my readers should still lack 3
skill to distinguish the precise meaning of each
word, I would have him know that it is not honest
shame that is the object of my criticism, but that
excess of modesty which is really a form of fear
deterring the soul from doing what is its duty to do,
and resulting in confusion of mind, regret that our
task was ever begun, and sudden silence. For who
can hesitate to give the name of fault to a feeling
that makes a man ashamed to do what is right? On 4
the other hand, I am not unwilling that the man who
has got to make a speech should show signs of
nervousness when he rises to his feet, should change
colour and make it clear that he feels the risks of his
position: indeed, if these symptoms do not occur
naturally, it will be necessary to simulate them.
But the feeling that stirs us should be due to the
realisation of the magnitude of our task and not to
fear: we should be moved, but not to the extent of
collapsing. But the best remedy for such excess
of modesty is confidence: however great our natural
timidity of mien, we shall find strength and support
in the consciousness of the nobility of our task.

There are also those natural instruments which, as 5
I mentioned above,[1] may be further improved by
care, such as voice, lungs and grace of carriage
and movement, all of which are of such importance

quīdem tantum valent, ut frequenter famam ingenii
faciant. Habuit oratores aetas nostra copiosiores,
sed, cum diceret, eminere inter aequales Trachalus
videbatur. Ea corporis sublimitas erat, is ardor
oculorum, frontis auctoritas, gestus praestantia, vox
quidem non, ut Cicero desiderat, paene tragoedorum,
sed super omnes, quos ego quidem audierim, tragoe-
6 dos. Certe cum in basilica Iulia diceret primo
tribunali, quattuor autem iudicia, ut moris est,
cogerentur, atque omnia clamoribus fremerent, et
auditum eum et intellectum et, quod agentibus
ceteris contumeliosissimum fuit, laudatum quoque
ex quattuor tribunalibus memini. Sed hoc votum
est et rara felicitas; quae si non adsit, sane sufficiat
ab iis, quibus quis dicit, audiri. Talis esse debet
orator, haec scire.

VI. Agendi autem initium sine dubio secundum
vires cuiusque sumendum est. Neque ego annos
definiam, cum Demosthenen puerum admodum
actiones pupillares habuisse manifestum sit, Calvus,
Caesar, Pollio multum ante quaestoriam omnes aetatem gravissima iudicia susceperint, praetextatos
egisse quosdam sit traditum, Caesar Augustus duodecim natus annos aviam pro rostris laudaverit.
2 Modus mihi videtur quidam tenendus, ut neque prae-

---

[1] de Or. I. xxviii. 128.
[2] Of the Centumviral Court. Four different cases were
being tried simultaneously.
[3] Demosthenes was 18, Crassus 19, Caesar 21, Asinius Pollio
22 and Calvus not much older. See Tac. Dial. 34.

as frequently to give a speaker the reputation for talent. Our own age has had orators of greater resource and power, but Trachalus appeared to stand out above all his contemporaries, when he was speaking. Such was the effect produced by his lofty stature, the fire of his eye, the dignity of his brow, the excellence of his gesture, coupled with a voice which was not almost a tragedian's, as Cicero[1] demands that it should be, but surpassed the voice of all tragedians that I have ever heard. At any 6 rate I remember that, when he was speaking in the Basilica Julia before the first tribunal, and the four panels of judges[2] were assembled as usual and the whole building was full of noise, he could still be heard and understood and applauded from all four tribunals at once, a fact which was not complimentary to the other pleaders. But gifts like these are such as all may pray for and few are happy enough to attain. And if we cannot achieve such fortune, we must even be content to be heard by the court which we are addressing. Such then should the orator be, and such are the things which he should know.

VI. The age at which the orator should begin to plead will of course depend on the development of his strength. I shall not specify it further, since it is clear that Demosthenes pleaded against his guardians while he was still a mere boy, Calvus, Caesar and Pollio[3] all undertook cases of the first importance before they were old enough to be qualified for the quaestorship, others are said to have pleaded while still wearing the garb of boyhood, and Augustus Caesar delivered a funeral oration over his grandmother from the public rostra when he was only twelve years old. In my opinion we should aim 2

propere destringatur immatura frons nec,[1] quidquid
est illud adhuc acerbum, proferatur; nam inde et
contemptus operis innascitur et fundamenta iaciuntur
impudentiae et, quod est ubicunque perniciosissimum,
3 praevenit vires fiducia. Nec rursus differendum est
tirocinium in senectutem; nam cotidie metus crescit,
maiusque fit semper quod ausuri sumus et, dum
deliberamus quando incipiendum sit, incipere iam
serum est. Quare fructum studiorum viridem et
adhuc dulcem promi decet, dum et veniae [2] spes est
et paratus favor et audere non dedecet et, si quid
desit operi, supplet aetas, et, si qua sunt dicta
4 iuveniliter, pro indole accipiuntur: ut totus ille
Ciceronis pro Sexto Roscio locus: *Quid enim tam
commune quam spiritus vivis, terra mortuis, mare fluctu-
antibus, litus eiectis?* Quae cum sex et viginti natus
annos summis audientium clamoribus dixerit, defer-
visse tempore et annis liquata iam senior idem
fatetur. Et hercule quantumlibet secreta studia
contulerint, est tamen proprius quidam fori profectus,

---

[1] nec, *Buttmann*: et, *MSS.*
[2] veniae, *Davisius*: venia et, *MSS.*

---

[1] *pro Rosc. Amer.* xxvi. 72.   *Orat.* xxx. 107.

at a happy mean. The unripe brow of boyhood should not be prematurely robbed of its ingenuous air nor should the young speaker's powers be brought before the public while yet unformed, since such a practice leads to a contempt for study, lays the foundations of impudence and induces a fault which is pernicious in all departments of life, namely, a self-confidence that is not justified by the speaker's resources. On the other hand, it is undesirable to 3 postpone the apprenticeship of the bar till old age: for the fear of appearing in public grows daily and the magnitude of the task on which we must venture continually increases and we waste time deliberating when we should begin, till we find it is too late to begin at all. Consequently it is desirable that the fruit of our studies should be brought before the public eye while it is still fresh and sweet, while it may hope for indulgence and be secure of a kindly disposition in the audience, while boldness is not unbecoming and youth compensates for all defects and boyish extravagance is regarded as a sign of natural vigour. Take for example the whole of the 4 well-known passage from Cicero's defence of Sextus Roscius:[1] "For what is more common than the air to the living, than the earth to the dead, than the sea to mariners or the shore to shipwrecked men?" etc. This passage was delivered at the age of twenty-six amid loud applause from the audience, but in later years[2] he acknowledges that the ferment of youth has died down and his style been clarified with age. And, indeed, however much private study may contribute to success, there is still a peculiar proficiency that the courts alone can give: for there the atmosphere is changed and the reality of the

alia lux, alia veri discriminis facies, plusque, si
separes, usus sine doctrina quam citra usum doctrina
5 valet. Ideoque nonnulli senes in schola facti stupent
novitate, cum in iudicia venerunt, et omnia suis
exercitationibus similia desiderant. At illic et iudex
tacet et adversarius obstrepit et nihil temere dictum
perit et, si quid tibi ipse sumas, probandum est, et
laboratam congestamque dierum ac noctium studio
actionem aqua deficit, et omisso magna semper
flandi tumore in quibusdam causis loquendum est;
6 quod illi diserti minime sciunt. Itaque nonnullos
reperias, qui sibi eloquentiores videantur, quam ut
causas agant. Ceterum illum, quem iuvenem tene-
risque adhuc viribus nitentem in forum deduximus,
et incipere quam maxime facili ac favorabili causa
velim, ferarum ut catuli molliore praeda saginantur,
et non utique ab hoc initio continuare operam et
ingenio adhuc alendo callum inducere, sed iam
scientem, quid sit pugna, et in quam rem studendum
7 sit, refici atque renovari. Sic et tirocinii metum,
dum facilius est audere, transierit, nec audendi

peril puts a different complexion on things, while, if
it is impossible to combine the two, practice without
theory is more useful than theory without practice.
Consequently, some who have grown old in the 5
schools lose their heads when confronted by the
novelty of the law courts and wish that it were
possible to reproduce all the conditions under which
they delivered their exercises. But there sits the
judge in silence, their opponent bellows at them, no
rash utterance passes unnoticed and all assumptions
must be proved, the clock cuts short the speech that
has been laboriously pieced together at the cost of
hours of study both by day and night, and there are
certain cases which require simplicity of language and
the abandonment of the perpetual bombast of the
schools, a fact which these fluent fellows completely
fail to realise. And so you will find some persons 6
who regard themselves as too eloquent to speak in
the courts. On the other hand, the man, whom we
conducted to the forum while still young and in the
charm of immaturity, should begin with as easy and
favourable a case as may be (just as the cubs of wild
beasts are brought up to start with on softer
forms of prey), and should not proceed straight
from this commencement to plead case after case
without a break, or cause his talents to set and
harden while they still require nourishment; on the
contrary, as soon as he has come to realise the nature
of the conflicts in which he will have to engage and
the object to which his studies should be directed, he
should take an interval of rest and refreshment.
Thus, at an age to which boldness is still natural, he 7
will find it easy to get over the timidity which invari-
ably accompanies the period of apprenticeship, and

facilitatem usque ad contemptum operis adduxerit. Usus est hac ratione M. Tullius, et cum iam clarum meruisset inter patronos, qui tum erant, nomen, in Asiam navigavit seque et aliis sine dubio eloquentiae ac sapientiae magistris, sed praecipue tamen Apollonio Moloni, quem Romae quoque audierat, Rhodi rursus formandum ac velut recoquendum dedit. Tum dignum operae pretium venit, cum inter se congruunt praecepta et experimenta.

VII. Cum satis in omni certamine virium fecerit, prima ei cura in suscipiendis causis erit; in quibus defendere quidem reos profecto quam facere vir bonus malet, non tamen ita nomen ipsum accusatoris horrebit, ut nullo neque publico neque privato duci possit officio, ut aliquem ad reddendam rationem vitae vocet. Nam et leges ipsae nihil valeant, nisi actoris idonea voce munitae; et si poenas scelerum expetere fas non est, prope est ut scelera ipsa permissa sint, et licentiam malis dari certe contra 2 bonos est. Quare neque sociorum querelas nec amici vel propinqui necem nec erupturas in rem publicam conspirationes inultas patietur orator, non poenae nocentium cupidus, sed emendandi vitia

will not, on the other hand, carry his boldness so far as to lead him to despise the difficulties of his task. This was the method employed by Cicero: for when he had already won a distinguished position at the bar of his day, he took ship to Asia and there studied under a number of professors of philosophy and rhetoric, but above all under Apollonius Molon, whose lectures he had attended at Rome and to whom he now at Rhodes entrusted the refashioning and recasting of his style. It is only when theory and practice are brought into a perfect harmony that the orator reaps the reward of all his study.

VII. When our orator has developed his strength to such a pitch that it is equal to every kind of conflict in which he may be called upon to bear his part, his first consideration should be to exercise care in the choice of the cases which he proposes to undertake. A good man will undoubtedly prefer defence to prosecution, but he will not have such a rooted objection to the task of accuser as to disregard his duty towards the state or towards individuals and refuse to call any man to render an account of his way of life. For the laws themselves would be powerless without the assistance of advocates equal to the task of supporting them; and to regard it as a sin to demand the punishment of crime is almost equivalent to the sanctioning of crime, while it is certainly contrary to the interest of the good to give the wicked free leave to work their will. Therefore, our 2 orator will not suffer the complaints of our allies, the death of friends or kinsmen, or conspiracies that threaten the common weal to go unavenged, while his conduct will be governed not by a passion to secure the punishment of the guilty, but by the

corrigendique mores. Nam qui ratione traduci ad
3 meliora non possunt, solo metu continentur. Itaque
ut accusatoriam vitam vivere et ad deferendos reos
praemio duci proximum latrocinio est, ita pestem
intestinam propulsare cum propugnatoribus patriae
comparandum. Ideoque principes in re publica viri
non detrectaverunt hanc officii partem, creditique
sunt etiam clari iuvenes obsidem rei publicae dare
malorum civium accusationem, quia nec odisse im-
probos nec simultates provocare nisi ex fiducia bonae
4 mentis videbantur; idque cum ab Hortensio, Lucullis,
Sulpicio, Cicerone, Caesare, plurimis aliis, tum ab
utroque Catone factum est, quorum alter appellatus
est sapiens, alter nisi creditur fuisse, vix scio, cui
reliquerit huius nominis locum. Neque[1] defendet
omnes orator idem, portumque illum eloquentiae
suae salutarem non etiam piratis patefaciet ducetur-
5 que in advocationem maxime causa. Quoniam tamen
omnes, qui non improbe litigabunt, quorum certe
bona pars est, sustinere non potest unus, aliquid
et commendantium personis dabit et ipsorum qui

---

[1] neque, *early edd.* : namque, *MSS.*

---

[1] *i. e.* Cato the Elder.

desire to correct vice and reform morals. For fear
is the only means of restraining those who cannot
be led to better ways by the voice of reason. Conse- 3
quently, while to devote one's life to the task of
accusation, and to be tempted by the hope of reward
to bring the guilty to trial is little better than making
one's living by highway robbery, none the less to rid
one's country of the pests that gnaw its vitals is
conduct worthy of comparison with that of heroes,
who champion their country's cause in the field of
battle. For this reason men who were leaders of the
state have not refused to undertake this portion of
an orator's duty, and even young men of high rank
have been regarded as giving their country a pledge
of their devotion by accusing bad citizens, since it
was thought that their hatred of evil and their
readiness to incur enmity were proofs of their confidence in their own rectitude. Such action was 4
taken by Hortensius, the Luculli, Sulpicius, Cicero,
Caesar and many others, among them both the Catos,
of whom one was actually called the Wise,[1] while if
the other is not regarded as wise, I do not know of
any that can claim the title after him. On the other
hand, this same orator of ours will not defend all and
sundry: that haven of safety which his eloquence
provides will never be opened to pirates as it is to
others, and he will be led to undertake cases mainly
by consideration of their nature. However, since 5
one man cannot undertake the cases of all litigants
who are not, as many undoubtedly are, dishonest, he
will be influenced to some extent by the character
of the persons who recommend clients to his protection and also by the character of the litigants
themselves, and will allow himself to be moved by

iudicio decernent, ut optimi cuiusque voluntate
moveatur; namque hos et amicissimos habebit vir
6 bonus. Summovendum vero est utrumque ambitus
genus vel potentibus contra humiles venditandi
operam suam vel illud etiam iactantius minores
utique contra dignitatem attollendi. Non enim fortuna causas vel iustas vel improbas facit. Neque
vero pudor obstet, quo minus susceptam, cum melior
videretur, litem cognita inter discendum iniquitate
7 dimittat, cum prius litigatori dixerit verum. Nam et
in hoc maximum, si aequi iudices sumus, beneficium
est, ut non fallamus vana spe litigantem. Neque
est dignus opera patroni, qui non utitur consilio,
et certe non convenit ei, quem oratorem esse
volumus, iniusta tueri scientem. Nam si ex illis,
quas supra diximus, causis falsum tuebitur, erit
tamen honestum quod ipse faciet.

8 Gratisne ei semper agendum sit, tractari potest.
Quod ex prima statim fronte diiudicare impru-
dentium est. Nam quis ignorat, quin id longe sit
honestissimum ac liberalibus disciplinis et illo, quem
exigimus, animo dignissimum, non vendere operam
nec elevare tanti beneficii auctoritatem, cum plera-

---

[1] XII. i. 36.

the wishes of all virtuous men; for a good man will naturally have such for his most intimate friends. But he must put away from him two kinds of 6 pretentious display, the one consisting in the officious proffering of his services to the powerful against those of meaner position, and the other, which is even more obtrusive, in deliberately supporting inferiors against those of high degree. For a case is not rendered either just or the reverse by the social position of the parties engaged. Nor, again, will a sense of shame deter him from throwing over a case which he has undertaken in the belief that it had justice on its side, but which his study of the facts has shown to be unjust, although before doing so he should give his client his true opinion on the case. For, if we judge aright, there is no greater 7 benefit that we can confer on our clients than this, that we should not cheat them by giving them empty hopes of success. On the other hand, no client that does not take his advocate into his counsel deserves that advocate's assistance, and it is certainly unworthy of our ideal orator that he should wittingly defend injustice. For if he is led to defend what is false by any of the motives which I mentioned above,[1] his own action will still be honourable.

It is an open question whether he should never 8 demand a fee for his services. To decide the question at first sight would be the act of a fool. For we all know that by far the most honourable course, and the one which is most in keeping with a liberal education and that temper of mind which we desiderate, is not to sell our services nor to debase the value of such a boon as eloquence, since there are not a few things which come to be regarded as

que hoc ipso possint videri vilia, quod pretium

9 habent? Caecis hoc, ut aiunt, satis clarum est, nec quisquam, qui sufficientia sibi (modica autem haec sunt) possidebit, hunc quaestum sine crimine sordium fecerit. At si res familiaris amplius aliquid ad usus necessarios exiget, secundum omnium sapientium leges patietur sibi gratiam referri, cum et Socrati collatum sit ad victum, et Zeno, Cleanthes, Chry-

10 sippus mercedes a discipulis acceptaverint. Neque enim video, quae iustior acquirendi ratio quam ex honestissimo labore et ab iis, de quibus optime meruerint, quique, si nihil invicem praestent, indigni fuerint defensione. Quod quidem non iustum modo, sed necessarium etiam est, cum haec ipsa opera tempusque omne alienis negotiis datum facultatem

11 aliter acquirendi recidant. Sed tum quoque tenendus est modus, ac plurimum refert et a quo accipiat et quantum et quousque. Paciscendi quidem ille piraticus mos et imponentium periculis pretia procul abominanda negotiatio etiam a mediocriter improbis aberit, cum praesertim bonos homines bonasque causas tuenti non sit metuendus ingratus;

cheap, merely because they have a price set upon
them. This much even the blind can see, as the 9
saying is, and no one who is the possessor of sufficient
wealth to satisfy his needs (and that does not imply
any great opulence) will seek to secure an income
by such methods without laying himself open to the
charge of meanness. On the other hand, if his
domestic circumstances are such as to require some
addition to his income to enable him to meet the
necessary demands upon his purse, there is not a
philosopher who would forbid him to accept this form
of recompense for his services, since collections were
made even on behalf of Socrates, and Zeno, Cleanthes
and Chrysippus took fees from their pupils. Nor 10
can I see how we can turn a more honest penny than
by performance of the most honourable of tasks and
by accepting money from those to whom we have
rendered the most signal services and who, if they
made no return for what we have done for them,
would show themselves undeserving to have been
defended by us. Nay, it is not only just, but
necessary that this should be so, since the duties of
advocacy and the bestowal of every minute of our
time on the affairs of others deprive us of all other
means of making money. But we must none the 11
less observe the happy mean, and it makes no small
difference from whom we take payment, what payment we demand, and how long we continue to do
so. As for the piratical practice of bargaining and
the scandalous traffic of those who proportion their
fees to the peril in which their would-be client
stands, such a procedure will be eschewed even by
those who are more than half scoundrels, more
especially since the advocate who devotes himself

12 quodsi sit futurus, malo tamen ille peccet. Nihil
ergo acquirere volet orator ultra quam satis erit; ac
ne pauper quidem tanquam mercedem accipiet, sed
mutua benivolentia utetur, cum sciat se tanto plus
praestitisse. Non enim, quia venire hoc beneficium
non oportet, oportet[1] perire. Denique ut gratus sit
ad eum magis pertinet qui debet.

VIII. Proxima discendae causae ratio, quod est
orationis fundamentum. Neque enim quisquam
ingenio tam tenui reperietur, qui, cum omnia quae
sunt in causa diligenter cognoverit, ad docendum
2 certe iudicem non sufficiat. Sed eius rei paucissimis
cura est. Nam ut taceam de negligentibus, quorum
nihil refert, ubi litium cardo vertatur, dum sint quae
vel extra causam ex personis aut communi tractatu
locorum occasionem clamandi largiantur, aliquos et
ambitio pervertit, qui partim tanquam occupati
semperque aliud habentes, quod ante agendum sit,
pridie ad se venire litigatorem aut eodem matutino
iubent, nonnunquam etiam inter ipsa subsellia
3 didicisse se gloriantur; partim iactantia ingenii, ut

---

[1] *Second* oportet *added by Buttmann.*

to the defence of good men and worthy causes will
have nothing to fear from ingratitude. And even if
a client should prove ungrateful, it is better that he
should be the sinner and not our orator. To con- 12
clude, then, the orator will not seek to make more
money than is sufficient for his needs, and even if he
is poor, he will not regard his payment as a fee, but
rather as the expression of the principle that one
good turn deserves another, since he will be well
aware that he has conferred far more than he receives.
For it does not follow that because his services
ought not to be sold, they should therefore be
unremunerated. Finally, gratitude is primarily the
business of the debtor.

VIII. We have next to consider how a case should
be studied, since such study is the foundation of
oratory. There is no one so destitute of all talent
as, after making himself thoroughly familiar with all
the facts of his case, to be unable at least to commu-
nicate those facts to the judge. But those who 2
devote any serious attention to such study are very
few indeed. For, to say nothing of those careless
advocates who are quite indifferent as to what the
pivot of the whole case may be, provided only there
are points which, though irrelevant to the case, will
give them the opportunity of declaiming in thunder-
ous tones on the character of persons involved or
developing some commonplace, there are some who
are so perverted by vanity that, on the oft-repeated
pretext that they are occupied by other business,
they bid their client come to them on the day preceding the trial or early on the morning of the day
itself, and sometimes even boast that they learnt up
their case while sitting in court; while others by 3

res cito accepisse videantur, tenere se et intelligere
prius paene quam audiant mentiti, cum multa et
diserte summisque clamoribus, quae neque ad
iudicem neque ad litigatorem pertineant, decanta-
verunt, bene sudantes beneque comitati per forum
4 reducuntur. Ne illas quidem tulerim delicias eorum,
qui doceri amicos suos iubent, quanquam minus mali
est, si illi saltem recte discant recteque doceant.
Sed quis discet tam bene quam patronus? Quomodo
autem sequester ille et media litium manus et
quidam interpres impendet aequo animo laborem
in alienas actiones, cum dicturis tanti suae non sint?
5 Pessimae vero consuetudinis libellis esse contentum,
quos componit aut litigator qui confugit ad patro-
num, quia liti ipse non sufficit, aut aliquis ex eo
genere advocatorum, qui se non posse agere confitentur, deinde faciunt id quod est in agendo diffi-
cillimum. Nam qui iudicare, quid dicendum, quid
dissimulandum, quid declinandum, mutandum, fingendum etiam sit, potest, cur non sit orator, quando,

---

[1] *Advocatus* is here used in its original sense. By Quintilian's time it had come also to mean "advocate," and is
often so used by him elsewhere.

way of creating an impression of extraordinary talent,
and to make it seem that they are quick in the up-
take, pretend that they have grasped the facts of
the case and understand the situation almost before
they have heard what it is, and then after chanting
out some long and fluent discourse which has nought
to do either with the judge or their client, but
awakens the clamorous applause of the audience,
they are escorted home through the forum, perspiring
at every pore and attended by flocks of enthusiastic
friends. Further, I would not even tolerate the 4
affectation of those who insist that their friends, and
not themselves, should be instructed in the facts
of the case, though this is a less serious evil, if the
friends can be relied upon to learn and supply the
facts correctly. But who can give such effective
study to the case as the advocate himself? How
can the intermediary, the go-between or interpreter,
devote himself whole-heartedly to the study of other
men's cases, when those who have got to do the
actual pleading do not think it worth while to get
up their own? On the other hand, it is a most 5
pernicious practice to rest content with a written
statement of the case composed either by the litigant
who betakes himself to an advocate because he finds
that his own powers are not equal to the conduct of
his case, or by some member of that class of legal
advisers [1] who admit that they are incapable of pleading, and then proceed to take upon themselves the
most difficult of all the tasks that confront the pleader.
For if a man is capable of judging what should be
said, what concealed, what avoided, altered or even
invented, why should he not appear as orator himself,
since he performs the far more difficult feat of making

429

6 quod difficilius est, oratorem facit? Hi porro non
tantum nocerent, si omnia scriberent uti gesta sunt.
Nunc consilium et colores adiiciunt et aliqua peiora
veris, quae plerique cum acceperunt, mutare nefas
habent et velut themata in scholis posita custodiunt.
Deinde deprehenduntur et causam, quam discere ex
suis litigatoribus noluerunt, ex adversariis discunt.

7 Liberum igitur demus ante omnia iis, quorum
negotium erit, tempus ac locum, exhortemurque
ultro, ut omnia quamlibet verbose et unde volent
repetita ex tempore exponant. Non enim tam
obest audire supervacua quam ignorare necessaria.

8 Frequenter autem et vulnus et remedium in iis
orator inveniet, quae litigatori in neutram partem
habere momentum videbantur. Nec tanta sit acturo
memoriae fiducia, ut subscribere audita pigeat.

Nec semel audisse sit satis; cogendus eadem
iterum ac saepius dicere litigator, non solum quia
effugere aliqua prima expositione potuerunt, praesertim hominem (quod saepe evenit) imperitum, sed

an orator? Such persons would not, however, do so 6
much harm if they would only put down all the
facts as they occurred. But as it is, they add sug-
gestions of their own, put their own construction on
the facts and insert inventions which are far more
damaging than the unvarnished truth. And then
the advocate as a rule, on receiving the document,
regards it as a crime to make any alteration, and
keeps to it as faithfully as if it were a theme set for
declamation in the schools. The sequel is that they
are tripped up and have to learn from their opponents the case which they refused to learn from their
own clients. We should therefore above all allow 7
the parties concerned ample time for an interview in
a place free from interruption, and should even
exhort them to set forth on the spot all the facts in
as many words as they may choose to use and allowing them to go as far back as they please. For it is
less of a drawback to listen to a number of irrelevant
facts than to be left in ignorance of essentials.
Moreover, the orator will often detect both the evil 8
and its remedy in facts which the litigant regarded
as devoid of all importance, one way or the other.
Further, the advocate who has got to plead the case
should not put such excessive confidence in his
powers of memory as to disdain to jot down what he
has heard.

Nor should one hearing be regarded as sufficient.
The litigant should be made to repeat his statements
at least once, not merely because certain points may
have escaped him on the occasion of his first statement, as is extremely likely to happen if, as is often
the case, he is a man of no education, but also that
we may note whether he sticks to what he originally

9 etiam ut sciamus an eadem dicat. Plurimi enim
mentiuntur et, tanquam non doceant causam, sed
agant, non ut cum patrono sed ut cum iudice
loquuntur. Quapropter nunquam satis credendum
est, sed agitandus omnibus modis et turbandus et
10 evocandus. Nam ut medicis non apparentia modo
vitia curanda sunt sed etiam invenienda quae latent,
saepe ipsis ea, qui sanandi sunt, occulentibus, ita
advocatus plura quam ostenduntur aspiciat. Nam
cum satis in audiendo patientiae impenderit, in
aliam rursus ei personam transeundum est, agendus-
que adversarius, proponendum quidquid omnino
excogitari contra potest, quidquid recipit in eiusmodi
disceptatione natura. Interrogandus quam infes-
11 tissime ac premendus. Nam dum omnia quaerimus,
aliquando ad verum, ubi minime exspectavimus,
pervenimus.

In summa optimus est in discendo patronus
incredulus. Promittit enim litigator omnia, testem
populum, paratissimas consignationes, ipsum denique
12 adversarium quaedam non negaturum. Ideoque
opus est intueri omne litis instrumentum; quod
videre non est satis, perlegendum erit. Nam frequentissime aut non sunt omnino, quae promittebantur,
aut minus continent aut cum alio aliquo nocituro
permixta sunt aut nimia sunt et fidem hoc ipso

said. For a large number of clients lie, and hold   9
forth, not as if they were instructing their advocate
in the facts of the case, but as if they were pleading
with a judge. Consequently we must never be too
ready to believe them, but must test them in every
way, try to confuse them and draw them out. For 10
just as doctors have to do more than treat the
ailments which meet the eye, and need also to
discover those which lie hid, since their patients
often conceal the truth, so the advocate must look
out for more points than his client discloses to him.
After he considers that he has given a sufficiently
patient hearing to the latter's statements, he must
assume another character and adopt the rôle of his
opponent, urging every conceivable objection that a
discussion of the kind which we are considering may
permit. The client must be subjected to a hostile 11
cross-examination and given no peace : for by en-
quiring into everything, we shall sometimes come
upon the truth where we least expect it.

In fact, the advocate who is most successful in
getting up his case is he who is incredulous. For
the client promises everything : the people, he says,
will bear witness to the truth of what he says, he can
produce documentary evidence at a moment's notice
and there are some points which he says his opponent
will not deny. It is therefore necessary to look into 12
every document connected with the case, and where
the mere sight of them is not sufficient, they must
be read through. For very frequently they are
either not at all what the client alleged them to be,
or contain less, or are mixed up with elements that
may damage our case, or prove more than is required
and are likely to detract from their credibility just

13 detractura quod non habent modum. Denique linum ruptum aut turbatam ceram[1] aut sine agnitore signa frequenter invenies ; quae, nisi domi excusseris, in foro inopinata decipient, plusque nocebunt destituta quam non promissa nocuissent. Multa etiam, quae litigator nihil ad causam pertinere crediderit, patronus eruet, modo per omnes, quos tradidimus, 14 argumentorum locos eat. Quos ut circumspectare in agendo et attentare singulos minime convenit, propter quas diximus causas, ita in discendo rimari necessarium est, quae personae, quae tempora et loca, instituta, instrumenta, cetera, ex quibus non tantum illud, quod est artificiale probationis genus, colligi possit, sed qui metuendi testes, quomodo sint refellendi. Nam plurimum refert, invidia reus an odio an contemptu laboret, quorum fere pars prima superiores, proxima pares, tertia humiliores premit.

15 Sic causam perscrutatus, propositis ante oculos omnibus quae prosint noceantve, tertiam deinceps personam induat iudicis, fingatque apud se agi

---

[1] turbatam ceram, *Salmasius* : turbata cetera, *B.*

---

[1] v. x. 20 *sqq.*   *i. e.* sources from which arguments may be drawn.

because they are so extravagant. Further, it will 13 often be found that the thread is broken or the seal tampered with or the signatures unsupported by witnesses. And unless you discover such facts at home, they will take you by surprise in court and trip you up, doing you more harm by forcing you to abandon them than they would have done had they never been promised you. There are also a number of points which the client regards as irrelevant to his case, which the advocate will be able to elicit, provided he go carefully through all the "dwelling-places" of argument which I have already described.[1] Now though, for reasons already mentioned, it is 14 most undesirable that he should hunt for and try every single one of those, while actually engaged in pleading his case, it is most necessary in the preliminary study of the case to leave no stone unturned to discover the character of the persons involved, the circumstances of time and place, the customs and documents concerned, and the rest, from which we may not merely deduce the proofs known as artificial, but may also discover which witnesses are most to be feared and the best method of refuting them. For it makes a great difference whether it be envy, hatred or contempt that forms the chief obstacle to the success of the defence, since of these obstacles the first tells most against superiors, the second against equals, and the third against those of low degree.

Having thus given a thorough examination 15 to the case and clearly envisaged all those points which will tell for or against his client, the orator must then place himself in the position of a third person, namely, the judge, and imagine that the

causam, et, quod ipsum movisset de eadem re
pronuntiaturum, id potentissimum, apud quemcunque
agetur, existimet. Sic eum raro fallet eventus, aut
culpa iudicis erit.

IX. Quae sint in agendo servanda, toto fere opere
exsecuti sumus; pauca tamen propria huius loci,
quae non tam dicendi arte quam officiis agentis[1]
continentur, attingam. Ante omnia ne, quod plerisque accidit, ab utilitate eum causae praesentis
2 cupido laudis abducat. Nam ut gerentibus bella
non semper exercitus per plana et amoena ducendus
est, sed adeundi plerumque asperi colles, expug-
nandae civitates quamlibet praecisis impositae rupi-
bus aut operum mole difficiles, ita oratio gaudebit
quidem occasione laetius decurrendi et aequo
congressa campo totas vires populariter explicabit;
3 at si iuris anfractus aut eruendae veritatis latebras
adire cogetur, non obequitabit nec illis vibrantibus
concitatisque sententiis velut missilibus utetur, sed
operibus et cuniculis et insidiis et occultis artibus
4 rem geret. Quae omnia non dum fiunt laudantur,
sed cum facta sunt; unde etiam cupidissimis

---

[1] agentis, *Obrecht* : agendis, *B.*

case is being pleaded before himself, and assume
that the point which would have carried most weight
with himself, had he been trying the case, is likely
to have the greatest influence with the actual judge.
Thus he will rarely be deceived as to the result of
the trial, or, if he is, it will be the fault of the judge.

IX. As regards the points to be observed in the
actual pleading, I have dealt with these in every
portion of this work, but there still remain a few on
which I must touch as being specially appropriate to
the present place, since they are concerned not so
much with the art of speaking as with the duties
of the advocate. Above all it is important that he
should never, like so many, be led by a desire to win
applause to neglect the interest of the actual case.
It is not always the duty of generals in the field to 2
lead their armies through flat and smiling country :
it will often be necessary to cross rugged mountain
ranges, to storm cities placed on inaccessible cliffs or
rendered difficult of access by elaborate fortifications.
Similarly oratory will always be glad of the opportunity of manœuvring in all its freedom and delight-
ing the spectator by the deployment of its full
strength for conflict in the open field ; but if it is 3
forced to enter the tortuous defiles of the law, or
dark places whence the truth has to be dragged
forth, it will not go prancing in front of the enemy's
lines nor launch its shafts of quivering and passionate
epigram of the fashion that is now so popular, but
will wage war by means of sap and mine and ambush
and all the tactics of secrecy.   None of these 4
methods win applause during their actual execution :
the reward comes after they have been carried to a
successful termination, when even the most ambitious

opinionis plus fructus venit. Nam cum illa dicendi
vitiosa iactatio inter plausores suos detonuit, resurgit
verae virtutis fortior fama, nec iudices a quo sint
moti, dissimulant, et doctis creditur, nec est orationis
5 vera laus nisi cum finita est. Veteribus quidem
etiam dissimulare eloquentiam fuit moris, idque
M. Antonius praecipit, quo plus dicentibus fidei
minusque suspectae advocatorum insidiae forent.
Sed illa dissimulari, quae tum erat, potuit; nondum
enim tantum dicendi lumen accesserat, ut etiam
per obstantia erumperet. Quare artes quidem et
consilia lateant et quidquid, si deprehenditur, perit.
6 Hactenus eloquentia secretum habet. Verborum
quidem delectus, gravitas sententiarum, figurarum
elegantia aut non sunt aut apparent. Sed vel
propter hoc ipsum ostendenda non sunt quod
apparent; aut si unum sit ex duobus eligendum,
causa potius laudetur quam patronus. Finem tamen
hunc praestabit orator, ut videatur optimam causam
optime egisse. Illud certum erit neminem peius

438

will reap a richer recompense than they could ever
have secured by other means. For so soon as the
thunders of applause awakened among their admirers
by these affected declamatory displays have died
away, the glory of true virtue rises again with
renewed splendour, the judges do not conceal who
it is has moved them, the well-trained orator wins
their belief and oratory receives its only genuine
tribute, the praise accorded it when its task is done.
The old orators indeed used to conceal their elo- 5
quence, a method which is recommended by Marcus
Antonius, as a means of securing that the speaker's
words should carry conviction and of masking the
advocate's real designs. But the truth is that the
eloquence of those days was capable of concealment,
for it had not yet attained that splendour of diction
which makes it impossible to hide its light under a
bushel. Therefore artifice and stratagem should be
masked, since detection in such cases spells failure.
Thus far, and thus only, may eloquence hope to enjoy
the advantages of secrecy. But when we come to 6
consider the choice of words, the weight essential
to general reflexions and the elegance demanded by
figures, we are confronted by elements which must
either strike the attention or be condemned to non-
existence. But the very fact that they strike the
attention is a reason why they should not flaunt
themselves obtrusively. And, if we have to make
the choice, I should prefer that it should be the
cause, and not the orator, to which we award our
praise. Nevertheless, the true orator will achieve
the distinction of seeming to speak with all the
excellence that an excellent case deserves. One
thing may be regarded as certain, that no one can

agere quam qui displicente causa placet; necesse
7 est enim extra causam sit quod placet. Nec illo
fastidio laborabit orator non agendi causas minores,
tanquam infra eum sint aut detractura sit opinioni
minus liberalis materia. Nam et suscipiendi ratio
iustissima est officium, et optandum etiam ut amici
quam minimas lites habeant; et abunde dixit bene,
quisquis rei satisfecit.

8   At quidam, etiamsi forte susceperunt negotia
paulo ad dicendum tenuiora, extrinsecus adductis
ea rebus circumlinunt ac, si defecerint alia, conviciis
implent vacua causarum, si contingit, veris, si minus,
fictis, modo sit materia ingenii mereaturque clamorem dum dicitur. Quod ego adeo longe puto ab
oratore perfecto, ut eum ne vera quidem obiecturum,
9 nisi id causa exigit, credam. Ea est enim prorsus
canina, ut ait Appius, eloquentia, cognituram male
dicendi subire; quod facientibus etiam male audiendi
praesumenda patientia est. Nam et in ipsos fit
impetus frequenter, qui egerunt, et certe petulan-

---

[1] A *cognitor* is one who represents another. The litigant
may abuse his opponent, but that does not justify his
advocate in doing so.

plead worse than he who wins applause despite the disapproval meted out to his case. For the inevitable conclusion is that the applause must have been evoked by something having no connexion with the case. Further, the true orator will not turn up his 7 nose at cases of minor importance on the ground of their being beneath his dignity or as being likely to detract from his reputation because the subject matter does not allow his genius full scope. For the strongest reason for undertaking a case is to be found in our duty towards our clients: nay, we should even desire the suits in which our friends are involved to be as unimportant as possible, and remember that the advocate who gives an adequate presentment to his case, has spoken exceeding well.

But there are some who, even although the cases 8 which they have undertaken give but small scope for eloquence, none the less trick it out with matter drawn from without and, if all else fails, fill up the gaps in their case with abuse of their opponents, true if possible, but false if necessary, the sole consideration that weighs with them being that it affords exercise for their talents and is likely to win applause during its delivery. Such conduct seems to me so unworthy of our perfect orator that, in my opinion, he will not even bring true charges against his opponents unless the case demand. For it is a 9 dog's eloquence, as Appius says, to undertake the task of abusing one's opponent,[1] and they who do so should steel themselves in advance to the prospect of being targets for like abuse themselves, since those who adopt this style of pleading are frequently attacked themselves, and there can at any rate be no doubt that the litigant pays dearly for the violence

tiam patroni litigator luit. Sed haec minora sunt
ipso illo vitio animi, quod maledicus a malefico non
10 distat nisi occasione. Turpis voluptas et inhumana
et nulli audientium bona gratia a litigatoribus
quidem frequenter exigitur, qui ultionem malunt
quam defensionem. Sed neque alia multa ad arbitrium eorum facienda sunt. Hoc quidem quis
hominum liberi modo sanguinis sustineat petulans
11 esse ad alterius arbitrium? Atqui etiam in advocatos partis adversae libenter nonnulli invehuntur;
quod, nisi si forte meruerunt, et inhumanum est
respectu communium officiorum, et cum ipsi qui
dicit inutile (nam idem iuris responsuris datur), tum
causae contrarium, cui[1] plane adversarii fiunt et
inimici, et quantulumcunque eis virium est, con-
12 tumelia augetur. Super omnia perit illa, quae
plurimum oratori et auctoritatis et fidei adfert,
modestia, si a viro bono in rabulam latratoremque
convertitur, compositus non ad animum iudicis sed
13 ad stomachum litigatoris. Frequenter etiam species
libertatis deducere ad temeritatem solet non causis
modo, sed ipsis quoque, qui dixerunt, periculosam.

---

[1] cui, *Halm*: qui, *B.*

of his advocate.   But such faults are less serious than
that which lies deep in the soul itself, making the
evil speaker to differ from the evil doer only in
respect of opportunity.   It is not uncommon for 10
the litigant to demand a base and inhuman gratifi-
cation of his rancour, such as not a single man among
the audience will approve, for it is on revenge rather
than on protection that his heart is set.   But in this,
as in a number of other points, it is the duty of the
orator to refuse to comply with his clients' desires.
For how can a man with the least degree of gentle-
manly feeling consent to make a brutal attack merely
because another desires it?   And yet there are some 11
who take pleasure in directing their onslaughts
against their opponents' counsel as well, a practice
which, unless they have deserved such attacks, shows
an inhuman disregard of the duties incumbent on the
profession, and is not merely useless to the speaker
(since he thereby gives his opponent the right to
reply in the same strain), but contrary to the
interests of his case, since it creates a hostile and
antagonistic disposition in the advocates attacked,
whose eloquence, however feeble it may be, will be
redoubled by resentment at the insults to which
they have been subjected.   Above all, it involves a 12
complete waste of one of the most valuable of an
orator's assets, namely that self-restraint which gives
weight and credit to his words, if he debases himself from an honest man into a snarling wrangler,
directing all his efforts not to win the goodwill of the
judge, but to gratify his client's spite.   Often too 13
the attractions of freedom of speech will lure him
into a rashness of language perilous not merely to
the interests of the case, but to those of the speaker

Nec immerito Pericles solebat optare, ne quod sibi
verbum in mentem veniret, quo populus offenderetur.
Sed quod ille de populo, id ego de omnibus sentio,
qui tantundem possunt nocere. Nam quae fortia
dum dicuntur videbantur, stulta cum laeserunt
vocantur.

14 Nunc, quia varium fere propositum agentium fuit,
et quorundam cura tarditatis, quorundam facilitas temeritatis crimine laboravit, quem credam fore in hoc

15 oratoris modum, tradere non alienum videtur. Adferet
ad dicendum curae semper quantum plurimum poterit. Neque enim hoc solum negligentis, sed mali
et in suscepta causa perfidi ac proditoris est, peius
agere quam possit. Ideoque ne suscipiendae quidem
sunt causae plures quam quibus suffecturum se sciat.

16 Dicet scripta quam res patietur plurima et, ut Demosthenes ait, si continget, et sculpta. Sed hoc aut
primae actiones aut quae in publicis iudiciis post
interiectos dies dantur permiserint; at cum protinus
respondendum est, omnia parari non possunt, adeo
ut paulo minus promptis etiam noceat scripsisse, si
alia ex diverso, quam opinati fuerint, occurrerint.

---

[1] This passage is our sole authority for the saying.

himself. It was not without good reason that Pericles used to pray that no word might occur to his
mind that could give offence to the people. But
what he felt with regard to the people, I feel with
regard to every audience, since they can cause just
as much harm to the orator as the people could
ever do to Pericles. For utterances which seemed
courageous at the moment of speaking, are called
foolish when it is found that they have given offence.

In view of the fact that there is commonly a great 14
variety in the aims which pleaders set before themselves and that the diligence shown by some is
branded as tedious caution, while the readiness of
others is criticised as rashness, I think that this will
be an appropriate place to set forth my views as to
how the orator may strike the happy mean. He will 15
show all the diligence of which he is capable in his
pleading. For to plead worse than he might have
done, is not merely an indication of negligence, but
stamps him as a bad man and a traitor, disloyal to the
cause which he has undertaken. Consequently he
must refuse to undertake more cases than he feels
he can manage. As far as possible he will deliver 16
only what he has written, and, if circumstances
permit, only what he has, as Demosthenes says,[1]
carved into shape. Such a practice is possible in
first hearings and also in subsequent hearings such as
are granted in the public courts after an interval of
several days. On the other hand, when we have to
reply on the spot, it is impossible to prepare everything: in fact for the less ready type of speaker, it
may, in the event of his opponents putting forward
arguments quite other than those which they were
expected to advance, be a positive drawback to have

17 Inviti enim recedunt a praeparatis et tota actione respiciunt requiruntque, num aliquid ex illis intervelli
atque ex tempore dicendis inseri possit; quod si fiat,
non cohaeret nec commissuris modo, ut in opere
male iuncto, hiantibus sed ipsa coloris inaequalitate

18 detegitur. Ita nec liber est impetus nec cura con-
texta, et utrumque alteri obstat; illa enim quae
scripta sunt retinent animum, non sequuntur. Itaque
in his actionibus omni, ut agricolae dicunt, pede stan-

19 dum est. Nam cum in propositione ac refutatione
causa consistat, quae nostrae partis sunt scripta esse
possunt, quae etiam responsurum adversarium certum
est (est enim aliquando certum) pari cura refelluntur.
Ad alia unum paratum adferre possumus, ut causam
bene noverimus, alterum ibi sumere, ut dicentem

20 adversarium diligenter audiamus. Licet tamen
praecogitare plura et animum ad omnes casus componere, idque est tutius stilo, quo facilius et omittitur

written anything. For it is only with reluctance 17
that such speakers will under such circumstances
consent to abandon what they have written, and
throughout their pleading keep looking back and
trying to discover whether any portion of their
manuscript can be saved from the wreck and inter-
polated into what they have to improvise. And if
they do make such interpolations, the result is a lack
of cohesion which is betrayed not merely by the
gaping of the seams where the patch has been unskilfully inserted, but by the differences of style.
Consequently, the vigour of their eloquence will be 18
hampered and their thought will lack connexion, each
of which circumstances reacts unfavourably upon the
other, since what is written trammels the mind
instead of following its lead. Therefore, in such
pleadings we must, as the rustic adage says, "stand
on all our feet." For since the case turns on the 19
propounding and refutation of arguments, it is
always possible to write out what we propose to
advance on our own behalf, and similar preparation
is also possible with regard to the refutation of such
replies as are absolutely certain to be made by our
adversary: for there are times when we have this
certainty. But with regard to all other portions of
our speech, the only preparation that is possible in
advance consists in a thorough knowledge of our
case, while there is a second precaution which may
be taken in court, consisting in giving our best
attention to our opponent's speech. On the other 20
hand, there is much that may be thought out in
advance and we may forearm our mind against all
possible emergencies, a course which is far safer
than writing, since a train of thought can easily be

cogitatio et transfertur. Sed sive in respondendo fuerit subito dicendum, sive quae alia ita exegerit ratio, non oppressum se ac deprehensum credet orator, cui disciplina et studium et exercitatio dederit 21 vires etiam facilitatis; quem armatum semper ac velut in procinctu stantem non magis unquam in causis oratio quam in rebus cotidianis ac domesticis sermo deficiet, nec se unquam propter hoc oneri subtrahet, modo sit causae discendae tempus; nam cetera semper sciet.

X. Superest ut dicam de genere orationis. Hic erat propositus a nobis in divisione prima locus tertius; nam ita promiseram me de arte, de artifice, de opere dicturum. Cum sit autem rhetorices atque oratoris opus oratio pluresque eius formae, sicut ostendam, in omnibus his et ars est et artifex. Plurimum tamen invicem differunt; nec solum specie, ut signum signo et tabula tabulae et actio actioni, sed genere ipso, ut Graecis Tuscanicae statuae, ut Asianus 2 eloquens Attico. Suos autem haec operum genera, quae dico, ut auctores, sic etiam amatores habent; atque ideo nondum est perfectus orator ac nescio an ars ulla, non solum quia aliud in alio magis eminet, sed quod non una omnibus forma placuit, partim

---

[1] II. xiv. 5.

abandoned or diverted in a new direction. But whether we have to improvise a reply, or are obliged to speak extempore by some other reason, the orator on whom training, study and practice have conferred the gift of facility, will never regard himself as lost or taken at hopeless disadvantage. He stands 21 armed for battle, ever ready for the fray, and his eloquence will no more fail him in the courts than speech will fail him in domestic affairs and the daily concerns of life: and he will never shirk his burden for fear of failing to find words, provided he has time to study his case: for all other knowledge will always be his at command.

X. The question of the "kind of style" to be adopted remains to be discussed. This was described in my original division [1] of my subject as forming its third portion: for I promised that I would speak of the art, the artist and the work. But since oratory is the work both of rhetoric and of the orator, and since it has many forms, as I shall show, the art and the artist are involved in the consideration of all these forms. But they differ greatly from one another, and not merely in *species,* as statue differs from statue, picture from picture and speech from speech, but in *genus* as well, as, for example, Etruscan statues differ from Greek and Asiatic orators from Attic. But these different kinds of 2 work, of which I speak, are not merely the product of different authors, but have each their own following of admirers, with the result that the perfect orator has not yet been found, a statement which perhaps may be extended to all arts, not merely because some qualities are more evident in some artists than in others, but because one single form

condicione vel temporum vel locorum, partim iudicio
cuiusque atque proposito.

3   Primi, quorum quidem opera non vetustatis modo
gratia visenda sunt, clari pictores fuisse dicuntur
Polygnotus atque Aglaophon, quorum simplex color
tam sui studiosos adhuc habet, ut illa prope rudia
ac velut futurae mox artis primordia maximis, qui
post eos exstiterunt, auctoribus praeferant, proprio
quodam intelligendi, ut mea opinio est, ambitu.

4   Post Zeuxis atque Parrhasius non multum aetate
distantes, circa Peloponnesia ambo tempora (nam
cum Parrhasio sermo Socratis apud Xenophontem
invenitur) plurimum arti addiderunt.   Quorum prior
luminum umbrarumque invenisse rationem, secundus

5   examinasse subtilius lineas traditur.   Nam Zeuxis
plus membris corporis dedit, id amplius atque
augustius ratus atque, ut existimant, Homerum
secutus, cui validissima quaeque forma etiam in
feminis placet.   Ille vero ita circumscripsit omnia,
ut eum legum latorem vocent, quia deorum atque
heroum effigies, quales ab eo sunt traditae, ceteri,

6   tanquam ita necesse sit, sequuntur.   Floruit autem
circa Philippum et usque ad successores Alexandri

---

¹ Of the painters mentioned in this and the following
sections Polygnotus of Thasos, son of Aglaophon, painted at
Athens in the middle of the 5th century B.C. Zeuxis of
Heraclea and Parrhasius of Ephesus flourished 420–390, while
the remainder are painters of the 4th century. Of these
Pamphilus of Sicyon was the teacher of Melanthius and
Apelles, the latter being the most famous painter of antiquity.

² *Memor.* III. x. 1.

³ *I.e.* by giving them roundness and solidity by his treatment of light and shade.

will not satisfy all critics, a fact which is due in part to conditions of time or place, in part to the taste and ideals of individuals.

The first great painters, whose works deserve 3 inspection for something more than their mere antiquity, are said to have been Polygnotus and Aglaophon,[1] whose simple colouring has still such enthusiastic admirers that they prefer these almost primitive works, which may be regarded as the first foundations of the art that was to be, over the works of the greatest of their successors, their motive being, in my opinion, an ostentatious desire to seem persons of superior taste. Later Zeuxis and Par- 4 rhasius contributed much to the progress of painting. These artists were separated by no great distance of time, since both flourished about the period of the Peloponnesian war: for example, Xenophon[2] has preserved a conversation between Socrates and Parrhasius. The first-mentioned seems to have discovered the method of representing light and shade, while the latter is said to have devoted special attention to the treatment of line. For 5 Zeuxis emphasised the limbs of the human body,[3] thinking thereby to add dignity and grandeur to his style : it is generally supposed that in this he followed the example of Homer, who likes to represent even his female characters as being of heroic mould. Parrhasius, on the other hand, was so fine a draughtsman that he has been styled the law-giver of his art, on the ground that all other artists take his representations of gods and heroes as models, as though no other course were possible. It was, however, from about the period of the reign 6 of Philip down to that of the successors of Alexander

pictura praecipue, sed diversis virtutibus. Nam
cura Protogenes, ratione Pamphilus ac Melanthius,
facilitate Antiphilus, concipiendis visionibus, quas
φαντασίας vocant, Theon Samius, ingenio et gratia,
quam in se ipse maxime iactat, Apelles est praestantissimus. Euphranorem admirandum facit, quod
et ceteris optimis studiis inter praecipuos et pingendi
fingendique idem mirus artifex fuit.

7 Similis in statuariis differentia.[1] Nam duriora et
Tuscanicis proxima Callon atque Hegesias, iam minus
rigida Calamis, molliora adhuc supra dictis Myron
fecit. Diligentia ac decor in Polyclito supra ceteros,
cui quanquam a plerisque tribuitur palma, tamen, ne
8 nihil detrahatur, deesse pondus putant. Nam ut
humanae formae decorem addiderit supra verum, ita
non explevisse deorum auctoritatem videtur. Quin
aetatem quoque graviorem dicitur refugisse nihil
ausus ultra leves genas. At quae Polyclito defue-
9 runt, Phidiae atque Alcameni dantur. Phidias tamen diis quam hominibus effingendis[2] melior artifex
creditur in ebore vero longe citra aemulum, vel si

---

[1] statuariis, *Christ*: statuis, *MSS.*
[2] effingendis, *Dukerus*: efficiendis, *MSS.*

---

[1] Callon of Aegina and Hegesias flourished in the latter
years of the 6th century. Calamis of Athens and Myron of
Eleutherae, first half of 5th century. Phidias of Athens and
Polyclitus of Argos, the two most famous sculptors of the
second half of 5th century. Praxiteles, middle of 4th
century. Lysippus and Demetrius, last half of 4th century.

that painting flourished more especially, although the different artists are distinguished for different excellences. Protogenes, for example, was renowned for accuracy, Pamphilus and Melanthius for soundness of taste, Antiphilus for facility, Theon of Samos for his depiction of imaginary scenes, known as φαντασίαι, and Apelles for genius and grace, in the latter of which qualities he took especial pride. Euphranor, on the other hand, was admired on the ground that, while he ranked with the most eminent masters of other arts, he at the same time achieved marvellous skill in the arts of sculpture and painting.

The same differences exist between sculptors. The 7 art of Callon and Hegesias [1] is somewhat rude and recalls the Etruscans, but the work of Calamis has already begun to be less stiff, while Myron's statues show a greater softness of form than had been achieved by the artists just mentioned. Polyclitus surpassed all others for care and grace, but although the majority of critics account him as the greatest of sculptors, to avoid making him faultless they express the opinion that his work is lacking in grandeur. For while he gave the human form an 8 ideal grace, he is thought to have been less successful in representing the dignity of the gods. He is further alleged to have shrunk from representing persons of maturer years, and to have ventured on nothing more difficult than a smooth and beardless face. But the qualities lacking in Polyclitus are allowed to have been possessed by Phidias and Alcamenes. On the other hand, Phidias is regarded 9 as more gifted in his representation of gods than of men, and indeed for chryselephantine statues he is without a peer, as he would in truth be, even if he

nihil nisi Minervam Athenis aut Olympium in Elide
Iovem fecisset, cuius pulchritudo adiecisse aliquid
etiam receptae religioni videtur; adeo maiestas
operis deum aequavit. Ad veritatem Lysippum ac
Praxitelen accessisse optime adfirmant. Nam Demetrius tanquam nimius in ea reprehenditur et fuit
similitudinis quam pulchritudinis amantior.

10 In oratione vero si species intueri velis, totidem
paene reperias ingeniorum quot corporum formas.
Sed fuere quaedam genera dicendi condicione temporum horridiora, alioqui magnam iam ingenii vim
prae se ferentia. Hinc sint Laelii, Africani, Catones
etiam Gracchique, quos tu licet Polygnotos vel
Callonas appelles. Mediam illam formam teneant L.
11 Crassus, Q. Hortensius. Tum deinde efflorescat non
multum inter se distantium tempore oratorum ingens
proventus. Hic vim Caesaris, indolem Caelii, sub-
tilitatem Calidii, diligentiam Pollionis, dignitatem
Messalae, sanctitatem Calvi, gravitatem Bruti, acumen Sulpicii, acerbitatem Cassii reperiemus; in iis
etiam, quos ipsi vidimus, copiam Senecae, vires
Africani, maturitatem Afri, iucunditatem Crispi,
12 sonum Trachali, elegantiam Secundi. At M.

had produced nothing in this material beyond his
Minerva at Athens and his Jupiter at Olympia in
Elis, whose beauty is such that it is said to have
added something even to the awe with which the
god was already regarded: so perfectly did the
majesty of the work give the impression of godhead.
Lysippus and Praxiteles are asserted to be supreme
as regards faithfulness to nature. For Demetrius is
blamed for carrying realism too far, and is less
concerned about the beauty than the truth of his
work.

Now, if we turn our attention to the various styles 10
of oratory, we shall find almost as great variety of
talents as there are of personal appearance. There
were certain kinds of oratory which, owing to the
circumstances of the age, suffered from lack of polish,
although in other respects they displayed remarkable
genius. In this class we may place orators such as
Laelius, Africanus, Cato, and even the Gracchi,
whom we may call the " Polygnoti " and " Callones "
of oratory. Among orators of the intermediate 11
type we may rank Lucius Crassus and Quintus
Hortensius. Then let us turn to a vast harvest of
orators who flourished much about the same period.
It is here that we find the vigour of Caesar, the
natural talent of Caelius, the subtlety of Calidius,
the accuracy of Pollio, the dignity of Messala, the
austerity of Calvus, the gravity of Brutus, the acumen
of Sulpicius and the bitterness of Cassius, while
among those whom we have seen ourselves we
admire the fluency of Seneca, the strength of Africanus, the mellowness of Afer, the charm of Crispus,
the sonority of Trachalus and the elegance of Secundus. But in Cicero we have one who is not, 12

Tullium non illum habemus Euphranorem circa plures
artium species praestantem, sed in omnibus, quae in
quoque laudantur, eminentissimum.   Quem tamen et
suorum homines temporum incessere audebant ut
tumidiorem et Asianum et redundantem et in re-
petitionibus nimium et in salibus aliquando frigidum
et in compositione fractum, exultantem ac paene,
13 quod procul absit, viro molliorem; postea vero quam
triumvirali proscriptione consumptus est, passim qui
oderant, qui invidebant, qui aemulabantur, adulatores
etiam praesentis potentiae non responsurum in-
vaserunt.   Ille tamen, qui ieiunus a quibusdam et
aridus habetur, non aliter ab ipsis inimicis male audire
quam nimiis floribus et ingenii affluentia potuit.
Falsum utrumque, sed tamen illa mentiendi propior
14 occasio.   Praecipue vero presserunt eum, qui videri
Atticorum imitatores concupierant.   Haec manus
quasi quibusdam sacris initiata ut alienigenam et
parum superstitiosum devinctumque illis legibus
insequebatur; unde nunc quoque aridi et exsuci et
15 exangues.   Hi sunt enim, qui suae imbecillitati sa-
nitatis appellationem, quae est maxime contraria,
obtendant; qui, quia clariorem vim eloquentiae
velut solem ferre non possunt, umbra magni nominis
delitescunt.   Quibus quia multa et pluribus locis

---

[1] *Cp.* x. i. 105 *sq.*   [2] *I. e.* Attic.

like Euphranor, merely distinguished in a number
of different forms of art, but is supreme in all the
different qualities which are praised in each individual
orator.[1] And yet even his own contemporaries
ventured to attack him on the ground that he was
bombastic, Asiatic, redundant, given to excessive
repetition, liable at times to be pointless in his
witticisms, sensuous, extravagant and (an outrageous
accusation!) almost effeminate in his rhythm. And 13
later, after he had fallen a victim to the proscrip-
tion of the second triumvirate, those who hated
and envied him and regarded him as their rival, nay,
even those who had flattered him in the days of his
power, attacked him now that he could no longer
reply. But that very man, who is now regarded
by some as being too jejune and dry, was attacked
by his personal enemies on no other ground than
that his style was too florid and his talents too little
under control. Both charges are false, but there is
more colour for the lie in the latter case than in
the former. Those, however, who criticised him 14
most severely were the speakers who desired to be
regarded as the imitators of Attic oratory. This
coterie, regarding themselves as the sole initiates in
the mysteries of their art, assailed him as an alien,
indifferent to their superstitions and refusing to be
bound by their laws. Their descendants are among
us to-day, a withered, sapless and anaemic band.
For it is they that flaunt their weakness under the 15
name of health, in defiance of the actual truth, and
because they cannot endure the dazzling rays of the
sun of eloquence, hide themselves beneath the
shadow of a mighty name.[2] However, as Cicero himself answered them at length and in a number of

Cicero ipse respondit, tutior mihi de hoc disserendi brevitas erit.

16 Et antiqua quidem illa divisio inter Atticos atque Asianos fuit, cum hi pressi et integri, contra inflati illi et inanes haberentur, in his nihil superflueret, illis iudicium maxime ac modus deesset. Quod quidam, quorum et Santra est, hoc putant accidisse, quod, paulatim sermone Graeco in proximas Asiae civitates influente, nondum satis periti loquendi facundiam concupierint, ideoque ea, quae proprie signari poterant, circuitu coeperint enuntiare ac
17 deinde in eo perseverarint. Mihi autem orationis differentiam fecisse et dicentium et audientium naturae videntur, quod Attici limati quidam et emuncti nihil inane aut redundans ferebant, Asiana gens tumidior alioqui atque iactantior vaniore etiam
18 dicendi gloria inflata est. Tertium mox, qui haec dividebant, adiecerunt genus Rhodium, quod velut medium esse atque ex utroque mixtum volunt; neque enim Attice pressi neque Asiane sunt abundantes, ut aliquid habere videantur gentis, aliquid
19 auctoris. Aeschines enim, qui hunc exilio delegerat

458

passages, it will be safer for me to be brief in my treatment of this topic.

The distinction between the Attic and the Asiatic 16 schools takes us back to antiquity. The former were regarded as concise and healthy, the latter as empty and inflated: the former were remarkable for the absence of all superfluity, while the latter were deficient alike in taste and restraint. The reason for this division, according to some authorities, among them Santra, is to be found in the fact that, as Greek gradually extended its range into the neighbouring cities of Asia, there arose a class of men who desired to distinguish themselves as orators before they had acquired sufficient command of the language, and who consequently began to express by periphrases what could have been expressed directly, until finally this practice became an ingrained habit. My own view, however, is that the 17 difference between the two styles is attributable to the character both of the orators and the audiences whom they addressed: the Athenians, with their polish and refinement, refused to tolerate emptiness and redundance, while the Asiatics, being naturally given to bombast and ostentation, were puffed up with a passion for a more vainglorious style of eloquence. At a later period, the critics, to whom 18 we owe this classification, added a third style, the Rhodian, which they asserted to lie midway between the two and to be a blend of both, since the orators of this school are neither so concise as the Attic nor redundant like the Asiatic school, but appear to derive their style in part from their national characteristics, in part from those of their founder. For 19 it was Aeschines who introduced the culture of

locum, intulit eo studia Athenarum, quae, velut sata
quaedam caelo terraque degenerant, saporem illum
Atticum peregrino miscuerunt.   Lenti ergo quidam
ac remissi, non sine pondere tamen neque fontibus
puris neque torrentibus turbidis, sed lenibus stagnis
similes habentur.

20   Nemo igitur dubitaverit, longe esse optimum genus
Atticorum.   In quo ut est aliquid inter ipsos commune, id est iudicium acre tersumque, ita ingeni-
21 orum plurimae formae.   Quapropter mihi falli multum
videntur, qui solos esse Atticos credunt tenues et
lucidos et significantes sed quadam eloquentiae fru-
galitate contentos ac semper manum intra pallium
continentes.   Nam quis erit hic Atticus?   Sit
Lysias; hunc enim amplectuntur amatores istius
nominis modum.   Non igitur iam usque ad Coccum
et Andocidem remittemur.   Interrogare tamen velim,
22 an Isocrates Attice dixerit.   Nihil enim tam est
Lysiae diversum.   Negabunt.   At eius schola principes oratorum dedit.   Quaeratur similius aliquid.
Hyperides Atticus?   Certe, at plus indulsit voluptati.   Transeo plurimos, Lycurgum, Aristogitona et

---

[1] The only Coccus known to us is stated by Suidas to
have been a pupil of Isocrates, whereas we should here
have expected Quintilian to refer to some orator of the
5th century contemporary with Andocides (closing decades
of 4th century).

Athens at Rhodes, which he had chosen as his place of exile : and just as certain plants degenerate as a result of change of soil and climate, so the fine Attic flavour was marred by the admixture of foreign ingredients. Consequently certain of the orators of this school are regarded as somewhat slow and lacking in energy, though not devoid of a certain weight, and as resembling placid pools rather than the limpid springs of Athens or the turbid torrents of Asia.

No one therefore should have any hesitation in pronouncing Attic oratory to be by far the best. But although all Attic writers have something in common, namely a keen and exact judgement, their talents manifest themselves in a number of different forms. Consequently I regard those critics as committing a serious error who regard only those authors as Attic who, while they are simple, lucid and expressive, are none the less content with a certain frugality of eloquence, and keep their hands modestly within the folds of their cloaks. For what author is there who answers to this conception? I am prepared to grant that there is Lysias, since he is the favourite model of the admirers of this school, and such an admission will save us from being referred to Coccus[1] and Andocides. But I should like to ask whether Isocrates spoke in the Attic style. For there is no author less like Lysias. They will answer in the negative. And yet it is to the school of Isocrates that we owe the greatest orators. Let us look for something closer. Is Hyperides Attic? Yes, they reply, but of an over-sensuous character. I pass by a number of orators, such as Lycurgus and Aristogeiton and their predecessors

his priores Isaeum, Antiphonta; quos ut homines
inter se genere similes, differentes dixeris specie.
23 Quid ille, cuius modo fecimus mentionem, Aeschines?
nonne his latior et audentior et excelsior? Quid
denique Demosthenes? non cunctos illos tenues et
circumspectos vi, sublimitate, impetu, cultu, compositione superavit? non insurgit locis? non figuris
gaudet? non translationibus nitet? non oratione
24 ficta dat tacentibus vocem? non illud iusiurandum
per caesos in Marathone ac Salamine propugnatores
rei publicae satis manifesto docet praeceptorem eius
Platonem fuisse? quem ipsum num Asianum appel-
labimus plerumque instinctis divino spiritu vatibus
comparandum? Quid Periclea? similemne credimus
Lysiacae gracilitati, quem fulminibus et caelesti
fragori comparant comici, dum illi conviciantur?
25 Quid est igitur, cur in iis demum, qui tenui venula
per calculos fluunt, Atticum saporem putent, ibi
demum thymum redolere dicant? Quos ego existimo, si quod in iis finibus uberius invenerint solum
fertilioremve segetem, negaturos Atticam esse, quod
plus, quam acceperit, seminis reddat, quia hanc eius
26 terrae fidem Menander eludit. Ita nunc, si quis ad
eas Demosthenis virtutes, quas ille summus orator

---

[1] *Georg.* 35 *sqq.* (Koerte); ἀπέδωκεν ὀρθῶς καὶ δικαίως, οὐ
πλέον, | ἀλλ' αὐτὸ τὸ μέτρον.

Isaeus and Antiphon; for though they have a certain *generic* resemblance, they may be said to differ in *species*. But what of Aeschines, whom I mentioned 23 just now? Is not his style ampler and bolder and more lofty than theirs? And what of Demosthenes himself? Did not he surpass all those simple and circumspect orators in force, loftiness, energy, polish and rhythm? Does he not rise to great heights in his *commonplaces*? Does he not rejoice in the employment of figures? Does he not make brilliant use of metaphor? Does he not lend a voice, a fictitious utterance to speechless things? Does not his famous 24 oath by the warriors who fell fighting for their country at Salamis and Marathon show that Plato was his master? And shall we call Plato an Asiatic, Plato who as a rule deserves comparison with poets instinct with the divine fire of inspiration? What of Pericles? Can we believe that his style was like the slender stream of Lysias' eloquence, when the comedians, even while they revile him, compare his oratory to the bolts and thunder of the skies? What is the 25 reason, then, why these critics regard that style which flows in a slender trickle and babbles among the pebbles as having the true Attic flavour and the true scent of Attic thyme? I really think that, if they were to discover a soil of exceptional richness and a crop of unusual abundance within the boundaries of Attica, they would deny it to be Attic, on the ground that it has produced more seed than it received: for you will remember the mocking comments passed by Menander [1] on the exact fidelity with which the soil of Attica repays its deposits. Well, then, if any man should, in addition to the 26 actual virtues which the great orator Demosthenes

habuit, tamen quae defuisse ei sive ipsius natura seu
lege civitatis videntur, adiecerit, ut adfectus con-
citatius moveat, audiam dicentem, *Non fecit hoc
Demosthenes ?* et si quid numeris exierit aptius (fortasse non possit, sed tamen si quid exierit) non erit
Atticum ? Melius de hoc nomine sentiant credantque
Attice dicere esse optime dicere.

27   Atque in hac tamen opinione perseverantes
Graecos magis tulerim. Latina mihi facundia, ut
inventione, dispositione, consilio, ceteris huius generis artibus similis Graecae ac prorsus discipula eius
videtur, ita circa rationem eloquendi vix habere
imitationis locum. Namque est ipsis statim sonis
durior, quando et iucundissimas ex Graecis litteras
non habemus, vocalem alteram, alteram consonantem,
quibus nullae apud eos dulcius spirant; quas mutuari
28 solemus, quotiens illorum nominibus utimur. Quod
cum contingit, nescio quomodo hilarior protinus
renidet oratio, ut in *Zephyris* et *Zophoris*. Quae si
nostris litteris scribantur, surdum quiddam et barbarum efficient, et velut in locum earum succedunt
29 tristes et horridae, quibus Graecia caret. Nam et
illa, quae est sexta nostrarum, paene non humana

---

[1] See **II.** xvi. 4. Quintilian alludes to an alleged law forbidding Athenian orators to appeal to the emotions in the
law courts.   [2] Φ and Υ.
[3] Friezes.   [4] F and U ; *zefuri* and *zofori.*

possessed, show himself to be the possessor of others,
that either owing to his own temperament or the
laws of Athens[1] Demosthenes is thought to have
lacked, and should reveal in himself the power of
strongly stirring the emotions, shall I hear one of
these critics protesting that Demosthenes never did
this? And if he produces something rhythmically
superior (an impossible feat, perhaps, but let us
assume it to be so), are we to be told that it is not
Attic? These critics would show finer feeling and
better judgement, if they took the view that Attic
eloquence meant perfect eloquence.

Still I should find this attitude less intolerable if 27
it were only the Greeks that insisted on it. For Latin
eloquence, although in my opinion it closely resembles
the Greek as far as invention, arrangement, judgement and the like are concerned, and may indeed be
regarded as its disciple, cannot aspire to imitate it
in point of elocution. For, in the first place, it is
harsher in sound, since our alphabet does not contain
the most euphonious of the Greek letters, one a
vowel and the other a consonant,[2] than which there
are none that fall more sweetly on the ear, and
which we are forced to borrow whenever we use
Greek words. The result of such borrowing is, for 28
some reason or other, the immediate accession to
our language of a certain liveliness and charm.
Take, for example, words such as *zephyri* and *zophori*:[3]
if they were spelt according to the Latin alphabet,
they would produce a heavy and barbarous sound.
For we replace these letters by others of a harsh
and unpleasant character,[4] from which Greece is
happily immune. For the sixth letter in our alphabet 29
is represented by a sound which can scarcely be

465

voce vel omnino non voce potius inter discrimina
dentium efflanda est; quae, etiam cum vocalem
proxima accipit, quassa quodammodo, utique quotiens
aliquam consonantium frangit, ut in hoc ipso *frangit*,
multo fit horridior. Aeolicae quoque litterae, qua
*servum cervum*que dicimus, etiamsi forma a nobis
repudiata est, vis tamen nos ipsa persequitur.
30 Duras et illa syllabas facit, quae ad coniungendas
demum subiectas sibi vocales est utilis, alias supervacua, ut *equos* hac et *aequum* scribimus; cum etiam
ipsae hae vocales duae efficiant sonum, qualis apud
Graecos nullus est, ideoque scribi illorum litteris
31 non potest. Quid? quod pleraque nos illa quasi
mugiente M[1] littera cludimus in quam[2] nullum Graece
verbum cadit: at illi *ny* iucundam et in fine praecipue
quasi tinnientem illius loco ponunt, quae est apud
32 nos rarissima in clausulis. Quid? quod syllabae
nostrae in B litteram et D innituntur adeo aspere,
ut plerique non antiquissimorum quidem, sed tamen
veterum mollire temptaverint non solum *aversa* pro
abversis dicendo, sed et in praepositione B litterae
33 absonam et ipsam S subiiciendo. Sed accentus
quoque, cum rigore quodam, tum similitudine ipsa,

---

[1] M *added by Halm.*
[2] quam, *Halm*: qua, *MSS.*

---

[1] *cp.* I. iv. 11.
[2] A sound approximating to our W.
[3] The sound of Q in itself does not differ from C. It
would therefore be useless, save as an indication that U and
another vowel are to follow. The U in this combination
following Q was, as Donatus later pointed out, "neither a
vowel nor a consonant," *i.e.* it was something between U
and V.

called human or even articulate, being produced by
forcing the air through the interstices of the teeth.
Such a sound, even when followed by a vowel, is
harsh enough and, as often as it clashes (*frangit*)
with a consonant,[1] as it does in this very word
frangit, becomes harsher still.   Then there is the
Aeolic digamma whose sound occurs in words such
as our *servus* and *cervus*; for even though we have
rejected the actual form of the letter, we cannot
get rid of that which it represents.[2]   Similarly the 30
letter Q, which is superfluous and useless save for
the purpose of attaching to itself the vowels by
which it is followed, results in the formation of
harsh syllables, as, for example, when we write *equos*
and *aequum*, more especially since these two vowels
together produce a sound for which Greek has no
equivalent and which cannot therefore be expressed
in Greek letters.[3]   Again, we have a number of 31
words which end with M, a letter which suggests
the mooing of a cow, and is never the final letter
in any Greek word: for in its place they use the
letters *ny*, the sound of which is naturally pleasant
and produces a ringing tone when it occurs at the
end of a word, whereas in Latin this termination is
scarcely ever found.   Again, we have syllables which 32
produce such a harsh effect by ending in B and
D, that many, not, it is true, of our most ancient
writers, but still writers of considerable antiquity,
have attempted to mitigate the harshness not merely
by saying *aversa* for *abversa*, but by adding an S
to the preposition *ab*, although S is an ugly letter
in itself.   Our accents also are less agreeable than 33
those of the Greeks.   This is due to a certain rigidity
and monotony of pronunciation, since the final

minus suaves habemus, quia ultima syllaba nec acuta
unquam excitatur nec flexa circumducitur, sed in
gravem vel duas graves cadit semper.   Itaque tanto
est sermo Graecus Latino iucundior, ut nostri poetae,
quotiens dulce carmen esse voluerint, illorum id
34 nominibus exornent.   His illa potentiora, quod res
plurimae carent appellationibus, ut eas necesse sit
transferre aut circumire; etiam in iis, quae de-
nominata sunt, summa paupertas in eadem nos
frequentissime revolvit; at illis non verborum modo,
sed linguarum etiam inter se differentium copia
est.

35   Quare qui a Latinis exiget illam gratiam sermonis
Attici, det mihi in eloquendo eandem iucunditatem
et parem copiam.   Quod si negatum est, sententias
aptabimus iis vocibus quas habemus, nec rerum
nimiam tenuitatem, ut non dicam pinguioribus,
fortioribus certe verbis miscebimus, ne virtus utraque
36 pereat ipsa confusione.   Nam quo minus adiuvat
sermo, rerum inventione pugnandum est.   Sensus
sublimes variique eruantur.   Permovendi omnes
adfectus erunt, oratio translationum nitore illumi-
nanda.   Non possumus esse tam graciles: simus
fortiores.   Subtilitate vincimur: valeamus pondere.
Proprietas penes illos est certior: copia vincamus.

---

[1] *I. e.* the last syllable and often the last *two* syllables
have the grave accent. See **I.** v. 22 *sqq.*
[2] *I.e.* because the names are not wholly adequate and
there are no satisfactory synonyms.

syllable is never marked by the rise of the acute accent nor by the rise and fall of the circumflex, but one or even two grave accents[1] are regularly to be found at the end. Consequently the Greek language is so much more agreeable in sound than the Latin, that our poets, whenever they wish their verse to be especially harmonious, adorn it with Greek words. A still stronger indication of the inferiority of Latin 34 is to be found in the fact that there are many things which have no Latin names, so that it is necessary to express them by metaphor or periphrasis, while even in the case of things which have names, the extreme poverty of the language leads us to resort to the same practice.[2] On the other hand, the Greeks have not merely abundance of words, but they have also a number of different dialects.

Consequently he who demands from Latin the 35 grace of Attic Greek, must first provide a like charm of tone and equal richness of vocabulary. If this advantage is denied us, we must adapt our thoughts to suit the words we have and, where our matter is unusually slight and delicate, must avoid expressing it in words which are, I will not say too gross, but at any rate too strong for it, for fear that the combination should result in the destruction both of delicacy and force. For the less help we 36 get from the language, the more must we rely on inventiveness of thought to bring us through the conflict. We must discover sentiments full of loftiness and variety, must stir all the emotions and illumine our style by brilliance of metaphor. Since we cannot be so delicate, let us be stronger. If they beat us for subtlety, let us prevail by weight, and if they have greater precision, let us outdo

37 Ingenia Graecorum etiam minora suos portus habent: nos plerumque maioribus velis movemur,
validior spiritus nostros sinus tendat; non tamen
alto semper feremur, nam et litora interim sequenda
sunt. Illis facilis per quaelibet vada accessus; ego
aliquid, non multo tamen, altius, in quo mea cumba
38 non sidat, inveniam. Neque enim, si tenuiora haec
ac pressiora Graeci melius, in eoque vincimur solo et
ideo in comoediis non contendimus, prorsus tamen
omittenda pars haec orationis, sed exigenda ut
optime possumus; possumus autem rerum et modo
et iudicio esse similes, verborum gratia, quam in
39 ipsis non habemus, extrinsecus condienda est. An
non in privatis et acutus et indistinctus et non super
modum elatus M. Tullius? non in M. Calidio
insignis haec virtus? non Scipio, Laelius, Cato in
eloquendo velut Attici Romanorum fuerunt? Cui
porro non satis est, quo nihil esse melius potest?

40 Adhuc quidam nullam esse naturalem putant
eloquentiam, nisi quae sit cotidiano sermoni simill-
ima, quo cum amicis, coniugibus, liberis, servis
loquamur, contento promere animi voluntatem
nihilque arcessiti et elaborati requirente; quid-

---

[1] Owing to the subtlety and delicacy of the Greek
language even second-rate talent will be able to win distinction in dealing with minor things. But the coarser and
more full-blooded nature of Latin makes this difficult.

them in fullness of expression. Even the lesser **37** orators of Greece have their own havens where they may ride in safety,[1] while we as a rule carry more sail. Let stronger gales fill our canvas, and yet let us not always keep the high seas; for at times we must cling to shore. The Greeks can easily traverse any shallows; I must find a deeper, though not much deeper, channel, that my bark may not run aground. For even though the Greeks surpass us **38** where circumstances call for delicacy and restraint, though we acknowledge their superiority in this respect alone, and therefore do not claim to rival them in comedy, that is no justification for our abandonment of this department of oratory, but rather a reason why we should handle it as best we can. Now we can at any rate resemble the Greeks in the method and judgement with which we treat our matter, although that grace of language, which our words cannot provide, must be secured by the admixture of foreign condiments. For example, is **39** not Cicero shrewd, simple and not unduly exalted in tone, when he deals with private cases? Is not Calidius also distinguished for the same virtue? Were not Scipio, Laelius and Cato the Attic orators of Rome? Surely we ought to be satisfied with them, since nothing can be better.

There are still some critics who deny that any **40** form of eloquence is purely natural, except that which closely resembles the ordinary speech of every-day life, which we use to our friends, our wives, our children and our slaves, a language, that is to say, which contents itself with expressing the purpose of the mind without seeking to discover anything in the way of elaborate and far-fetched phraseology.

quid huc sit adiectum, id esse adfectationis et
ambitiosae in loquendo iactantiae, remotum a veri-
tate fictumque ipsorum gratia verborum, quibus
solum natura sit officium attributum, servire
41 sensibus: sicut athletarum corpora, etiamsi validiora
fiant exercitatione et lege quadam ciborum, non
tamen esse naturalia atque ab illa specie, quae sit
concessa hominibus, abhorrere. Quid enim, inquiunt,
attinet circuitu res ostendere et translationibus, id
est aut pluribus aut alienis verbis, cum sua cuique
42 sint adsignata nomina? Denique antiquissimum
quemque maxime secundum naturam dixisse contendunt: mox poetis similiores exstitisse, etiamsi
parcius, simili tamen ratione, falsa et impropria
virtutes ducentes. Qua in disputatione nonnihil
veri est, ideoque non tam procul, quam fit a quibus-
43 dam, recedendum a propriis atque communibus. Si
quis tamen, ut in loco dixi compositionis, ad necessaria, quibus nihil minus est, aliquid melius adiecerit,
non erit hac calumnia reprehendendus. Nam mihi
aliam quandam videtur habere naturam sermo
vulgaris, aliam viri eloquentis oratio; cui si res
modo indicare satis esset, nihil ultra verborum

---

[1] XI. ch. 4.

And they hold that whatever is added to this simplicity lays the speaker open to the charge of affectation and pretentious ostentation of speech, void of all sincerity and elaborated merely for the sake of the words, although the sole duty assigned to words by nature is to be the servants of thought. Such language may be compared to the bodies of 41 athletes, which although they develop their strength by exercise and diet, are of unnatural growth and abnormal in appearance. For what, say these critics, is the good of expressing a thing by periphrasis or metaphor (that is, either by a number of words or by words which have no connexion with the thing), when everything has been allotted a name of its own? Finally, they urge that all the earliest orators 42 spoke according to the dictates of nature, but that subsequently there arose a class of speakers resembling poets rather than orators, who regarded false and artificial methods of expression as positive merits; they were, it is true, more sparing than the poets in their use of such expressions, but none the less worked on similar lines. There is some truth in this contention, and we should therefore be careful not to depart from the more exact usage of ordinary speech to the extent that is done by certain orators. On the other hand, that is no 43 reason for thus calumniating the man who, as I said in dealing with the subject of artistic structure,[1] succeeds in improving upon the bare necessaries of style. For the common language of every day seems to me to be of a different character from the style of an eloquent speaker. If all that was required of the latter was merely to indicate the facts, he might rest content with literalness of language, without

proprietatem elaboraret; sed cum debeat delectare,
movere, in plurimas animum audientis species
impellere, utetur his quoque adiutoriis, quae sunt
44 ab eadem nobis concessa ñatura. Nam et lacertos
exercitatione constringere et augere vires et colorem
trahere naturale est. Ideoque in omnibus gentibus
alius alio facundior habetur et eloquendo dulcis
magis (quod si non eveniret, omnes pares essent);
at idem homines aliter de re alia[1] loquuntur et
servant personarum discrimina. Ita, quo quisque
plus efficit dicendo, hoc magis secundum naturam
eloquentiae dicit.

45 Quapropter ne illis quidem nimium repugno, qui
dandum putant nonnihil etiam temporibus atque
auribus nitidius aliquid atque adfectius postulantibus.
Itaque non solum ad priores Catone Gracchisque, sed
ne ad hos quidem ipsos oratorem adligandum puto.
Atque id fecisse M. Tullium video, ut cum plurimum[2]
utilitati, tum partem quandam delectationi daret;
cum et suam se rem agere diceret, ageret autem
46 maxime litigatoris. Nam hoc ipso proderat, quod
placet. Ad cuius voluptates nihil equidem quod

---

[1] at idem homines aliter de re alia loquuntur, *Halm*: et
idem homines al⊤ de re allocuntur, *G*.
[2] plurimum, *Christ*: omnium, *G*.

further elaboration. But since it is his duty to delight and move his audience and to play upon the various feelings, it becomes necessary for him to employ those additional aids which are granted to us by that same nature which gave us speech. It is, in fact, as natural to do this as to harden the **44** muscles, increase our strength and improve our complexion by means of exercise. It is for this reason that among all nations one man is regarded as more eloquent and more attractive in his style than another (since if this were not the case, all speakers would be equal); but the same men speak differently on different subjects and observe distinctions of character. Consequently the more effective a man's speaking, the more in accordance with the nature of eloquence will it be.

I have, therefore, no strong objection even to the **45** views expressed by those who think that some concession should be made to the circumstances under which we speak and to the ears of the audience which require something more polished and emotional than ordinary speech. For this reason I consider that it would be absurd to restrict an orator to the style of the predecessors of Cato and the Gracchi, or even of those orators themselves. And I note that it was the practice of Cicero, while devoting himself in the main to the interests of his case, to take into account the delectation of his audience as well, since, as he pointed out, his own interests were concerned as well as those of his client, although of course the latter were of paramount importance. For his very charm was a valuable asset. I do not know what **46** can be added by way of improvement to the charms of his style, except perhaps the introduction of

addi possit invenio, nisi ut sensus nos quidem dicamus
plures.   Neque enim non [1] fieri potest salva tracta-
tione causae et dicendi auctoritate, si non crebra
haec lumina et continua fuerint et invicem offecerint.
47 Sed me hactenus cedentem nemo insequatur ultra.
Do tempori, ne hirta toga sit, non ut serica; ne
intonsum caput, non ut in gradus atque anulos comp-
tum, cum eo quod, si non ad luxuriam ac libidinem
referas, eadem speciosiora quoque sint, quae honesti-
48 ora.   Ceterum hoc, quod vulgo sententias vocamus,
quod veteribus praecipueque Graecis in usu non fuit
(apud Ciceronem enim invenio), dum rem contineant
et copia non redundent et ad victoriam spectent,
quis utile neget? Feriunt animum et uno ictu frequenter impellunt et ipsa brevitate magis haerent
et delectatione persuadent.
49   At sunt qui haec excitatiora lumina, etiamsi dicere
permittant, a componendis tamen orationibus ex-
cludenda arbitrentur.   Quocirca mihi ne hic quidem
locus intactus est omittendus; nam plurimi [2] erudi-

---

[1] non *added by Buttmann.*
[2] nam plurimi, *Halm*: ā plurimis, *G.*

---

[1] For this ever-recurring technical term there is no
adequate translation. It means a "reflexion couched in
aphoristic or epigrammatic form."

something more in the way of brilliant reflexions to suit the taste of our own times. For this can be done without injury to the treatment of our case or impairing the authority of our language, provided that such embellishments are not too frequent or continuous, and do not mutually destroy the effects which they were designed to produce. I am ready 47 to go so far along the path of concession, but let no man press me further. I concur in the fashion of the day to the extent of agreeing that the toga should not be long in the nap, but not to the extent of insisting that it should be of silk: I agree that the hair should be cut, but not that it should be dressed in tiers and ringlets, since we must always remember that ornaments, unless they be judged from the standpoint of the fop and the debauchee, are always effective in proportion to their seemliness. But with regard to those passages to which we give 48 the name of *reflexions*,[1] a form of ornament which was not employed by the ancients and, above all, not by the Greeks, although I do find it in Cicero, who can deny their usefulness, provided they are relevant to the case, are not too diffuse and contribute to our success? For they strike the mind and often produce a decisive effect by one single blow, while their very brevity makes them cling to the memory, and the pleasure which they produce has the force of persuasion.

There are, however, some who, while allowing 49 the actual delivery of such specially brilliant forms of ornament, think that they should be excluded from the written speech. Consequently I must not dismiss even this topic without a word of discussion. For a number of learned authorities

torum aliam esse dicendi rationem, aliam scribendi
putaverunt; ideoque in agendo clarissimos quosdam
nihil posteritati mansurisque mox litteris reliquisse,
ut Periclem, ut Demaden; rursus alios ad componendum optimos actionibus idoneos non fuisse, ut
50 Isocraten; praeterea in agendo plus impetus plerumque et petitas vel paulo licentius voluptates,
commovendos enim esse ducendosque animos imperitorum; at quod libris dedicatum in exemplum edatur,
id [1] tersum ac limatum et ad legem ac regulam compositum esse oportere, quia veniat in manus doctorum
51 et iudices artis habeat artifices. Quin illi subtiles
(ut sibimet ac multis persuaserunt) magistri παράδειγμα
dicendo, ἐνθύμημα scribendo esse aptius tradiderunt.
Mihi unum atque idem videtur bene dicere ac bene
scribere, neque aliud esse oratio scripta quam monu-
mentum actionis habitae. Itaque nullas non, ut
opinor, debet habere virtutes,[2] virtutes dico, non
vitia. Nam imperitis placere aliquando quae vitiosa
52 sint, scio. Quo different igitur? Quodsi mihi des
consilium iudicum sapientium, perquam multa recidam
ex orationibus non Ciceronis modo, sed etiam eius,
qui est strictior multo, Demosthenis. Neque enim

---

[1] at quod . . . dedicatum . . . edatur id, *Halm*: ad quos
. . . dedicatorum . . . edantur et, *G*.
[2] *second* virtutes *added by Buttmann*.

---

[1] See v. xi. 1. Parallels and especially historical ones.
[2] See v. xiv. 1 *sqq.* A form of syllogism.

have held that the written and the spoken speech
stand on different footings, and that consequently
some of the most eloquent of speakers have left
nothing for posterity to read in durable literary form,
as, for example, is the case with Pericles and Demades.
Again, they urge that there have been authors, like
Isocrates, who, while admirable writers, were not
well-fitted for actual speaking; and, further, that 50
actual pleading is characterised by a greater energy
and by the employment, almost verging on license,
of every artifice designed to please, since the minds
of an uneducated audience require to be moved and
led.   On the other hand, the written speech which
is published as a model of style must be polished
and filed and brought into conformity with the
accepted rules and standards of artistic construction,
since it will come into the hands of learned men
and its art will be judged by artists.   These subtle 51
teachers (for such they have persuaded themselves
and others that they are) have laid it down that
the παράδειγμα [1] is best suited for actual speech and
the ἐνθύμημα [2] for writing.   My own view is that
there is absolutely no difference between writing
well and speaking well, and that a written speech
is merely a record of one that has actually been
delivered.   Consequently it must in my opinion
possess every kind of merit, and note that I say
merit, not fault.   For I know that faults do sometimes meet with the approval of the uneducated.
What, then, will be the difference between what is 52
written and what is spoken?   If I were given a jury
of wise men, I should cut down a large number of
passages from the speeches not only of Cicero, but
even of Demosthenes, who is much more concise.

adfectus omnino movendi erunt, nec aures delectatione mulcendae, cum etiam prooemia supervacua
esse apud tales Aristoteles existimet; non enim
trahentur his illi sapientes; proprie et significanter
53 rem indicare, probationes colligere satis est.   Cum
vero iudex detur aut populus aut ex populo, laturique
sint sententiam indocti saepius atque interim rustici,
omnia quae ad obtinendum, quod intendimus, prodesse credemus adhibenda sunt; eaque et cum dicimus promenda et cum scribimus ostendenda sunt,
si modo ideo scribimus, ut doceamus quomodo dici
54 oporteat.   An Demosthenes male sic egisset, ut
scripsit, aut Cicero? aut eos praestantissimos oratores
alia re quam scriptis cognoscimus?   Melius egerunt
igitur an peius?   Nam si peius, sic potius oportuit dici,
ut scripserunt; si melius, sic potius oportuit scribi,
55 ut dixerunt.   Quid ergo?   Semper sic aget orator,
ut scribet?   Si licebit, semper.   Si vero quando[1]
impediant brevitate tempora a iudice data, multum
ex eo, quod oportuit[2] dici, recidetur; editio habebit
omnia.   Quae tamen[3] secundum naturam iudicantium

---

[1] Si vero quando, *Wölfflin*: steterunt quae, *G.*
[2] oportuit, *Christ*: potuit, *MSS.*
[3] quae tamen, *Halm*: quaedam, *G.*

---

[1] *Rhet.* iii. 13.

For with such a jury there would be no need to appeal to the emotions nor to charm and soothe the ears, since according to Aristotle[1] even exordia are superfluous, if addressed to such persons, as they will have no influence upon judges who are truly wise: it will be sufficient to state the facts with precision and significance and to marshal our array of proofs. Since, however, our judges are the 53 people, or drawn from the people, and since those who are appointed to give sentence are frequently ill-educated and sometimes mere rustics, it becomes necessary to employ every method that we think likely to assist our case, and these artifices must not merely be produced in speech, but exhibited in the written version as well, at least if in writing it our design is to show how it should be spoken. If 54 Demosthenes or Cicero had spoken the words as they wrote them, would either have spoken ill? And is our acquaintance with either of those two great orators based on anything save their writings? Did they speak better, then, or worse than they wrote? If they spoke worse, all that can be said is that they should have spoken as they wrote, while, if they spoke better, they should have written as they spoke. Well, you ask, is an orator 55 then always to speak as he writes? If possible, always. If, however, the time allowed by the judge is too short for this to be possible, he will have to cut out much that he should have said, but the published speech will contain the omitted passages. On the other hand, such passages as were uttered merely to suit the character of the judges will not be published for the benefit of posterity, for fear that they should seem to indicate

dicta sunt, non ita posteris tradentur, ne videantur
56 propositi fuisse, non temporis. Nam id quoque
plurimum refert, quomodo audire iudex velit, atque
eius vultus saepe ipse rector est dicentis, ut Cicero
praecipit. Ideoque instandum iis quae placere in-
tellexeris, resiliendum ab iis quae non recipientur.
Sermo ipse, qui facillime iudicem doceat, aptandus.
Nec id mirum sit, cum etiam testium personis aliqua
57 mutentur. Prudenter enim, qui cum interrogasset
rusticum testem, an Amphionem nosset, negante eo,
detraxit aspirationem breviavitque secundam eius
nominis syllabam, et ille eum sic optime norat.
Huiusmodi casus efficient, ut aliquando dicatur aliter
quam scribitur, cum dicere, quomodo scribendum est,
non licet.
58 Altera est divisio, quae in tres partes et ipsa
discedit, qua discerni posse etiam recte dicendi
genera inter se videntur. Namque unum subtile,
quod ἰσχνὸν vocant, alterum grande atque robustum,
quod ἁδρὸν dicunt, constituunt; tertium alii, medium
ex duobus, alii floridum (namque id ἀνθηρὸν ap-
59 pellant) addiderunt. Quorum tamen ea fere ratio
est, ut primum docendi, secundum movendi,
tertium illud, utrocumque est[1] nomine, delectandi
sive, ut alii dicunt, conciliandi praestare videatur officium; in docendo autem acumen, in con-

---

[1] utrocumque est, *Halm* : est ultrorumque, *G.*

---

[1] Not in any extant work.
[2] The witness did not recognise the name correctly
pronounced *Amphĭon*, but recognised it when pronounced
Ampĭon.
[3] *subtilis* (*lit.* = finely woven) applied to style has three
meanings : (*a*) refined, (*b*) precise, (*c*) plain. See Sandys on
Cic. *Or.* vi. 20.

the author's deliberate judgement instead of being
a mere concession to the needs of the moment.
For it is most important that we should know how 56
the judge is disposed to listen, and his face will
often (as Cicero[1] reminds us) serve as a guide to
the speaker. Consequently we must press the points
that we see commend themselves to him, and draw
back from those which are ill-received, while our
actual language must be so modified that he will
find our arguments as intelligible as possible. That
this should be necessary is scarcely surprising, when
we consider the alterations that are frequently
necessary to suit the characters of the different
witnesses. He was a shrewd man who, when he 57
asked a rustic witness whether he knew Amphion,
and the witness replied that he did not, dropped
the aspirate and shortened the second syllable,[2]
whereupon the witness recognised him at once.
Such situations, when it is impossible to speak as
we write, will sometimes make it necessary to speak
in language other than that which we use in
writing.

There is another threefold division, whereby, 58
it is held, we may differentiate three styles of
speaking, all of them correct. The first is termed
the plain[3] (or ἰσχνόν), the second grand and
forcible (or ἁδρόν), and the third either intermediate or florid, the latter being a translation
of ἀνθηρόν. The nature of these three styles is, 59
broadly speaking, as follows. The first would seem
best adapted for instructing, the second for moving,
and the third (by whichever name we call it) for
charming or, as others would have it, conciliating
the audience; for instruction the quality most

ciliando lenitas, in movendo vis exigi videatur.
Itaque illo subtili praecipue ratio narrandi proban-
dique consistet, sed saepe id[1] etiam detractis ceteris
60 virtutibus suo genere plenum.   Medius hic modus
et translationibus crebrior et figuris erit iucundior,
egressionibus amoenus, compositione aptus, sententiis
dulcis, lenior tamen ut amnis lucidus quidem sed
61 virentibus utrinque ripis[2] inumbratus.   At ille, qui
saxa devolvat et *pontem indignetur* et ripas sibi faciat,
multus et torrens iudicem vel nitentem contra feret
cogetque ire, qua rapiet.   Hic orator et defunctos
excitabit ut Appium Caecum, apud hunc et patria
ipsa exclamabit, aliquandoque ut Ciceronem in ora-
62 tione contra Catilinam in senatu alloquetur.   Hic et
amplificationibus extollet orationem, et in superla-
tionem quoque erigetur.   *Quae Charybdis tam vorax?*
et *Oceanus medius fidius ipse.*   Nota sunt enim iam
studiosis haec lumina.   Hic deos ipsos in congressum
prope suum sermonemque deducet: *Vos enim Albani
tumuli atque luci; vos, inquam, Albanorum obrutae arae,*

---

[1] saepe id, *Halm* : que id, *G.*
[2] ripis inumbratus, *Meyer* : sipisim umbratus *and the like,
MSS.*

---

[1] Verg. *Aen.* viii. 728.
[2] See III. viii. 54.   "Cicero in the *pro Caelio* makes both
Appius Caecus and her brother Clodius address Clodia, the
former rebuking her for her immorality, the latter exhorting
her thereto."
[3] *Phil.* II. xxvii. 67.   The passage continues: "could
scarce, methinks, have swallowed with such speed so many
things, scattered in so many places."

needed is acumen, for conciliation gentleness, and
for stirring the emotions force. Consequently it is
mainly in the plain style that we shall state our
facts and advance our proofs, though it should be
borne in mind that this style will often be sufficiently
full in itself without any assistance whatever from
the other two. The intermediate style will have 60
more frequent recourse to metaphor and will make
a more attractive use of figures, while it will introduce alluring digressions, will be neat in rhythm
and pleasing in its reflexions : its flow, however, will
be gentle, like that of a river whose waters are clear,
but overshadowed by the green banks on either side.
But he whose eloquence is like to some great torrent 61
that rolls down rocks and " disdains a bridge " [1] and
carves out its own banks for itself, will sweep the
judge from his feet, struggle as he may, and force
him to go whither he bears him. This is the orator
that will call the dead to life (as, for example, Cicero
calls upon Appius Caecus [2]); it is in his pages
that his native land itself will cry aloud and at
times address the orator himself, as it addresses
Cicero in the speech delivered against Catiline in
the senate. Such an orator will also exalt his style 62
by amplification and rise even to *hyperbole*, as when
Cicero [3] cries, " What Charybdis was ever so vora-
cious ! " or " By the god of truth, even Ocean's
self," etc. (I choose these fine passages as being
familiar to the student). It is such an one that
will bring down the Gods to form part of his
audience or even to speak with him, as in the
following, " For on you I call, ye hills and groves
of Alba, on you, I say, ye fallen altars of the
Albans, altars that were once the peers and equals

sacrorum populi Romani sociae et aequales. Hic iram, hic misericordiam inspirabit, hoc dicente iudex deos [1] appellabit et flebit et per omnes adfectus tractatus huc atque illuc sequetur nec doceri desiderabit.

63 Quare si ex tribus his generibus necessario sit eligendum unum, quis dubitet hoc praeferre omnibus et validissimum alioqui et maximis quibusque causis

64 accommodatissimum? Nam et Homerus brevem quidem cum iucunditate et propriam, id enim est *non deerrare verbis,* et carentem supervacuis eloquentiam Menelao dedit, quae sunt virtutes generis illius primi, et ex ore Nestoris dixit *dulciorem melle profluere sermonem,* qua certe delectatione nihil fingi maius potest; sed summam expressurus [2] in Ulixe facundiam et magnitudinem illi vocis et vim orationis nivibus hibernis [3] et copia verborum atque impetu

65 parem tribuit. *Cum hoc* igitur *nemo mortalium contendet; hunc ut deum homines intuebuntur.* Hanc vim et celeritatem in Pericle miratur Eupolis, hanc fulminibus Aristophanes comparat, haec est vere dicendi facultas.

66 Sed neque his tribus quasi formis inclusa eloquentia est. Nam ut inter gracile validumque tertium aliquid constitutum est, ita horum inter se intervalla sunt,

---

[1] hoc dicente iudex deos apellabit et flebit, *Madrig*: hoc dicente iudet appellavit et flevit, *G.*

[2] expressurus, *M. Seyffert*: regressurus est, *G.*

[3] vocis . . . hibernis, *Seyffert*: vicisset cum orationi similibus, *G.*

---

[1] *pro Mil.* xxxi. 85.

[2] *Il.* iii. 214. The words which Quintilian translates by *non deerrare verbis* are οὐδ᾽ ἀφαμαρτοεπής, "no stumbler in speech," rather than "correct in speech."

of the holy places of Rome."[1] This is he that will inspire anger or pity, and while he speaks the judge will call upon the gods and weep, following him wherever he sweeps him from one emotion to another, and no longer asking merely for instruction. Wherefore if one of these three styles has to be 63 selected to the exclusion of the others, who will hesitate to prefer this style to all others, since it is by far the strongest and the best adapted to the most important cases? For Homer himself assigns 64 to Menelaus[2] an eloquence, terse and pleasing, exact (for that is what is meant by "making no errors in words") and devoid of all redundance, which qualities are virtues of the first type: and he says that from the lips of Nestor[3] flowed speech sweeter than honey, than which assuredly we can conceive no greater delight: but when he seeks to express the supreme gift of eloquence possessed by Ulysses[4] he gives a mighty voice and a vehemence of oratory equal to the snows of winter in the abundance and the vigour of its words. "With him then," he says, "no mortal 65 will contend, and men shall look upon him as on a god."[5] It is this force and impetuosity that Eupolis admires in Pericles, this that Aristophanes[6] compares to the thunderbolt, this that is the power of true eloquence.

But eloquence cannot be confined even to these 66 three forms of style. For just as the third style is intermediate between the grand and the plain style, so each of these three are separated by interspaces

[3] *Il.* i. 249. [4] *Il.* iii. 221.
[5] A blend of *Il.* iii. 223 and *Od.* viii. 173.
[6] *Ach.* 530. "Then in his wrath Pericles the Olympian lightened and thundered and threw all Greece into confusion."

atque inter haec ipsa mixtum quiddam ex duobus
67 medium est eorum. Nam et subtili plenius aliquid
atque subtilius et vehementi remissius atque ve-
hementius invenitur, ut illud lene aut ascendit ad
fortiora aut ad tenuiora summittitur. Ac sic prope
innumerabiles species reperiuntur, quae utique aliquo
momento inter se differant: sicut quattuor ventos
generaliter a totidem mundi cardinibus accepimus
flare, cum interim plurimi medii et eorum varia
nomina et quidam etiam regionum ac fluminum
68 proprii deprehenduntur. Eademque musicis ratio
est, qui, cum in cithara quinque constituerunt sonos,
plurima deinde varietate complent spatia illa nervorum, atque his, quos interposuerunt, inserunt
alios, ut pauci illi transitus multos gradus habeant.

69 Plures igitur etiam eloquentiae facies, sed stultissimum quaerere, ad quam se recturus sit orator, cum
omnis species, quae modo recta est, habeat usum,
atque id ipsum non sit oratoris, quod vulgo genus
dicendi vocant. Utetur enim, ut res exiget, omnibus, nec pro causa modo, sed pro partibus causae.
70 Nam ut non eodem modo pro reo capitis et in
certamine hereditatis et de interdictis ac spon-

---

[1] *cp.* **II. x.** 5 and **IV. ii. 61.** *Sponsio* (= wager) was a form
of lawsuit in which the litigant promised to pay a certain
sum of money if he lost his case. The *interdict* was an order
issued by the praetor commanding or prohibiting certain
action.

which are occupied by intermediate styles compounded of the two which lie on either side. For 67 there are styles fuller or plainer than the plain, and gentler or more vehement than the vehement, while the gentler style itself may either rise to greater force or sink to milder tones. Thus we may discover almost countless species of styles, each differing from the other by some fine shade of difference. We may draw a parallel from the winds. It is generally accepted that there are four blowing from the four quarters of the globe, but we find there are also a large number of winds which lie between these, called by a variety of names, and in certain cases confined to certain districts and river valleys. The 68 same thing may be noted in music. For after assigning five notes to the lyre, musicians fill up the intervals between the strings by a variety of notes, and between these again they interpose yet others, so that the original divisions admit of a number of gradations.

Eloquence has, therefore, a quantity of different 69 aspects, but it is sheer folly to inquire which of these the orator should take as his model, since every species that is in itself correct has its use, and what is commonly called *style of speaking* does not depend on the orator. For he will use all styles, as circumstances may demand, and the choice will be determined not only by the case as a whole, but by the demands of the different portions of the case. For just as he will not speak in the same way when 70 he is defending a client on a capital charge and when he is speaking in a lawsuit concerned with an inheritance, or discussing interdicts and suits taking the form of a wager,[1] or claims in connexion with

sionibus et de certa credita dicet, sententiarum
quoque in senatu et contionum et privatorum con-
siliorum servabit discrimina, multa ex differentia
personarum, locorum temporumque mutabit, ita in
eadem oratione aliter concitabit,[1] aliter conciliabit,
non ex iisdem haustibus iram et misericordiam petet,
alias ad docendum alias ad movendum adhibebit
71 artes. Non unus color prooemii, narrationis, argumentorum, egressionis, perorationis servabitur. Dicet
idem graviter, severe, acriter, vehementer, concitate,
copiose, amare, comiter, remisse, subtiliter, blande,
leniter, dulciter, breviter, urbane, non ubique similis,
72 sed ubique par sibi. Sic fiet cum id, propter quod
maxime repertus est usus orationis, ut dicat utiliter
et ad efficiendum quod intendit potenter, tum
laudem quoque nec doctorum modo sed etiam vulgi
consequatur.

73 Falluntur enim plurimum, qui vitiosum et corruptum dicendi genus, quod aut verborum licentia
exultat aut puerilibus sententiolis lascivit aut immo-
dico tumore turgescit aut inanibus locis bacchatur
aut casuris, si leviter excutiantur, flosculis nitet aut
praecipitia pro sublimibus habet aut specie libertatis
insanit, magis existimant populare atque plausibile.
74 Quod quidem placere multis nec infitior nec miror.

---

[1] aliter concitabit, *added by Halm.*

loans, so too he will preserve a due distinction
between the speeches which he makes in the senate,
before the people and in private consultations, while
he will also introduce numerous modifications to
suit the different persons and circumstances of time
and place. Thus in one and the same speech he
will use one style for stirring the emotions, and
another to conciliate his hearers; it is from different
sources that he will derive anger or pity, and the
art which he employs in instructing the judge will
be other than that which he employs to move him.
He will not maintain the same tone throughout his 71
exordium, statement of fact, arguments, digression and
peroration. He will speak gravely, severely, sharply,
with vehemence, energy, fullness, bitterness, or
geniality, quietly, simply, flatteringly, gently, sweetly,
briefly or wittily; he will not always be like himself, but he will never be unworthy of himself.
Thus the purpose for which oratory was above all 72
designed will be secured, that is to say, he will
speak with profit and with power to effect his aim,
while he will also win the praise not merely of the
learned, but of the multitude as well.

They make the gravest mistake who consider that 73
the style which is best adapted to win popularity
and applause is a faulty and corrupt style of speaking
which revels in license of diction or wantons in
childish epigram or swells with stilted bombast or
riots in empty commonplace or adorns itself with
blossoms of eloquence which will fall to earth if
but lightly shaken, or regards extravagance as
sublime or raves wildly under the pretext of free
speech. I am ready to admit that such qualities 74
please many, and I feel no surprise that this should

Est enim iucunda auribus ac favorabilis qualiscunque
eloquentia et ducit animos naturali voluptate vox
omnis, neque aliunde illi per fora atque aggerem
circuli; quo minus mirum est, quod nulli non
75 agentium parata vulgi corona est. Ubi vero quid
exquisitius dictum accidit auribus imperitorum,
qualecunque id est, quod modo se ipsi posse desperent, habet admirationem, neque immerito; nam
ne illud quidem facile est. Sed evanescunt haec
atque emoriuntur comparatione meliorum, ut lana
tincta fuco citra purpuras placet; at si contuleris
Tyriae eam[1] lacernae, conspectu melioris obruatur,
76 ut Ovidius ait. Si vero iudicium his corruptis acrius
adhibeas ut fucinis[2] sulfura, iam illum, quo fefellerant,
exuant[3] mentitum colorem et quadam vix enarrabili
foeditate pallescant. Lucent igitur haec citra solem,
ut quaedam exigua animalia igniculi videntur in
tenebris. Denique mala multi probant, nemo im-
probat bona.

77   Neque vero omnia ista, de quibus locuti sumus,
orator optime tantum sed etiam facillime faciet.
Neque enim vim summam dicendi et os[4] admira-

[1] Tyriae eam, *Halm*: etiam, *MSS*.
[2] fucinis, *Buttmann*: fucinus, *G*.
[3] illum quo fefellerant exuant, *Buttmann*: illud quod
fefellerat exuat, *G*.   [4] os, *Halm*: eos, *G*.

[1] The *agger* of Servius Tullius, which served as a promenade.
The nearest modern parallel may be found in the "Hyde
Park orator."   [2] *Rem. Am.* 707 *sqq.*

be the case. For any kind of eloquence is pleasing and attractive to the ear, and every effort of the voice inspires a natural pleasure in the soul of man; indeed this is the sole cause of those familiar gatherings in the Forum or on the Old Wall,[1] so that there is small reason for wonder if any pleader is safe to draw a ring of listeners from the crowd. And when 75 any unusually precious phrase strikes the ears of an uneducated audience, whatever its true merits, it wakens their admiration just for the very reason that they feel they could never have produced it themselves. And it deserves their admiration, since even such success is hard to attain. On the other hand, when such displays are compared with their betters, they sink into insignificance and fade out of sight, for they are like wool dyed red that pleases in the absence of purple, but, as Ovid[2] says, if compared with a cloak of Tyrian dye, pales in the presence of the fairer hue. If, however, we test 76 such corrupt eloquence by the touchstone of a critical taste, as, for example, we test inferior dyes with sulphur, it will lay aside the false brilliance that deceived the eye and fade to a pallor almost too repulsive to describe. Such passages shine only in the absence of the sunlight, just as certain tiny insects seem transformed in the darkness to little flames of fire. Finally, while many approve of things that are bad, no one disapproves of that which is good.

But the true orator will not merely be able to 77 achieve all the feats of which I have spoken with supreme excellence, but with the utmost ease as well. For the sovereign power of eloquence and the voice that awakens well-deserved applause will

tione dignum infelix usque ad ultimum sollicitudo persequitur, quae[1] oratorem macerat et coquit aegre verba vertentem et perpendendis coagmentandisque
78 eis intabescentem. Nitidus ille et sublimis et locuples circumfluentibus undique eloquentiae copiis imperat. Desinit enim in adversa niti, qui pervenit in summum. Scandenti circa ima labor est; ceterum quantum processeris, mollior clivus ac laetius solum.
79 Et si haec quoque iam lenius supina perseverantibus studiis evaseris, inde fructus illaborati offerunt sese et omnia sponte proveniunt; quae tamen cotidie nisi decerpantur, arescunt. Sed et copia habeat[2] modum, sine quo nihil nec laudabile nec salutare est, et nitor ille cultum virilem et inventio iudicium.
80 Sic erunt magna non nimia, sublimia non abrupta, fortia non temeraria, severa non tristia, gravia non tarda, laeta non luxuriosa, iucunda non dissoluta, grandia non tumida. Similis in ceteris ratio est ac tutissima fere per medium via, quia utriusque ultimum vitium est.

XI. His dicendi virtutibus usus orator in iudiciis, consiliis, contionibus, senatu, in omni denique officio boni civis finem quoque dignum et optimo viro et opere sanctissimo faciet, non quia prodesse unquam

---

[1] quae, *Halm*: nec, *MSS.*
[2] habeat, *Heindorf*: habet, *MSS.*

be free from the perpetual distress of harassing anxiety which wastes and fevers the orator who painfully corrects himself and pines away over the laborious weighing and piecing together of his words. No, our orator, brilliant, sublime and 78 opulent of speech, is lord and master of all the resources of eloquence, whose affluence surrounds him. For he that has reached the summit has no more weary hills to scale. At first the climber's toil is hard, but the higher he mounts the easier becomes the gradient and the richer the soil. And 79 if by perseverance of study he pass even beyond these gentler slopes, fruits for which none have toiled thrust themselves upon him, and all things spring forth unbidden; and yet if they be not gathered daily, they will wither away. But even such wealth must observe the mean, without which nothing is either praiseworthy or beneficial, while brilliance must be attended by manliness, and imagination by soundness of taste. Thus the works 80 of the orator will be great not extravagant, sublime not bombastic, bold not rash, severe but not gloomy, grave but not slow, rich but not luxuriant, pleasing but not effeminate, grand but not grandiose. It is the same with other qualities : the mean is safest, for the worst of all faults is to fly to extremes.

XI. After employing these gifts of eloquence in the courts, in councils, in public assemblies and the debates of the senate, and, in a word, in the performance of all the duties of a good citizen, the orator will bring his activities to a close in a manner worthy of a blameless life spent in the pursuit of the noblest of professions. And he will do this, not because he can ever have enough of doing good,

495

satis sit et illa mente atque illa facultate praedito
non optandum operis pulcherrimi quam longissimum
tempus, sed quia decet hoc quoque prospicere, ne
2 quid peius, quam fecerit, faciat.   Neque enim
scientia modo constat orator, quae augetur annis,
sed voce, latere, firmitate; quibus fractis aut im-
minutis aetate seu valetudine cavendum est, ne quid
in oratore summo desideretur, ne intersistat fati-
gatus, ne quae dicet parum audiri sentiat, ne se
3 quaerat priorem.   Vidi ego longe omnium, quos
mihi cognoscere contigit, summum oratorem, Domi-
tium Afrum valde senem, cotidie aliquid ex ea
quam meruerat auctoritate perdentem, cum agente
illo, quem principem fuisse quondam fori non erat
dubium, alii, quod indignum videatur, riderent, alii
erubescerent; quae occasio fuit de[1] illo dicendi,
4 *malle eum deficere quam desinere.*   Neque erant illa
qualiacunque mala sed minora.

Quare antequam in has aetatis veniat insidias,
receptui canet et in portum integra nave perveniet.
Neque enim minores eum, cum id fecerit, studiorum
fructus prosequentur.   Aut ille monumenta rerum
posteris aut, ut L. Crassus in libris Ciceronis destinat,

---

[1] de *added by Halm.*

---

[1] By "finish" is meant "retire from pleading."

or because one endowed with intellect and talents such as his would not be justified in praying that such glorious labours may be prolonged to their utmost span, but for this reason, that it is his duty to look to the future, for fear that his work may be less effective than it has been in the past. For the 2 orator depends not merely on his knowledge, which increases with the years, but on his voice, lungs and powers of endurance. And if these be broken or impaired by age or health, he must beware that he does not fall short in something of his high reputation as a master of oratory, that fatigue does not interrupt his eloquence, that he is not brought to realise that some of his words are inaudible, or to mourn that he is not what once he was. Domitius 3 Afer was by far the greatest of all the orators whom it has been my good fortune to know, and I saw him, when far advanced in years, daily losing something of that authority which his merits had won for him; he whose supremacy in the courts had once been universally acknowledged, now pleaded amid the unworthy laughter of some, and the silent blushes of others, giving occasion to the malicious saying that he had rather "faint than finish."[1] And 4 yet even then, whatever his deficiencies, he spoke not badly, but merely less well.

Therefore before ever he fall a prey to the ambush where time lies in wait for him, the orator should sound the retreat and seek harbour while his ship is yet intact. For the fruits of his studies will not be lessened by retirement. Either he will bequeath the history of his own times for the delight of after ages, or will interpret the law to those who seek his counsels, as Lucius Crassus proposes

iura quaerentibus reddet aut eloquentiae componet
artem aut pulcherrimis vitae praeceptis dignum os
5 dabit.   Frequentabunt vero eius domum optimi
iuvenes more veterum et vere dicendi viam velut ex
oraculo petent.   Hos ille formabit quasi eloquentiae
parens, et ut vetus gubernator litora et portus et
quae tempestatum signa, quid secundis flatibus, quid
adversis ratio poscat, docebit, non humanitatis solum
communi ductus officio, sed amore quodam operis.
6 Nemo enim minui velit id, in quo maximus fuit.   Quid
porro est honestius quam docere quod optime scias?
Sic ad se Caelium deductum a patre Cicero profitetur; sic Pansam, Hirtium, Dolabellam in morem
7 praeceptoris exercuit cotidie dicens audiensque.   Ac
nescio an eum tunc beatissimum credi oporteat fore,
cum iam secretus et consecratus, liber invidia, procul
contentionibus famam in tuto collocarit et sentiet[1]
vivus eam, quae post fata praestari magis solet,
venerationem et, quid apud posteros futurus sit,
videbit.

8   Conscius sum mihi, quantum mediocritate valui,

---

[1] sentiet, *Obrecht*: sententia et, *G.*

---

[1] *de Or.* I. xlii. 190.   [2] *pro Cael.* iv. 10.

to do in the *de Oratore*[1] of Cicero, or compose some treatise on the art of oratory, or give worthy utterance to the sublimest ideals of conduct. His house 5 will, as in the days of old, be thronged by all the best of the rising generation, who will seek to learn from him as from an oracle how they may find the path to true eloquence. And he as their father in the art will mould them to all excellence, and like some old pilot will teach them of the shores whereby their ships must sail, of the harbours where they may shelter, and the signs of the weather, and will expound to them what they shall do when the breeze is fair or the tempest blows. Whereto he will be inclined not only by the common duty of humanity, but by a certain passion for the task that once was his, since no man desires that the art wherein he was once supreme should suffer decay or diminution. And what can be more honourable 6 than to teach that which you know surpassing well? It was for this that the elder Caelius brought his son to Cicero, as the latter[2] tells us, and it was with this intent that the same great orator took upon himself the duties of instructor, and trained Pansa, Hirtius and Dolabella by declaiming daily before them or hearing them declaim. And I know not whether 7 we should not deem it the happiest moment in an orator's life, when he has retired from the public gaze, the consecrated priest of eloquence, free from envy and far from strife, when he has set his glory on a pinnacle beyond the reach of detraction, enjoys, while still living, that veneration which most men win but after death, and sees how great shall be his renown amid generations yet unborn.

I can say with a good conscience that, as far as 8

quaeque antea scierim, quaeque operis huiusce gratia
potuerim inquirere, candide me atque simpliciter in
notitiam eorum, si qui forte cognoscere voluissent,
protulisse. Atque id viro bono satis est, docuisse
9 quod scierit. Vereor tamen, ne aut magna nimium
videar exigere, qui eundem virum bonum esse et
dicendi peritum velim, aut multa, qui tot artibus in
pueritia discendis morum quoque praecepta et
scientiam iuris civilis praeter ea, quae de eloquentia
tradebantur, adiecerim, quique haec operi nostro
necessaria esse crediderint, velut moram rei per-
10 horrescant et desperent ante experimentum. Qui
primum renuntient sibi, quanta sit humani ingenii
vis, quam potens efficiendi quae velit, cum maria
transire, siderum cursus numerosque cognoscere,
mundum ipsum paene dimetiri, minores, sed diffi-
ciliores artes potuerint. Tum cogitent, quantam
rem petant, quamque nullus sit hoc proposito prae-
11 mio labor recusandus. Quod si mente conceperint,
huic quoque parti facilius accedent, ut ipsum iter
neque impervium neque saltem durum putent. Nam
id, quod prius quodque maius est, ut boni viri simus,

my poor powers have permitted, I have published frankly and disinterestedly, for the benefit of such as might wish to learn, all that my previous knowledge and the researches made for the purpose of this work might supply. And to have taught what he knows is satisfaction enough for any good man. I fear, however, that I may be regarded as setting 9 too lofty an ideal for the orator by insisting that he should be a good man skilled in speaking, or as imposing too many subjects of study on the learner. For in addition to the many branches of knowledge which have to be studied in boyhood and the traditional rules of eloquence, I have enjoined the study of morals and of civil law, so that I am afraid that even those who have regarded these things as essential to my theme, may be appalled at the delay which they impose and abandon all hope of achievement before they have put my precepts to the test. I would ask them to consider how great are the 10 powers of the mind of man and how astonishing its capacity for carrying its desires into execution: for has not man succeeded in crossing the high seas, in learning the number and the courses of the stars, and almost measuring the universe itself, all of them accomplishments of less importance than oratory, but of far greater difficulty? And then let them reflect on the greatness of their aims and on the fact that no labour should be too huge for those that are beckoned by the hope of such reward. If they can 11 only rise to the height of this conception, they will find it easier to enter on this portion of their task, and will cease to regard the road as impassable or even hard. For the first and greatest of the aims we set before us, namely that we shall be good

voluntate maxime constat; quam qui vera fide
induerit, facile eas, quae virtutem docent, artes
12 accipiet. Neque enim aut tam perplexa aut tam
numerosa sunt quae praecipiuntur,[1] ut non paucorum
admodum annorum intentione discantur. Longam
enim facit operam quod repugnamus; brevis est
institutio vitae honestae beataeque, si credas. Natura
enim nos ad mentem optimam genuit, adeoque discere
meliora volentibus promptum est, ut vere intuenti
13 mirum sit illud magis malos esse tam multos. Nam
ut aqua piscibus, ut sicca terrenis, circumfusus nobis
spiritus volucribus convenit, ita certe facilius esse
oportebat secundum naturam quam contra eam vivere.
Cetera vero, etiamsi aetatem nostram non spatio
senectutis sed tempore[2] adolescentiae metiamur,
abunde multos ad discendum annos habent. Omnia
14 enim breviora reddet ordo et ratio et modus. Sed
culpa est in praeceptoribus prima, qui libenter de-
tinent quos occupaverunt, partim cupiditate diutius
exigendi mercedulas, partim ambitione, quo difficilius
videatur[3] esse quod pollicentur, partim etiam in-
scientia tradendi vel negligentia. Proxima in nobis,
qui morari in eo quod novimus, quam discere quae

---

[1] praecipiuntur, *Buttmann* : praemuntur, *G.*
[2] tempore, *early edd.* : corpore, *G.*
[3] videatur esse, *added by Halm.*

men, depends for its achievement mainly on the will to succeed: and he that truly and sincerely forms such resolve, will easily acquire those forms of knowledge that teach the way to virtue. For 12 the precepts that are enjoined upon us are not so complex or so numerous that they may be acquired by little more than a few years' study. It is repugnance to learn that makes such labour long. For if you will only believe it, you will quickly learn the principles that shall lead you to a life of virtue and happiness. For nature brought us into the world that we might attain to all excellence of mind, and so easy is it for those to learn who seek for better things, that he who directs his gaze aright will rather marvel that the bad should be so many. For 13 as water is the natural element of fish, dry land for creatures of the earth and the circumambient atmosphere for winged things, even so it should be easier to live according to nature than counter to her will. As regards other accomplishments, there are plenty of years available for their acquisition, even though we measure the life of man not by the span of age, but by the period of youth. For in every case order and method and a sense of proportion will shorten our labour. But the chief fault 14 lies with our teachers, in that they love to keep back the pupils they have managed to lay their hands on, partly from the desire to draw their miserable fees for as long as possible, partly out of ostentation, to enhance the difficulty of acquiring the knowledge which they promise to impart, and to some extent owing to their ignorance or carelessness in teaching. The next most serious fault lies in ourselves, who think it better to linger over what we have learned

15 nondum scimus, melius putamus. Nam ut de nostris
potissimum studiis dicam, quid attinet tam multis
annis quam in more est plurimorum (ut de his, a
quibus magna in hoc pars aetatis absumitur, taceam)
declamitare in schola et tantum laboris in rebus
falsis consumere, cum satis sit modico tempore imaginem veri discriminis et dicendi leges comperisse ?

16 Quod non eo dico, quasi[1] sit unquam omittenda
dicendi exercitatio, sed quia non in una sit eius
specie consenescendum. Res varias[2] cognoscere et
praecepta vivendi perdiscere et in foro nos experiri
potuimus, dum scholastici sumus. Discendi ratio
talis, ut non multos poscat annos. Quaelibet enim
ex iis artibus, quarum habui mentionem, in paucos
libros contrahi solet; adeo non est infinito spatio
ad traditionem opus. Reliqua est exercitatio,[3] quae
17 vires cito facit, cum fecit, tuetur. Rerum cognitio
cotidie crescit, et tamen quam multorum ad eam
librorum necessaria lectio est, quibus aut rerum
exempla ab historicis aut dicendi ab oratoribus
petuntur, philosophorum quoque consultorumque
opiniones, si utilia velimus legere non, quod ne fieri

---

[1] quasi, *Halm* : qua, *G.*
[2] Res varias, *added by Halm.*
[3] ad traditionem, *Halm* : ac traditione, *G.* : exercitatio
added by Halm.

than to learn what we do not yet know. For ex- 15
ample, to restrict my remarks mainly to the study
of rhetoric, what is the use of spending so many
years, after the fashion now so prevalent (for I will
say nothing of those who spend almost their whole
lives), in declaiming in the schools and devoting so
much labour to the treatment of fictitious themes,
when it would be possible with but slight expenditure
of time to form some idea of what the true conflicts
are in which the orator must engage, and of the
laws of speaking which he ought to follow?   In 16
saying this, I do not for a moment mean to suggest
that we should ever omit to exercise ourselves in
speaking. I merely urge that we should not grow old
over one special form of exercise. We have been in a
position to acquire varied knowledge, to familiarise
ourselves with the principles that should guide our
life, and to try our strength in the courts, while we
were still attending the schools. The theory of speaking is of such a nature that it does not demand
many years for its acquisition. For any one of the
various branches of knowledge which I have mentioned will, as a rule, be found to be comprised in
a few volumes, a fact which shows that instruction
does not require an indefinite amount of time to be
devoted to it. The rest depends entirely on practice,
which at once develops our powers and maintains
them, once developed.   Knowledge increases day 17
by day, and yet how many books is it absolutely
necessary to read in our search for its attainment, for
examples of facts from the historians or of eloquence
from the orators, or, again, for the opinions of the
philosophers and the lawyers, that is to say, if we
are content to read merely what is useful without

quidem[1] potest, omnia? Sed breve nobis tempus
18 nos facimus. Quantulum enim studiis partimur?
Alias horas vanus salutandi labor, alias datum fabulis
otium, alias spectacula, alias convivia trahunt. Adiice
tot genera ludendi et insanam corporis curam, pere-
grinatio, rura, calculorum anxiam sollicitudinem,
invitamenta libidinum et vinum et flagrantibus omni
genere voluptatum animis[2] ne ea quidem tempora
19 idonea, quae supersunt. Quae si omnia studiis im-
penderentur, iam nobis longa aetas et abunde satis
ad discendum spatii viderentur vel[3] diurna tantum
computantibus tempora ut nihil noctes, quarum bona
pars omni somno longior est, adiuvarent. Nunc com-
putamus annos, non quibus studuimus, sed quibus
20 viximus. Nec vero si geometrae et musici[4] et gram-
matici ceterarumque artium professores omnem suam
vitam, quamlibet longa fuerit, in singulis artibus
consumpserunt, sequitur ut plures quasdam vitas ad
plura discenda desideremus. Neque enim illi didicerunt haec usque in senectutem, sed ea sola didicisse
contenti fuerunt ac tot annos non in percipiendo
exhauserunt, sed in praecipiendo.[5]
21 Ceterum, ut de Homero taceam, in quo nullius
non artis aut opera perfecta aut certe non dubia

---

[1] si utilia, *Christ* : sicuti alia, *MSS.*: quod ne fieri quidem,
Halm : quod quidem, *MSS.*

[2] *The text is as corrected by Halm. The MSS. give a variety
of readings. The chief alterations involved by Halm's correction
are* invitamenta *for* multae causae, multae eam, etc., *and*
flagrantibus *for* flagitiis. *The other changes are of the simplest
and most ordinary character.*

[3] vel, *Buttmann* : ut, *MSS.*

[4] et musici, *added by Halm (erasure in G).*

[5] sed in praecipiendo, *Halm* : ✳✳✳ p̄✳✳ p✳✳✳do *G.*

attempting the impossible task of reading everything? But it is ourselves that make the time for 18 study short: for how little time we allot to it! Some hours are passed in the futile labour of ceremonial calls, others in idle chatter, others in staring at the shows of the theatre, and others again in feasting. To this add all the various forms of amusement, the insane attention devoted to the cultivation of the body, journeys abroad, visits to the country, anxious calculation of loss and gain, the allurements of lust, wine-bibbing and those remaining hours which are all too few to gratify our souls on fire with passion for every kind of pleasure. If all this 19 time were spent on study, life would seem long enough and there would be plenty of time for learning, even though we should take the hours of daylight only into our account, without asking any assistance from the night, of which no little space is superfluous even for the heaviest sleeper. As it is, we count not the years which we have given to study, but the years we have lived. And indeed 20 even although geometricians, musicians and grammarians, together with the professors of every other branch of knowledge, spend all their lives, however long, in the study of one single science, it does not therefore follow that we require several lives more if we are to learn more. For they do not spend all their days even to old age in learning these things, but being content to have learned these things and nothing more, exhaust their length of years not in acquiring, but in imparting knowledge.

However, to say nothing of Homer, in whom we 21 may find either the perfect achievements, or at any rate clear signs of the knowledge of every art,

vestigia reperiuntur, (ut Eleum Hippiam transeam,
qui non liberalium modo disciplinarum prae se
scientiam tulit, sed vestem et anulum crepidasque,
quae omnia manu sua fecerat, in usu habuit, atque
ita se praeparavit, ne cuius alterius opere egeret,)
illusisse tot malis, quot[1] summa senectus habet,
universae Graeciae credimus Gorgian, qui quaerere
22 auditores de quo quisque vellet iubebat. Quae
tandem ars digna litteris Platoni defuit? Quot
saeculis Aristoteles didicit, ut non solum, quae ad
philosophos atque oratores pertinent, scientia com-
plecteretur, sed animalium satorumque naturas omnes
perquireret? Illis haec invenienda fuerunt, nobis
cognoscenda sunt. Tot nos praeceptoribus, tot exemplis instruxit antiquitas, ut possit videri nulla
sorte nascendi aetas felicior quam nostra, cui do-
23 cendae priores elaborarunt. M. igitur Cato idem
summus imperator, idem sapiens, idem orator, idem
historiae conditor, idem iuris, idem rerum rusticarum
peritissimus fuit inter tot operas militiae, tantas
domi contentiones, rudi saeculo, litteras Graecas
aetate iam declinata didicit, ut esset hominibus
documento ea quoque percipi posse quae senes con-
24 cupissent. Quam multa, paene omnia, tradidit Varro!
Quod instrumentum dicendi M. Tullio defuit? Quid

---

[1] tot malis quot, *Bonnell*: tot ✳✳✳✳s quod, *G.*

and to pass by Hippias of Elis, who not merely
boasted his knowledge of the liberal arts, but wore
a robe, a ring and shoes, all of which he had made
with his own hands, and had trained himself to be
independent of external assistance, we accept the
universal tradition of Greece to the effect that
Gorgias, triumphant over all the countless ills in-
cident to extreme old age, would bid his hearers
propound any questions they pleased for him to
answer. Again in what branch of knowledge 22
worthy of literary expression was Plato deficient?
How many generations' study did Aristotle require to embrace not merely the whole range of
philosophical and rhetorical knowledge, but to
investigate the nature of every beast and plant.
And yet they had to discover all these things which
we only have to learn. Antiquity has given us all
these teachers and all these patterns for our imitation,
that there might be no greater happiness conceivable
than to be born in this age above all others, since
all previous ages have toiled that we might reap the
fruit of their wisdom. Marcus Cato was at once a 23
great general, a philosopher, orator, historian, and
an expert both in law and agriculture, and despite
his military labours abroad and the distractions of
political struggles at home, and despite the rudeness
of the age in which he lived, he none the less
learned Greek, when far advanced in years, that he
might prove to mankind that even old men are
capable of learning that on which they have set
their hearts. How wide, almost universal, was the 24
knowledge that Varro communicated to the world!
What of all that goes to make up the equipment of
an orator was lacking to Cicero? Why should I say

plura? cum etiam Cornelius Celsus, mediocri vir
ingenio, non solum de his omnibus conscripserit
artibus, sed amplius rei militaris et rusticae et medi-
cinae praecepta reliquerit, dignus vel ipso proposito,
ut eum scisse omnia illa credamus.

25   At perficere tantum opus arduum et nemo perfecit.
Ante omnia sufficit ad exhortationem studiorum,
capere id rerum naturam nec,[1] quidquid non est
factum, ne fieri quidem posse; tum omnia, quae
magna sunt atque admirabilia, tempus aliquod quo
26 primum efficerentur habuisse.   Nam et poesis ab
Homero et Vergilio tantum fastigium accepit et
eloquentia a Demosthene atque Cicerone.   Denique
quidquid est optimum, ante non fuerat.   Verum
etiam si quis summa desperet (quod cur faciat, cui
ingenium, valetudo, facultas, praeceptores non deerunt?), tamen est, ut Cicero ait, pulchrum in
27 secundis tertiisque consistere.   Neque enim, si quis
Achillis gloriam in bellicis consequi non potest,
Aiacis aut Diomedis laudem aspernabitur, nec qui
Homeri non fuerunt, Tyrtaei.[2]   Quin immo si hanc
cogitationem homines habuissent, ut nemo se meli-
orem fore eo qui optimus fuisset, arbitraretur, ii ipsi,
qui sunt optimi, non fuissent, neque post Lucretium

---

[1] nec, *Zumpt* : eo, *AG.*
[2] non fuerunt, *G* : non tyrthei, *second hand of A, written
in over an erasure.*

---

[1] *Or.* i. 4.

more, since even Cornelius Celsus, a man of very ordinary ability, not merely wrote about rhetoric in all its departments, but left treatises on the art of war, agriculture and medicine as well. Indeed the high ambition revealed by his design gives him the right to ask us to believe that he was acquainted with all these subjects.

But, it will be urged, to carry out such a task is 25 difficult and has never been accomplished. To which I reply that sufficient encouragement for study may be found in the fact, firstly, that nature does not forbid such achievement and it does not follow that, because a thing never has been done, it therefore never can be done, and secondly, that all great achievements have required time for their first accomplishment. Poetry has risen to the heights 26 of glory, thanks to the efforts of poets so far apart as Homer and Virgil, and oratory owes its position to the genius of Demosthenes and Cicero. Finally, whatever is best in its own sphere must at some previous time have been non-existent. But even if a man despair of reaching supreme excellence (and why should he despair, if he have talents, health, capacity and teachers to aid him?), it is none the less a fine achievement, as Cicero[1] says, to win the rank of second or even third. For even if a soldier 27 cannot achieve the glory of Achilles in war, he will not despise fame such as fell to the lot of Ajax and Diomede, while those who cannot be Homers may be content to reach the level of Tyrtaeus. Nay, if men had been obsessed by the conviction that it was impossible to surpass the man who had so far shown himself best, those whom we now regard as best would never have reached such distinction, Lucretius

ac Macrum Vergilius nec post Crassum et Hortensium
28 Cicero, sed nec illi, qui post eos fuerunt. Verum
ut transeundi spes non sit, magna tamen est dignitas
subsequendi. An Pollio et Messala, qui iam Cicerone
arcem tenente eloquentiae agere coeperunt, parum
in vita dignitatis habuerunt, parum ad posteros
gloriae tradiderunt? Alioqui pessime de rebus
humanis perductae in summum artes mererentur,
29 si, quod optimum, idem ultimum[1] fuisset. Adde
quod magnos modica quoque eloquentia parit fructus
ac, si quis haec studia utilitate sola metiatur, paene
illi perfectae par est. Neque erat difficile vel veteribus vel novis exemplis palam facere, non aliunde
maiores opes, honores, amicitias, laudem praesentem,
futuram hominibus contigisse, nisi indignum litteris
esset, ab opere pulcherrimo, cuius tractatus atque
ipsa possessio plenissimam studiis gratiam refert,
hanc minorem exigere mercedem, more eorum, qui
a se non virtutes sed voluptatem, quae fit ex virtu-
30 tibus, peti dicunt. Ipsam igitur orandi maiestatem,
qua nihil dii immortales melius homini dederunt et
qua remota muta sunt omnia et luce praesenti ac
memoria posteritatis carent, toto animo petamus
nitamurque semper ad optima, quod facientes aut
evademus in summum aut certe multos infra nos
videbimus.

---

[1] idem ultimum, *added by Buttmann.*

and Macer would never have been succeeded by
Virgil, nor Crassus and Hortensius by Cicero, nor
they in their turn by those who flourished after
them. But even though we cannot hope to surpass **28**
the great, it is still a high honour to follow in their
footsteps. Did Pollio and Messala, who began to
plead when Cicero held the citadel of eloquence,
fail to obtain sufficient honour in their lifetime or
to hand down a fair name to posterity? The arts
which have been developed to the highest pitch
of excellence would deserve but ill of mankind if
that which was best had also been the last of its
line. Add to this the further consideration that **29**
even moderate eloquence is often productive of
great results and, if such studies are to be measured
solely by their utility, is almost equal to the perfect
eloquence for which we seek. Nor would it be difficult
to produce either ancient or recent examples to show
that there is no other source from which men have
reaped such a harvest of wealth, honour, friendship
and glory, both present and to come. But it would
be a disgrace to learning to follow the fashion of those
who say that they pursue not virtue, but only the
pleasure derived from virtue, and to demand this
meaner recompense from the noblest of all arts, whose
practice and even whose possession is ample reward
for all our labours. Wherefore let us seek with all **30**
our hearts that true majesty of oratory, the fairest
gift of god to man, without which all things are
stricken dumb and robbed alike of present glory and
the immortal record of posterity; and let us press
forward to whatsoever is best, since, if we do this,
we shall either reach the summit or at least see
many others far beneath us.

31   Haec erant, Marcelle Victori, quibus praecepta
dicendi pro virili parte adiuvari posse per nos videbantur, quorum cognitio studiosis iuvenibus si non
magnam utilitatem adferet, at certe, quod magis
petimus, bonam voluntatem.

Such, Marcellus Victorius, were the views by **31**
the expression of which it seemed to me that I
might, as far as in me lay, help to advance the
teaching of oratory. If the knowledge of these
principles proves to be of small practical utility to
the young student, it should at least produce what
I value more,—the will to do well.

INDEX OF NAMES

517

INDEX OF NAMES

INDEX OF NAMES

INDEX OF NAMES

INDEX OF NAMES

INDEX OF NAMES

INDEX OF NAMES

INDEX OF NAMES

526

INDEX OF NAMES

INDEX OF NAMES

INDEX OF NAMES

INDEX OF NAMES

530

INDEX OF NAMES

INDEX OF NAMES

INDEX OF WORDS

533

INDEX OF WORDS

INDEX OF WORDS

bipennis from *pinnus*, I. iv. 20.
bos clitellas, V. xi. 21.
βρασμός, XI. iii. 55.
βραχυλογία, VIII. iii. 82; IX. iii. 50 and 99.
Bruges, I. iv. 15.
Bruti, I. vi. 31.
Burri, I. iv. 25.

C, I. vii. 28; I. xi. 5.
caelibes, I. vi. 36.
caesim dicere, IX. iv. 126.
caldus, calidus, I. vi. 19.
calefacere for *calfacere*, I. vi. 21.
Calypsonem, I. v. 63.
Camillus, I. v. 32.
canina eloquentia, XII. ix. 9.
cano, canto, dico, VIII. vi. 38.
Canobus, I. v. 13.
canon Alexandrinorum, I. iv. 3; X. 54.
Canopitae, I. v. 13.
cantare, XI. i. 56; XI. iii. 57 *sqq.*
canticum, I. viii. 2; I. x. 23; IX. i. 35; XI. iii.167.
cantus, XI. iii. 23, 60 and 172.
cantus = tyre of wheel, I. v. 8.
Capitolium, I. vi. 31.
capsis, I. v. 66.
caput (how carried), XI. iii. 68 *sqq.*
caput = status, III. vi. 2, 21, 89; III xi. 3 and 27.
casamo, I. v. 8.
Cassantra, I. iv. 16.
cassus for *casus*, I. vii. 20.
Castor, XI. ii. 11; quantity of -o, I. v. 60.
castrata respublica, VIII. vi. 15.
casus, I. iv. 26; I. v. 45 and 61; I. vi. 22; VIII. iii. 20.
Cato, quantity of -o, VII. ix. 13.
causa (a category), III. vi. 27; =αἰτία, III. xi. 5 and 10; =τὸ συνέχον, III. xi.24; = quaestio finita or ὑπόθεσις, III. v. 7; kinds of causae, III. iii. 15; III. iv. 1 *sqq.*; III. x. 1 and 3; IV. i. 40.
causidicus, XII. i. 25.
caussa, I. vii. 20.
centumviri, III. x. 3; IV. i. 57; IV. ii. 3; v. ii. 1; v. x. 115; VII. iv. 11 and 20; XI. i. 78; XI. iii.138.
cerae, X. iii. 30 *sqq.*
ceratinae, I. x. 5.
cerno, VII. ix. 2.

cervix, I. xi. 9; XI. iii. 82; (use in the singular), VIII. iii. 35.
cervom, I. vii. 26.
Cethegus, I. v. 23.
χαλινοί, I. i. 37.
χαλκευτική, II. xxi.10.
χαρακτηρισμός, IX. iii. 99.
chenturiones, I. v. 20.
chironomia, I. xi. 17.
choreus, IX. iv. 80 *sqq.*, 103 *sqq.*, 140.
choronae, I. v. 20.
χρειώδες, I. ix. 5.
chria, I. ix. 3 *sqq.*; II. iv. 26.
χρονός, III. vi. 25.
cinctura, XI. iii. 138 *sqq.*
circuitus = periodus, IX. iii. 122 and 124; XI. i. 26; = περίφρασις, VIII. vi. 59.
circum, I. v. 25 *sq.*
circumducta syllaba = περισπωμένη, I. v. 35.
circumductio, IX. iv. 118; XI. iii. 39.
circumductum = periodus, IX. iv. 22.
circumlocutio, VIII. vi. 61.
circumscriptio = periodus, IX. i. 35 and 91; IX. iv. 124.
circumstantia = περίστασις,V. x. 104.
clamos, I. iv. 13.
clarigatio, VII. iii. 13.
classis, I. ii. 23 and 24; I. vi. 33; X. v. 21.
clausula, VIII. v. 13; IX. iii. 45; IX. iv. 18, 45, 61 *sqq.*, 70, 93.
cogitatio, X. vi. 1 *sqq.*
cognatio, ix. ii. 105.
collectio, IX. ii. 103.
collectiva quaestio, VII. i. 60.
collegit, not *conlegit*, XI. iii. 35.
colli (plural), I. vi. 42.
collum (carriage of), I. xi. 82.
color, IV. ii. 88, 91, 94 *sqq.*; VI. v. 5; VII. i. 40, 53; X. i. 116; X. vi. 5; XI. i. 85; XII. i. 33; XII. viii. 6.
columa for *columna*, I. vii. 29; columna rostrata, I. vii. 12.
comam in gradus frangere, I. vi. 44.
comici, I. vii. 22; I. viii. 8; XII. ii. 22.
commentatio = ἐνθύμημα, V. x. 1.
commentum = ἐνθύμημα, V. x. 1; IX. ii. 107.
commiseratio, I. i. 107.
commissura verborum, VII. x. 16; IX. iv. 37; XII. ix. 17.
commoratio, IX. i. 27; IX. ii. 4.

INDEX OF WORDS

INDEX OF WORDS

INDEX OF WORDS

INDEX OF WORDS

exitus = ἐκβάσεις, V. x. 86.
exordium, IV. i. 1 *sqq.*, 5, 7, 11, 16, 28, 30, 42, 58, 62, 71, 72, 76; XI. iii. 161.
expecto and *exspecto*, I. vii. 4.
expectorat, VIII. iv. 31.
explanatio (figure), IX. i. 27; IX. ii. 2.
expositio, III. ix. 7; IV. ii. 50; VII. ii. 26; XI. i. 53.
exsecratio, IX. i. 32; IX. ii. 3.
extemporalis actio, X. vi. 6; X. vii. 18; XI. ii. 3.
extenuatio, IX. i. 27; IX. ii. 3.

F, I. iv. 14; XII. x. 29.
fabricari, IX. iii. 6.
face for *fac*, I. v. 21.
faciem for *faciam*, I. vii. 23.
facere (category), III. vi. 24.
facetum, VI. iii. 20.
faciliter, I. vi. 17.
faedus for *haedus*, I. v. 14.
fari, VIII. iii. 27.
fasciatim, I. iv. 20.
favor, VIII. iii. 34.
femur, I. vi. 22.
feminina positio, I. iv. 24.
fero, I. iv. 29; I. vi. 26.
ferrum for *gladius*, VIII. vi. 20; *ferrum* and *mucro*, X. i. 11.
fides = πίστεις, V. x. 8 and 10 *sqq.*
Figulatum, VIII. iii. 32.
figura = σχῆμα, I. v. 5; I. viii. 16; II. xiii. 11; VII. iv. 28; VI. iii. 70; VIII. vi. 67; IX. *passim.*
figuratus, VIII. iii. 59; IX. i. 13 and 14; IX. ii. 65 *sqq.* and 88.
Fimbriatum, VIII. iii. 32.
finis = finitio, IV. iv. 3; V. x. 54, etc.
finitae questiones, III. v. 7; VIII. Pr. 8.
finitio, III. v. 10; V. x. 36 and 54 *sqq.*; VI. iv. 4; VII. iii. 1 *sqq.*, 19 *sqq.*; VII. x. 1 *sqq.*; IX. iii. 91.
finitiva causa, VII. iii. 36; see also status.
firmamentum causae = συνέχον, III. xi. 1, 9, 19.
fletur, I. iv. 28.
flexa littera, syllaba, I. v. 23 and 30; XII. x. 33.
Floralia, I. v. 52.
fluctuatur and *fluctuat*, IX. iii. 7.
fordeum for *hordeum*, I. iv. 14.
forma = species, V. x. 62.
formulae, III. vi. 69; VII. iv. 20.

formularii, XII. iii. **11.**
fraudator, I. iv. 28.
frugalis, I. vi. 17.
funis, I. vi. 5.
Furii for *Fusii*, I. iv. 13.

G, I. vii. 12.
Gaius indicated by C., I. vii. 28.
Galbae, I. iv. 25.
galliambi, IX. iv. 6.
Gallica verba, I. v. 57.
gallus, VII. ix. 2.
γελοῖον, VI. iii. 22.
geminatio, I. iv. 10; I. vii. 14; VIII. v. 18; IX. i. 33; IX. iii. 28, 45, 47; IX. iv. 119.
gemma, VIII. vi. 6.
generalis quaestio, III. v. 9; III. vi. 21; VII. i. 49 and 58; VII. ii. 1 *sqq.*; X. v. 13; XII. ii. 18.
γένεσις = coniectura, III. vi. 53.
geometria, I. x. 34 *sqq.*
gestus, I. xi. 3 and 16; XI. iii. 65 *sqq.*, 88 *sqq.*, 102, 109, 117, 125, 181.
gladiola, I. vi. 42.
gladius and *ensis*, X. i. 11; and *mucro*, X. i. 11 and 14; *gladia*, I. v. 6.
γλῶσσαι, I. i. 35.
glossemata, I. viii. 15.
Glycerium, I. iv. 24.
Gnaeus, I. vii. 29.
γνῶμαι, VIII. v. 3.
Gracci, I. v. 20.
graculi, I. vi. 27.
gradatio (figure), IX. i. 34; IX. iii. 54.
grammatice, I. iv. 4, 5, 6; I. v. 54; I. viii. 12; I. x. 17; II. i. 1 *sqq.* and 4.
grammaticus, I. ii. 14; I. iv. 1 *sqq.*; I. viii. 21; II. xiv. 3; IX. iv. 53; X. i. 54.
gravis (accent), I. v. 22 *sqq.*
gubernator for *agitator*, VIII. vi. **9.**
gurdi, I. v. 57.
guttur, I. vi. 22.

H, I. v. 19 *sqq.*
habere (category), III. vi. 24.
ἁδρόν, XII. x. 58.
ἁρμονία, I. x. 12.
haruspex, I. vii. **9.**
have, I. vi. 21.
Hecoba, I. v. 16.
ἥμερον, III. vi. 28.
hendecasyllabi, I. viii. 6.

539

INDEX OF WORDS

540

INDEX OF WORDS

INDEX OF WORDS

542

INDEX OF WORDS

INDEX OF WORDS

INDEX OF WORDS

545

INDEX OF WORDS

INDEX OF WORDS

scribendi ars, I. i. 27, 28, 34 *sq.*; I.
vii. 1, 28, 30; X. iii. 1 *sqq.*, 10, 30;
X. v 1 *sqq.*; XII. ix. 16; XII. x.
49 *sqq.*
scripsere and *scripserunt*, I. v. 44.
scriptum et voluntas, III. vi. 88; VII
i. 49 *sqq.*; VII. v. 5 *sq.*; VII. vi. 1 *sqq.*;
VII. vii. 1; VII. viii. 1; VII. x. 1 *sqq.*;
cp. also III. vi. 37; VII. i. 13; VII.
v. 5.
sedes argumentorum, V. x. 20 and
100; V. xii. 17.
seiunctio, IX. i. 28; IX. ii. 2.
σημεῖον, V. ix. 9; ἄλυτον, V. ix. 3;
(in rhythm), IX. iv. 51.
semivocales, I. iv. 6; I. vii. 14.
senarius, IX. iv. 72 *sq.*, 75, 125, 140.
senatus, I. vi. 27; (derivation), I. vi.
33.
sensa, VIII. v. 1.
sensus, VIII. v. 1 *sq.* = sententiae
XII. x. 46.
sententiae, I. viii. 9; I. ix. 3; II. xi.
3; II. xii. 7; III. viii. 65; VI. iii.
36; VII. i. 44; VII. iv. 29; VIII. v.
passim; IX. ii. 107; IX. iii. 76
and 98; X. i. 60; XII. ix. 3; XII.
x. 48.
sententiolae, XII. x. 73.
sequens = ἐπίθετον, VIII. vi. 40.
Serani, I. iv. 25.
sermocinatrix, III. iv. 10.
servom, I. vii. 26.
servus, I. iv. 8 and 11.
sescuplex pes, IX. iv. 47.
sibe for *sibi*, I. vii. 24.
signa, V. viii. 1; V. ix. 3 *sqq.*; V. x. 74.
significatio = ἔμφασις, IX. i. 27; IX.
ii. 3.
silva, X. iii. 17.
similia, V. x. 73; V. xi. 1 *sqq.*; IX.
iii. 75 *sqq.*
similitudo, V. x. 1; V. xi. 22 *sqq.*;
VIII. iii. 72 *sqq.*; VIII. vi. 8 and 49;
IX. i. 31; IX. ii. 2.
simulatio (figure), IX. ii. 26.
singularia, V. i. 16; IX. iii. 20.
sitiunt segetes, VIII. vi. 6.
toleae, VIII. ii. 8.
solitaurilia, I. v. 67.
soloecismus, I. v. 4, 34 *sqq.*, 51.
sotadei, I. viii. 6; IX. iv. 6 and 90.
spartum, VIII. i. 2.
species, V. x. 25 *sqq.*; VII. i. 23 *sq.*
spes, I. vi. 26.

Spinther, VI. iii. 57.
spondeus, IX. iv. 48 *sq.*, 80, 88, 97, 101.
sponsiones, VII. v. 3.
στάσις = status, III. vi. 3.
status = στάσις, III. vi. *passim*; VII.
iv. 15; VII. v. 2 and 5; VII. vi.
1 *sqq.*; VII. vii. 1 *sqq.*; VII. viii.
1 *sqq.*; VII. x. 1; IX. i. 8; XII. ii. 19.
stella, I. vi. 35.
stercus curiae, VIII. vi. 15.
stlites and *stlocus*, I. iv. 16.
στοιχεῖα, III. iii. 13.
suasoria, II. i. 8; II. iv. 5; III. viii.
1 *sqq.*; VII. iv. 2; VIII. Pr. 9.
subiectio (figure), IX. iii. 98.
sublatio, IX. iv. 48 and 55.
substantia, III. vi. 39; IX. i. 8.
Subura, I. vii. 29.
Sufenas, I. v. 62.
suggestio, IX. ii. 15.
Sullae, I. iv. 25.
sullaturit, VIII. iii. 32; VIII. vi. 32.
sulpur, I. vi. 22.
suovetaurilia, I. v. 67.
superiectio = hyperbole, VIII. vi. 67.
superlatio, IX. i. 29; IX. ii. 3; XII. x.
62.
sustentatio, IX. ii. 23.
syllaba, I. i. 26, 30 *sqq.*, 37; IX. iv.
84, 85, 92, 93; XII. x. 32, 33.
syllogismus, III. vi. 15 *sqq.*, 43, 88; v
x. 3 and 6; V. x. 36; V. xiv. 14,
20, 24 *sqq.*; VII. iii. 11; VII. viii.
1 *sqq.*; VII. x. 1 *sqq.*; IX. iv. 57.
syllogisticus status, V. x. 6.
συμβεβηκότα, III. vi. 36; κατα συμβε-
βηκός, III. vi. 56.
σύμβολον, I. vi. 28.
συναίρεσις, V. i. 22.
συναλοιφή, I. v. 17; IX. iv. 36 and
109.
συναθροισμός, VIII. iv. 27.
σύνδεσμος, I. iv. 18.
συνέχον, II. xi. 1 and 9.
synecdoche, VIII. vi. 19 *sqq.*; IX i.
5; IX. iii. 58 *sqq.*
συνοικείωσις, IX. iii. 64.
συνωνυμία, VIII. iii. 16; IX. iii. 45.
συντελικὴ στάσις, IX. vi. 47.
σύντομος, IV. ii. 42.
syntonorum modi, IX. iv. 142.

talpae oculis capti, IX. iii. 6.
ταπείνωσις, VIII. iii. 48.
taurus, VIII. ii. 13.

547

INDEX OF WORDS

INDEX OF WORDS

THE LOEB CLASSICAL LIBRARY

VOLUMES ALREADY PUBLISHED

Latin Authors

AMMIANUS MARCELLINUS. Translated by J. C. Rolfe. 3 Vols.

APULEIUS: THE GOLDEN ASS (METAMORPHOSES). W. Adlington (1566). Revised by S. Gaselee.

ST. AUGUSTINE: CITY OF GOD. 7 Vols. Vol. I. G. E. McCracken. Vol. II. and VII. W. M. Green. Vol. III. D. Wiesen. Vol. IV. P. Levine. Vol. V. E. M. Sanford and W. M. Green. Vol. VI. W. C. Greene.

ST. AUGUSTINE, CONFESSIONS OF. W. Watts (1631). 2 Vols.

ST. AUGUSTINE, SELECT LETTERS. J. H. Baxter.

AUSONIUS. H. G. Evelyn White. 2 Vols.

BEDE. J. E. King. 2 Vols.

BOETHIUS: TRACTS and DE CONSOLATIONE PHILOSOPHIAE. Rev. H. F. Stewart and E. K. Rand. Revised by S. J. Tester.

CAESER: ALEXANDRIAN, AFRICAN and SPANISH WARS. A. G. Way.

CAESER: CIVIL WARS. A. G. Peskett.

CAESER: GALLIC WAR. H. J. Edwards.

CATO: DE RE RUSTICA; VARRO: DE RE RUSTICA. H. B. Ash and W. D. Hooper.

CATULLUS. F. W. Cornish; TIBULLUS. J. B. Postgate; PERVIGILIUM VENERIS. J. W. Mackail.

CELSUS: DE MEDICINA. W. G. Spencer. 3 Vols.

CICERO: BRUTUS, and ORATOR. G. L. Hendrickson and H. M. Hubbell.

[CICERO]: AD HERENNIUM. H. Caplan.

CICERO: DE ORATORE, etc. 2 Vols. Vol. I. DE ORATORE, BOOKS I. and II. E. W. Sutton and H. Rackham. Vol. II. DE ORATORE, Book III. De Fato; Paradoxa Stoicorum; De Partitione Oratoria. H. Rackham.

CICERO: DE FINIBUS. H. Rackham.

CICERO: DE INVENTIONE, etc. H. M. Hubbell.

CICERO: DE NATURA DEORUM and ACADEMICA. H. Rackham.

CICERO: DE OFFICIIS. Walter Miller.

CICERO: DE REPUBLICA and DE LEGIBUS: SOMNIUM SCIPIONIS. Clinton W. Keyes.

CICERO: DE SENECTUTE, DE AMICITIA, DE DIVINATIONE. W. A. Falconer.

CICERO: IN CATILINAM, PRO FLACCO, PRO MURENA, PRO SULLA. New version by C. Macdonald.

CICERO: LETTERS TO ATTICUS. E. O. Winstedt. 3 Vols.

CICERO: LETTERS TO HIS FRIENDS. W. Glynn Williams, M. Cary, M. Henderson. 4 Vols.

CICERO: PHILIPPICS. W. C. A. Ker.

CICERO: PRO ARCHIA POST REDITUM, DE DOMO, DE HARUSPICUM RESPONSIS, PRO PLANCIO. N. H. Watts.

CICERO: PRO CAECINA, PRO LEGE MANILIA, PRO CLUENTIO, PRO RABIRIO. H. Grose Hodge.

CICERO: PRO CAELIO, DE PROVINCIIS CONSULARIBUS, PRO BALBO. R. Gardner.

CICERO: PRO MILONE, IN PISONEM, PRO SCAURO, PRO FONTEIO, PRO RABIRIO POSTUMO, PRO MARCELLO, PRO LIGARIO, PRO REGE DEIOTARO. N. H. Watts.

CICERO: PRO QUINCTIO, PRO ROSCIO AMERINO, PRO ROSCIO COMOEDO, CONTRA RULLUM. J. H. Freese.

CICERO: PRO SESTIO, IN VATINIUM. R. Gardner.

CICERO: TUSCULAN DISPUTATIONS. J. E. King.

CICERO: VERRINE ORATIONS. L. H. G. Greenwood. 2 Vols.

CLAUDIAN. M. Platnauer. 2 Vols.

COLUMELLA: DE RE RUSTICA. DE ARBORIBUS. H. B. Ash, E. S. Forster and E. Heffner. 3 Vols.

CURTIUS, Q.: HISTORY OF ALEXANDER. J. C. Rolfe. 2 Vols.

FLORUS. E. S. Forster; and CORNELIUS NEPOS. J. C. Rolfe.

FRONTINUS: STRATAGEMS and AQUEDUCTS. C. E. Bennett and M. B. McElwain.

FRONTO: CORRESPONDENCE. C. R. Haines. 2 Vols.

GELLIUS, J. C. Rolfe. 3 Vols.

HORACE: ODES AND EPODES. C. E. Bennett.

HORACE: SATIRES, EPISTLES, ARS POETICA. H. R. Fairclough.

JEROME: SELECTED LETTERS. F. A. Wright.

JUVENAL and PERSIUS. G. G. Ramsay.

LIVY. B. O. Foster, F. G. Moore, Evan T. Sage, and A. C. Schlesinger and R. M. Geer (General Index). 14 Vols.

LUCAN. J. D. Duff.

LUCRETIUS. W. H. D. Rouse. Revised by M. F. Smith.

MANILIUS. G. P. Goold.

MARTIAL. W. C. A. Ker. 2 Vols.

MINOR LATIN POETS: from PUBLILIUS SYRUS to RUTILIUS NAMATIANUS, including GRATTIUS, CALPURNIUS SICULUS, NEMESIANUS, AVIANUS, and others with "Aetna" and the "Phoenix." J. Wight Duff and Arnold M. Duff.

OVID: THE ART OF LOVE and OTHER POEMS. J. H. Mosley. Revised by G. P. Goold.

OVID: FASTI. Sir James G. Frazer.

OVID: HEROIDES and AMORES. Grant Showerman. Revised by G. P. Goold

OVID: METAMORPHOSES. F. J. Miller. 2 Vols. Vol. 1 revised by G. P. Goold.

OVID: TRISTIA and EX PONTO. A. L. Wheeler.

PERSIUS. Cf. JUVENAL.

PETRONIUS. M. Heseltine; SENECA; APOCOLOCYNTOSIS. W. H. D. Rouse.

PHAEDRUS AND BABRIUS (Greek). B. E. Perry.

PLAUTUS. Paul Nixon. 5 Vols.

PLINY: LETTERS, PANEGYRICUS. Betty Radice. 2 Vols.

PLINY: NATURAL HISTORY. Vols. I.–V. and IX. H. Rackham. VI.–VIII. W. H. S. Jones. X. D. E. Eichholz. 10 Vols.

PROPERTIUS. H. E. Butler.

PRUDENTIUS. H. J. Thomson. 2 Vols.

QUINTILIAN. H. E. Butler. 4 Vols.

REMAINS OF OLD LATIN. E. H. Warmington. 4 Vols. Vol. I. (ENNIUS AND CAECILIUS.) Vol. II. (LIVIUS, NAEVIUS, PACUVIUS, ACCIUS.) Vol. III. (LUCILIUS and LAWS OF XII TABLES.) Vol. IV. (ARCHAIC INSCRIPTIONS.)

SALLUST. J. C. Rolfe.

SCRIPTORES HISTORIAE AUGUSTAE. D. Magie. 3 Vols.

SENECA, THE ELDER: CONTROVERSIAE, SUASORIAE. M. Winterbottom. 2 Vols.

SENECA: APOCOLOCYNTOSIS. Cf. PETRONIUS.

SENECA: EPISTULAE MORALES. R. M. Gummere. 3 Vols.

SENECA: MORAL ESSAYS. J. W. Basore. 3 Vols.

SENECA: TRAGEDIES. F. J. Miller. 2 Vols.

SENECA: NATURALES QUAESTIONES. T. H. Corcoran. 2 Vols.

SIDONIUS: POEMS and LETTERS. W. B. Anderson. 2 Vols.

SILIUS ITALICUS. J. D. Duff. 2 Vols.

STATIUS. J. H. Mozley. 2 Vols.

SUETONIUS. J. C. Rolfe. 2 Vols.

TACITUS: DIALOGUS. Sir Wm. Peterson. AGRICOLA and GERMANIA. Maurice Hutton. Revised by M. Winterbottom, R. M. Ogilvie, E. H. Warmington.

TACITUS: HISTORIES AND ANNALS. C. H. Moore and J. Jackson. 4 Vols.

TERENCE. John Sargeaunt. 2 Vols.

TERTULLIAN: APOLOGIA and DE SPECTACULIS. T. R. Glover. MINUCIUS FELIX. G. H. Rendall.

VALERIUS FLACCUS. J. H. Mozley.

VARRO: DE LINGUA LATINA. R. G. Kent. 2 Vols.

VELLEIUS PATERCULUS and RES GESTAE DIVI AUGUSTI. F. W. Shipley.

VIRGIL. H. R. Fairclough. 2 Vols.

VITRUVIUS: DE ARCHITECTURA. F. Granger. 2 Vols.

Greek Authors

ACHILLES TATIUS. S. Gaselee.

AELIAN: ON THE NATURE OF ANIMALS. A. F. Scholfield. 3 Vols.

AENEAS TACTICUS, ASCLEPIODOTUS and ONASANDER. The Illinois Greek Club.

AESCHINES. C. D. Adams.

AESCHYLUS. H. Weir Smyth. 2 Vols.

ALCIPHRON, AELIAN, PHILOSTRATUS: LETTERS. A. R. Benner and F. H. Fobes.

ANDOCIDES, ANTIPHON, Cf. MINOR ATTIC ORATORS.

APOLLODORUS. Sir James G. Frazer. 2 Vols.

APOLLONIUS RHODIUS. R. C. Seaton.

THE APOSTOLIC FATHERS. Kirsopp Lake. 2 Vols.

APPIAN: ROMAN HISTORY. Horace White. 4 Vols.

ARATUS. Cf. CALLIMACHUS.

ARISTIDES: ORATIONS. C. A. Behr. Vol. I.

ARISTOPHANES. Benjamin Bickley Rogers. 3 Vols. Verse trans.

ARISTOTLE: ART OF RHETORIC. J. H. Freese.

ARISTOTLE: ATHENIAN CONSTITUTION, EUDEMIAN ETHICS, VICES AND VIRTUES. H. Rackham.

ARISTOTLE: GENERATION OF ANIMALS. A. L. Peck.

ARISTOTLE: HISTORIA ANIMALIUM. A. L. Peck. Vols I.–II.

ARISTOTLE: METAPHYSICS. H. Tredennick. 2 Vols.

ARISTOTLE: METEOROLOGICA. H. D. P. Lee.

ARISTOTLE: MINOR WORKS. W. S. Hett. On Colours, On Things Heard, On Physiognomies, On Plants, On Marvellous Things Heard, Mechanical Problems, On Indivisible Lines, On Situations and Names of Winds, On Melissus, Xenophanes, and Gorgias.

ARISTOTLE: NICOMACHEAN ETHICS. H. Rackham.

ARISTOTLE: OECONOMICA and MAGNA MORALIA. G. C. Armstrong; (with METAPHYSICS, Vol. II.).

ARISTOTLE: ON THE HEAVENS. W. K. C. Guthrie.

ARISTOTLE: ON THE SOUL. PARVA NATURALIA. ON BREATH. W. S. Hett.

ARISTOTLE: CATEGORIES, ON INTERPRETATION, PRIOR ANALYTICS. H. P. Cooke and H. Tredennick.

ARISTOTLE: POSTERIOR ANALYTICS, TOPICS. H. Tredennick and E. S. Forster.

ARISTOTLE: ON SOPHISTICAL REFUTATIONS.
On Coming to be and Passing Away, On the Cosmos. E. S. Forster and D. J. Furley.

ARISTOTLE: PARTS OF ANIMALS. A. L. Peck; MOTION AND PROGRESSION OF ANIMALS. E. S. Forster.

ARISTOTLE: PHYSICS. Rev. P. Wicksteed and F. M. Cornford. 2 Vols.

ARISTOTLE: POETICS and LONGINUS. W. Hamilton Fyfe; DEMETRIUS ON STYLE. W. Rhys Roberts.

ARISTOTLE: POLITICS. H. Rackham.

ARISTOTLE: PROBLEMS. W. S. Hett. 2 Vols.

ARISTOTLE: RHETORICA AD ALEXANDRUM (with PROBLEMS. Vol. II). H. Rackham.

ARRIAN: HISTORY OF ALEXANDER and INDICA. 2 Vols. Vol. I. P. Brunt. Vol. II. Rev. E. Iliffe Robson.

ATHENAEUS: DEIPNOSOPHISTAE. C. B. Gulick. 7 Vols.

BABRIUS AND PHAEDRUS (Latin). B. E. Perry.

ST. BASIL: LETTERS. R. J. Deferrair. 4 Vols.

CALLIMACHUS: FRAGMENTS. C. A. Trypanis. MUSAEUS: HERO AND LEANDER. T. Gelzer and C. Whitman.

CALLIMACHUS, Hymns and Epigrams, and LYCOPHRON. A. W. Mair; ARATUS. G. R. Mair.

CLEMENT OF ALEXANDRIA. Rev. G. W. Butterworth.

COLLUTHUS. Cf. OPPIAN.

DAPHNIS AND CHLOE. Thornley's Translation revised by J. M. Edmonds: and PARTHENIUS. S. Gaselee.

DEMOSTHENES I.: OLYNTHIACS, PHILIPPICS and MINOR ORATIONS. I.–XVII. AND XX. J. H. Vince.

DEMOSTHENES II.: DE CORONA and DE FALSA LEGATIONE. C. A. Vince and J. H. Vince.

DEMOSTHENES III.: MEIDIAS, ANDROTION, ARISTOCRATES, TIMOCRATES and ARISTOGEITON, I. and II. J. H. Vince.

DEMOSTHENES IV.–VI.: PRIVATE ORATIONS and IN NEAERAM. A. T. Murray.

DEMOSTHENES VII: FUNERAL SPEECH, EROTIC ESSAY, EXORDIA and LETTERS. N. W. and N. J. DeWitt.

DIO CASSIUS: ROMAN HISTORY. E. Cary. 9 Vols.

DIO CHRYSOSTOM. J. W. Cohoon and H. Lamar Crosby. 5 Vols.

DIODORUS SICULUS. 12 Vols. Vols. I.–VI. C. H. Oldfather. Vol. VII. C. L. Sherman. Vol. VIII. C. B. Welles. Vols. IX. and X. R. M. Geer. Vol. XI. F. Walton. Vol. XII. F. Walton. General Index. R. M. Geer.

DIOGENES LAERTIUS. R. D. Hicks. 2 Vols. New Introduction by H. S. Long.

DIONYSIUS OF HALICARNASSUS: ROMAN ANTIQUITIES. Spelman's translation revised by E. Cary. 7 Vols.

DIONYSIUS OF HALICARNASSUS: CRITICAL ESSAYS. S. Usher. 2 Vols.

EPICTETUS. W. A. Oldfather. 2 Vols.

EURIPIDES. A. S. Way. 4 Vols. Verse trans.

EUSEBIUS: ECCLESIASTICAL HISTORY. Kirsopp Lake and J. E. L. Oulton. 2 Vols.

GALEN: ON THE NATURAL FACULTIES. A. J. Brock.

THE GREEK ANTHOLOGY. W. R. Paton. 5 Vols.

GREEK ELEGY AND IAMBUS with the ANACREONTEA. J. M. Edmonds. 2 Vols.

THE GREEK BUCOLIC POETS (THEOCRITUS, BION, MOSCHUS). J. M. Edmonds.

GREEK MATHEMATICAL WORKS. Ivor Thomas. 2 Vols.

HERODES. Cf. THEOPHRASTUS: CHARACTERS.

HERODIAN. C. R. Whittaker. 2 Vols.

HERODOTUS. A. D. Godley. 4 Vols.

HESIOD AND THE HOMERIC HYMNS. H. G. Evelyn White.

HIPPOCRATES and the FRAGMENTS OF HERACLEITUS. W. H. S. Jones and E. T. Withington. 4 Vols.

HOMER: ILIAD. A. T. Murray. 2 Vols.

HOMER: ODYSSEY. A. T. Murray. 2 Vols.

ISAEUS. E. W. Forster.

ISOCRATES. George Norlin and LaRue Van Hook. 3 Vols.

[ST. JOHN DAMASCENE]: BARLAAM AND IOASAPH. Rev. G. R. Woodward, Harold Mattingly and D. M. Lang.

JOSEPHUS. 9 Vols. Vols. I.–IV. H. Thackeray. Vol. V. H. Thackeray and R. Marcus. Vols. VI.–VII. R. Marcus. Vol. VIII. R. Marcus and Allen Wikgren. Vol. IX. L. H. Feldman.

JULIAN. Wilmer Cave Wright. 3 Vols.

LIBANIUS. A. F. Norman. Vols. I.–II.

LUCIAN. 8 Vols. Vols. I.–V. A. M. Harmon. Vol. VI. K. Kilburn. Vols. VII.–VIII. M. D. Macleod.

LYCOPHRON. Cf. CALLIMACHUS.

LYRA GRAECA. J. M. Edmonds. 3 Vols.

LYSIAS. W. R. M. Lamb.

MANETHO. W. G. Waddell: PTOLEMY: TETRABIBLOS. F. E. Robbins.

MARCUS AURELIUS. C. R. Haines.

MENANDER. I New edition by W. G. Arnott.

MINOR ATTIC ORATORS (ANTIPHON, ANDOCIDES, LYCURGUS, DEMADES, DINARCHUS, HYPERIDES). K. J. Maidment and J. O. Burtt. 2 Vols.

MUSAEUS: HERO AND LEANDER. Cf. CALLIMACHUS.

NONNOS: DIONYSIACA. W. H. D. Rouse. 3 Vols.

OPPIAN, COLLUTHUS, TRYPHIODORUS. A. W. Mair.

PAPYRI. NON-LITERARY SELECTIONS. A. S. Hunt and C. C. Edgar. 2 Vols. LITERARY SELECTIONS (Poetry). D. L. Page.

PARTHENIUS. Cf. DAPHNIS and CHLOE.

PAUSANIAS: DESCRIPTION OF GREECE. W. H. S. Jones. 4 Vols. and Companion Vol. arranged by R. E. Wycherley.

Philo. 10 Vols. Vols. I.–V. F. H. Colson and Rev. G. H. Whitaker. Vols. VI.–IX. F. H. Colson. Vol. X. F. H. Colson and the Rev. J. W. Earp.

Philo: two supplementary Vols. (*Translation only.*) Ralph Marcus.

Philostratus: The Life of Apollonius of Tyana. F. C. Conybeare. 2 Vols.

Philostratus: Imagines; Callistratus: Descriptions. A. Fairbanks.

Philostratus and Eunapius: Lives of the Sophists. Wilmer Cave Wright.

Pindar. Sir J. E. Sandys.

Plato: Charmides, Alcibiades, Hipparchus, The Lovers, Theages, Minos and Epinomis. W. R. M. Lamb.

Plato: Cratylus, Parmenides, Greater Hippias, Lesser Hippias. H. N. Fowler.

Plato: Euthyphro, Apology, Crito, Phaedo, Phaedrus, H. N. Fowler.

Plato: Laches, Protagoras, Meno, Euthydemus. W. R. M. Lamb.

Plato: Laws. Rev. R. G. Bury. 2 Vols.

Plato: Lysis, Symposium, Gorgias. W. R. M. Lamb.

Plato: Republic. Paul Shorey. 2 Vols.

Plato: Statesman, Philebus. H. N. Fowler; Ion. W. R. M. Lamb.

Plato: Theaetetus and Sophist. H. N. Fowler.

Plato: Timaeus, Critias, Clitopho, Menexenus, Epistulae. Rev. R. G. Bury.

Plotinus: A. H. Armstrong. Vols. I.–III.

Plutarch: Moralia. 17 Vols. Vols. I.–V. F. C. Babbitt. Vol. VI. W. C. Helmbold. Vols. VII. and XIV. P. H. De Lacy and B. Einarson. Vol. VIII. P. A. Clement and H. B. Hoffleit. Vol. IX. E. L. Minar, Jr., F. H. Sandbach, W. C. Helmbold. Vol. X. H. N. Fowler. Vol. XI. L. Pearson and F. H. Sandbach. Vol. XII. H. Cherniss and W. C. Helmbold. Vol. XIII 1–2. H. Cherniss. Vol. XV. F. H. Sandbach.

Plutarch: The Parallel Lives. B. Perrin. 11 Vols.

Polybius. W. R. Paton. 6 Vols.

Procopius: History of the Wars. H. B. Dewing. 7 Vols.

Ptolemy: Tetrabiblos. Cf. Manetho.

Quintus Smyrnaeus. A. S. Way. Verse trans.

Sextus Empiricus. Rev. R. G. Bury. 4 Vols.

Sophocles. F. Storr. 2 Vols. Verse trans.

Strabo: Geography. Horace L. Jones. 8 Vols.

Theophrastus: Characters. J. M. Edmonds. Herodes, etc. A. D. Knox.

7

THEOPHRASTUS: ENQUIRY INTO PLANTS. Sir Arthur Hort, Bart. 2 Vols.

THEOPHRASTUS: DE CAUSIS PLANTARUM. G. K. K. Link and B. Einarson. 3 Vols. Vol. I.

THUCYDIDES. C. F. Smith. 4 Vols.

TRYPHIODORUS. Cf. OPPIAN.

XENOPHON: CYROPAEDIA. Walter Miller. 2 Vols.

XENOPHON: HELLENCIA. C. L. Brownson. 2 Vols.

XENOPHON: ANABASIS. C. L. Brownson.

XENOPHON: MEMORABILIA AND OECONOMICUS. E. C. Marchant. SYMPOSIUM AND APOLOGY. O. J. Todd.

XENOPHON: SCRIPTA MINORA. E. C. Marchant. CONSTITUTION OF THE ATHENIANS (Athenians.) G. W. Bowersock